PIONEER TRAILS WEST

PIONEER TRAILS WEST

By

THE WESTERN WRITERS OF AMERICA

DON WORCESTER, *Editor*

The CAXTON PRINTERS, Ltd.
Caldwell, Idaho
1985

PIONEER TRAILS WEST

Includes index. 1. Trails — West (U.S.) — History. 2. West (U.S.) — Description and travel. 3. Overland journeys to the Pacific. 4. Frontier and pioneer life — West (U.S.) I. Worcester, Donald Emmet, 1915-. II. Western Writers of America.

F591.P56   1985   978'.02   84-15592
ISBN 0-87004-304-8

Printed and Bound in the United States of America by
The Caxton Printers, Ltd.
Caldwell, Idaho 83605
141449

To the trailblazers and pathfinders
of Early America

CONTENTS

Chapter *Page*

ILLUSTRATIONS

MAPS

FOREWORD

In the early nineteenth century, Thomas Carlyle suggested that the milestones dotting the road of progress in mankind's history were the results of actions taken by great people who molded events for good or evil: History is the record of "innumerable biographies." Maybe he was right. Maybe people of different nationalities, sexes, sizes, and capacities for good and evil take this planet and bend it to their will. However, when one contemplates and then discards that explanation, he does so because it is much more reasonable to suggest that the flow of events mold people and their actions rather than the other way around. Do people make the times or do times make the people? That question has been argued for centuries and, alas, will continue to be debated interminably, for no particularly good reason, for generations to come. The truth is that everything affects everything else. History is ever evolving; it is shaped by everything that comes its way, but unfortunately we do not write about it that way. It is much more convenient to pretend that Carlyle was right and to continue the bad habit of narrating only the lives of "great" people or the facts about major events. It is easier to package the Civil War, Napoleon Bonaparte, the Great Depression, or

Marco Polo than it is to deal with subjects deemed minor. However, our convenience packaging should never be presented or accepted as "the way things happened," even though historians, unlike cigarette packages, are not required to warn others that it is intellectually unhealthy to believe that the American Revolution can be understood clearly if we see it through the eyes of George Washington or if we would only realize the significance of Burgoyne's failure before Saratoga.

In truth, the continuing joy experienced in historical research stems from the fact that, despite the paucity of historical evidence remaining once an event has happened or once a person has been buried, it is putting the pieces of the puzzle back together again into a logical whole that brings us pleasure and satisfaction. For example, like most other folks I spent years studying the various trends, battles, and leaders that parade across the stage of American history during the Civil War as I sought reasons why the conflict seemed inevitable to some, was so bitterly fought throughout, and left us as a nation with problems just as complex as those we had before Fort Sumter started the bloodbath. Then I happened upon a small collection of letters written by two unschooled private soldiers from Livingston County, Illinois, who served from 1862 to the end of the conflict in the Illinois 129th Regiment and wrote back home to kin about what it was really like to meet death daily in the guise of enemy soldiers, epidemics, poisonous snakes, and diarrhea. One of the brothers survived the conflict, but he was never again the same apple-cheeked, trusting, optimistic person he was when he left family and friends in 1862 to answer the call to arms. It was only then that I realized that Laforest Dunham — a lost soul among so many others — was just as important a part of the drama as was Ulysses S. Grant or Jefferson Davis. His descent into hell mirrors well America's posture during four incredible years, and his emergence at war's end as a selfish, unfeeling, and uncaring exponent of the "self before all else" philosophy also reflects the inevitable curse that plagues a people who try to solve problems by killing each other. It is no accident that in 1865 a tired America — North as well as South — entered a thirty-year period when caring gave way to exploitation, and progress was defined as making white people out of Western Indians and Southern ex-slaves. The spirit of a nation almost died with Lincoln in 1865, and that fact is more clearly seen in the letters of an unknown private soldier than in the career of his conquering commanding general. Yet how is the package presented on the library shelf?

I suspect that the foregoing is a careless, long-winded means of suggesting that we have stumbled our way through the process of historical discovery by giving much more attention to the large stones on the road than the much more numerous smaller ones. In defense of this statement, I would suggest that the movement of people from place to place in America was and is a characteristic of our culture and history that must be understood if we hope to understand ourselves; yet we have given scant attention to that trait. We have published series of volumes paying tribute to the major rivers in the United States that have moved people and goods — offered river by river in individual volumes — but the effort lacks cohesiveness because there is no attempt to tie all those rivers together into a meaningful whole discussing travel. Rivers and lakes were used by different people the country over to get from one place to another, and they were used simultaneously — not, as the series addresses them, one by one. Is there any connection in the way towns sprouted up along the Hudson River as compared, let us say, to the Columbia River? Which rivers were units unto themselves and which led to other rivers that took travelers Lord knows where? How do lakes and oceans fit into the story? How was national and local commerce affected? Is it important to know that most East Coast rivers run west to east rather than north to south? On and on the queries go. They are interrelated and cannot be answered adequately in a volume discussing only the Missouri River. In short, I suspect that the history of rivers and their overall effect on this country's history has yet to be written, but we have at least started the task. The same is true for railroading, which has received some, but not enough, attention.

To carry this linking effort one step further, it is important to understand that people traveled by more than one means as they made their way into, over, and across America. Water travel was important, but it was oceanic as well as inland in nature, and the shortcomings of rivers — particularly the fact that travel was almost totally limited to the downstream direction until the invention of the steamboat — made them of secondary importance to other modes of travel. We used oceans, rivers, lakes, tributaries, canals, railroads, and overland trails with much success during pre-twentieth century days, and we changed the face of a continent long before airplanes flew above us and super highways cut ribbons of concrete through our countryside in every conceivable direction.

A study of all these travel options, if we could link their histories into an understandable whole, would be an empty effort if we did not spend a good deal of our time reconstructing the history of America's most important and most neglected means of early travel — overland trails. If Laforest Dunham is as true a spokesman as one can find to lay bare the tragedy of 1861-1865, then I submit that the foot and wagon trails of America do the same thing for the history of travel in America. It would be fruitless to compare the various modes of travel in an effort to show, for example, that foot trails were cheaper and safer, and that they offered such luxuries as the ability to travel in both directions, links with

other trails that allowed you to change directions, and towns or forts along the way that offered a variety of opportunities and diversity not available to travelers on waterways. The truth is that overland travel was not cheaper than water, and it certainly was not safer on those trails where bands of cutthroats waited to rob or kill you for booty or Indians waited to avenge wrongs that seemed to be without end. Also, travel by trail was not glamorous or joyful as portrayed by the likes of Gene Autry and friends riding along neat as a pin and singing their woes away. Trails are central to the travel story because they were used by more folks than all other means of transportation put together, and they took those people to more different places. Trails were, indeed, the way to go.

Like the rivers that bless our land, trails were gifts of nature that made travel possible in a land more than 3,000 miles wide and pockmarked with generous barriers to easy movement — numerous mountain ranges, deserts, and open, windy prairies, where ambush by Mother Nature as well as Indians made life more than interesting. And these paths were gifts to white, European interlopers from the animals and Native Americans, whom the intruders immediately started slaughtering. The first thoroughfares through North America, save for the time-obliterated paths of mastodon, musk ox, and Mound Builders, were the oft-used paths made by buffalo and deer in seasonal migrations and between feeding grounds and salt licks. Many of these faint paths were hammered into routes by countless hoofs instinctively following watersheds and the crests of ridges in an effort to avoid spring and summer mud and winter snowdrifts. These routes were gifts to Indians, who used them as they trailed game to various hunting grounds and as they stalked each other over what came to be called "warriors' paths." These same paths were later valuable to Spanish, English, and French explorers and were eagerly adopted by the pioneers who followed them.

Buffalo traces were characteristically north and south, but the trails that buffalo and deer charted east to west and back again through the Cumberland Gap of Virginia-Tennessee, along the New York watershed, from the Potomac River through the Allegheny divide to the Ohio headwaters, and through the Blue Ridge Mountains to Upper Kentucky became the highways of commerce and population, along with the Ohio and Mississippi rivers that carried succeeding generations of settlers to the Mississippi River for more than two centuries. Sen. Thomas Hart Benton of Missouri later saluted these pathfinding animals by stating that the buffalo blazed the way for the railroads from the East Coast to the Pacific Ocean. The claim may have been somewhat of an overstatement, but it is important to note that animal trails, refined by thousands of Indians over centuries, offered new residents in North America the gift of movement. In truth, I cannot visualize how they would have gotten about without these trails.

Does it not seem unusual that historians have paid so little attention to

the evolution and history of various trails in the United States? As mentioned above, we have written a good deal about water travel — up and down our Atlantic and Pacific coasts and in the intriguing Caribbean, where America's southern coastline shares space with numerous important and strategic islands. *Moby Dick, Two Years Before The Mast,* and countless other historical treatises and novels recount vividly the role played by ships sailing along the thousands of miles of coastline that define the United States on three sides; indeed, the importance of sea travel to the evolution of the nation has not been overstated. To a lesser degree we have studied major lakes, rivers, and water as a national resource — not as a cohesive whole deserving understanding but at least as problems needing attention as we view filthy waterways, oil spills, decreasing clean water supplies, and dying wildlife. Need is rekindling an interest in the whole topic of water, even its use for travel as we build inland waterways, at dreadful cost, to move goods to coastal ports by water rather than by overused roads and underattended rail lines.

However, other than several published volumes in McGraw Hill's unfinished *American Trail Series,* research has been lacking on overland trails, or trails that utilize both water and overland routes along the way. In the inland South, for example, much has been written about the travel role played by such waterways as the Mississippi, Ohio, Tennessee, and Cumberland rivers, but what about important overland routes, such as the Natchez Trace (from Nashville,

Tennessee to Natchez, Mississippi), Gaines Trace (from north-central Alabama at Muscle Shoals to the Natchez Trace), Three-Chopped Way (from Natchez, Mississippi, across the inland South to Milledgeville, Georgia), or Jackson's Military Road (from Columbia, Tennessee, to Madisonville, Louisiana)? All these routes evolved out of animal and Indian paths, and all became major trails that moved people across the hundreds of inland miles comprising the fast-evolving Cotton South of the early nineteenth century. Yet precious little has been written about any of these routes except the Natchez Trace; only when one consults individual state histories does something on the subject appear in print. Yet all influenced the peopling of a nation and the expansion of an economic system; most stand as forgotten pages in a chapter of our history yet to be told.

I would suggest, for a number of reasons, that the Natchez Trace is one of America's most interesting trails. It is significant because it has been memorialized by a fine volume, *The Devil's Backbone,* written by Jonathan Daniels. Also, it has been reconstructed and perpetuated by our national and various state governments; today one can ride the length of that route through beautiful landscape approximating the vista seen by those on foot or horseback around 1800. It is truly a preserved page in our history that deserves to be seen by all who enjoy a restoration job well done.

The Trace is important for many other reasons. It was the first overland route (dating from 1801) that tied an interior Southern growth area — the Nashville Basin — with the lower Mississippi River. More often than not it was a one-way route, from Natchez to Nashville, serving the needs of Northern farmers and Southern planters who floated their goods for sale down the various inland rivers to the Mississippi River and then New Orleans. There the goods and the flatboat were sold, and, with cash in their pockets, the young men returned to their families by way of the Natchez Trace, after spending the first night in a Natchez inn. The presence of people with money naturally attracted thieves who preyed on unsuspecting victims as they walked or rode home over what came to be called the "Bloody Trace." The most notorious was the Samuel Mason Gang, a group of cutthroats who wreaked havoc from 1801 to 1803. Their special trademark was to scrawl the name "Mason" on the ground with the victim's blood. They were captured and escaped more times than thieves in a grade B cowboy movie, but finally they were captured, tried, and hanged on February 8, 1804. Their heads were cut off, mounted on pikes, and displayed for all to see north and south of Natchez.

How many tales of woe and joy can each major trail in America tell? Hundreds, I suspect, and all deserve to be known. The little bit we know about the Natchez Trace begs the question of when we might learn more about trails that contributed much to the history of various states and regions. What about the Cumberland Gap — a magnificently beautiful sliver of hope that allowed thousands of easterners to make their way through a seemingly impenetrable mountain range to the blue grass country of Kentucky? What about overland routes joined together by strange and interesting canals constructed in New York, Pennsylvania, and Ohio? Have you ever wanted to give form and substance to the numerous cattle trails that gave us cities like Fort Worth and Oklahoma City, and quaint but important towns like Abilene and Salina, Kansas? Well, so have I. The northern winter wind and the southern summer wind that blow unmolested up and down the Great Plains make that region seem to be the coldest and the hottest in America. And those winds have blown sand over the tracks of the Chisholm Trail, almost — not totally — obliterating deep ruts caused by thousands of cattle passing decades ago to Kansas slaughterhouses. The trail was an important one and should be seen and studied; it gave birth to a section and changed, in more than one way, the American way of life.

After all other routes are studied and given places of honor in our history and our hearts, there will always remain the Oregon Trail, standing before us with a majesty rivaled only by the mighty Mississippi itself. I know some may disagree and cast their vote for "most significant trail" to the various Indian Trails of Tears from Georgia and elsewhere to Indian Territory. Or, in the arena where suffering reigns supreme, many nod knowingly and appreciatively when they contemplate the conquest of adversity by Latter-day Saints, who were unwelcome in Illinois and on the bloody trail westward to the

Great Salt Lake. I know that the trails followed by Missouri Fur Company trappers were important threads of commerce, bringing forth entrepreneurs and great wealth rivaled only, in enterprise and audacity, by trails bringing miners to California and then inland to Colorado, Idaho, and anywhere else rumors of gold or silver moved adventurers to gamble all on the harsh odds against finding that one great strike. Cowboys and Indians, miners and Mormons, missionaries seeking lost souls and soldiers seeking recalcitrant Indians preferring freedom to reservation life — all, yes all, moved by overland trails waiting to be rediscovered so they can share secrets with those of us eager to learn.

Still, above all the rest, there is the Oregon Trail. I admit partiality to this trail because I can drive less than fifty miles from my home and touch the deep rutted seams that continue to defy change. I can stand on this southern Idaho ground and hear the sound of wind carrying the laughter of men and women nearing The Dalles in Oregon and the sobs of those burying their own in the prairie or on the side of some mountain through which the Oregon Trail wound. It was a magnificent curved thread from the flatlands around Independence, Missouri, to the awesome beauty of America's most majestic sight — Mt. Hood, Oregon. And it was a long 2,000-mile thread that took all who challenged it through the heat and wind of the Great Plains to the Continental Divide and beyond, offering for relief along the way only a handful of forts where one could refresh and start again or give up.

The wind suggests more than the sounds of laughter and crying. It offers, too, the realization that those who laugh and cry, all of whom have a tale to tell about why they left the relative security of a rich but small Indiana farm, or what it's like to get pregnant or give birth along a route that tested the bravest and the strongest, or how adventure and the need to see beyond the next mountain motivates many to taunt danger and to die seeking answers. It's not that the folks on the Oregon Trail were better or braver than others going elsewhere on overland routes (for myriad reasons — even to deliver the mail); rather, it is the majesty of the enterprise and the odds facing all those who gambled that they could court so much potential danger and still reach an unseen goal 2,000 miles away. There were easier things to do than make your way through Crow and Blackfoot country and live to tell about it! How many steps are there in 2,000 miles? How many horses and oxen are needed to make the trip? And what about water, food, clothing, weapons? Each traveler on the Oregon Trail embarked with the knowledge that death or, at best, failure was the surest possibility; yet the decision to try gaining the brass ring by challenging unbelievable odds is the reality that pleases me most as I stand and view the deeply cut ruts made by wagons loaded with hope and tired souls approaching Fort Boise, not many miles from the Oregon border. When are hope and optimism overwhelmed by the sureness of failure? Obviously never —

and that is the message the Oregon Trail passes on to us today.

They came through this country, and I salute every one of them. They also came through your country, whether you reside in the Berkshires of Connecticut and Massachusetts, the Hot Springs of Arkansas, or the wine country of California. All states have trails that years ago carried people of different colors and beliefs to a place they wanted to reach; or moved goods of all kinds to market, from corn to beaver pelts; or offered the option to the unsettled to find a way station that might, indeed, be "the place," but more likely was not. You may not be able to find these trails, as I can the Oregon Trail here in Idaho, and that is sad. They are there, probably hidden in the form of a railroad track or a super highway or a secondary road. As Indian paths evolved out of routes followed by buffalo and deer, and pioneers made countless trails out of Indian paths, smart engineers followed many of those trails when they built railroads, adding yet another dimension to the history of American traffic.

To be remembered, a trail does not have to be as magnificently preserved as the Natchez Trace or cut as deeply into the landscape as is some of the Oregon Trail; it should, though, be recorded in books available to all in local libraries. A start in that direction has been the fine volumes in the *American Trails Series* mentioned earlier. An intensification of that start is, I suspect, the true significance of this volume, and I salute all who labored assiduously to offer bits and pieces about this or that trail in the chapters that follow. All the trails discussed here are important, but at no time does the editor claim that these trails are the only ones that passed muster or are worthy of inclusion. Rather, what is presented here are a few morsels that challenge and entice. This volume gains significance because it addresses a subject too long neglected in favor of the more glamorous topics that "play well in Peoria" and everywhere else. Do we need another life of Abraham Lincoln or another revisionist view of the Constitution, Reconstruction, or even Watergate? Maybe so, if repetition is your game, but I suggest that those who have overlooked travel as an important and exciting subject — and overland trails as a worthy subdivision of that topic — had better look again. These trails carried the hopes and aspirations of thousands seeking a new life, escaping the law, riding the Butterfield Stage, driving cattle, chasing Indians, being chased by Indians. People used the trails for many of the same reasons we use highways today, save for the joy of a day of sightseeing. We ought, as historians and students of history, to tip our hats to those who went before and offered us ruts along the Oregon Trail — meaningful symbols rivaling footprints on the moon.

This is a book that suggests that the "smaller rocks" of history are more numerous and deserve just as careful attention as do the "larger rocks." Let us accept that message as a challenge to carry forward the research on the story of America's overland trails in the days ahead. The volume tantalizes, asks more questions than it answers, and suggests that illumination will have to wait until the bibliography on this subject is fuller. The poet wrote: "I will not follow where the path may lead, but I will go where there is no path and I will leave a trail." I suspect this means that the trails willed to us by buffalo and deer seeking new feeding grounds, Native Americans seeking game and each other, and early pioneers seeking riches or a new life, need to be attended by a new, more contemporary breed of trailblazers — those who record the story and enhance our knowledge of travel as an element in the evolution of a country. This volume is a beginning, not an end. If it does not generate complementary volumes, it will stand as a symbol of futility instead of illumination. Much remains to be done. Centuries ago the Prophet Jeremiah warned against half-finished projects when he said:

> The harvest is ended;
> the summer is over;
> and we are not saved.

Arthur H. DeRosier, Jr.

John Phillip Weyerhaeuser, Jr.
Professor of History
The College of Idaho

PIONEER TRAILS WEST

INDIAN AND BUFFALO TRAILS

By Don Worcester

The buffalo, Sen. Thomas Hart Benton extravagantly proclaimed, blazed the way for the railroads to the Pacific. Although this is an exaggeration, buffalo "roads" or trails were important avenues to the interior and through various mountain ranges. They were much used by Indians, fur traders, and pioneers in the East as well as the West, especially through rough country and wherever water was scarce.

The frontier explorers who first crossed the Appalachians found buffalo roads and Indian trails the best routes for travel. Thomas Walker, who reached central Kentucky in the mid eighteenth century, recalled that "We kept . . . along the Indian road . . . . A large Buffalo Road goes from that Fork to the Creek over the West Ridge, which we took and found the Ascent and Descent tolerably easie." Walker's party encountered only one obstacle, a buffalo bull which disputed their right-of-way.

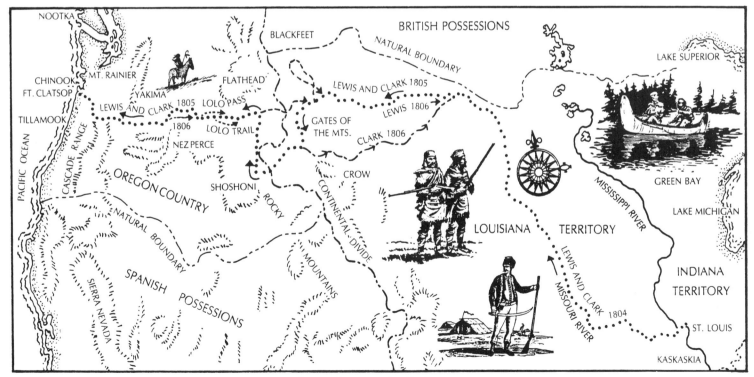

Indian Trails Across the Rockies

Buffalo roads through mountain gaps or passes were invariably well graded. As Col. Richard I. Dodge observed concerning the buffalo, "He seems to have a natural antipathy to the exertion of going up or down steep places." Many men have commented on the buffalo's facility in selecting easy travel routes. George Washington wrote in 1784 concerning Sandy Creek, West Virginia, "At the Crossing of this Creek, McCullock's path, which owes its origen to Buffaloes, being no other than their tracks from one lick to another and consequently crooked and not well chosen, strikes off from the New Road." For a buffalo road to be useful to a traveler, both must have the same destination.

Because of the numerous salt licks in Kentucky, there were dozens of well-worn buffalo roads to them from all directions. Indians followed these routes, making Kentucky a meeting place and an Indian battleground long before the coming of the whites.

The buffalo found not only the best passes through the mountains but also the safest river crossings. Frontiersmen learned that the buffalo generally crossed a river where another stream entered it; at these junctions sand bars formed, which simplified the crossing. Pioneers with wagons took advantage of the buffalo roads across rivers as well as through mountains.

There were many Indian trails that did not follow the buffalo, trails used by war, hunting, or trading parties. Since the Indians of the East customarily traveled in single file, their trails were narrow, suitable for men on foot or horseback but not necessarily for wagons. Portage trails, followed by Indians or traders carrying canoes from the head of one stream over a divide to the head of another, often crossed trails that followed the high ground between watersheds. These crossroads were frequently chosen as the sites of trading posts. Some, like Detroit, Michigan, and Portage, Wisconsin, became settlements.

The buffalo were obliged to move frequently to find grass, and they changed ranges with the seasons. The extent of their movements between summer and winter east of the Mississippi is not known. Because of the mountain ranges, they may have moved east and west as much as north and south. The search for grass, not cooler or warmer temperatures, governed their seasonal movements.

The old buffalo roads had a significant influence on the location of some of the interior settlements, such as Louisville, Frankfort, and Lexington, Kentucky, and Cincinnati, Ohio, which were built along well-traveled buffalo routes. The early railroad builders also followed buffalo roads through the mountains. As Archer Butler Hulbert observed, "The greater marvel is that these early pathfinders chose routes, even in the roughest districts, which the tripod of the white man cannot improve upon. A rare instance of this is the course of the Baltimore and Ohio railway between Grafton and Parkersburg in West Virginia. That this is one of the roughest rides . . . is well known to all who have passed that way, and that so fine a road could be put through such a rough country is one of the marvels of engineering science." The railroad followed the old-time thoroughfare of buffalo and Indians.

Joel A. Allen, writing in the 1870s, remarked that "Ordinarily . . . the buffalo shows commendable sagacity in respect to his choice of routes, usually choosing the easiest grades and the most direct courses, so that a buffalo trail can be depended upon as affording the most feasible road possible through the region it traverses." Similarly, W. T. Hornaday, writing a decade later, noted that "The trail of a herd in search of water is usually as good a piece of engineering as could be executed by the best railway surveyor, and is governed by precisely the same principles. It always follows the level of the valley, swerves around the high points, and crosses the stream repeatedly in order to avoid climbing up from the level."

West of the Mississippi there were many more buffalo and Indian trails. On the Great Plains between Texas and the Saskatchewan the buffalo usually grazed north three or four hundred miles in the spring and back to the south a similar distance in the

Courtesy Smithsonian Institution   *Photo by Edward S. Curtis*

Slow Bull, Oglala Sioux warrior, participating in the Hunka ceremony fall. There were many buffalo roads within these ranges in all parts of the plains, but the Great Buffalo Road covering the entire distance between Texas and northern Canada was a myth.

Trails to grass and water were most numerous on the plains, corresponding somewhat to the salt-lick trails of Kentucky. Buffalo trails radiated in all directions from water sources; between the water and the numerous grazing grounds the trails split many times. Frontiersmen in search of water had only to follow the trails away from the forks.

One peculiarity of buffalo trails was explained by Buffalo Jones. A buffalo trail, he noted, "cannot be found anywhere that is longer than four hundred yards without a change of direction, but the general course of the herd would be comparatively straight for a distance of thirty or forty miles." Because the buffalo cannot see directly in front, "they are compelled to keep one side or the other turned in the general direction in which they are going. Not being good travelers sideways, they look ahead with one eye and to the rear with the other, deflecting to the right and then to the left for a distance of two or three hundred yards."

Lewis and Clark were the first American explorers to discover the value of buffalo roads and Indian trails in the trans-Mississippi West, especially for finding the best river crossings and the easiest routes through the mountains. They followed the Lolo or Northern Nez Perce Trail part of the way through the Rockies. The trail passes around the northern edge of the Bitterroot Mountains. It was one of several routes by which Plateau tribes such as the Nez Perces, Shoshones, and Flatheads crossed over the mountains to the buffalo ranges of Montana and Wyoming.

Unlike buffalo roads, Indian trails did not always follow the longer, easier grades. Lewis and Clark "continued our march along the Indian road which led us over steep hills and deep hollows." A century later their route up Lolo Creek served as the stagecoach road from Missoula to Boyle's Springs, Montana. The Lolo Trail was surveyed by Lt. John Mullan in 1854 and was used as a military road by Gen. O. O. Howard in 1876-1877 during the Nez Perce war.

On their return eastward across the mountains in 1806 Lewis and Clark traveled part of the way by separate routes. Lewis sought the Cokahlahishkit (modern Big Blackfoot) or buffalo road river, which some tribes followed when going to the plains to hunt. The Indians assured him that it would lead to the falls of the Missouri. The trail forked, they told him; both branches led to the falls, but the left fork was the best route to follow. "The Indians informed us that there is an excellent road from the three forks of the Missouri through a low gap in the mountains to the East fork of Clark's river which passes down that fork to its junction and up on the west side of the main fork to Travelers Rest creek which they travel with their families in six days; the distance must be about 150 miles." Lewis and Clark found that the Indians' knowledge of trails, terrain, and landmarks was accurate and valuable.

When Lewis was crossing the mountains in June, the snow was still deep. He and his men were able to keep on the trail by watching for marks on trees which the Indians' pack animals had made by rubbing against them as they passed. The Nez Perce told Lewis that farther south there was a longer trail that was free of snow by June, but he took the shorter route.

Clark, meanwhile, explored another trail to the falls of Missouri. Near modern Trail Creek, Montana, he crossed the divide over Gibbon's Pass. "I observe the appearance of the old buffalow road . . . on this side of the mountain (*proving that formerly Buffs roved there and also that this is the best route, for the Buffs and the Indians always have the best route and now both were joined*)," Clark wrote.

In July Clark crossed the most southerly branch of the Gallatin River "and struck an old buffalow road (the one our Indn. woman meant) which I kept continuing nearly the same course up the middle fork, crossed it and camped on a small branch of the middle fork at the northeast side at the commencement of the gap in the mountain — the road leading up this branch, served other roads, all old, came in from the

Arapaho camp with buffalo meat drying, near Fort Dodge, Kansas

right and left." Concerning this route, Peter Koch commented: "When I first came to Bozeman in 1870, the main 'buffalo road' crossed Sour Dough (or Bozeman) creek about half a mile above the cemetery and entered the foothills through a low depression through the bluff. It kept the foothills until it crossed the East Gallatin in a little more than two miles, opposite old Fort Ellis. It was very plain and deeply worn. Clark may have followed that all the way." At the Yellowstone, Clark observed a "great crossing place of the buffalow."

Courtesy National Park Service

Cheyenne family — chief American Horse with his wives and children, 1891

In August 1809 British fur trader-scientist David Thompson was exploring in the Rockies and reached the point where the "Great Road of the Flat Heads" left the Kootenai River and continued to the Flathead River. He was, at the time, near the present Idaho-Montana border. Later he was directly opposite the 'Skeetshoo road' by which the Indians traveled from Clark's Fork to the Spokane River. Thompson returned on the "Saleesh road to the buffalo," which went eastward into Montana.

English naturalist John Bradbury, who accompanied the Astorians to the upper Missouri, was on the Niobrara River in 1811. "Along the bluffs," he wrote, "we observed excellent roads made by the buffaloes. These roads I had frequent opportunities of examining, and am of the opinion that no engineer could have laid them out more judiciously."

W. P. Hunt and the Astorians continued overland to the Pacific Coast. They crossed the Bighorn Mountains by a route that became a highway and followed an Indian trail across the Wind River range and through Union Pass. From the Snake River they followed another Indian trail which later was followed by emigrants to Oregon.

Indian and buffalo trails were found all over the plains, from far north to far south. In 1905 an old Blackfoot medicine man, Brings-down-the-Sun, explained to Walter McClintock that "There is a well known trail we call the Old North Trail. It runs north and south along the Rocky Mountains. No one knows how long it has been used by the Indians. My father told me it originated in the migration of a great tribe of Indians from the distant north to the south, and all the tribes have, ever since, continued to follow in their tracks." The trail forked where Calgary is now located. The main trail went south near modern Helena, Montana, and along the eastern slope of the Rockies to a country "inhabited by a people with dark skins, and long hair falling over their faces (Mexico)." Blackfoot raiding parties did reach Mexico in the eighteenth century; David Thompson told of one that in 1787 returned with a Spanish packtrain.

In 1865 a Dr. John McDougall was in the central Battle River country of Alberta, Canada. "In the course of years," he wrote, "I have travelled thousands of miles along buffalo paths, and often I have wondered at and admired the instinctive knowledge of engineering skill manifested in the selection of ground and route made by these wandering herds . . . . If one was in doubt as to a crossing let him follow the path of a buffalo." A few years later McDougall was in the upper Bow River Valley. "This time we traveled by a new route through the hills. Old buffalo trails were our bridle paths, and through spots and scenes wonderfully picturesque . . . these instinctive engineers of nature led us on."

Officers who served in the Indian fighting army of the West frequently commented on buffalo roads and Indian trails. Gen. J. F. Rusling wrote in the 1870s concerning the buffalo: "They are a sure guide up and down the bluffs; many are so precipitous that safe ascent or descent elsewhere seems impossible. But the buffalo, by a wise instinct seems to have hit just the right path."

Richard I. Dodge, who served many years on the plains, noted that "When travelling unmolested the buffalo is extremely careful in his choice of grades by which to pass from one creek to another; so much so indeed that, though a well-defined buffalo trail may not be a good waggon road, one may rest well assured that it is the best route to be had." Dodge added that the buffalo's reluctance to travel over bad ground did not indicate an inability to do so. "When frightened he will, with perfect impunity, climb banks or plunge down precipices where it would be impossible, or certain death, to a horse to follow."

On the southern plains buffalo and Indian trails were also useful to travelers. In the 1530s Cabeza de Vaca did not see any trails in Texas, but a few years later Coronado's men followed "paths down into the ravines, made by the cows."

After the New Mexicans made a lasting peace with the Comanches in the 1780s, citizens and Pueblo Indians made annual visits to the plains to trade with the Comanches, Kiowas, and other tribes, and to hunt buffalo. The traders became known as Comancheros; the hunters were called Ciboleros — *cíbola* was an Indian word for buffalo. Both the traders and the hunters eventually used two-wheeled carts, with the result that they left easily followed trails from the eastern settlements of New Mexico. In 1820 Stephen Long saw a well-worn trail following the Canadian River eastward. By the 1840s both hunters and traders used

wagons. In 1845 Lt. J. W. Abert reported that the route along the Canadian had the appearance of a wagon road. A few years later Cap. Randolph B. Marcy called it "the old Mexican Cart road." An emigrant in his party wrote that on the Canadian "you find large, broad wagon tracks made by the Ciboleros or buffalo hunters, and the Comanche traders, which lead you to the settlements." One Comanchero trail led to a canyon near modern Lubbock, Texas.

Many buffalo trails ran north and south across Texas. One, the Old Buffalo Trail, reached Buffalo Springs in Sherman County from the northwest and continued on to the Agua Frio. Another crossed the Canadian near Old Tascosa in Oldham County and hit the Tierra Blanca near Vega in Deaf Smith County. In September 1841 the Texas-Santa Fe expedition reached this crossing. Peter Gallagher, a member of the expedition, saw many horse trails worn into the limestone. "The Indian Trail in this valley is the Largest trail we found on the Plains," he wrote. "I think it the Main Indian Route from the Head of the Red River across the Llano Estacado to the Pecos River."

The Great Comanche War Trail used on raids into Mexico crossed Hemphill County. There were two main branches which led into the main route from the north, and three forks into Mexico where the main trail reached the Rio Grande. The Comanches followed buffalo trails most of the way. There were many other buffalo and Indian trails running north from Texas, and the later trail herds heading for Kansas used the buffalo crossing of the Red and other rivers.

In 1849 Captain Marcy set out from Fort Smith, Arkansas, to find the best wagon route to Santa Fe. On the way across the Llano Estacado he reported that "From the Sand hills our road followed an old Comanche trail until we turned to the left." A small lake that provided the only water in one region he named Mustang Pond, because of the trails made by wild horses that led to it. "The trails in this vicinity," he added, "all concentrate at the water." This was valuable information for anyone traveling through the region.

Marcy's Comanche guide told him there was a good wagon route farther south which did not enter the Llano Estacado. "There is a Comanche trail leading over this route," Marcy wrote, "and it would undoubtedly be the best between this point and Chihuahua."

On his return trip Marcy followed the southern route and found that his Comanche guide had been correct. He recommended it as the best wagon road to California. It became a famous road and was heavily traveled during the gold rush. It was later abandoned in favor of the Southern Overland Mail Route.

In 1852 Marcy led another expedition, this time to the headwaters of the Red River. "Taking an old Comanche trail," he wrote when he had reached mountains, "I followed it into a narrow defile in the mountains, which

Courtesy U.S. Fish and Wildlife Service

Grazing buffalo — Wichita mountains wildlife refuge

led me up through a very tortuous and rocky gorge, where the well-worn path indicated that it had been travelled for many years."

These are but a few of the multitude of buffalo and Indian trails that provided avenues for Americans pushing westward from the Atlantic seacoast to the Pacific. Many of them became wagon roads and ultimately highways or railroad routes. Some of the trails discussed in the following chapters had been used by buffaloes and Indians long before the coming of the whites.

THE WILDERNESS ROAD

By Earl Wade

For centuries southern Indian warriors had followed the tracks of wandering buffaloes through the rugged Appalachian Mountains into the land that they called "Ken-ta-kee," meaning "among the meadows." In the eighteenth century thousands of American long hunters, farmers, and land speculators traveled over the Indian trail, known as the Warriors Path, into the land that the white man often labeled "Kaintuck." They transformed the Warriors Path into

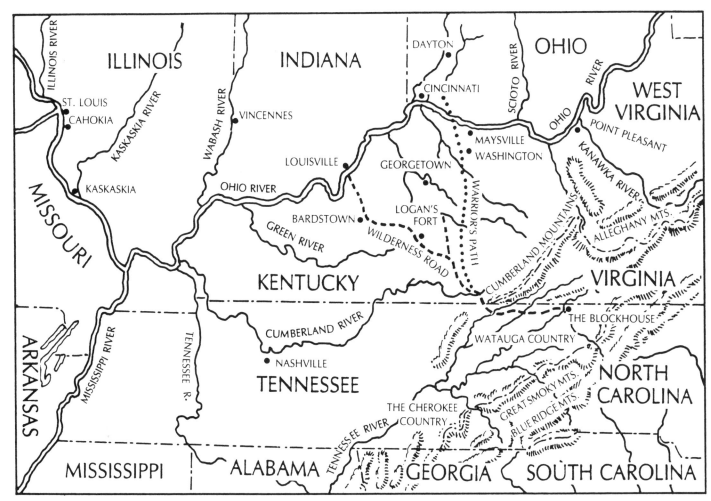

The Wilderness Road Through the Cumberland Gap

one of the best-known pioneer trails, the Wilderness Road.

For a brief period during the last three decades of the eighteenth century, this pioneer trail was by far the most significant link between the old colonial frontier and the trans-Appalachian settlements in Kentucky and Tennessee. By the beginning of the nineteenth century these two new states and a bridgehead to the trans-Mississippi West stood as monuments to "American's first highway to the west."

It was largely geography that determined the location of the first highway to the West. Stretching from Maine to Georgia, the Appalachian chain presented a major barrier to Americans who desired to move westward into the Ohio River Valley. The northernmost route to that valley ran through the Hudson and Mohawk river valleys of New York to the Great Lakes and the Old Northwest.

A second major route, later destined to be part of the National Road of the nineteenth century, cut through the mountains of western Pennsylvania. It led from the Potomac River through western Maryland to Pittsburgh, where the confluence of the Monongahela and Allegheny rivers form the Ohio — the major gateway of the future into the rich valley. The third route through the Appalachians came with the white man's discovery of the Cumberland Gap in 1750, which proved to be the earliest pioneer trail of easy passage through the mountains to the West. "As though hollowed by the Creator's hand for the sole purpose of opening a way from the seaboard to the interior of the continent," Archer B. Hulbert wrote, "the trough between the Blue Ridge and Cumberland ranges was early found to lead surely but circuitously westward."

The Appalachian barrier fell with the discovery of the southern route through the Cumberland Gap. Whether the Creator opened the way from the seaboard to the interior or persistence finally reaped its reward, the discovery of the gap and the Warriors Path into Kentucky sent a flood of people into the interior, flowing through Virginia's Shenandoah Valley towards the headwaters of the Clinch and Holston rivers of southwest Virginia and eastern Tennessee. Pioneers by the thousands flowed down these valleys into east Tennessee to strike the Wilderness Road where it turned northwest through the Appalachians into Kentucky.

The lack of heavy Indian concentrations in the region of "Ken-ta-kee" helped promote the southernmost route through the Appalachians. On the two northern routes, pioneers had to contend with powerful and often hostile Indian opposition. Among the northern tribes, the Iroquois, Delawares, and Shawnees were ready to repel pioneers who braved the difficult, mountainous valleys to invade Indian hunting grounds. From the Cumberland Gap south, the mountains could not easily be flanked because of the Cherokees, Catawbas, and Upper Creeks. The largely open territory between the Tennessee and Ohio rivers also lay between the northern and southern concentrations of Indians east of the Mississippi and served as hunting grounds and a battlefield. The area was not settled by great numbers of Indians but was often fought over, particularly by the northern Shawnees and the southern Cherokees, who turned "Ken-ta-kee" into a "dark and bloody ground." Yet, because no strong Indian concentrations lived there to stem the tide of pioneers when they spilled through the gap, the days of Indian hunting grounds in Kentucky were numbered.

Until 1763, however, American pioneers had to wait to challenge the Indians and the elements because of the influence of French and Spanish civil, religious, and military agents in the backcountry from Canada to Florida. By that year Britain had fought four major wars involving both the United Kingdom's New World European rivals and its American colonies — King William's War, 1689-1697; Queen Anne's War, 1702-1713; King George's War, 1740-1748; and the French and Indian War, 1754-1763. As far as American colonists were concerned, each war had been a French and Indian war, with an occasional Spanish and Indian conflict in the South. These wars had involved Indian allies on all sides. Until Britain's rivals had been defeated and removed, hostile tribes and the formidable mountain barriers combined to delay the western stream of pioneers until the Treaty of Paris of 1763.

Meanwhile, Old World immigrants continued to flow into the British colonies, particularly into tolerant Pennsylvania. Instead of pushing on to the west, these new arrivals moved north and south into the backcountry of the Atlantic colonies. Northern movement was discouraged by Indians, rugged land, poor access routes to the backcountry, and avaricious land speculators. On the other hand, opportunities for land to the south drew tens of thousands down the Great Valley Road from Philadelphia through the Shenandoah Valley of Virginia into eastern Tennessee, the western Carolinas, and ultimately into Kentucky over the Wilderness Road.

Religious, economic, and political conditions that existed in the Old World during the early eighteenth century sent thousands of Germans and Scotch-Irish to the New World, where they frequently acquired land without benefit of title. Even in tolerant Pennsylvania these squatters eventually encountered civilization's laws and displeasures. "It was against the laws of God and nature," according to one defiant Scotch-Irish, "that so much land should be idle while so many Christians wanted it to labor on to raise their bread." Although he spoke what many thought, the majority eventually had to move. With opportunities limited for the moment to the north and west, these immigrants and others turned southward toward Virginia and North Carolina on the Great Valley Road, sometimes referred to as the Irish Road because so many Scotch-Irish traveled it.

Cheap land and freedom of worship attracted thousands to the backcountry of Virginia and North Carolina. In Pennsylvania, land prices jumped more than 50 percent between 1719 and 1732, rising from ten to more than fifteen pounds per hundred acres. In Maryland the cost of one hundred acres was only five pounds in 1738, but in the backcountry of Virginia and North Carolina land ranged in price from free grants in return for settlement to a modest three shillings for one square mile (640 acres). And after 1738 Virginia and North Carolina promised freedom of worship to Presbyterians, which gave even greater impetus to the southern movement by the Calvinist Germans and Scotch-Irish. Land, religious freedom, and fate carried the American westward movement on a southern course close to its first highway to the West — the Wilderness Road through the Cumberland Gap into Kentucky.

Dr. Thomas Walker discovered the Cumberland Gap in 1750. He was the Virginia agent for the Loyal Land Company, a speculation company that had secured a grant of 800 thousand acres in territory beyond the Appalachians claimed in the colony's charter. On March 6, 1750, Walker departed from his home near Charlottesville with five companions — Ambrose Powell, William Tomlison, Colby Chew, Henry Lawless, and John Hughes — to "go to the Westward in order to discover a proper place for settlement." This mission was the first time that white men were known to pass through the gap on the Warriors Path. By April 13 the party had arrived at the gap that Walker later named for the Duke of Cumberland. In his journal Dr. Walker described his first observations. On the south side of the gap, he wrote, the incline was gentle with a "plain Indian Road" visible, where the gap may be seen "at a considerable distance," but "the Mountain on the North Side of the Gap is very Steep and Rocky."

By April 23 the Walker party had passed through the gap and proceeded northwest to cross the Cum-

berland River near the modern community of Barbourville, Kentucky. There Dr. Walker executed the main goal of the mission when he established a "settlement," as the land grant required, for the Loyal Land Company. For the next five days Walker, Powell, and Chew explored the mountainous land about them in search of good land for the company. Their colleagues, who stayed in the base camp on the Cumberland River, built a "house 12 by 8, clear'd and broke up some ground, and planted Corn, and Peach Stones." This was the first recorded house built in Kentucky by white men, but the "settlement" soon collapsed. Walker returned on April 28, and the entire party left on April 30, never to return.

Dr. Walker failed to find great tracts of good land for the Loyal Land Company or to settle any permanent station in the land grant area, yet he had been so close to the rich meadows of Kentucky! If he had continued to the north and northwest along the "plain Indian Road" (the Warriors Path that he described in his journal) Dr. Walker's mission would have ended in triumph. Instead, he turned east and northeast through eastern Kentucky, across modern West Virginia, and back to his home in Virginia, completing a great circle in four months and seven days. He arrived home on July 16, 1750, much discouraged, not realizing the significance of his discovery of the Cumberland Gap and the Warriors Path to "Ken-ta-kee."

In the same year that Dr. Walker made his fruitless trip for the Loyal Land Company, Christopher Gist, an explorer for the rival Ohio Land

Company, discovered the good land that Dr. Walker had so narrowly missed. The Ohio company's grant provided for 200 thousand acres between the Monongahela and Great Kanawha rivers and another 300 thousand acres along the Ohio River. Gist left his home on the Yadkin River in North Carolina during October, and on the following March 12, 1751, he entered Kentucky, after traveling north and then west down the Ohio River. On May 18 he had completed his assignment and returned to the Yadkin River Valley. Like Dr. Walker, he made a great circle in his explorations and encountered more mountainous than good land, but he had seen the fertile, level land in the Ohio River Valley. John Findley followed Gist down the Ohio the next year until he was captured by Shawnees, and Thomas Bullitt and his party of surveyors arrived at the Falls of the Ohio,

later Louisville, Kentucky, in 1753. However, the great imperial struggle between Britain and France for colonies and commerce soon slowed the westward thrust from the Atlantic colonies toward the Ohio River Valley.

Christopher Gist's report created much excitement among investors of the Ohio Land Company, offset by news that the French were building a series of forts from Lake Erie to the site of modern Pittsburgh, which thoroughly alarmed both supporters and foes of the company. If the French were successful, it meant for American colonials the end of western trade and land opportunities and the emergence of an extremely hostile frontier. Gov. Robert Dinwiddie moved quickly to protect Virginia's interests, as well as his own, for he was an investor in the Ohio company. He ordered young George Wash-

Cumberland Gap National Historical Park — Visitor Center Pinnacle Drive

ington into the backcountry to warn the French. By late 1753 Washington had delivered the governor's message to the French that they were encroaching on territory claimed by Virginia. When the French ignored his warning, Washington advised Dinwiddie that his only option was to remove the French by force.

Governor Dinwiddie elected to send Washington to the forks of the Ohio to build a fort and secure for Virginia the gateway to the west. By the time Washington had executed the order in April 1754, the French were already building Fort Duquesne. Following a brief skirmish with a French scouting party near that fort, Washington ordered Fort Necessity built in anticipation of a French attack. On July 3, 1754, the French defeated Washington and took Fort Necessity. Washington was released to inform Virginia, the American colonies, and Britain that the Ohio River Valley and the West belonged to France. Although Britain and France were technically at peace for the next two years, the last of the four great colonial conflicts had begun in 1754 as the French and Indian War. Further exploration of "Ken-ta-kee" had to await the outcome of that war.

In the meantime the flow of people down the Great Valley Road from Pennsylvania through Virginia into North Carolina continued unabated. One pioneer family that sought a new life in North Carolina was that of Squire Boone from Berks County, Pennsylvania. Troubled because he was "disowned" by his Quaker neighbors in the Society of Friends, and encouraged because land was both available and cheap in North Carolina, Boone moved his family to the Yadkin River Valley in 1752. Among the members of Squire Boone's family was young Daniel Boone, the future pathfinder of the Wilderness Road to Kentucky. At the age of eighteen he was already an expert marksman and hunter.

Late in 1754 Daniel Boone joined the North Carolina militia, commanded by Maj. Edward B. Dobbs, as a wagoner and blacksmith. In 1755 the unit moved north to Fort Cumberland on the Maryland border to join other colonial troops and British regulars. British Maj. Gen. Edward Braddock arrived that same year to take command of the combined forces. In June he began a long, slow march to disaster — cutting a supply road ahead of units advancing toward the French at Fort Duquesne at the forks of the Ohio River. On July 9, 1755, the French and their Indian allies attacked and decisively defeated the British army. Braddock, mortally wounded, ordered a retreat, which turned into chaos.

Since Daniel Boone was a wagoner and blacksmith he was not expected to take part in the fighting. Various accounts agree that Boone was at the rear of Braddock's supply train when the French routed the front units and forced a disorganized retreat toward the wagons. Seeing the breakdown in front of them, the wagoners slashed their horses traces and retreated on horseback, with Boone among them. Eventually he made his way back to his father's cabin in the Yadkin Valley of North Carolina.

Although his brief war experience in 1755 was disastrous, Boone had heard first-hand accounts of the excellent land beyond the Appalachians, especially the land of "Kenta-kee." John Findley, a wagoner with the Pennsylvania militia, related to Boone his recent experiences as trader, explorer, and Indian captive in Kentucky. Christopher Gist, a scout for Braddock's army, had explored Kentucky for the Ohio Land Company at the beginning of the decade, and the Boones and Gists were family friends from the Yadkin Valley. Dr. Thomas Walker, who in 1750 had discovered the Cumberland Gap while on a mission for the Loyal Land Company, was also with Braddock's army, although there is no evidence that Walker talked with Boone. The stories of better land across the mountains created in Boone a lifelong wanderlust.

For the next ten years the trailblazer of the Wilderness Road farmed, roamed, and fought over much of western Virginia, eastern Tennessee, and western North Carolina. He had married Rebecca Bryan and settled down as a farmer in the Yadkin Valley when war once again touched his life. In 1759 the Cherokees went on the warpath. Because of the turbulent conditions on the Yadkin frontier during the next year, Boone took his young family into Virginia, where he worked briefly as a wagoner. Before the year was finished, however, he began to roam down the Holston Valley and then into the Watauga to hunt for animal pelts in Cherokee country. Evidence of his trip into eastern Tennessee remained until the twentieth century on a tree in the Boone's Creek community of Washington County, where he had carved on a beech tree:

"D. Boon Cilled A. Bar on tree in the year 1760." In 1761 he joined the North Carolina militia to fight the Cherokees, but the war soon ended. Boone moved his family back to the Yadkin, where his hunting and trapping trips became increasingly frequent.

The French and Indian War also ended, with the Treaty of Paris in 1763, but new problems prevented thousands of Americans, like Boone, from visiting the lands beyond the Appalachians. In the spring of 1763 Ottawa Chief Pontiac led his warriors against Fort Detroit and ignited an Indian explosion on the western frontier. The causes of the rebellion were many, but they may be reduced to a single problem: Too many white men were encroaching on Indian lands. The British government struggled to develop a western policy, but Pontiac's rebellion made that goal extremely difficult.

Acting in this emergency with little knowledge and much poor judgment, Lord Hillsborough, president of the Board of Trade, advised King George III to halt colonial westward expansion at the crest of the Appalachians, to open the newly acquired territories of Canada and Florida to Americans, to prohibit private land purchases from Indians, and to stop unlicensed trade between the colonials and Indians. King George accepted Hillsborough's suggestions in good faith and issued the now famous Royal Proclamation of 1763.

The Proclamation, together with Pontiac's rebellion, spelled trouble from the west for the crown and eastern colonials. The proclamation overlooked the reality of colonials already living west of the demarcation line, which, with the lack of an adequate defense against Indians on the western frontier, caused a major split between east and west.

By 1768 the demarcation line had been pushed west by the Fort Stanwix Treaty with the Iroquois in the north and the Hard Labor Treaty with the Cherokees in the south. In 1770 the Cherokees agreed to a further expansion to meet objections by Virginia. Pontiac's rebellion acted as a catalyst for several outstanding western complaints against the east. Heavy taxes, eastern tax collectors, eastern judges and civil officials, and eastern centers of judicial and civil authority had irritated westerners for years. These and other grievances, combined with the lack of protection as demonstrated again during Pontiac's rebellion, caused a split. Indifference to their frontier problems and a dangerous frontier had turned most westerners against the east. In the South many of these disenchanted frontiersmen joined the Regulator Movement and eventually were among the first settlers to seek a new life in Kentucky over the Wilderness Road.

The long hunter and the trader, however, blazed the trail to Kentucky. Shortly after Pontiac's rebellion was crushed, American long hunters and traders had illegally begun to hunt and trade in "Ken-ta-kee." James Smith and Issac Lindsey explored and hunted throughout southern Kentucky beginning in 1766. John Findley crossed northern Kentucky to trade with Indians, while James Harrod and Michael Stoner explored and hunted in southern Kentucky. Ben Cutbirth (or Cutbird) ventured overland from North Carolina through Kentucky and Tennessee to the Mississippi River and then down the river to New Orleans.

To complete the cutting edge of the frontier, the land speculator and farmer had to make their appearances. In Kentucky, Daniel Boone was to be a little of each. Back in the Yadkin Valley Boone had scratched out a meager living by farming and hunting, but in 1764 his chances for land speculation improved when he became an agent of Judge Richard Henderson. Henderson financed Boone's trips in return for information on land in the territory that he hunted. In his missions on the frontier, Boone asked long hunters about the quality of land they had crossed in their travels. Boone had heard about the Cutbirth trip to New Orleans. His brother-in-law had been a member of the party, and Cutbirth was married to Boone's niece. He also remembered the stories of Kentucky told around the campfires of the ill-fated march by Braddock on Fort Duquesne. Boone continued to hunt for himself and explore for Judge Henderson in the valleys of the Tennessee and Holston until 1767. He had not entered Kentucky, but stories of the bluegrass region soon would lead both Henderson and Boone there.

Boone made his first trip to Kentucky during the winter of 1767-68. He failed to find the quality land described by long hunters and traders, but he returned home in the spring with a profit from successful hunting and trapping.

Fate brought an unexpected guest to the Boone house in Yadkin Valley that spring. John Findley, who had served with Boone during the Braddock disaster and who had been a trader and explorer in Kentucky as recently as 1767, arrived to persuade Boone to accompany him through the Cumberland Gap into Kentucky. Findley had heard of the gap while he was a captive of Indians in Kentucky before the French and Indian War, and Boone had learned from the long hunters of an overland passageway to Kentucky. If Boone would help him, Findley was sure he could find the gap. Boone seized the opportunity. Findley remained Boone's houseguest during the winter of 1768-69, while they planned their spring trip into Kentucky.

On May 1, 1769, Boone and Findley, with four companions, left Boone's house "to wander through the wilderness . . . in quest of the country of Kentucke." No doubt Judge Henderson played a significant role in financing the trip, because it was well supplied. Three of the men — Joseph Holden, James Mooney, and William Cooley — were designated as "camp keepers," hired to release the other three for hunting and exploring. Squire Boone, Daniel's brother, planned to follow the group to Kentucky with fresh supplies after the crops were harvested in the late autumn.

Since Boone had explored and hunted for Henderson around the headwaters of the Tennessee River in the Holston, Clinch, and Powell valleys, the trip to the gap was unexpectedly easy. Earlier long hunters had blazed the trail to the gap; there it joined the Warriors Path, which was also plainly marked, as Dr. Walker had indicated in his journal in 1750.

Cumberland Gap Historical Pass — on the wilderness road

The Boone party followed this path for some distance and then turned west to the headwaters of the west branch of the Rockcastle River. By June 7, 1769, they had established their base camp at Station Camp Creek. They divided into pairs to hunt and explore, setting a time for all to return to the base camp.

For several months the men hunted, explored, and prepared their pelts without any trouble. On December 22, 1769, the serenity and isolation ended when Daniel and his brother-in-law, John Stewart, were captured by an Indian hunting party. "A number of Indians rushed out of a thick cane-brake upon us," Boone wrote, "and made us prisoners. The time of our sorrow was now arrived . . . . The Indians plundered us of what we had, and kept us in confinement seven days." Boone and Stewart escaped their captors, but they had lost the fruit of their labors.

In late December, during the Boone party's greatest moment of despair, Squire Boone and Alexander Neely arrived with fresh supplies from North Carolina. John Findley and the three camp keepers decided, however, that they had seen enough and departed, leaving the Boone brothers, Stewart, and Neely in Kentucky. Soon there would only be two. John Stewart failed to return from a hunting trip shortly after Findley left, and Alexander Neely decided to return to his people in North Carolina. The Boone brothers hunted and trapped through the winter. On May 1, 1770, exactly a year after the trip had begun, Squire Boone packed the horses with their furs and skins and returned to the Yadkin settlement for supplies.

Daniel Boone was now alone in the Kentucky wilderness. "I was happy," he observed, "in the midst of dangers and inconveniences. In such a diversity it was impossible I should be disposed to melancholy." During this period of solitude, without the luxury of powder and ball to continue the commercial hunt, he explored much of the Kentucky country.

On July 27, 1770, Squire Boone returned from North Carolina and met his brother at their old campsite. By autumn the Boones had accumulated enough furs and skins for Squire to make another trip to the settlements. Daniel remained in the wilderness alone for the second time to scout the land. After Squire's return the brothers hunted together until March of 1771. Thinking it not safe to remain any longer in Kentucky, they headed toward the Cumberland Gap and home. In May they were almost home when Indians jumped them and seized everything — furs, skins, horses, and guns. After two years in the wilderness the Boones returned home with little to show for their effort but the knowledge of Kentucky that Daniel had gained. In the end this knowledge offset any material losses that the brothers had suffered.

Despite his adversity Boone determined to return with his family to Kentucky, which he esteemed "a second paradise." Two years passed before he attempted the move, during which he sold the farm and everything else that could not be carried or used in the new home. He also convinced five families in the Yadkin settlements to join him. This hardy group, soon to be joined by forty men in Powell Valley, departed on September 25, 1773, for "Ken-ta-kee."

The little band of pioneers failed to reach the promised land. Indians attacked as they were about to enter Kentucky and forced them to retreat to the Clinch Valley settlements for protection. Boone was discouraged by the failure and disheartened by the death of James, his eldest son, in the Indian attack. The future appeared even more gloomy, for the Indians were restless all along the western frontier. Thus collapsed the first effort at permanent settlement over the trail that would soon become the Wilderness Road. For the moment Kentucky had to wait.

In the summer of 1774 Indian restlessness on the frontier erupted into the open warfare of Lord Dunmore's War. It was a war for western land. The westward expansion that followed the collapse of Pontiac's rebellion revived Indian resistance. With considerable provocation, the powerful Shawnees renewed their attacks on the white settlements along a 350-mile frontier. Lord Dunmore, the royal governor of Virginia, issued a general alert for the frontier and sent a warning to the surveyors who were at work in Kentucky. Daniel Boone and Michael Stoner of the Clinch settlements were chosen to deliver the warning, since the northern route down the Ohio River had been blocked by the Shawnees. The southern overland route through the Cumberland Gap remained open, but the mission required the special talents and knowledge of Boone. For sixty-two days he and Stoner traveled through Kentucky spreading the

alarm. Their warning saved most of the Kentucky frontiersmen.

When Boone returned to Clinch Valley he became the local commander of three forts that anchored Virginia's southern defense in Dunmore's War. Although Boone and his men experienced several raids, the main development in the brief war came with Dunmore's effort to break the strength of the Shawnees in the north. His strategy involved a two-pronged attack on the Shawnee heartland north of the Ohio River. Lord Dunmore led one colonial army and Col. Andrew Lewis the other. The divided colonials courted disaster. On October 9, 1774 the main Shawnee war party caught Colonel Lewis and his men at Point Pleasant near the juncture of the Great Kanawha and Ohio rivers. The colonials repulsed the Shawnee attack and turned disaster into victory. Lewis' triumph opened the way for Lord Dunmore to settle with the Shawnees on highly favorable terms for western settlers and eastern speculators. Dunmore's War had completed the opening of the West.

Boone left the militia on November 20, 1774. The opportunities in Kentucky never seemed better; his dream of new land in the wilderness was at hand.

Now that there was peace with the Indians, thousands of land-seeking pioneers in Virginia and North Carolina were eager to push into the interior. Boone's old friend, Judge Henderson, had organized the Louisa Company in August 1774 to take advantage of the opportunity, planning to lease land from the Cherokees, now the sole claimants of "Ken-ta-kee."

By January of 1775, however, he had decided on outright purchase of the land from the Cherokees, and he engaged Boone to help him.

Henderson's company name also changed with his intentions. The Louisa Company became the Transylvania Company, with the avowed purpose of establishing Kentucky as the fourteenth British colony. Henderson asked Boone to assist the Transylvania Company in the purchase of the "dark and bloody ground" of Kentucky. "This I accepted," Boone stated, and he "undertook to mark out a road in the best passage from the settlement through the wilderness of Kentucke."

Henderson negotiated with Cherokee chiefs at Sycamore Shoals on the Watauga River (Elizabethton, Tennessee) between March 14 and 17, 1775, for some twenty million acres in Kentucky. Daniel Boone had already departed for the wilderness with a "number of enterprising men" to carry out Henderson's order to mark out a road. Beginning at the Long Island of the Holston River (Kingsport, Tennessee), Boone led his party of thirty axmen through the familiar Clinch and Powell valleys to Cumberland Gap and the Warriors Path.

From the gap he followed the Indian trail for several miles and then turned onto a buffalo trace bearing to

Courtesy Washington University Gallery of Art, St. Louis   *Painting by George Caleb Bingham*
Daniel Boone escorting settlers through the Cumberland Gap

the northwest. After the party crossed Rockcastle River, the task of opening the Wilderness road became extremely difficult. "On leaving that River," Felix Walker wrote in his journal, "we had to . . . cut our way through a country of about twenty miles, entirely covered with dead brash [sic] . . . . At the end of which we arrived at the commencement of a cane country . . . about thirty miles through thick cane and reed." After they emerged from the cane territory, Walker reported that "we began to discover the pleasing and rapturous appearance of the plains of Kentucky."

Indian raids, however, soon interrupted the "pleasing and rapturous" plain. Several men in the Boone party, including Walker himself, were killed by Indians in the march to the Kentucky River. By April 1, 1775, Boone had completed the road to the river. In less than a month, more than 200 miles of wilderness road (not much more than a rough pathway in places) had been marked or cut by the Boone woodsmen from Holston Valley to the Kentucky River. Land fever infected Boone's men and prevented them from preparing proper defensive fortifications. That work began when Judge Henderson arrived at their camp to supervise the construction of Boonesborough.

To make his dream of a Transylvania colony a reality, Henderson had to secure assistance from the other new settlements or stations in Kentucky — Harrodsburg, Boiling Springs, and St. Asaph. Like Henderson, land speculators and Virginia frontiersmen had moved to take advantage of the new situation in Kentucky. They and the colony of Virginia looked upon this upstart from North Carolina as an interloper, for Virginia had claimed this land in its colonial charter of 1609. Despite his neighbors' attitude toward him and his proposed colony, Henderson called the Boonesborough Assembly on May 22, 1775, in an effort to gain its support. Delegates from each station gathered at Boonesborough to discuss a government for the new colony.

Trouble began almost immediately. Not only were there strong objections from Henderson's Kentucky neighbors, but both the crown and shortly thereafter the Continental Congress turned down his proposal for a new colony or state. The assembly promulgated a set of laws to govern the new "colony," but with the outbreak of the American Revolution they were ignored even in Boonesborough. In January 1777 Henderson's dream ended when the Virginia assembly voted to add the whole of Kentucky as the westernmost county of Virginia.

The Virginia assembly rewarded Henderson handsomely, nevertheless, for his excellent work in opening the Wilderness Road by awarding him some 200 thousand acres on the Ohio River. He had failed to create a colony, but thousands of people would travel west over the Wilderness Road. Civilization began to arrive on the Kentucky frontier as early as September of 1775, when Rebecca and Jemima Boone became the first white women to settle on the new land. They were the first of many to come over the Wilderness Road. Settlement now was to be permanent, even though many years of danger lay ahead.

During the American Revolution the west faced constant threats from Indian raids, which the British encouraged. Boonesborough and the other Kentucky settlements were often attacked. Even though Daniel Boone played a major role in the defense of Boonesborough during the Revolution, George Rogers Clark of Harrodsburg easily overshadowed him in the West. Clark's victories — Kaskaskia, Cahokia, Vincennes, and others — failed to win the West for Americans, but they kept the Wilderness Road protected, and the frontier remained open. Even during the Revolution, therefore, people continued to flow through the gap on the Wilderness Road into Kentucky or Tennessee.

After peace was established at the conclusion of the American Revolution, Kentucky's population began to expand rapidly. From a dozen backwoodsmen in 1775 the region's population had grown to twelve thousand by the end of the war. A decade later the population had expanded to a hundred thousand. This tremendous growth allowed Kentucky to become the fifteenth state in the Union in 1792. The Wilderness Road had contributed thousands of people to swell the new state's population. Soon after the road was built, a western branch was opened. North of London, Kentucky, the new route turned off to the northwest toward Crab Orchard and then on to Louisville and the Ohio River, opening other areas to settlement.

In 1796 Isaac Shelby, first governor of the state of Kentucky, authorized the improvement of the Wilderness Road so that wagons "loaded with a ton weight, may pass with ease, with four good horses." Daniel Boone applied for the job of improving the road that he had blazed. "I think My Self intiteled to ofer . . . as I marked out that Rode in March 1775 and never Re'd anything for my trubel . . . and think My Self as capable of marking and cutting as any other man." Even though Boone thought himself still capable, Governor Shelby evidently believed that at sixty-two Boone was no longer fit for hard service. He did not give Boone the job.

As Boone faded into Kentucky's history, the Wilderness Road also became less and less important. American pioneers took the water highways to the west and increasingly bypassed the isolated Wilderness Road. For a short period during the last third of the eighteenth century, however, this road that followed in part a great Indian trail, the Warriors Path, opened the West, populated two states — Kentucky and Tennessee — and established a bridgehead to the land west of the Mississippi River.

Tennessee became the sixteenth state in the Union in 1796. Many people who had come down the Great Valley Road made their way by the Clinch or Holston rivers to the Tennessee River and then into central Tennessee — or they went through the Cumberland Gap on the Wilderness Road to the Cumberland River in Kentucky and then turned west and south on that river to Nashville, the heart of the modern state. Tennessee and Kentucky continued to grow until the last great Indian confederation east of the Mississippi

River was broken during the War of 1812; then the rich land of the Deep South and the Old Northwest replaced the lure of Kentucky and Tennessee. It was not until the Civil War that the Wilderness Road again played a role in the history of Kentucky or Tennessee.

Boone's Wilderness Road has not been forgotten. Today there are several major efforts underway to have Boone's trail from the Yadkin River in North Carolina to the Kentucky River in Kentucky declared a National Historical Trail by the federal government. Passageway for the trail through the Cumberland Gap is already assured by the Cumberland Gap National Park. In that park, covering twenty thousand acres, one can find a short section of the early Wilderness Road and Warriors Path protected for the future. A short drive through the beautiful gap into Kentucky brings one to the Dr. Thomas Walker State Park, named in memory of the first white man to discover the Cumberland Gap and to establish a "settlement" in that state. A few miles to the north is London, where one can visit the Levi Jackson State Park, dedicated to the people who took the Wilderness Road and helped build Kentucky. These twentieth-century efforts to preserve the brief but important history of the Wilderness Road celebrate the triumph of the American pioneer and the trails he followed to the West.

THE MOHAWK*

By Ronnie Day

When the earth's convulsions had ceased and the glaciers covering the present state of New York had melted away, a depression ten to fifty miles wide was left which divided the Adirondack Mountains in the north from the Catskills in the south. In the Adirondack highlands, a stream which the Indians were to call Tenonanatche, "the river flowing through the mountains," sprang up, ran south almost to the edge of the Lake Erie-Ontario plain and then at what is today Rome, turned back sharply to the east. At Little Falls the Mohawk cut a deep gorge through a pre-glacial divide, the only major barrier separating east and west, went on to spill over the falls at Cohoes, and shortly thereafter effected a juncture with the Hudson River.

"The Valley of the Mohawk has no pretentions to sublimity," Francis Parkman observed in the summer of 1845. "Its hills are not high, but the river winds like a snake in the interval between, with trees fringing its banks, forming a rich and picturesque landscape." He was "getting a stronger relish for quiet beauties," he added almost as an afterthought. Parkman had been traveling through the old northwest gathering material for his *History of the Conspiracy of Pontiac* and was making his way home by train from Niagara Falls. Looking ahead to the time when he would cast the struggle between the French and English for dominion over North America as a romantic epic of monumental proportions, he jotted down in his journal his observations of the Mohawk and handed out cheap cigars and pipes to the descendants of the Iroquois in an unsuccessful attempt to gain information. "They are the worst people in the world to extract information from," he noted disgustedly, "the eternal grunted 'yas' of acquiescence follows every question you may ask, without distinction."

When Parkman used the descriptive phrase "quiet beauties," he was no doubt comparing the Mohawk with Niagara Falls to the west, which he had just visited, and the White Mountains nearer his home, of which he was so fond. But it was accurate, and in the patches of countryside preserved among superhighways, railroads, and sprawling in-

---

*I have used Mohawk throughout as the general geographic term to denote the region. This choice is largely a matter of personal convenience, yet it was, after all, the Mohawk route which made possible the Iroquois Trail, the early turnpikes, the Erie Canal, and the early railroads.

dustrial cities, this is the view a tourist still sees in the last quarter of the twentieth century. "Leather-stocking Country," a 1980 New York State tourist guide calls the lower Mohawk, conjuring up Cooper's tales of idealized heroes struggling in a romanticized wilderness setting. The accompanying picture is an image of Parkman's words. One first sees a small, white rural church surrounded by fading green fields sloping down to the river, then low hills with the woodlands in the first stage of autumnal foliage rolling away into the distance.

This idyllic image, however, can be deceptive. When the Mohawk River cut through the divide at Little Falls, it created the lowest passageway through the Appalachian Mountains between the St. Lawrence River and the end of the chain in Georgia. This gorge became a natural highway by land and water — the two cannot be separated — which connected the Great Lakes and the West with New York City. The river and valley formed the vital link in a route which became a microcosm of the evolution of transportation in the United States from the time of Columbus to the present day. The Iroquois Trail, the Mohawk and Seneca (also called the Great Genesee Road) turnpikes, the Erie Canal, the New York Central Railroad, the New York State Barge Canal, the Old Mohawk and Seneca Road motor turnpikes, and Interstate 90 all follow approximately the same routes.

Possession of such a strategic route was bound to be contested, and was — from the days when Iroquois warriors glided silently along the narrow paths to those when railroad moguls

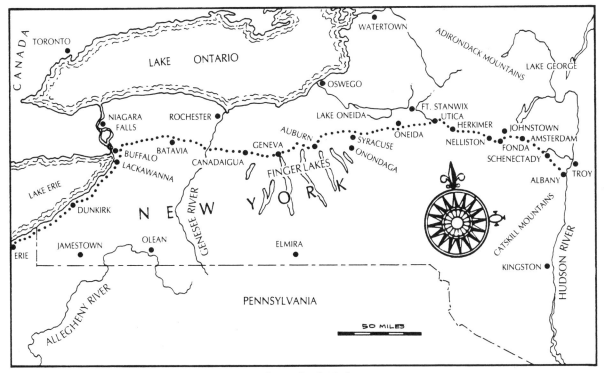

The Mohawk Trail

plotted and schemed in the Victorian drawing rooms of New York mansions. The first two centuries of this struggle, the seventeenth and eighteenth, were bloody. "As Belgium was the buffer state in the World War," T. Ward Clarke wrote in his history, *The Bloody Mohawk,* published on the eve of America's entry into the Second World War, "so the Mohawk Valley was the vortex of North American conflict for over two hundred years." The earth mixed with the ashes of Iroquois captives burned alive at the stake and soaked up the blood of the French, English, and Americans, both Patriot and Tory. The prize was control of the Iroquois Trail.

The history of the Iroquois (the Five Nations — Mohawk, Oneida, Onondaga, Cayuga, and Seneca; later the Six Nations with the inclusion of the Tuscarora in 1714) is shrouded in myth, confused by silly analogies, and still largely explained by conjecture. Sometime between the fourteenth and early sixteenth centuries, the Iroquois peoples either migrated or were driven by more powerful enemies into the Mohawk and western New York region. According to legend, Deganawidah and his disciple, Hiawatha, later the subject of Longfellow's popular poem, conceived of a covenant designed to establish permanent peace among the Five Nations. The fierce and powerful Mohawks, "the maneaters," whose fortified places or castles dotted the lower Mohawk, first took up the covenant chain, and the western tribes, Oneida, Onondaga, Cayuga, and Seneca, joined in succession.

At least as it functioned in the period before the subjugation and eventual disperson of the Six Nations, the Iroquois League has been the source of considerable misunderstanding. An eighteenth century English administrative official, Cadwallader Colden, laid the basis for exaggerated claims for the league's effectiveness in his history of the Iroquois. An Irish-born graduate of the University of Edinburgh removed to the provinces, Colden had imbibed some of the 18th century European Enlightenment's infatuation with classical civilization and so sprinkled his account with comparison to the Romans. In this vein, for example, he wrote that "an old Mohawk Sachem in a poor Blanket and a dirty Shirt, may be seen issuing his Orders with as arbitrary an Authority as a Roman Dictator." A rapidly changing American perspective contributed further to the exaggerated view of the Iroquois League. Some of the Founding Fathers on occasion referred to the league as the predecessor of the U.S. Constitution. The romantic historians of the nineteenth century, writing with the excessive idealism so typical of them, went both Colden and the Founding Fathers one better and portrayed the Iroquois as the Greeks of America.

Whether European or American, the historians should have known better. They had ample evidence, from the time of the Greek city states to the coalitions which finally succeeded in defeating Napoleon, of how effective such leagues and confederations were, even among the civilized peoples of Europe. And certainly the Iroquois were not civilized. They were American Indians living in a stone-age society and having nothing in common with the Greeks and Romans except the instinct for survival. Probably through little choice of their own they had settled in a strategic crucible, surrounded on all sides by powerful tribal enemies. If warpaths led from the Mohawk in all directions, the reverse was also true. Geography dictated peace as the only wise course — and the Iroquois, while primitive, were not stupid. A metaphor they used to describe their league is illustrative. The Five Nations constituted a long house or council lodge. The Mohawks guarded the eastern door, the Senecas the western. With the two most powerful nations guarding the entrances, a relative degree of security could be attained.

This loose confederation rested on the first communications network established along the Mohawk route, the famed Iroquois Trail. The Iroquois, wrote the British trader John Long, "express peace by the metaphor of a tree, whose top they say will reach the sun, and whose branches extend far abroad, not only that they may be seen at a great distance, but to afford them shelter and repose." If the strategic Mohawk passage formed the trunk and the villages of the Five Nations the branches, then the massive root system anchoring the great tree of peace was the Iroquois Trail.

The water route of the Iroquois Trail ran from the Hudson to Oswego on Lake Ontario. With two portages, one at Cohoes Falls near the mouth and the other at Little Falls where the river dropped forty feet in half a mile, the Mohawk River was navigable under conditions of normal rainfall as far as Rome, where it turns north and ceases to be of any use. A third portage over a low ridge was necessary to make the connection with Wood Creek, a shallow stream which flowed west for thirty miles into Lake Oneida. The actual distance separating the two streams was about a mile, but in dry weather, such as occurs in late summer, the distance was increased to six or eight miles. Crossing Lake Oneida, a swift, easy passage in calm weather, the water route continued to Lake Ontario by way of the Oswego River, a stream a British military report described as "extremely difficult and hazardous" to navigate because of rifts, rocks, and a swift current. "The principal obstruction," the report noted, "is twelve miles short of Oswego, and is a fall of about eleven feet perpendicular. The portage here is by land, not exceeding forty yards, before they launch for the last time."

The land route, the Iroquois Trail proper, ran from the Hudson to Niagara. Like modern railroads and highways, the main artery followed the Mohawk River west through the mountains to Utica, where it struck overland through the great watershed between the rivers flowing north into the lakes and those flowing south into the Susquehanna and Allegheny rivers. For two hundred miles through or near what is today the cities of Oneida, Syracuse, Auburn, Canadaigua, and Batavia, the trail ran west to join the Niagara River just south of the falls, connecting en route the major villages of the Five Nations. Important trails ran north to join the Lake George-Champlain route to Montreal on the St. Lawrence; others followed the creeks and valleys south to the headwaters of the Delaware, Susquehanna, and Allegheny rivers.

A maze of lesser trails connected all the important points within this area. These trails were beaten paths, perhaps fifteen inches wide. They passed around obstacles such as fallen trees, avoided open spaces except those near villages, crossed streams at fords, and ran slightly beneath the crests of ridges in order to avoid exposure. To the Europeans who first penetrated the area, the trails presented a vast wilderness labyrinth. "We proceeded early in the morning," a Dutch resident of Fort Orange (Albany) traveling in the lower Mohawk Valley wrote in 1635, "and after a long march we took a wrong path that was the most walked upon; but as the savages knew the paths better than we did they returned with us, and after eleven leagues of marching, we arrived, the Lord be praised and thanked, at Fort Orange."

The coming of the Europeans in the seventeenth century increased the strategic importance of the Iroquois Trail and drastically altered the Iroquois way of life. In 1609, the same year that Henry Hudson's *Half Moon* sailed up the river which now bears his name to the site of present-day Albany, a Mohawk war party ran into their traditional enemies, the Algonquins, at Lake Champlain. On the day of battle the Mohawks launched their attack in the time-honored manner, only to see the enemy ranks part and a white man, in armor and holding an arquebus loaded with four balls, step forward. Samuel de Champlain raised his

weapon to his cheek and fired. Two of the three Mohawk chiefs were killed instantly, and the third fell mortally wounded. "Seeing their chiefs dead," Champlain wrote, "they lost courage, and took to flight, abandoning their camp and fort, and fleeing into the woods, whither I pursued them, killing still more of them." In this manner, as dramatic as any Hollywood screenwriter could contrive, a culture of wood and flint met one of steel and gunpowder. The effect was comparable to the launching of *Dreadnought* in the early twentieth century, or the nuclear bombing of Japan four decades later.

Survival for the Iroquois now hinged on their being able to compete in the arms race with their traditional enemies, and from the beginning they were at a disadvantage. The medium of exchange was fur. But the Dutch were more reluctant than the French to place guns in the hands of Indians, and the Iroquois by and large were excluded from the French trade network by the pattern of tribal warfare which had existed prior to the European settlement. By their location the Mohawks had access to the Dutch trade, but this was rendered worthless when the supply of pelts in the Iroquois region was depleted around 1640. In desperation the more powerful elements of the Iroquois League sought an accommodation with the French and, when that proved futile, resorted to war in an attempt to gain their share — or, as some have argued, to control the fur trade. "All trade is a kind of warfare," Sir Josiah Child wrote in 1688, describing current mercantilist policies of the European states.

Forced by circumstances beyond their control into the logical extension of this concept, the Iroquois destroyed the Huron trading empire north of the Great Lakes, crippled the Susquehanna to the south, and made at least one foray in strength into the Illinois country.

The Iroquois trade wars gained them a terrible and exaggerated reputation among the whites. "They are indeed the fiercest and most formidable people in North America," Colden wrote. "I have been told by Old Men in New England, who remembered the Time when the Mohawks made War on their Indians, that as soon as a single Mohawk was discover'd in the Country, their Indians raised a Cry from Hill to Hill, A Mohawk!, A Mohawk! upon which they all fled like Sheep before Wolves." Unfortunately for the Iroquois, the French Jesuits had a virtual monopoly over the early written history, and they painted them with a bloody brush. The picture survived long after the Iroquois were either destroyed or dispersed. Ever the romantic, Parkman called the Iroquois the kinsmen of wolves. In the early 1960s, when the McCarthy era was grudgingly giving ground before the lure of Camelot, a historian compared the Iroquois to the Nazis. The war machine of the Iroquois, he wrote, expanding on both the Iroquois and the German myths, "was as horribly effective as that of the Nazis in 1940, and was built on the same principles of ruthlessness and the application of explosive force against enemies who were unprepared."

Actually, the bloodthirstiness of the Iroquois, the effectiveness of their league, and the success of their wars have all been greatly exaggerated. The cultural anthropologist, Anthony F. C. Wallace in his *The Death and Rebirth of the Seneca* has restored common sense to an appraisal of the Iroquois: "The major functions of Iroquois warfare — its consequences, both intended and unintended for the Iroquois way of life and their situation in the world — were, in the early part of the century, threefold: to maintain an emotional equilibrium in individuals who were strongly motivated to avenge, or replace, murdered kinfolk, and thereby maintain the social equilibrium of kinship units; to extend, or at least maintain, Iroquois political influence over other tribal groups, and thus provide access by trade or hunting to land rich in peltries; and to perpetuate a political situation in which the threat of retaliation against either party could be used to play off the British and the French against one another."

Events beyond Iroquois control, however, thwarted this policy. By their wars against the Hurons and other tribes they gained no more than a respite. As in a game of chess, the French and English moved their pieces into position on the board of the Mohawk-Great Lakes regions. Before the end of the seventeenth century the French moved into the western interior by way of the St. Lawrence River, filling the power vacuum resulting from the Iroquois wars and effectively eliminating the role of Indian middlemen in the fur trade. They built Fort Frontenac on the St. Lawrence at the outlet of Lake Ontario in 1673 and, when attempts at establishing a fort at Niagara failed because of Seneca opposition, built a fort and trading post at Detroit in 1701. The French were thus in a position to dominate the western fur trade.

The English, however, moved quickly to check their opponent. They had taken New York from the Dutch in 1664 and after 1689 had been waging a global struggle against France for European dominance and colonial empire. Utilizing the Mohawk-Lake Ontario route, the British jumped the intervening 150 miles of wilderness and established a fort and trading post at Oswego in the 1720s. The French immediately countered by building a fort at Niagara in an attempt to intercept the western trade before it reached Oswego. But the English could dangle before the Indians the lure of cheaper goods brought over the Mohawk-Oswego route. One French official sailing to Niagara in 1726 counted 100 canoes loaded with peltry passing by on their way to Oswego.

Once again the Iroquois found themselves encircled, caught between two enemies advancing on a collision course. During the lull in the Anglo-French wars in the early eighteenth century, they took part in the flourishing fur trade as well as they could, complaining about prices and of being cheated, and attempted to maintain neutrality between the two European giants steadily encroaching upon them. The first two of the series of Anglo-French wars, The War of the League of Augsburg (1689-97) and the War of the Spanish Succession (1701-1714), had been largely

European Wars fought to curb the ambitions of Louis XIV. When the wars resumed near the middle of the eighteenth century, however, the major theaters of operation shifted to the colonies. Because of the strategic value of the Mohawk, the Iroquois found neutrality to be impossible. In the three major conflicts fought to decide the ownership of the North American continent — the War of the Austrian Succession (1744-48), the Seven Years War (1756-63), and the War of the American Revolution (1776-83) — the Iroquois were ultimately destroyed as a power of any consequence.

During this half century and more of conflict, the Mohawk-Oswego route of the Iroquois Trail formed the base of the most strategic triangle in North America. At midcentury the French held Canada and the English the eastern seaboard. The contested area was the western territory between the Appalachian Mountains and the Mississippi River. From Montreal, their major military base in New France, the French had moved up the St. Lawrence, across Lakes Ontario and Erie, and down the Allegheny to the Ohio. Niagara was the key to this line of penetration, and to neutralize it the English had made the move to Oswego. Now the triangle was in place. It can be seen easily on any map of the area. The right side is formed by the Albany-to-Montreal route along the Hudson River, Lakes George and Champlain, and the Richelieu River; the left by the St. Lawrence River and Lake Ontario; the base by the Oswego-Mohawk route.

In his finest work, *Montcalm and*

Wolfe, Parkman described in a poetic passage the route from Albany to Montreal as it was in 1757. "Spring came at last, and the Dutch burghers of Albany heard, faint from the far height, the clamor of the wild fowl, streaming in long files northward to their summer home. As the aerial travellers winged their way, the seat of war lay spread beneath them like a map. First the blue Hudson, slumbering among its forests, with the forts along its banks . . . . Then a broad belt of dingy evergreen; and beyond, released from wintry fetters, the glistening breast of Lake George."

On northward, Parkman's wild fowl flew. "They looked down on Ticonderoga, with the flag of the Bourbons waving on its ramparts; and next on Crown Point with its tower of stone. Lake Champlain now spread before them, widening as they flew: on the left, the mountain wilderness of the Adirondacks, like a stormy sea congealed; on the right, the long procession of the Green Mountains; and, far beyond, on the dim verge of the eastern sky, the White Mountains throned in savage solitude." On the wild fowl flew. "They passed over the bastioned square of Fort St. John, Fort Chambly guarding the rapids of the Richelieu, and the broad belt of the St. Lawrence, with Montreal seated on its bank." There Parkman left them "to build their nests and hatch their brood among the fens of the lonely North."

In the hues and shades of Sir Walter Scott's north and James Fenimore Cooper's wilderness, Parkman set the stage on which his Byronic he-

roes, Montcalm and Wolfe, would act out the drama which ended with the clash of armies on the Plains of Abraham at Quebec and the death of both men. His vision ran north-south not east-west (for which he has been criticized by historians who pose as prophets of the past).

Had some of Parkman's wild fowl broken off at Albany and flown west over the Mohawk in 1757 they would have looked down on a French spy carefully making his way from Oswego to the Hudson. Viewing the area with the practical eyes of an expert observer rather than those of the romantic historian, he methodically reported the distances of the carrying places, the condition of the few primitive roads, the number of militia available, and the angles of fire from the forts still standing on the lower Mohawk. He noted also the ruins of forts, burned either by the attacking French or the retreating English. They stood as grim reminders that in the second year of the second war, the passage of armies back and forth through the Mohawk had begun.

During the opening round of the prolonged conflict, King George's War (as the colonists called the War of the Austrian Succession), the Mohawk was relatively untouched. From the beginning the war was ineptly prosecuted on both sides. The Iroquois, the decisive factor, were kept loyal to England largely through the efforts of their trusted friend and adopted brother — the entrepreneur, soldier, and extraordinary Indian agent, Sir William Johnson of Johnstown. The war ended in 1748 in an agreement which was more of a truce than a peace treaty — and not a very well-honored truce at that. The French acted quickly to strengthen their line of fortifications; the English moved in 1754 to block them. The attempt under Joshua Fry and George Washington to occupy a fort at the juncture of the Allegheny and Monongahela rivers (the present site of Pittsburgh) ended in defeat, and the French occupied the fort, naming it Fort Duquesne.

All pretense of peace was now dropped, and the English planned an all-out attack on New France. With their usual penchant for violating the military principle of concentration of force, they decided in 1755 to attack four points with four armies from four bases. The first army would take Cape Breton, Nova Scotia, the key to the Gulf of St. Lawrence, from Boston; a second under General Braddock would attack Fort Duquesne, the key to the Ohio Valley, from Virginia; a third under Sir William Johnson would take Crown Point, the key to the Lakes George-Champlain route to Montreal, from Albany; and the fourth under Governor Shirley of Massachusetts, would march over the Mohawk route to Oswego and from there attack Niagara, which was the key to it all.

The result was disaster. Braddock's army was annihilated in the Pennsylvania wilderness. After a fierce battle, Johnson was stopped at Lake George. Shirley's campaign against Niagara was hampered by supply difficulties and his own procrastination and ended without an attack ever being launched. To make the already bad military situation worse, the French struck back quick-

ly. One expedition burned two hastily erected English forts at the Great Carrying Place between the Mohawk River and Wood Creek; another captured Oswego, the only remaining English stronghold in the west.

Reeling from one defeat after the other, and with their Iroquois allies wavering, the English seemed on the verge of losing North America. But again, as his accounts show, Johnson used every means at his disposal and kept the Iroquois in the alliance against France. In England William Pitt assumed office. A brilliant war minister, his aim was no less than the destruction of the French empire. In 1758 he sent two competent generals, Jeffrey Amherst and James Wolfe, to America with a large army. The fortress of Louisburg surrendered to them in late summer. Forts Frontenac and Duquesne fell the same year to English and Colonial forces.

With the overwhelming forces now at their disposal, the English planned a three-pronged attack for 1759 aimed at the conquest of New France. One army under Wolfe would take Quebec by way of the St. Lawrence; a second under Amherst would open the Lakes George-Champlain route to Montreal; and the third under Prideaux, with Johnson in command of the Iroquois, would advance over the Mohawk route to capture Niagara. In preparation for the campaign the English at last fortified the upper Mohawk. A modern fortress, Stanwix, costing sixty thousand pounds and accommodating a garrison of four hundred, was built at the Great Carrying Place. Smaller forts were built at the major ford sixteen miles downriver (present Utica), at each end of Lake Oneida, and at the falls of the Oswego. To facilitate the portage, especially in the dry season, a wagon road was cut from Fort Stanwix to the eastern end of Lake Oneida, and a dam and floodgates were built to store water for the passage of boats down Wood Creek.

The "year of victories," the relieved English were to call 1759. Wolfe took Quebec. Amherst forced the French to abandon Ticonderoga and Crown Point, opening the route to Montreal. In June five thousand men under Prideaux marched over the Mohawk to join Johnson and his Iroquois at Oswego. Prideaux was killed during the siege of Niagara when an English cannon burst. Johnson took command and pressed the siege until the French surrendered. All that was left of New France was a strip of the St. Lawrence River on each side of Montreal.

The final British offensive was launched in 1760 as another three-pronged attack, this time against Montreal. One force proceeded up the St. Lawrence, a second by way of Lakes George-Champlain and the Richelieu River. The bulk of the army went up the Mohawk to Oswego, crossed Lake Ontario, and advanced down the St. Lawrence. In September the French surrendered to the overwhelming forces converged upon them, and New France disappeared from the map.

For the first time since the beginning of settlement, American colonists were freed from the imminent threat of a European enemy. The way was clear for expansion west. When the western tribes under Pontiac rose against the encroaching whites and turned the frontiers into a battleground from 1763 to 1765, Johnson was able through his prestige and influence with the Iroquois to keep them neutral. In 1768 he negotiated the Fort Stanwix Treaty with the Indians, marking out a boundary line beyond which the white settlers agreed not to encroach. Beginning at a point on Wood Creek between Fort Stanwix and Lake Oneida, the demarcation line ran south to the Delaware, crossed west to the Susquehanna, then to a point just above Pittsburgh and down the Ohio to the mouth of the Tennessee River. By these terms the Mohawk River was opened to the whites up to Rome. During the interval between the French Wars and the outbreak of the American Revolution, settlement inched up the river toward Stanwix and spread out into the Schoharie and Cherry valleys.

The Mohawk settlements constituted an international smorgasbord created out of the turmoil of the eighteenth century. The Dutch had been in the valley since the founding of Schenectady in 1661, three years before the English conquest. In the early eighteenth century Palatine German refugees, victims of French aggression, were sent to the area in an English project to start production of naval stores for the Royal Navy. The scheme failed, and the Germans were finally left to fend for themselves as best they could. Following the abortive uprisings of 1715 and 1745, a great many Scots were transported to America, some settling in the Mohawk. The discharge of the officers and men of the Highland regiments which had served in the Seven Years War further increased the Scottish complexion of the white settlements.

With a large non-English population firmly entrenched, with the removal of Sir William Johnson's counsel by his death in 1774, with the western Iroquois nations growing more apprehensive over the white advance, and with the strategic value of the Iroquois Trail still of the utmost importance, the stage was set for the American Revolutionary War — the bloodiest episode in Mohawk history. When the war broke out the powerful Tory families, led by the Johnsons and Butlers, fled the Mohawk. But the Patriots' triumph was brief. The dispossessed Tories formed military units and planned to retake their lands. Except for the Oneidas and Tuscaroras (who remained neutral and thus split the confederation) the Iroquois honored their traditional alliance with the British. Occupying the former French position in Canada, the British could be expected to use the strategic triangle to attack the Americans, now in control of the old English position along the Mohawk. All along the Mohawk to Fort Stanwix the Patriots built forts, some new and some converted from private houses and churches.

The blow fell in 1777. As was their custom, the British divided their forces. One army was to attack up the Hudson from New York City. The second was to attack over the Montreal-Lakes George-Champlain route. A third was to follow the Oswego-Mohawk route, and a fourth was to come from Niagara by way of the Schoharie. The objective was to separate New England from the rest of the colonies so the colonial rebellion could be crushed. Gen. Barry St. Leger commanded the force of 400 British regulars, 600 Tories, and 300 Mohawks which was to conquer the Mohawk. Setting out in July, St. Leger began the march to Fort Stanwix, with warriors from the Seneca and Cayugas joining him on the way. The advance was slow, and the Patriots obstructed it even more by felling trees across Wood Creek. On August 2 the siege of Fort Stanwix began. A Patriot relief force under Gen. Nicholas Herkimer, son of a Palatine refugee, ran into an ambush in early August in the Oriskany swamp and, in the savage fighting which followed, kept the battlefield but lost so many men that relief of Fort Stanwix was impossible. The Indians and Tories, however, were so badly handled in the fight that their worth was considerably reduced. Fort Stanwix held, and, as the siege continued, the British invasion fell apart. The attack up the Schoharie was repulsed. On August 22 Benedict Arnold relieved Fort Stanwix and sent St. Leger's forces into retreat, more by daring than by force. The main British army under Burgoyne, trapped between Lake George and Albany, surrendered October 17, 1777.

With the destruction of the British grand design in the wilderness of the Mohawk-Hudson angle of the strategic triangle, the major theater of operations shifted south. The war along the Mohawk developed into a savage frontier conflict. Tories and Iroquois attacked the settlements. In reprisal the Patriots carried fire and sword throughout the Indian lands. The destruction of lives and property left the area all but wasteland. "To account for this large reduction [of the population around Herkimer]," Col. Marinus Willett, one of the more brilliant American commanders, wrote Washington in 1781, "I do not think I am wild in my calculations, when I say that one-third of them have been killed, or carried captive by the enemy; one-third have removed to the interior parts of the country; and one-third deserted to the enemy."

A legacy of bitterness and hatred was left. "Our patriotism in those early days was measured by our dislike of the British," the feminist leader, Elizabeth Cady Stanton, recalled in her memoirs. As a child she had seen the marks of tomahawks on the balustrades of Sir William Johnson's mansion at Johnstown and had listened to tales of the bloody deeds done in the valley. "At home and at school," she wrote, "we were educated to hate the English." Confronted with the controversies which the war along the Mohawk still seems to breed, a historian writing in 1941 explained that "Where people have suffered terribly, it is understandable that they should hate violently." As late as 1976 another historian was forced to devote both the preface and an appendix of a new and excellent biography of Sir William Johnson to an examination of the biased and sometimes deliberately fraudulent histories of the area.

Despite a century first of traders and then of armies passing over the Iroquois Trail, the country was still largely wilderness. Some improvements in transportation were made, especially on the Mohawk-Oswego

water route. The early fur traders replaced the small, fragile bark canoes with larger, sturdier boats, the bateaux (from the French for boat). The Swedish botanist, Peter Kalm, who visited Albany in 1749, described these craft as board-built of white pine, with flat bottoms and sharp prows fore and aft. Kalm thought they were round, as they probably were on the Hudson, but on the treacherous Mohawk and Oswego rivers, they were propelled by men with poles. "They are chiefly made use of for carrying goods, by means of the rivers, to the Indians," he wrote, "that is, when those rivers are open enough for the battoes to pass through, and when they need not be carried by land a long way." Fleets of these boats left Schenectady each spring for a rendezvous with the Indians in the trading sheds at Oswego.

During the wars a few more minor improvements were made. A larger boat was introduced, described in 1756 as being twice the size of the older craft. To handle these larger boats, work parties cleared brush and trees from the upper Mohawk and Wood Creek, cut the wagon road at the Great Carrying Place, and built sluices at Fort Stanwix to divert water into Wood Creek. Wagons were introduced at the portages to facilitate the carriage of goods. Sleds were used where the ground was marshy, such as at Little Falls.

Roads, with the exception of the short one between Albany and Schenectady, were either primitive (as in the lower Mohawk) or nonexistent (as in the upper reaches and along the main Iroquois Trail). Noting that a large herd of cattle had been driven with ease over the Mohawk route to supply Shirley at Oswego during the Seven Years War, the early New York historian, William Smith, wrote in 1756 that "a good road might be made from Schenectady to Oswego." But until the West was settled and roads for travel and commerce were needed, the old Indian trails sufficed.

The dramatic change in transportation on the Mohawk occurred after the United States had achieved independence. It proved to be an overture to the general revolution in American transportation. In 1800 the major turnpikes were chartered. In 1825 the Erie Canal was completed. In 1831 the first railroad was built from Albany to Schenectady. Section by section it was extended west until, in 1853, the rails were consolidated into the New York Central system, which connected New York City and Buffalo. Turnpike, canal, railroad — all followed the old Iroquois Trail. Together they created the greatest gateway to the West on the North American continent.

Shortly after the end of the American Revolutionary War, settlers, many of them veterans, moved into the upper Mohawk Valley and repopulated the area. During the next few years the Iroquois who remained in New York (some had migrated to British Canada) were dispossessed of their lands by the usual means of purchase, fraud, and expropriation, and scattered settlements were established westward toward Lake Erie. Patrick Campbell, a Scotsman traveling in America to investigate the possibility of settling his countrymen there, passed through the Genesee and Mohawk country in March 1792 "at-

tended with an old faithful servant, a Dog, and gun, only." He found a largely unsettled wilderness with all but impassable roads, even for a horse, a few crude taverns "such as . . . are called in Scotland small tippling houses," and a sprinkling of rough-mannered, strong-minded settlers. "After crossing this lake [Cayuga], I put up at the house of a gunsmith, one Harris, who kept a tavern, and who assured me he could make a riffled gun of iron to his liking, that would hit an egg at a hundred and thirty paces," Campbell wrote. "This man kept me up till very late reading Paine's *Rights of Man,* of which he seemed very fond, arguing, and making commentaries on every passage as we went along."

Always on the alert for agricultural information, Campbell learned that the cost of transporting any article from Albany to Lake Seneca was two dollars per hundredweight. Herein was the problem with the western country. Without roads, settlers could not migrate into the area in any great numbers because they could not transport their produce to market. To remedy this, the New York legislature in 1794 provided for a road to be built from Utica to the Genesee River and, four years later, provided for the extension of the Great Genesee Road, as it was known, to Lake Erie. State lotteries, a popular means of the day for raising revenue, were authorized to help finance the building and maintenance of this road. Despite the lobbying of farmers, landowners, and speculators, the legislature, made up of easterners, showed little inclination to spend money on western roads. Under these circumstances, turnpikes seemed to be the solution to western transportation difficulties, and in 1800 the Seneca Road Company and the Mohawk Turnpike and Bridge Company were chartered. The first would take over, extend, and maintain the Great Genesee Road, and the latter would build a turnpike through the Mohawk Valley. Together the two roads would constitute an east-west road from Albany to the Genesee. The legislative act provided that the road was to be graded properly and surfaced with gravel or broken stone to a depth of fifteen inches. Timothy Bigelow, who traveled the length of the turnpikes in 1805, reported that the new section being built between Albany and Schenectady was "constructed in a very durable manner, with a pavement covered with hard gravel."

Along this road — and the numerous other toll roads like it built in the first two decades of the nineteenth century — wagons hauled freight and stagecoaches carried passengers and mail, until they were eclipsed first by the canal and then by the railroad. During the fighting in and around the Great Lakes during the War of 1812, men and supplies moved west over the traditional water routes and these new roads. Although a distinct improvement over the old Iroquois Trail, the turnpikes still had not solved the basic problem: a swift and inexpensive way to haul bulk freight.

This was to be accomplished by the Erie Canal, De Witt Clinton's "Big Ditch." For some time there had been talk of improving western transportation by building canals. In the usual American manner, some saw a canal to Lake Erie as the impossible vision of fools, while others saw it as the salvation of the West. One of the latter was George Washington, a firm believer in canals throughout his life. Visiting the Mohawk at the end of the war in 1783, he wrote Francois de Chastellux, a general in Rochambeau's army, that he "could not help taking a more extensive view of the vast inland navigation of these United States, from maps and the information of others, and could not but be struck by the immense extent and importance of it, and with the goodness of providence, which has dealt its favors to us with so profuse a hand. Would to God we may have the wisdom enough to improve them."

Before the turn of the century some improvement was made. Elkanah Watson, a man who was interested in all things mechanical and agricultural (he came to be known as the father of the county fair), toured the Mohawk in 1788. He had made an extensive study of European canals and on the basis of this knowledge believed a canal to be feasible. The immediate result of his visit was the formation in 1792 of the Western Inland Lock Navigation Company to open a waterway from the Hudson to Erie. While the company never got around to building the canal — indeed such a project was far beyond its financial resources — it did make some significant improvements. Locks and short canals built at Little Falls, German Flats, and Rome allowed the use of the much larger ten-ton Durham boats, which utilized sails in addition to poles and oars on a short distance of the river. As minor as this accomplishment might seem, it resulted in the reduction of freight rates between Schenectady and Utica from fourteen to five dollars a ton and gave added proof for the claims of the proponents of the canal.

When the Erie Canal was finally built (begun in 1817 and completed in 1825) after years of political squabbling and backbreaking labor, it quickly became America's entry into the wonders of the world of that era. The canal had a total length of 363 miles, a width of 40 feet at the top and 28 feet at the bottom and a depth of four feet. It crossed elevations and rivers by means of 83 locks and 18 aqueducts. The Erie followed the course of the Mohawk River to Utica, then struck west through the Genesee country to the little Lake Erie village of Buffalo, rebuilt after being burned by the British in the War of 1812.

The first of the great American canals, the Erie was by far the most successful financially. At four miles an hour enforced speed limit, thousands of freighters carried heavy cargo on the currentless waters at a rate which put the wagoners out of business. (Flour rode the entire distance for a penny a ton, for example.) Passenger packets carried tourists and immigrants west. Complete with saloon, dining table, and berths, the best of these packets constituted the most advanced mode of transportation in the early nineteenth century — even though Captain Marryat, an officer in the Royal Navy more famous as a novelist, sneered at the pretensions of the packet captains. Charles Dickens claimed that the berths were so small he mistook them for bookshelves, un-

til he was made aware that the passengers were to be the library. The emigrant boats were a different matter. Between 1825 and 1850 the canal carried west the bulk of the first huge wave of European immigration in the nineteenth century. The greater the number which could be packed aboard, the greater the profit, and many immigrant packets resembled floating sardine cans.

In this mass of humanity being funneled west along a forty-foot strip of water, the frontier Baptist and Methodist ministers plied their trade with the determination of pickpockets on an English hanging day. They faced no easy task. Like their brethren on the high seas, the canal sailors were a rough lot, given to drinking, brawling, and swearing. Some of the backwoodsmen, though uneducated, were natural philosophers who openly disputed the validity of the Bible. At Little Falls, Bigelow met several people who told him flatly that "Adam could not have been the first man, or he must have lived much longer ago than the Scriptures declare, because it . . . must be more than five thousand years for the Mohawk to have broken through the rocks, as it has done at those falls."

With the advent of railroads near midcentury, the Erie Canal lost much of its earlier importance. Like the wagons and wagoners before it, the Erie lost out to speed, already an American mania much noticed by foreign travelers. The second great wave of immigration came to America following the Civil War. The bulk of these settlers passed along the Mohawk aboard the New York Central, heading for the slums of western cities and the vast reaches of the Great Plains. One, for example, was O. E. Rolvaag, the chronicler of the Norwegian exodus to America. Although Per Hansa and his wife, Beret, the characters in Rolvaag's novel, *Giants in the Earth,* came to the plains by way of Quebec and Detroit, the experience of their creator was more typical. He landed in New York in the late summer of 1896. In his pocket he had a railroad ticket sent to him by his uncle, an American dime, and a Norwegian copper piece. Rolvaag existed on tobacco and a loaf of bread for the three days and nights he rode the trains west.

Today, like much of the rest of America, the old hunting ground of the Iroquois is a patchwork of picturesque countryside and industrial cities. Rochester and Buffalo, created by the Erie Canal, and Schenectady, the home of General Electric, are the most important. About the latter, a devotee to the cult of progress wrote in 1925 that the engineer "has torn from the skies the secret of electricity and he uses it as a giant slave to do his work. Nor is his thirst for mechanical power in any degree assuaged. Rather his career of mastery is just begun. . . . And it is Schenectady, N.Y. — in the historic Mohawk Valley — that the leaders of this wonderful electrical industry make their home." Of course, there is another more recent view of Schenectady, General Electric, and the progress of the world in general; for this, the reader should see Kurt Vonnegut's *Cat's Cradle* and *Palm Sunday.*

The Mohawk route running through the quiet countryside to connect the cities has also changed considerably. The New York Barge Canal has replaced both the Mohawk River and the Old Erie Canal, Interstate 90 the Mohawk and Seneca Turnpikes. Amtrak trains pass over the tracks of the New York Central. Although Fort Stanwix in Rome has been restored, the main defense establishment is just outside town: Griffiss Air Force Base, a bomber and interceptor base which is also the headquarters of the Northern Communications Area. Yet what the author of a tour guide for the Old Mohawk Turnpike wrote in 1924 still holds true. "It affords, to the automobilist, an unfolding panorama of unrivaled pictorial and human interest — a view in brief of America and an outlook upon the thrilling chapters of American history."

The Mohawk also lives on as myth and as symbol, both more important in the collective consciousness of a people than volumes of the so-called accurate histories written by academics. In the Great Depression year of 1936, for example, Walter D. Edmond's historical novel about the bitter fighting in the Revolutionary War, *Drums Along the Mohawk,* was published. It quickly received most of the rewards the American public can bestow on a work of fiction. The noted historian Allan Nevins reviewed the book favorably in *The Saturday Review of Literature,* comparing it with Harold Frederic's earlier novel on the same subject, *In the Valley,* a book Elizabeth Cady Stanton thought "true to nature." The Book of the Month Club chose *Drums Along the Mohawk* as a selection, and Twentieth-Century Fox made it into a movie. William

Faulkner, forced for a time to support himself in Hollywood, wrote the screen treatment.

World War II came, and at its end — as seems to be the American custom following each of its wars — a great purge of all things immoral, unpatriotic and thus un-American began. During the hysterical years of the McCarthy era, when patriotic groups across the country kept a constant watch for dangerous and subversive books, J. D. Salinger's *Catcher in the Rye* and D. H. Lawrence's *Lady Chatterley's Lover* provided the largest and most provocative targets. But on occasion *Drums Along the Mohawk* would appear on someone's list of books either to be banned or burned. What made the book objectionable to Americans as far away as Michigan and Tennessee during the nineteen fifties and sixties? Nevins provided the explanation in his review written twenty years earlier. Edmond's characters, he wrote, are portrayed "as living beings with the same virtues, the same vices, the same heroisms and follies, and much the same hopes and fears as their descendents in rural areas of the Mohawk today. By earthy speech (not without an infusion of modern slang), by earthy instincts and acts (not without a very modern quantum of sex), he brings them down from the heroic plane to that of everyday flesh and blood." What Nevins saw as modern realism, the book burners saw as a Communist attempt to subvert the morals and patriotism of America's youth.

A fictional account of the American struggle against the British and their Tory and Iroquois allies thus became a symbol of the American fear of a sometimes dimly perceived, but usually exaggerated, enemy during the Cold War. But then, today the most modern fighter planes are parked in the shadow of old Fort Stanwix, guardian of the great gateway to North America. Perhaps it is no coincidence.

THE NATCHEZ TRACE
By Maurice Boyd

The Northern Tip

Each summer, long ago, a small Shawnee band came to their campsite and burial ground atop the Dividing Ridge in southwestern Kentucky between the Great Lakes and the Gulf. The ridge overlooked the "Dark and Bloody Ground" west and south to the Cumberland River. From their vantage point the Shawnees rested while they gathered nuts from the giant walnut and hickory trees and feasted on the abundant rabbits, squirrels, and deer. Their campsite was nestled immediately west of the peak in a horseshoe-shaped ring of rock ledges, where an everlasting spring emerged from a limestone fault. On the rising slope south of the campsite was their burial ground.

One fall the Shawnee band, suddenly attacked by an unknown enemy, abandoned their belongings and attempted to flee. Many died in the attack, and the few survivors crept back to place their dead on the burial ground and cover them with huge boulders. The survivors left, never to return, and the campsite and burial ground were covered anew each year by a heavy blanket of leaves and natural growth.

Many years later a Scotch-Irish family came down the Ohio and Cumberland rivers to trade with Col. James Robertson's settlers on the bluffs of the Cumberland at Nashborough. The family journeyed north and homesteaded the land on the ridge with the everlasting spring. For the next seven generations they uncovered Shawnee artifacts at the former campsite. A thicket of young trees now lined the great stones placed on the burial ground, and both then and now the graves lay untouched. But amidst the tools uncovered at the campsite were Chickasaw and Cherokee goods which the Shawnees had acquired by trade or war on the trail leading southward.

The Shawnees' hunting range had dipped south beyond the Cumberland to the Tennessee River. An ancient human and animal trail from the north passed by the ridge and divided, one fork veering west and the other continuing south. The west fork led to the "Land Between the Rivers," a region of mystery and danger twenty-seven miles distant, formed by the parallel routes of the Cumberland and Tennessee rivers as they flowed northward to the Ohio River. The south fork led past Nashborough through Cherokee hunting grounds to the Tennessee River, merging with the Path to the

Chickasaw Nation. Both the Cumberland and Tennessee rivers flowed west for a short distance before turning north and intersecting the first Shawnee fork across western Kentucky en route to their separate junctions with the Ohio River, shortly before it in turn emptied into the Mississippi.

All the streams and rivers below the Great Lakes between the Appalachians and the Rocky Mountains deposit their waters eventually into the powerful Mississippi. The Native Americans and later the European immigrants followed this long, turbulent water route by canoe or barge down the Mississippi to the land of the Natchez Indians at White Apple Village, later called Natchez. These travelers could not row upstream against the strong current of the giant river, so they necessarily returned to their northern homes by land.

The European newcomers discovered that the only route overland was a long, dangerous, and narrow foot trail through the wilderness formed from several shorter ancient paths. From Natchez it originally had been called the Path to the Choctaw Nation, since that trail was the first encountered from the south; however, when the destination of most travelers became Nashborough (Nashville), it was called the Road to Nashville. Slave traders at this northern terminus, preferring a cheaper method than boats to move blacks south to the Louisiana plantations, selected the overland trail. Called the Road to Natchez, it included the Path to the Chickasaw Nation, several human and animal

trails through the next two hundred miles of wilderness, the Path through the Choctaw Nation down to the great Bayou Pierre, and finally a trail to Natchez. The entire Trace from Nashville to Natchez measured six hundred miles.

The Trace, or paths, existed before the Spaniards discovered the New World. In the fall of 1540 Don Hernando de Soto crossed the Trace from the east and moved north on it among the Chickasaw villages. It was a narrow lane through the brush used by deer and buffaloes, Chickasaws and traveling tribes. De Soto's demand for two hundred Chickasaw females as *tamenes,* or carriers, resulted in a furious night attack upon his party. He and his survivors left the path and struggled west to the Mississippi River, where De Soto died after a brief illness. The few Spanish survivors of this trek eventually received credit in white men's books for discovering the Natchez Trace and the Mississippi River, both already well known to Indians.

The Southern Tip

In 1716 the French, under Sieur Jean Baptiste Lemoyne de Bienville, were the first settlers at the southern end of the Trace at Natchez. With forty-nine men Bienville captured the Choctaw chief through trickery and ransomed him to the tribe for twenty-five hundred pieces of acacia wood and the bark of three thousand cypress trees. With this material he completed his fort beside the Natchez dwellings on the bluff overlooking the river. The ancient name for the Indian site was White Apple Village, but Bienville called his settlement

Fort Rosalie, after the Duchess de Pontchartrain, wife of the French minister of marine. Three hundred miles up the Mississippi, beyond the marshes and site of the future New Orleans, the outpost of the French empire was established.

By 1720 three hundred French colonists and their black slaves had opened the first plantations in the vicinity of Fort Rosalie. In 1729 an Indian uprising against Chopart, Bienville's inept successor, resulted in the death of 144 French men, 35

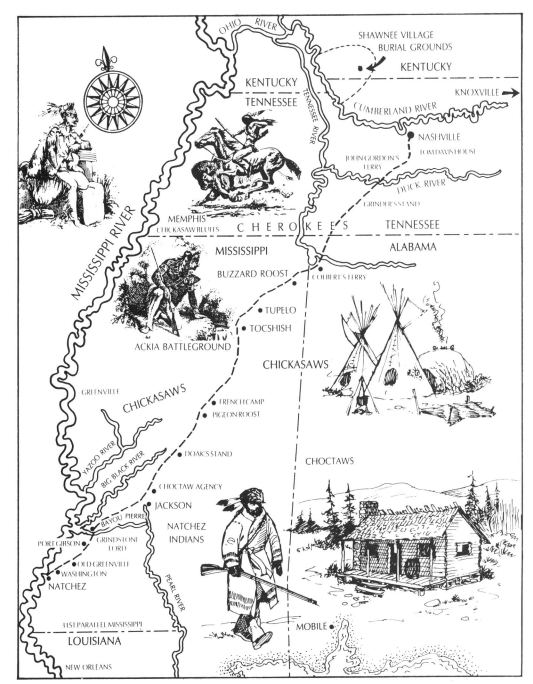

The Natchez Trace

women, and 56 children. The Indians spared two white men, most women, the half-grown children, and the blacks. All pregnant women and infants were killed.

The French from New Orleans retaliated, killing most of the Natchez Indians and sending captives into slavery in the West Indies. The few Natchez Indians who escaped made their way north and merged with the Chickasaws, who disliked the French and were friendly to the British.

In 1736 French forces under Pierre d'Artaguiette came from Illinois to defeat their Chickasaw enemies. At Pontotoc Ridge near Tupelo, where De Soto's party was almost destroyed in 1540, the Chickasaws completely defeated the French. D'Artaguiette and twenty other Frenchmen were tied to stakes, pierced with scores of fat pine splinters which were set afire, and slowly burned to death. Two months later Bienville returned from France and brought forces from the gulf, but he was defeated at Ackia and returned to Mobile. For the next thirty years the French permitted Natchez to pass into obscurity.

In 1763, at the Peace of Paris, the French government gave the land south of the 31st parallel and east of the Mississippi to the Spaniards, together with all Louisiana territory west of the Mississippi. Natchez and the land east of the river and north of the 31st parallel went to Britain. From then until the American Revolution only a few traders came to Natchez. It was no longer a thriving settlement, although the English monarch gave some land grants to men like Col. Anthony Hutchins.

Kentucky Traders and the Northern Terminus

After 1775 activity developed at the northern end of the Trace when Richard Henderson traded with a few Cherokees and presumably received thousands of acres of Kentucky land from the tribe. Soon afterward, Henderson sent Daniel Boone with his settlers into Kentucky. The permanent settlement of land north of the Trace had begun.

Slightly farther south, on Christmas Day, 1779, Col. James Robertson arrived on a bluff above the Cumberland River, the site of future Nashville. Impressed with the location, he met Col. John Donelson in 1780 at the junction of the Cumberland and Ohio rivers in Kentucky and persuaded him to bring his settlers to the Cumberland bluff. The northern terminus of the Trace was now permanently established.

In 1787 Gen. James Wilkinson, a flamboyant man of questionable character, took two flatboats and a smaller vessel down the rivers out of Kentucky to Natchez. The news of his trading success encouraged other Kentuckians and Ohio Valley settlers to explore the market in Natchez. In 1790 more than sixty flatboats stopped at Natchez with crops and goods from Kentucky, Tennessee, and the Ohio Valley. Two hundred and fifty traders returned home by the Natchez Trace through Nashville.

Boom Years on the Trace

Although trade from Nashville to Natchez was already significant by

1795, two events that year caused commercial activity to burgeon between the two towns. First, the United States and Spain signed the Treaty of San Lorenzo el Real, which opened the Mississippi River to American trade and fixed the U.S. border forty miles below Natchez. Second, Eli Whitney's cotton gin reached Natchez, revolutionizing plantation life in the region and creating an even greater demand for goods from Kentucky and Ohio river valleys. The last Spanish troops left Natchez in March 1798, and the town became the western outpost of the young United States.

To celebrate these developments, traders and settlers cut brush, cane, and trees to burn and permanently mark the boundary line. Excessive heat from the fire produced repeated explosions of air from the cane, which sounded like exploding bullets. Multitudes of animals emerged from the burning swampland — including birds of all kinds, serpents, small toads and giant bullfrogs, rabbits and squirrels, deer and crocodiles. The coming of the U.S. flag and cotton launched the boom years for Natchez and the Trace.

Boats by the hundreds and men by the thousands soon came down the river to Natchez, selling their goods and returning by the Trace. The rivermen floated down the current in boats of various types: light skiffs; northern birchbark canoes; pirogues — hollowed tree trunks fastened together with planks; bateaux — flat-bottomed boats tapered at each end; barges and keelboats. The most popular and picturesque of all, however, were the great Kentucky flatboats, known as broadhorns but also called arks or New Orleans boats. Propelled by the current and human muscle, they averaged 15 feet in width and 40 feet in length. Made of logs and planks which were sold for lumber at the end of the trip, the flatboats often had pens for horses, cattle, and pigs. They also carried tobacco, flour, whiskey, and the skins of beaver, otter, and buffalo, in addition to other products from the central United States.

The boatmen were called "Kaintucks" regardless of their origin. Mark Twain declared them rough and hardy, rude and uneducated, brave and suffering, drinkers and frolickers, reckless and prodigal, jolly and foul-witted, braggarts and often broke, but generally trustworthy and faithful to their promises, dutiful and often magnanimous. Samuel Woodworth wrote their song, which might appropriately be called "The Kaintuck Rivermen's Song:"

> We are a hardy, freeborn race,
> Each man to fear a stranger;
> What e'er the game, we join the
>   chase,
> Despising toil and danger;
> And if a daring foe annoys,
> No matter what his force is,
> We'll show him that Kentucky
>   boys
> Are alligator horses.

The rivermen constantly risked death from treacherous river currents, floods, robbers, poisonous snakes, crocodiles, and the famous "Trace sickness." Known today as yellow fever, it had a devastating effect upon both inhabitants and visitors from early Spanish days until the twentieth century.

From the outset of their journey the boatmen were beset with danger. The Cumberland River flowed out of Kentucky into the Ohio River fifty miles below Cave-in-the-Rock, the first of several stations where outlaws lurked to loot and murder flatboatmen. As late as 1828 a young Illinois trader named Abe Lincoln was attacked by seven men as his flatboat drifted downriver to Natchez; he fought them off and saved his cargo, but for the rest of his life he wore a scar from the encounter.

The perils of the journey found the boatmen ready for a boisterous celebration when they reached Natchez and sold their cargo. They usually disregarded the aristocratic plantation owners living in the stately mansions on the bluff, preferring the attractions at Natchez-below-the-Hill. Here they discarded their work problems, frustrations, and some of their earnings at King's and Walton's taverns before visiting Madame Aivoges' well-decorated house of girls or the hovels of half-naked white, yellow, and black women who took men to their rumpled beds for small sums. All women of colored or mixed races were required to wear brightly colored headdresses called *tignons*. In Natchez the wearer was regarded as a target of amiable availability.

The red-haired, green-eyed Madame Aivoges was reputed to be the ultimate of prostitutes, and she kept a house of desirable white and octoroon girls available for a price. Legend says that she placed her young son in a fashionable eastern school, anonymously maintaining him throughout his childhood and adolescence. As a young man he visited a school acquaintance in Natchez at a plantation on the bluff. He went below the hill one evening for some thrill and sport and discovered his mother and her business. He killed her in anger at the discovery.

The "king of the keelboatmen" was Mike Fink, who apparently died undeservedly on a tavern floor in Natchez. According to legend he could work, drink, and fight harder and shoot straighter than anyone on earth. Allegedly he could shoot the head off a wild turkey in full flight at one hundred yards. One night after drinking and quarreling with a friend named Carpenter, Mike lapsed into a mellow mood and suggested that he and Carpenter should renew their friendship by an overt act. They agreed that Mike should shoot a cup of whiskey off Carpenter's head. Everyone knew Mike could easily do so at close quarters, but Carpenter collapsed unconscious after the shot was fired. The giggling Fink humorously declared, "Carpenter, you've spilt your whiskey." Another friend of Carpenter's believing him dead, killed Fink before Carpenter regained consciousness. Fink's shot had passed between the cup and skull, only creasing Carpenter's scalp and temporarily knocking him out.

With the trading boom, the government decided in 1797 to use the Trace as the official postal road between Nashville and Natchez. The first postmasters were John Gordon at Nashville and Abiah Hunt at Natchez. In 1801 the government attempted to improve the Trace for mail riders like John Swaney, who left an account of incidents on the Trace. After difficult negotiations with the Choctaws and the Chickasaws, the army cleared and widened the path sufficiently for wagons to make the trip but did not build a road. The Trace was fairly good near the terminal towns, but the middle two hundred miles remained wild and unimproved. In some places the Trace was rerouted, as at Colbert's Crossing on the Tennessee River where the half-breed Chickasaw chief wanted a better crossing and a new ferryboat, storehouses, stables, and kitchens built for him at government expense. The chief refused the request to place some white families along the road in his territory to maintain accommodations for mail riders and travelers. He believed his family could handle the business more appropriately.

Washington officials named the partly cleared mail path the Columbian Highway, but its users still called it the Natchez Road or the Nashville Road, depending on which direction they were headed. Stopping places for travelers were operated by Choctaws, Chickasaw half-breeds, and a few white settlers at strategic places.

Before returning up the Trace, the traders bought needed supplies for the trip. They ground meal from roasted Indian corn and enjoyed the fritters made from the meal sweetened with honey and fried in buffalo or bear oil. Their basic fare was dried beef, hard biscuits, and whatever game and berries they could find on the trail. The trip required eighteen to twenty-one days, and the more affluent travelers bought horses from

men like Philip Nolan, a romantic opportunist who rounded up wild Opelousas in Spanish Texas and sold them in Natchez for $50 each. Nolan is undeservedly remembered as "The Man Without A Country" because more than sixty years later Edward Everett Hale selected his name from a Natchez list to create a fictional parable of treason. Nolan was killed in 1801 by a "random" bullet fired by a Spanish soldier under orders from the Spanish governor of New Orleans. The official justification stated that Nolan was rounding up wild horses without a license. Nolan was buried where he died, along the small river near Waco, Texas, which today bears his name. The true reason probably involved economic and political considerations which included Governor Gayoso, Gen. James Wilkinson, who was secretly on the Spanish payroll, and others.

Intrigue and murder were not the prerogatives of politicians alone. Merchant Anthony Glass of Natchez sold goods to travelers, noting who had the most money. He learned of their departure dates, often with the help of women and tavern workers below the hill. He then informed professional robbers, who shared the gain with him after robbing and sometimes killing the travelers on the Trace. Occasionally Glass apparently did the job himself, as in the case of a wealthy man named Campbell from Kentucky, who was murdered and robbed on the Trace while accompanied only by Glass.

The Trace: Natchez to Greenville

Before embarking on the Trace all travelers and postriders checked their powder and bullets, guns and knives. They were well aware of the dangers. Andrew Jackson, a frequent traveler of the Trace, once said he had never met a Kaintuck traveler without his rifle, whiskey, and deck of cards. Whether walking or riding, each person preferred to travel in the company of others for safety; even the postriders reported how often they were joined by fearful companions.

The first identifiable location, twelve miles up the trail, was Washington; the next was Bruinsburg, where Andrew Jackson and Rachel had lived in a log cabin shortly after their marriage in 1791. The first stop usually was Old Greenville, twenty-eight miles north of Natchez. The village acquired its name from two brothers, Abner and Thomas Marston Green, Jr., early plantation owners in the region and business associates of Andrew Jackson. The path was worn clear from Natchez to Greenville, but the incidence of robbery was high because of the activities of merchant Glass and his associates.

Samuel Mason and his son, two of Glass' proteges, worked this part of the Trace. Glass originally had introduced Mason to people in Natchez as a rich up-country plantation owner, and he looked the part with his polished boots, riding crop, and gentlemanly manner. Eventually the Masons were identified and flogged for robbing a popular planter named Baker. Angered by the punishment, the Masons dropped their gentility and became the terrors of the entire Trace for years.

Not until Gov. William Claiborne put a reward of $2,000 on the elder

Mason's head — dead or alive — was he stopped. The two men, identifying themselves as John Setton and James Mays, presented Mason's head at the Circuit Court in Greenville. They testified they discovered him asleep in his swamp hideout, tomahawked him, and severed his head. They had wrapped the head inside a ball of blue clay to prevent decay. After the clay was removed, several independent witnesses identified the head as Mason's, but postrider Swaney was not certain. In any event, Mason was never heard from again.

An ironic postscript to the story developed during identification proceedings. A gentleman known as Captain Stump from Kentucky rode into Greenville and saw the horses of Setton and Mays in the tavern's stable. The animals had been stolen from Stump and his murdered companion on the Trace two months earlier. Stump entered the courtroom and declared that the reward-seeker called Setton was the infamous Wiley Harpe, a robber sought throughout the Mississippi and Ohio valleys. Boatmen who knew Harpe were summoned, and their testimony was affirmative. Both Harpe and Mays were identified as outlaws.

On February 8, 1804, Harpe and Mays were hanged in Old Greenville. Their heads were elevated on spikes and placed on the Trace, Harpe's at the north edge of Greenville and Mays at the south end. Travelers making the perilous passage could now be assured that some robbers had reaped the whirlwind.

The Trace:
Greenville to Port Gibson

As travelers departed northward from Greenville, they encountered the marshes and swamps of Bayou Pierre. It has always been a beautiful, enchanting place, with natural green splendor where earth's creatures live beyond man's incursions. The trail here was beaten low and smooth in the soft soil, beneath the natural level of the ground. Roots and vines covered the sides facing the path.

The next major stop was Port Gibson in the heart of the bayou, founded by Sam Gibson, a South Carolinian who came to the Bayou Pierre in 1788. He was a hunter and stockman, gardener and beekeeper, orchardist and gristmill operator, and after 1795 the operator of a cotton gin. His settlement was distinguished by its church and by the myriads of mosquitoes and horseflies which plagued inhabitants and travelers alike. Many contracted "Trace sickness" (yellow fever) in the Bayou Pierre, only to die farther up the trail.

Of those who came to the Trace grasping for gold, none had a golden hand larger or more dramatic than the one on the spire of the Presbyterian Church in Port Gibson. A wooden church was on the site in 1807 when Aaron Burr landed nearby en route to his arrest and trial in Richmond. Its first permanent full-time pastor was the Reverend Zebulon Butler, who arrived from Pennsylvania in 1828. Soon afterward a brick church replaced the wooden structure. Jonathan Daniels, in his excellent book on the Natchez Trace entitled *The Devil's Backbone,* has the following to say about Zebulon Butler and the Golden Hand:

> [On the church spire] the cross is replaced by a great gleaming hand, with thumb and three fingers closed, its index finger pointing imperatively to heaven. Tired travelers saw it long ago . . . .
> [The pulpit mannerism of the Reverend Mr. Butler,] the upraised and clenched hand with the index finger pointing heavenward . . . became so much a part of his powerful preaching that members of his church took it as the symbol of his work and their worship.

Zebulon Butler dared the scorn and anger of powerful interests when he became involved in the emancipation question. The will of Capt. Isaac Ross, a plantation owner south of Port Gibson who died in 1836, provided that most of his slaves should be freed and transported to Liberia by the American Colonization Society. Ross' daughter handed the slaves to the pastor and an associate while legislators attempted to nullify the will. Butler never wavered, and finally in 1849 the provisions of the will were fulfilled.

During the Civil War, General Grant passed the town and church on the way to Vicksburg, and he declared the place too beautiful to burn. Mark Twain, as a riverboat pilot, used the towering spire to chart his course. And today The Golden Hand still stands as erectly as did the Reverend Mr. Butler against his critics.

The Trace:
Port Gibson to Le Fleur's Bluff

From Port Gibson the Trace led to Grindstone Ford, about ten miles distant, where the waters of the river giving Bayou Pierre its name often proved to be a hazard. The heavy rains in the region frequently swelled the bayou and caused delay. Impatient travelers used rafts to transport their provisions to the other side, and men and horses often swam.

The bayou pours into the Mississippi a few miles west, at Bruinsburg, but travelers continued northward through the bayou territory to Le Fleur's Bluff. The legend of Andrew Jackson bringing his bride Rachel to his log cabin overlooking the Mississippi at Bruinsburg holds a magnetism today not known in the boom years on the Trace.

From the deep, beaten path through the bayou the trail pointed into the ancient territory of the Choctaws. The path became rockier and rougher as the hilly ground provided poor footing and slowed passage. The woods and prairie presented a more barren appearance. Travelers often experienced the first signs of sickness and exhaustion on this stretch of the Trace. They were grateful to find one of the houses that provided meager accommodations. Supper and breakfast often consisted only of mush and milk; bed was cover in a barn, cabin room, or more often under the trees or in the traveler's own tent. The charge for these limited services was twenty-five cents a night.

By the 1790s more than five hundred men, sought elsewhere for capital crimes punishable by death, had settled as refugees along the Trace and taken Choctaw and Chickasaw wives. They and honest settlers produced numerous half-breeds who became a part of the history of the Trace.

The sister of the great Choctaw Chief Pushmataha married a Frenchman. Their daughter, the dazzling Rebecca Cravat, married a French Canadian named Louis Le Fleur. Le Fleur set up a trading post and traveling stand at Le Fleur's

Courtesy Natchez Trace State Park
A portion of the Natchez Trace

Bluff, the present site of Jackson, Mississippi. Later Louis established another stand northward on the Trace at French Camp. He and Rebecca became wealthy, and one of their eleven children, Greenwood Le Fleur, became the Choctaw *mingo* or chief upon the death of his uncle, Pushmataha.

Historically, Pushmataha is remembered as the chief who ceded Choctaw lands in Alabama and Mississippi to the U.S. government in 1805 for a down payment of $500 and an annuity of $150 as long as he was chief of the Choctaws. Pushmataha often spoke of his mystical origin by proclaiming: "I had no father; I had no mother. The lightning split the living oak, and Pushmataha sprang forth." His nephew seldom spoke of either his French father or grandfather, but he, too, was as strong as the oak.

The Trace: Jackson to French Camp

The traffic on the Trace encouraged Choctaws and Chickasaws, settlers and widows to set up overnight stands for travelers. More than thirty-five were once listed, not including the notorious "houses of entertainment" designed to fleece both travelers and army personnel. Every wayfarer knew that a thief, once caught and released, would carry one of three marks: thirty-nine lashes on the back; the brand of "H" on one cheek and "T" on the other (Horse Thief); or partially missing ears, occasioned when the culprit was nailed by the ears to the pillory and released by being cut loose from the nailed ears. Many horsemen and trampers

learned to their regret that not all thieves had been or would be caught.

From Jackson northward past the nearby Clinton settlement, the next major stop was the Choctaw agency. The best known of the agents was Silas Dinsmore, a responsible, hardworking man who tried to fulfill his job. It was his duty, among others, to require all masters traveling with blacks on the Trace to show their ownership papers. Owners and nonowners resisted the requirement; even legitimate owners frequently lacked proper proof of ownership. Andrew Jackson particularly disliked Dinsmore and once boasted that he refused to wait with his blacks for Dinsmore to appear at the agency.

Isaac Franklin and Nathan Bedford Forrest grew rich from the slave traffic down the Trace. In 1800 only thirty-five hundred blacks were in Mississippi; by 1810 the number had risen to seventeen thousand; by 1820 there were eighty thousand. Exactly how many came by the Trace no one knows. Wayfarers heading north often gave accounts of meeting parties of slaves headed south. The Choctaw agency was a bustling site with too much activity and responsibility for a single agent. Dinsmore was finally removed summarily, undoubtedly as a result of political pressure that reached Washington, D.C.

Still in Choctaw territory, the Trace reached Doak's Stand, forty miles north of the agency. The stand was established by William Doak in 1810. It was here in 1820 that Pushmataha faced Andrew Jackson for the last time as principal spokesman for the Choctaw Nation.

In the meeting of all the Choctaw

mingoes with Jackson and other U.S. officials, the humor of Pushmataha saved an impasse and possible disaster to the tribe in an uneven power game. After breaking the tension with light and amusing comments about past experiences, Pushmataha gave away more land than his people desired. Jackson obtained less than he sought, however, for he coveted virtually all of the Choctaw territory. The Choctaws exchanged six million acres of their land for a lesser tract west of the Mississippi between the Arkansas and Red rivers in Oklahoma Territory. In short, all land from Doak's Stand south to the Natchez District was opened to settlers. Within a few years the territory, divided into nine counties, was filled with new settlers, and the Choctaw sun was setting.

Beyond Doak's Stand the next fifty miles of the Trace passed through the northern edge of Choctaw territory before reaching the last two Choctaw stands. Pigeon Roost stood about eight miles from the Chickasaw line and derived its name from the immediate region where passenger pigeons roosted by the thousands. Originally Pigeon Roost had been the last Choctaw stand, but Louis Le Fleur in his later years placed a new stand directly on the boundary facing the wilderness and the Chickasaw Nation. In 1830, when the Choctaws were given the option to move into Oklahoma Territory or accept small farms in Mississippi, many of the Le Fleur family, now known as Leflore, stayed and accepted bits of their former tribal land.

The Trace:
French Camp to Colbert's Ferry

The ancient trail passing through the wilderness to the villages was a narrow lane beaten by animals and Indians. Running roughly north and south, it filed past Chickasaw villages to the Tennessee River. From Le Fleur's French Camp the path first led to the Chickasaw agency near the Ackia battleground, where the Choctaws defeated Bienville's French forces in 1736. Often called the most decisive but least remembered battle in American history, it forced the French to retire to Natchez and Mobile and left the northern end of the Trace for Anglo-Saxon settlers.

The next stand was Tocshish, near present Tupelo, the heart of the Chickasaw Nation. A Scotsman named John McIntosh had drifted into the tribal villages, adopted the life of the Chickasaws, and established his stand. Sometimes called McIntoshville, it was better known as Tocshish Stand, marking 310 miles to Natchez and 290 to Nashville. This was the station where fresh horses awaited postriders at the halfway point on the Trace.

Fifteen miles northeast lay Tupelo, in the heart of the Chickasaw villages. The Trace did not pass through Tupelo itself, although many travelers stopped to trade in the villages. By the time the weary wayfarers reached this point, they suffered from exhaustion and fever. Many needed to recover for the last part of the journey, and the moderately healthy ones took the opportunity to experience a final debauch before hitting the trail.

From Tupelo eighty miles north to the Tennessee River, a Chickasaw family with the unlikely name of Colbert controlled the stands. Their name was known to everyone who traveled over the Trace.

The family origin goes back to James Logan Colbert, a Scottish Highlander who fought for the Jacobite Pretender to the English throne in 1715 and lost. In 1736 he arrived in the southern colonies and moved directly into the wilderness. Becoming a cultural Chickasaw, he preyed upon Spanish posts and riverboats. He supported the British and became known to the Spaniards as a pirate, for in 1782 he seized a Spanish boat on the Mississippi carrying forty-five hundred Spanish pesos and the wife of the Spanish commander at St. Louis. He retained the pesos and exchanged the talkative Spanish lady for hostages held by the Spaniards in New Orleans.

Colbert had several Chickasaw wives, numerous sons and daughters, and 150 slaves. His sons became influential on the Trace, operating stands for the military and travelers and charging exorbitant prices. They held a monopoly on services through most of the Chickasaw territory. Among the more prominent were Levi Colbert's Stand eight miles short of the Tennessee River. George Colbert, the leader of the clan, completely controlled ferry traffic on the Trace at the Tennessee River.

The biggest obstacle on the Trace was the Tennessee River, a quarter to one-half mile wide at the crossing. Its banks were populated by Chickasaws at Colbert's Ferry, but those who ventured along the banks be-yond the Trace might find marauding Creeks or Cherokees — or unfriendly Shawnees from the north. Rafts were used to cross the river because no bridge or ferry existed, at least not originally. The river current was usually strong enough to carry away anyone who ventured into water more than four feet deep. Rafts starting on the south side often landed far downstream. George Colbert's experience and skill were needed.

Colbert literally blackmailed the young U.S. government into providing him with a ferry and buildings at a new location in exchange for permission to clear the Trace for the post road. His original stand at the river resembled others on the Trace. Cattle skins hanging on fences, animal droppings, and refuse of all kinds produced disagreeable odors and an overall sense of filth. Little wonder that Colbert drove a hard bargain with Gen. James Wilkinson and the federal government.

Once across the Tennessee the returnees dared not drop their precautions, for professional robbers found weary travelers an easy target. On the edge of the Chickasaw country between the Tennessee and the Duck rivers was a canebrake with an overhanging rock that formed a false cave. It was easy to defend, and Joseph Thompson Hare and his gang hid and rested there after robbing many Trace travelers.

Hare was the epitome of the romantic highwayman. He was intelligent and literate, sentimental and religiously mystical. Regarding himself as a Horseman of the Apocalypse, he demanded a special code of honor from his associates. A young man in his gang, for instance, "married" many young women for their handsome dowries and then deserted them. Hare accepted his roguish actions until the young man prepared to "marry" a young Spanish nun. To Hare this was sacrilegious, and he beat the young man until he was senseless.

Hare was not, however, a barroom brawler. He wore the finest clothes money could buy, and he possessed elegant manners, a finely modulated voice, and gentlemanly good taste. On the Trace he did not kill during his robberies unless forced to do so. His demise came because of his style of operation. He robbed a drover and spared the man's life. The man immediately gathered a posse and captured the highwayman. Hare was sent to jail for five years and never returned to the Trace. Years later, however, he was hanged in Maryland for robbing a night mail coach.

The capture of Hare removed only one threat from the Trace. The next stop north of Hare's hiding place was a stand owned by Robert E. Grinder, reputed to be part Indian. Whether he stole from the lodgers at his stand has never been determined. Twenty miles away, Mom Murrell operated a tavern, brothel, and thieves market, but Grinder did not have Murrell's reputation. Nevertheless, shortly after Grinder's Stand opened, it became the site of one of the most perplexing deaths on the Trace.

On October 10, 1810, a distraught Meriwether Lewis and a party of three men were caught in a rainstorm on the Trace. Two of his packhorses bolted with his valuable papers. While the other men hunted for the

horses, Lewis went to Grinder's Stand. The inn consisted of two log houses and a barn. Only Mrs. Grinder and their two children were there; Grinder was supposedly at his farm on Swan Creek.

The other members of Lewis' party finally arrived with the horses and were housed in the barn, about a hundred yards from the Grinder cabin, where Lewis had a room. According to Mrs. Grinder, Lewis had a few drinks, talked to himself, then asked his men for a bearskin and buffalo robe and retired to his room. Shortly thereafter she heard a pistol shot in his room and a heavy thud. Then there was another shot, and Lewis appeared at her door crying that he was wounded and asking for water.

Mrs. Grinder and the two children stayed in the kitchen until daybreak, when the children called Lewis' servants. He was still alive when the servants arrived, although he had a wound in his side and one in his head. Two hours later he died.

Lewis, who won fame as a member of the Lewis and Clark expedition to Oregon, had served as governor of upper Louisiana and was a trusted friend of President Thomas Jefferson. Whether he killed himself, as officially declared, or was the victim of foul play by Grinder, the servants, or some unknown assailant, will never be known. Lewis became another statistic devoured by the Trace.

Beyond Grinder's place lay John Gordon's Ferry at the Duck River. This crossing was a popular stop before the last lap into Nashville. The Trace was broad and clear from the river onward. Good food and better lodging were available at Gordon's, which was the first stop on the post road out of Nashville. For travelers completing a journey of eighteen days or more, the sight of Nashville and frontier civilization must have been exciting. Undoubtedly many were grateful and gave thanks for their deliverance.

Within a few years, however, the Trace would lose its importance. Robert Fulton's invention of the steamboat altered trading practices in the Mississippi and Ohio valleys. Nicholas Roosevelt built a steamboat in Pittsburgh, called it the *New Orleans,* and in 1811 sailed it all the way to Natchez. From that date, steam-powered boats could take upstream all traders prosperous enough to pay the fare. The gambling, "houses of entertainment," and robbery shifted to the riverboats and the river shores.

The demise of the Trace coincided generally with the capitulation and departure of the Chickasaw Nation. As early as 1805 the Chickasaws had ceded their lands north of the "big bend" in the Tennessee River, and settlers had occupied the region between the Duck and Tennessee rivers. In 1816 the tribe ceded thirteen thousand square miles on both banks of the Tennessee River above and below Muscle Shoals in Alabama. By the Treaty of Pontotoc in 1832 the Chickasaws signed a document similar to the final Choctaw Treaty of 1830. They exchanged their ancient tribal territory for land west of the Mississippi in Oklahoma Indian country. Most of the Colberts moved with the Chickasaws, as thousands of settlers bought and occupied the tribal lands.

The Trace gradually returned to its original wilderness state and was difficult to locate and reconstruct in the twentieth century when the federal government and the states decided to replace it with a paved highway. Research and guesswork reproduced the Trace, which now daily accommodates thousands of travelers and hundreds of giant trucks along a trail of unparalleled beauty.

Today the Natchez Trace Parkway runs from Natchez to Nashville. Historical events on the Trace are recounted on roadside markers and monuments; the legends are retold. The reconstructed cabins of Col. James Robertson stand on the Nashville bluff above the Cumberland River for all to see and remember.

The Parkway ends at Nashville, but U.S. Highway 41 runs north along the old Shawnee path leading to the Dividing Ridge. The highway passes a dense wood; three hundred yards from its shoulders, under gently falling leaves and underbrush, rest the Shawnee remains of camp and war, the Chickasaw goods, and the bones of warriors who once walked the Trace. They rest silent and unremembered.

THE TRAIL OF TEARS
By R. David Edmunds

There were many trails west, traveled by a wide variety of emigrants and wayfarers, but almost all the travelers had one thing in common: They went willingly, seeking either economic opportunity or a place of refuge. The Cherokees were different, for they trudged west in sorrow, often at gunpoint, leaving behind most of their possessions as well as their homeland. The saga of their journey, aptly named the Trail of Tears, remains one of the darkest pages in American history.

For centuries the Cherokee Nation was located in the region surrounding the southern Appalachians. A tribal people, the Cherokees originally were grouped into loosely organized villages held together by family or kinship ties. Prior to the nineteenth century they had no centralized government but counseled among themselves during periods of crisis or to ameliorate intratribal disputes. Cherokee families lived in bark-roofed log cabins organized into villages located along streams in protected valleys. Men hunted, trapped, and traded, while women cared for the small fields of corn, squash, and pumpkins. All enjoyed the fruit from orchards of

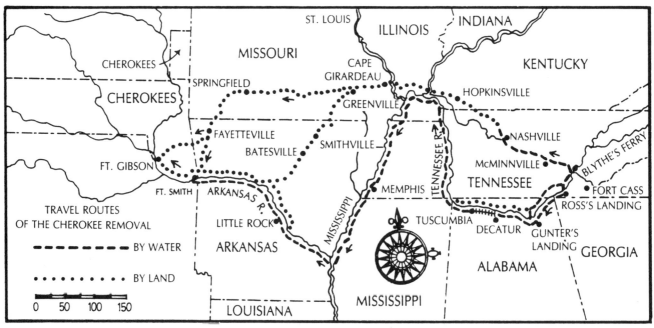

The Trail of Tears

plums and peaches surrounding the villages. By the mid-eighteenth century many also kept small herds of swine, often penned near the village or allowed to forage in the nearby forest. In the Revolutionary War the Cherokees first favored the British, but after the Americans conducted several campaigns against their villages they made a necessary if reluctant peace with the colonists.

The years following the American Revolution brought profound changes to the Cherokee people. In the last decades of the 1700s large numbers of white men entered Cherokee country, and many married into the tribe. These marriages produced a growing number of mixed-bloods who exercised an expanding influence within the tribe. Indeed, new white ideas or practices were not limited to the mixed-bloods, for by the turn of the century many full bloods also adopted much of the European or American life style. Some Cherokees still clung to the old ways, but others, emulating their white neighbors, established fine plantations, erected large houses, planted cotton, and purchased black slaves. Enterprising tribesmen also ventured into other traditionally white economic activities. Adapting to their changing world, former Cherokee warriors became blacksmiths, millers, ferry owners, carpenters, cobblers, tanners, merchants, teamsters, teachers, and ministers of the gospel. If the old Warrior's Path was gone, many Cherokees were willing to walk the white man's road to economic self-sufficiency.

The Cherokees changed in other ways. By the 1820s many adopted the clothing of white men, and Cherokee plantation owners and their wives dressed in garb resembling that of their Anglo-American neighbors. Some Cherokee homes were filled with furniture purchased in eastern cities, and wealthy families drove purebred horses hitched to elegant carriages. The tribe took great pains, moreover, to educate its people. Missionaries had been active among the Cherokees for decades, and in 1801 the Moravians opened a mission school at Spring Place in modern Georgia. Soon other schools were established, and within twenty years large numbers of Cherokee children were enrolled in classes throughout the nation. In 1821 Sequoya, also known as George Guess, perfected a Cherokee alphabet or syllabary consisting of eighty-five characters. Within ten years more than half of the Cherokee people could read and write in their own language. In the same year (1812) the *Cherokee Phoenix,* a tribal newspaper, began publication at New Echota, Georgia, and provided the Indians with local, national, and world news, in addition to various commercial information. The publishers of the *Phoenix* also produced pamphlets, hymnals, and other books in the Cherokee language, which were distributed among the Indians. At the same time other Cherokees continued to study English. By the 1830s much of the tribe was bilingual, and a growing number of educated Cherokees were literate in both languages.

The Cherokee political structure underwent a similar transition. In 1808 the tribe established a National Council, which passed the first written laws governing the tribe. One year later a standing committee of thirteen members was appointed, which began to assume control over political affairs within the Cherokee Nation. Soon known as the National Committee, it attempted to defend Cherokee sovereignty against claims by both state and federal governments. In 1820 the Cherokee homeland was apportioned into eight separate districts, each sending four delegates to the National Council for two-year terms. The delegates were chosen in popular elections within each district and were paid for their services. Five years later, in 1825, the national Committee decided to check its own power by decreeing that no acts of a public character (including the cession of tribal lands) could be passed by the committee without the consent of all the Cherokee people in council. They also voted to establish a formal capital of the Cherokee Nation at New Echota. Finally, in 1827 the tribe established a formal constitutional government quite similar to that of the United States. A tribal constitutional convention created three branches of government, with a bicameral legislature, a principal and assistant chief, and a tribal court system. Legislators served two-year terms and were elected from the separate districts within the nation. The chiefs served four years and were chosen by the combined legislative bodies. John Ross, a prominent mixed-blood of only one-eighth Cherokee lineage, was elected as the first principal chief of the tribe.

The federal government encouraged the Cherokees to make these changes. Throughout the first quarter of the nineteenth century officials in Washington urged the Cherokees and other tribes to adopt white ways and to settle down as farmers. Since game was becoming scarce, the government warned the tribesmen that they must give up their old ways of hunting and trapping. Only by farming could they hope to remain on their ancient homelands. Accepting the government's injunction, the Cherokees assumed that if they made the desired changes they would be allowed to stay on their lands in Georgia and Tennessee. Indeed, of all the tribes within the United States hadn't they most closely followed the president's wishes? Didn't white people refer to them and to their neighbors (the Creeks, Choctaws, Chickasaws, and part of the Seminoles) as the "civilized tribes"?

By 1828 the Cherokee population numbered between eighteen and nineteen thousand. They owned 22,000 cattle, 1,300 slaves, 2,000 spinning wheels, 700 looms, 31 gristmills, 10 sawmills, and 8 cotton gins. They maintained an 18-school educational system. They were rapidly adopting the white man's way of life. Surely such "progress" guaranteed them their homelands.

They were sorely mistaken. Although the government had assured the Cherokees they could remain in the East, federal officials had also promised Georgia that they would encourage the Indians to relinquish their lands within that state and move west of the Mississippi. White settlers in Georgia and Alabama were anxious to acquire the Cherokee farmlands, and they exerted pressure upon state and local officials to remove the Indians. In 1828 Cherokee fortunes darkened considerably when gold was discovered in the upland regions of their homeland. The Indians were also discouraged by federal election returns that year, for Andrew Jackson became the seventh president of the United States.

A former frontiersman from Tennessee, Jackson was sympathetic to Georgia and her attempts to extend state sovereignty over Cherokee lands within her borders. In 1830 he pushed his Indian Removal Bill through Congress, and the fate of the Cherokees was sealed. The bill provided that the federal government would purchase Indian lands east of the Mississippi and then provide for the removal of Indian people to new homes in the West. The state of Georgia, meanwhile, increased its harrassment of Cherokee tribesmen, sending the state militia into the Cherokee Nation and encouraging white squatters to settle on Cherokee farmlands. State laws were passed forbidding the Cherokee government to function within Georgia (except to ratify land cessions), and forbidding the tribesmen to mine gold in their homeland. More ominously, state officials established a lottery through which Cherokee plantations were to be raffled off to white Georgians.

Besieged on all sides, the Cherokees decided to fight the white man on his own terms. John Ross and other Cherokee leaders traveled to Washington, where they pointed out to both the president and congressmen that the Indians were suffering injustice. The Cherokees also took their case into the federal court system. Asserting that they were an inde-

pendent nation, they argued that the federal government had recognized their sovereignty through its treaties with the tribe, and therefore the state of Georgia had no legal right to extend its control over their homeland. In *Cherokee Nation vs Georgia* the Supreme Court denied that the Cherokees were an independent nation, claiming instead that the tribe constituted a "domestic dependent nation" of Indians. But in *Worcester vs Georgia* the court ruled in the Cherokees' favor. Chief Justice John Marshall stated that Georgia had no authority to extend her laws over the tribesmen. Although the Cherokees danced in celebration, their triumph was short-lived. President Jackson refused to enforce the court's decision, and Georgia increased its pressure against the hapless tribesmen.

By 1835 state and federal pressures upon the Cherokee people began to achieve the desired effect. Although Ross continued to lobby against removal, some Cherokees believed that their case was hopeless and that the tribe should move west. Led by Major Ridge, John Ridge (his son), and Elias Boudinot, these tribesmen argued that the tribe should secure the best possible terms from the government and then move to Arkansas and eastern Oklahoma, where scattered groups of Cherokees had already taken up residence. In the fall of 1835 federal agents negotiated a removal treaty with the Ridge faction, but the majority of the tribe refused to ratify the document. Then, on December 29, 1835, while Ross was absent in Washington, officials signed the Treaty of New Echota with Ridge and his followers. Although the majority of the tribe again disapproved, the government declared the treaty valid. Ridge and his followers promptly left for Oklahoma, but Ross and the remaining Cherokees used all their influence to prove that the agreement was a fraud.

Ultimately they failed. On May 23, 1836, in a close contest, the U. S. Senate ratified the treaty by a single vote. Jackson signed the treaty, which provided that the Cherokee homelands now belonged to the United States. The Indians could remain in the East no longer than 1838. During that two-year period they must settle all their affairs and prepare for removal. They were to receive 13.8 million acres in Arkansas and Oklahoma and $5 million to pay for the cost of removal and all legitimate claims against the tribe by white men.

Dumbfounded by the series of events that seemed to be overwhelming them, Ross and his followers accepted the loss of tribal lands but repeatedly petitioned the government to allow them to retain their individual farms and homesteads. They agreed to accept citizenship within the states of Georgia and Tennessee if they could remain. But the federal government turned a deaf ear to their pleas. Cherokee lands in Georgia were already being overrun by white squatters, who seized Cherokee property and actually forced many Indian families from their homes. When the few federal troops assigned to protect the Cherokees attempted to intervene, the Georgia militia supported the squatters. Many Indians fled Georgia, taking

refuge in the Smoky Mountain region of Tennessee and North Carolina.

Between May 1836 and May 1838 about one thousand Cherokees voluntarily agreed to accept removal. Part of these people were members of the Ridge faction, but others simply accepted the inevitable and decided to go west at the earliest opportunity. The remaining Indians rallied around Ross and refused to leave their homeland. Alarmed by their stubbornness, settlers in Georgia now wondered if the "civilized" Cherokees might not revert to their former ways and take to the warpath against those who usurped their land and property. In a futile effort to maintain peace in the region, the government ordered Gen. John E. Wool to disarm the tribesmen. The Cherokees voluntarily complied with the order, but Wool became so disgusted with the lawlessness of the squatters that he resigned his command.

In April 1838 Gen. Winfield Scott was ordered to prepare the Indians for their journey west. The small force of regular troops stationed in the Indian country was augmented by a regiment of infantry, six companies of dragoons, and artillery. For additional assistance, Scott was authorized to ask the governors of Georgia, Tennessee, North Carolina, and Alabama for four thousand militia and volunteers. By late May he commanded a force of about ninety-five hundred soldiers. The government had meanwhile constructed stockades at strategic locations along major rivers in the Cherokee Nation. Once the Cherokees were rounded up, the government had no intention of letting them escape again.

On May 23, 1838, exactly two years after the Treaty of New Echota had been ratified by the Senate, troops spread across the Cherokee Nation to arrest the hapless Indians. Although the tribesmen had been aware of the newly constructed detention camps, many were surprised by the government's actions. They still believed that, since they had never signed nor accepted the ill-begotten Treaty of New Echota, they were not bound by its terms. They were sadly mistaken. Squads of federal troops and militamen ranged across the countryside, barging into cabins and seizing Cherokee families at their breakfast tables. Other Indians were arrested as they worked in their fields or rode along the dust-covered highways. They were herded together, and men, women, and children were marched under armed guard to the detention camps.

Many of the Cherokees had little opportunity to retain their property. Some were allowed to stuff a few family heirlooms into duffle bags, but many were forced to abandon clothing, tools, furniture, and livestock. Although the federal troops generally acted with restraint, the undisciplined militiamen were quick to take advantage of the Indians' distress. Militia officers seized Cherokee property or demanded that Cherokee landholders still living on their homesteads sign fraudulent notes of indebtedness in exchange for additional time to pack household goods into other wagons. The officers could then assert they had liens against the farms, and when the

lands were opened up for white settlement, the liens gave them a valid claim to the real estate. As soon as the soldiers marched the Indians away, bands of white men descended upon many of the farms, pillaging whatever was left of the Cherokees' belongings. This frontier riffraff was so lawless that they often fought among themselves over the spoils, resulting in numerous beatings, stabbings, and gunshot wounds. Others even attacked wagons hired by the army to haul bedding and cooking utensils from the Cherokee homes to the detention camps. Teamsters were beaten or killed, and loaded wagons were looted or stolen. On some of the larger plantations, enterprising Georgians even exhumed Cherokee graves, searching for any jewelry that might have been buried with the corpses.

If the government seizure of the Indians was tragic, life in the detention camps was worse. The stockades were constructed of split logs, sixteen feet high and sharpened at the top. Since the enclosures were roofless, federal officials allowed the Cherokees to construct temporary shelters of brush and canvas to afford some protection from the summer sun and occasional thunderstorms. But the dozen detention camps were horribly overcrowded. Throughout the summer of 1838 more than fourteen thousand Cherokees sweltered in the heat, provisioned on a diet usually served in military prisons: salt pork and flour. Sanitary facilities were abominable. Water was in short supply and often so stagnant it reeked. Latrines consisted of slit trenches dug in opposite corners of the stockade and shielded by tarpaulins, but the sanitary facilities were entirely inadequate for such large numbers. Disease took a heavy toll. The few army doctors with the troops did their best, but dysentery, measles, whooping cough, and influenza swept through the camps, carrying off children, the aged, and those Cherokees who seemed to have lost their will to continue.

On June 6, 1838, the first detachment of about eight hundred Cherokees was loaded aboard six flatboats at Ross's Landing on the Tennessee river. Hoping to carry them west by a water route, the government rented several steamboats to tow the flatboats down the Tennessee to the Ohio, then to the Mississippi, and finally up the Arkansas to new Cherokee lands in Oklahoma. The first steamboat brought the Cherokees as far downstream as Decatur, Alabama. There the Tennessee became unnavigable, and the Indians were unloaded. Lt. Edward Deas, conductor of the emigration, arranged for a train to transport the tribesmen overland to Waterloo, where the river again became navigable and the Cherokees could be reloaded aboard boats. But when they reached Decatur, Deas found that the train could carry only about half the Indians. He escorted the first group to Waterloo, but when the train returned for the remainder, he found that many had fled. Abandoning any hope of overtaking them in the forest, Deas loaded the remaining tribesmen on the train and proceeded to Waterloo, where a head count indicated that his party now consisted of only 489 Indians.

At Waterloo the diminished party boarded two double-decked keelboats and, accompanied by another steamer, again descended the Tennessee. Afraid he might lose more of his emigrants, Deas kept the vessels moving night and day, stopping only to secure wood for the steamboat. After reaching the Arkansas, shallow water prevented traveling at night, so the Cherokees were allowed to camp along the riverbank. By this time the Indians were so far from their homes they were anxious to reach their final destination. They eventually were put ashore near Sallisaw, Oklahoma, during the third week in June. Although Deas had lost over a third of his Indians through desertions, no Cherokees in his party had died en route to the West.

The second group of Cherokee immigrants was less fortunate. On the thirteenth of June 875 more Indians left Ross's Landing for the West, supervised by R. H. K. Whitley, five assistants, three interpreters, and two physicians. Following in the first party's wake, they also sailed downstream in flatboats, portaged by rail from Decatur to Waterloo, and then boarded a large keelboat towed by the steamer *Smelter*. Between Ross's Landing and Waterloo, about two dozen Indians slipped away from evening camps, and three died: a child and an old woman from illness, and a man who was run down by the train used in the removal. Three more children died before they reached the mouth of the Arkansas. Along the way Indians in twos and threes continued to desert the nightly camps. At Little Rock the party transferred to the steamship *Tecumseh,* whose shallow draft was better suited to plying the Arkansas. But the river fell so rapidly that the *Te-*

Courtesy Woolaroc Museum — Bartlesville, Oklahoma

The Trail of Tears — a painting by Robert Lindneux

cumseh grounded on a sandbar near Lewisburg, and Whitley was forced to unload the Indians on the riverbank.

Whitley's party had stopped each evening to make camp, so it journeyed more slowly than the first group. By now it was mid-July, and Arkansas sweltered under high temperatures and a drought. The Cherokees in this second party had, moreover, been forced to remain longer in the pestilential detention camps. Many were ill, and they carried their diseases with them, spreading infection in the crowded vessels. Whitley searched through the surrounding countryside, hiring wagons to carry the ailing Indians and their supplies the rest of the way to Oklahoma. Finally, on July 20, all but eighty of the Cherokees set out overland. Those left behind, too ill with measles to walk, were loaded into wagons and eventually followed their kinsmen.

The trek across western Arkansas took a heavy toll. Traveling at a snail's pace, more and more of the Indians succumbed to illness. Whitley's journal indicates that the expedition was forced to bury three or four Indians each day. By August 1 almost three hundred of the Cherokees were so ill they could not continue. Camping near Lee's Creek, the party stayed several days at the same location. The Cherokees, disgusted with the government's provisions of salt pork and flour, purchased green corn and peaches from surrounding farmers. Much to Whitley's chagrin, they wolfed down large quantities of the produce. Because of their weakened physical condition, the corn and peaches provoked an epidemic of the

"bloody flux," which carried off dozens. Finally, a few days later, the survivors straggled into the Cherokee Nation. Of the original 875 emigrants, 602 eventually arrived in Oklahoma. Seventy had died; the rest had melted into the forests.

On June 17, four days after Whitley's party started west, the third detachment of 1,070 Cherokees left Ross's Landing. In those four days the Tennessee River had dropped so precipitously that it was no longer navigable. Capt. J. B. Drane, superintendent of the third removal party, marched his charges overland to Waterloo. En route about one hundred of the Indians slipped away. When the expedition reached Tuscumbia, they were informed that General Scott, concerned about their health and safety, had postponed any further immigration until fall. By autumn the temperatures would moderate, and the fall rains might provide adequate water for navigation. The rest of the Cherokees could remain in the East until October.

When the Indians in the third party learned of Scott's decision, they immediately petitioned their removal agents to return to Georgia and Tennessee. The agents refused. Angered, more than three hundred Cherokees seized their baggage from the freight wagons and scattered into the forest. Federal troops, augmented by local militia units, apprehended most of the fugitives and escorted them to Waterloo, where they were forced onto flatboats. En route to Arkansas they suffered an outbreak of measles. Large numbers continued to flee each evening as the party made camp. On their arrival in Oklahoma the party numbered 722. The 350 missing tribesmen had either died or escaped. Federal officials were unsure just how many of the absences to attribute to either cause.

John Ross had spent the early summer in Washington, pleading in vain with the government to allow the Indians to remain in the East. When he returned to Tennessee in mid-July he was shocked by reports of the hardships encountered by the emigrants and by conditions in the detention camps. Learning of Scott's order of postponement, Ross and several other Cherokee leaders proposed to the general that the Indians be allowed to conduct their own removal. Ross asked that the expeditions be resumed in September under Cherokee control. The tribe would organize the removal parties, arrange for their own transportation and provisions, and police themselves en route. Funds for the removal would come from the War Department and from annuities owed to the tribe. In the meantime the Cherokees would be free to leave the detention camps but would reassemble for removal shortly before their departure date. If the government agreed to this proposal, Cherokees still in the detention camps promised to honor their part of the agreement.

Over the protests of state and local officials Scott agreed, genuinely relieved to be free of the responsibility for removing the Cherokees. Cherokee morale quickly improved. The fourteen thousand Indians remaining in the East used the next few weeks to collect what was left of their property and to arrange for their journey. Since they planned to travel overland, Ross and his associates collected a large number of wagons and draft animals and contracted with suppliers along the route for provisions. Ross also took great pains to collect the records of the Cherokee Nation, so that its government could be reconstructed in the West.

Not all the Indians in the detention camps cooperated with Ross. Although Major Ridge and his family already were in the West, about seven hundred of his followers who had not been able to emigrate immediately after the Treaty of New Echota had been detained with the other Cherokees. They were opposed to Ross, and since they had proved cooperative, federal officials agreed to transport them west as a separate party. They were rewarded with increased travel allowances and permitted to take large amounts of their personal property. Under the supervision of Lt. Edward Deas, they left Tennessee in early October. They traveled quite comfortably and arrived in the West in early January.

The drought which had plagued the South during the summer of 1838 continued into September, so the departure date for Ross and his followers was postponed until early October. Ross and his advisers planned to remove the remaining Indians in thirteen parties of slightly more than one thousand each. All would follow a similar route: northwest through Nashville, then across Kentucky to the Ohio River, crossing over to pass through the tip of southern Illinois, then across southern Missouri or northern Arkansas to Oklahoma. Ross estimated the journey would take approximately twelve weeks and, since parties would be leaving every two or three days, some of the groups might join or pass slower-moving companies ahead of them.

The Cherokees had agreed to assemble at Rattlesnake Springs, near the Cherokee Agency in Tennessee. On October 1 the site was crowded with Indians. At noon 1,103 Cherokees led by John Benge and Assistant Chief George Lowrey paused briefly while Ross led the tribe in prayer. They then bid farewell to their friends and started toward Nashville. Almost all were either on foot or horseback; the wagons were piled high with baggage, and only the very young, aged, or infirm were allowed to ride. Assigned to keep order, a small number of Cherokee Light Horse Guards flanked the column on either side. The first day they traveled only about five miles.

Three days later a second detachment set out. Others followed in their path, until by the end of October nine parties were en route from Tennessee to Oklahoma. Four other parties left during the first two weeks of November. Ross and his advisers had assumed that information regarding the journey would be passed back to the following parties by those preceding them. They were correct but, unfortunately, most of the communications did little to bolster the spirits of the later expeditions. Although most of the Cherokees preferred to participate in removals they had organized themselves, they had underestimated the hardships they would encounter. A southern people, many did not realize that as they traveled north toward the Ohio they were marching into oncoming winter. Ironically, the show-ers that broke the drought and permitted their departure now turned into cold autumn rains, which fell incessantly as they trudged across Kentucky. Muddy roads became quagmires as thousands of Indians, their livestock, and wagons passed over (or through) them in seemingly endless succession. Small streams usually fordable overflowed their banks, providing further obstacles for the weary emigrants. Elijah Hicks, in charge of the second party to leave Tennessee, reported that his people were "very loath to go on, and unusually slow in preparing for starting each morning." Cherokee officials leading other parties sent Ross similar statements and warned those remaining at the departure camp to bring plenty of heavy waterproof clothing.

Health problems that had plagued them while in the detention camps reappeared. Many of the aged, unaccustomed to the hardships of the trail and dispirited by the entire removal process, lost their will to live. Wet, cold, and jolted unmercifully in the baggage wagons, these Cherokees succumbed to a multitude of maladies, not the least of which was pneumonia. Young children also seemed particularly susceptible to respiratory ailments, and eyewitnesses wrote vivid descriptions of Cherokee mothers striving desperately to save their dying infants. Measles again made an unwelcome appearance, as did a nameless "coughing sickness" which carried away tribesmen of all ages.

In a grim encore of events in Georgia, the emigrating Cherokees again fell victim to unscrupulous whites.

The Indians had contracted with various suppliers to provide them with food and other commodities at certain locations along their route, but when they arrived at these way stations they sometimes found the food unfit for human consumption. One unscrupulous frontier merchant even supplied the Indians with corn for their personal use that the army had condemned as unfit for horses. Although the cost of all foodstuffs purchased prior to the removal was established by legal contract, the Cherokees found that any additional provisions bought en route cost double, triple, or even seven times the usual price. Ferry owners asked similar fees, and even land owners whose real estate abutted the trails charged a tax for any livestock or wagons straying onto their property. When the Cherokees camped for the evening their livestock and freight wagons were targets for hoodlums and sneak thieves, and although the Light Horse Guards patrolled the camps, they had no authority to arrest intruders. Sometimes the Indians seized pilferers and enacted their own justice, but such retribution was dangerous. Complaints by apprehended (and bruised) freebooters brought out local officials, who were rarely sympathetic to the Cherokees.

By December the autumn rains had turned to snow. The frozen ground provided a better roadway for the wagons, but many of the Cherokees were ill-prepared for winter weather. In early January 1839 the Midwest was chilled by a mass of Arctic air, and temperatures plummeted. Several of the parties already had crossed over into Missouri, but

five contingents camped together, shivering in the Mississippi River bottoms of southern Illinois. All five of the parties had been able to cross the Ohio from Kentucky, but when they reached the Mississippi they found it choked with ice, and ferry captains refused to leave the Illinois shore. Many of the Cherokees had little winter clothing, and almost all of them were forced to seek shelter in makeshift tents constructed of canvas and blankets. Lewis Ross, elder brother of Chief John Ross, eventually purchased additional blankets and clothing, but many elderly Cherokees died and were buried in the river bottoms. Finally, in mid-January, they were able to ferry across to Cape Girardeau and continue.

John Ross rode with the last group of Cherokees to leave Tennessee in mid-November. His party numbered only 228, and it soon overtook Peter Hilderbrand's contingent of 1,800 tribesmen, merging with them in Kentucky. Accompanying Ross was his wife, Quatie, and several children. She was in poor health, and, although she did not complain, she suffered intensely as the caravan wound its way toward the northwest, Aware of her deteriorating physical condition, Ross was convinced that she would not survive the overland trek across Illinois and Missouri to Oklahoma. When the party reached the Ohio he used personal funds to charter the small steamboat *Victoria* to carry his family and other debilitated Indians by water to Little Rock, Arkansas. The *Victoria,* although small, was stoutly constructed and could weather the iceflows in the Mississippi.

The steamer arrived at Little Rock

on February 1, 1839, where the Cherokees went ashore to prepare for the last leg of their journey. The weather was cold, and the ailing Mrs. Ross gave part of her blankets to the mother of a child stricken with whooping cough. The child recovered, but the frail Cherokee woman contracted pneumonia. Already weakened by her ordeals in Georgia and on the trail, she no longer had the strength to resist the infection. Within a few hours she was dead. Ross buried her in a shallow grave beside the Arkansas River, and the Cherokees trudged on to Oklahoma.

The first of these final emigrants arrived in their new homeland on January 4. Other groups continued to straggle in throughout the following twelve weeks. Most had crossed southern Missouri to Springfield, then turned south through Fayetteville. A few had crossed northern Arkansas via Batesville and Lewisburg. On the final leg of their journey they had met with a mixed reception. Frightened by the large numbers of Indians emigrating through their communities, many white settlers refused to have any contact with them. Other allowed the Cherokees to camp on their farms and even to seek shelter in their farm buildings. The last party of Cherokees reached Oklahoma on March 25, 1839. The removal was over.

The process had taken a terrible toll. Census figures are inaccurate at best, but government documents indicate that prior to the removals there were about nineteen thousand Cherokees living east of the Mississippi. Approximately twenty-five hundred died in the roundups and in the deten-

tion camps. A total of 16,500 Cherokees were removed between 1835 and 1840, but some of them fled and sought refuge in the Smoky Mountains. Of the Indians removed in 1838, almost fifteen hundred died and, like Quatie Ross, were buried along the trail. There were altogether four thousand deaths in a population of nineteen thousand.

American historians still argue over the merits of the Cherokees' case and the government's motives in removing them. Some scholars state that Andrew Jackson and other politicians wanted to move the Indians to the West to protect them from state and local interests in Georgia. These historians assert that during the 1830s the federal government had neither the means nor the inclination to protect the Indians in their eastern homelands. Any strong defense of Cherokee rights might have precipitated a major confrontation with states' rights advocates in the South, a confrontation that could have splintered the Union. Undoubtedly the Cherokees suffered during their removal but, according to these scholars, they would have suffered more if they had continued to reside in Georgia. Removal was, therefore, the best of several bad alternatives.

Yet how does one rationalize the deaths of four thousand people? Some Indians were killed resisting arrest, and the federal government did not intentionally spread disease in the detention camps. In a similar vein, weren't Ross and his advisers responsible for those Cherokees who died in the tribal-sponsored removal beginning in October 1838? But such queries ignore the basic issue. The Cherokees were illegally removed from land rightfully theirs and forced west against their will. In a country founded upon the principle that all men "are endowed by their Creator with certain inalienable Rights, that among these are Life, Liberty, and the pursuit of Happiness," such a sequence of events is unconscionable. The Trail of Tears remains a dark trail, a sad trail, for all Americans.

THE CAMINO REAL: CALIFORNIA'S MISSION TRAIL

By W. Michael Mathes

The history of the Camino Real de las Californias is essentially that of exploration for mission sites, the founding of fifty-one missions from San José del Cabo to Sonoma, and the establishment of supply and commu-

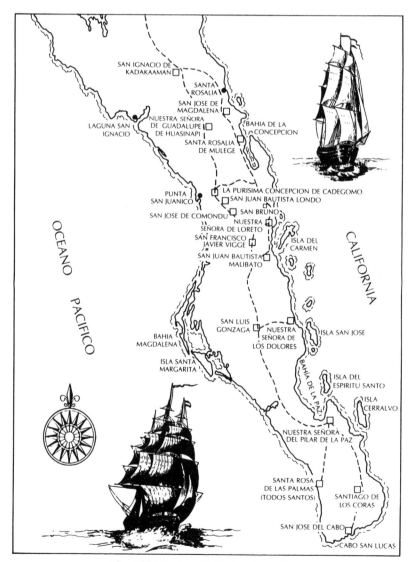

The Old Missions Trail, Southern Part

nication routes from 1683 to 1823. Although occasionally used for the movement of troops and settlers, the Camino Real was, until 1835, primarily a means of moving cattle, horses, mules, and other stock from mission to mission and of distributing mail and directives.

California's rugged terrain, extremes in climate, and isolation presented insurmountable obstacles to colonization for 150 years following its discovery by Spain. Such capable explorers and navigators as Fernando Cortés in 1535, Juan Rodríguez Cabrillo in 1542, Sebastián Vizcaíno in 1596 and 1602, and Francisco de Ortega in 1632-1636 found that the vagaries in weather in the Gulf of California and along the Pacific Coast made supply by sea to the distant outpost all but impossible, while the land itself was incapable of attracting and supporting large civilian settlements. Thus, activity in California was restricted to coastal exploration, and the establishment of land communication was considered untenable.

As a result of these failures to colonize, the Spanish crown recognized that the only means of achieving settlement was through the establishment of missions — religious centers designed to evangelize and acculturate native peoples who, in time, would come to form the nucleus of civilian settlement in the region. The founding of such missions in isolated frontier areas required personnel with a high level of religious motivation, patience, and stamina, as well as competence in building, farming, exploring, and mapping. It would be

just such men, missionaries of the Jesuit, Franciscan, and Dominican orders, who would, between 1683 and 1823, open the Camino Real de las Californias, a trail extending for almost three thousand kilometers from Cabo San Lucas to Sonoma.

In January 1683, following extensive preparation to insure success in a mission enterprise, Admiral Isidro de Atondo y Antillón, with a small complement of soldiers and Jesuit Fathers Eusebio Francisco Kino and Matías Goñi, sailed from Sinaloa to begin the long-desired settlement of California. After extensive exploration of the gulf coast a site with adequate water was discovered, and there Kino founded his base camp, Mission San Bruno, on October 5. Occupied with building and planting during the first year, additional land exploration was delayed, although a small camp was established at Londó (San Isidro). On December 14, 1684, Atondo and Kino set out from Londó in search of a route westward to the Pacific Coast. Five days later the party reached the waterhole of Comondú and on December 23 entered the great arroyo of La Purísima. Reaching the Pacific shore on December 30, the expedition returned via the same trail to San Bruno on January 13, 1685, having established the first land route in the Californias.

A month later, on February 16, Atondo and Goñi explored southward along the gulf coast, reaching the arroyo of Conchó (San Dionisio-Loreto) four days later, the waterholes of Notrí and Chuenqué (Puerto Escondido) on the 25th, and the arroyo of Ligüí on the 27th, when the expedition turned back due to the impassible terrain. Reaching San Bruno on March 6, Atondo and Goñi had succeeded in extending the earlier transpeninsular trail southward some seventy kilometers. Despite the exploration and the labors of Kino, Mission San Bruno was failing, and in May 1685 a decision was made to abandon the enterprise.

Upon returning to Mexico City, Kino persisted in his support of a permanent mission in California. Initial exploration had been made, land routes had been established and, most importantly, water sources had been located. Fortunately, Kino's enthusiasm was transmitted to his fellow Jesuits, Juan María de Salvatierra, Juan de Ugarte, and Francisco María Píccolo, who immediately began the collection of alms to finance a new attempt at settlement. By 1697 sufficient aid was secured, and Salvatierra prepared to leave for California from the Sinaloa coast.

Reaching San Bruno on October 10, 1697, Salvatierra decided to sail southward to Conchó, discovered by Atondo and Goñi twelve years earlier. On October 18 he determined that it would be the site of his first mission, Nuestra Señora de Loreto.

... Early on the morning of Friday, October 18, we reached the bay shaped like a half-moon. As we viewed the area from the ship, it all appeared green. The bay must be about four or five miles across.

The site seemed ideal to me .... The lowland of the valley where we were forms a small lake of somewhat brackish water but suitable for the animals. Beyond the valley, on the other side, it spreads out into an extensive area covered by reeds.

Despite severe hardships during the first year, Loreto survived, and, through support of his fellow Jesuits and the expanding Pious Fund, Salvatierra commenced exploration for additional mission sites. In March 1699 San Juan Bautista was founded at Londó, and on May 10 Father Francisco María Píccolo explored westward into the steep Sierra de la Giganta. Between June 1 and 12 Píccolo and ten soldiers spent days moving stones and clearing thick brush to open a road to the arroyo of Biaundó where, in October, the mission of San Francisco Xavier was founded.

Still highly dependent upon transgulf supply, Salvatierra made several voyages to Sonora and Sinaloa, and upon his returns in 1701 and 1703 he selected the Río Mulegé as a site for future expansion. With the arrival of Father Juan María Basaldua and Brother Pedro de Ugarte, such expansion was possible. On July 12, 1705, Salvatierra and Ugarte founded Mission San Juan Bautista Ligüí to the south of Loreto, while on November 21 of the same year Basaldua established Santa Rosalía de Mulegé. Further growth occurred in the summer of 1708 with the founding of Mission San José de Comondú by Fathers Salvatierra, Juan de Ugarte, and Julián Mayorga and the establishment of the site of La Purísima Concepción de Cadegomó by Píccolo and Capt. Esteban Rodríguez Lorenzo in 1712. Both sites were first visited by Atondo and Kino in 1684.

Although the first fifteen years of

Jesuit expansion had been generally limited to areas previously explored during the expeditions of 1684-1685, the influx of personnel and assured permanency permitted the undertaking of new expeditions to the north and south of Loreto, extending the radius of land communication. As was the case with earlier foundations, well-defined trails (which followed the most practical route from the standpoints of terrain, available water, and pasture) were opened by the Jesuits to provide supply and messenger service between the respective missions, with all roads radiating from Loreto. The clearing of brush, moving of rocks, building of stream fords, and marking of routes were carefully engineered to permit easy passage of mule trains and to prevent misdirection. Often as wide as five meters, these trails were, for all practical intents, roads.

On November 13, 1716, Píccolo, accompanied by three soldiers and two Indian guides, explored inland from Mulegé to the spring of Cadacaamán and on the 19th selected the site for a future mission. Three years later, on March 3, 1719, Father Clemente Guillén, Rodríguez Lorenzo, and a party of twelve soldiers and seventeen Indians left Loreto and proceeded southwesterly across the Sierra de la Giganta to the arroyo of Chiriyaquí (San Damián) where, on March 17, they found a suitable mission site. Continuing exploration to Bahía Magdalena on the Pacific Coast, they returned to Loreto on April 14. The need for a lumber source to construct the brigantine, *El Triunfo de la Cruz,* led to

further exploration. In September, 1719 the travels of Fathers Juan de Ugarte and Sebastián de Sistiaga to the west of Mulegé resulted in the discovery of a potential mission site at Huasinapí.

Long considered of major importance for settlement, the Bay of La Paz, explored by Cortés, Vizcaíno, and Atondo, became the object of expansion following the launching of *El Triunfo de la Cruz,* and on November 3, 1720, Fathers Jaime Bravo and Juan de Ugarte sailed from Loreto to found Mission Nuestra Señora del Pilar de La Paz. While sea communications with the new mission would be far more rapid, a land route was less dangerous, and on November 11 Guillén set out from Ligüí to open such a route southward along the rugged, mountainous coast. On the 18th he reached the spring of Apaté:

> About a league up the wash we explored and the explorers found running water. Part of it comes from two springs in a limestone mountain, and the rest comes from the high area of the mountain range. This watercourse has two flatland areas which could be easily irrigated . . .

and selected it as a site for a future mission. Continuing southward he reached La Paz on December 6. Due to the extensive badlands along the coast, Guillén was dissatisfied with the land route to La Paz. On his return to Loreto on January 10, 1721, he proceeded in a northwesterly course, reaching the water hole of San Hilario four days later and Chiriyaquí on the 18th. He then followed the trail he had established a year earlier to Loreto.

This active exploration led to the founding of new missions, not only at La Paz but also at Nuestra Señora de Guadalupe Huasinapí on December 12, 1720, Nuestra Señora de los Dolores Apaté in August 1721, and La Purísima Concepcíon de Cadegomó in September 1722. Furthermore, with La Paz as a southern base expansion was possible to the Cape Region. On August 17, 1721, Fathers Ignacio María Nápoli and Jaime Bravo began exploration southward to Bahía de las Palmas where, on the 24th, they established Mission Santiago.

In 1722 Father Nicolás Tamaral established specific routes from La Purísima to Guadalupe and Comondú, thus creating a transsierra trail connecting the missions of Loreto, San Javier, Comondú, La Purísima, Guadalupe, and Mulegé — and, with Loreto as the focal point, with those of Ligüí, Dolores, La Paz, and Santiago. Similarly, the following year Bravo explored southward from La Paz to the Pacific Coast and established the site of Todos Santos, which he connected by trail with Santiago in 1724.

The founding of Mission San Ignacio at Cadacaamán on January 20, 1728, by Father Juan Bautista Luyando not only led to the extension of the La Purísima-Guadalupe trail to the mission but also created a base for expansion northward through the great central desert of the peninsula. Such activity was delayed, however, by the long-standing priority of a port in California for the Manila gal-

leon. Thus, on March 24, 1730, Father Visitor José de Echeverría and Tamaral left La Paz to establish Mission San José del Cabo to the south of Santiago on the 30th of that month.

Northerly expansion was further delayed by the Pericú uprising of October 1734, which resulted in the martyrdom of Fathers Carranco and Tamaral and the forced abandonment of La Paz, Santiago, San José del Cabo, and Todos Santos. Thus the road from Loreto to the south ceased to be a route for supplies and communications and was transformed, from 1734 to 1737, into a military road for troop movement under Esteban Rodríguez Lorenzo, Francisco Cortés y Monroy, and Manuel Bernal de Huidobro. Although the latter succeeded in re-establishing order, the southern missions would never fully recover, and this southern route would languish until the discovery of silver at Santa Ana, north of Santiago, in 1748 by Manuel de Ocio, a retired soldier from Loreto. Nevertheless, in 1740, Rodríguez Lorenzo included in an official itinerary the southern route from Cabo San Lucas via San José and San Bartolo to Santa Ana, the branch from Todos Santos via Santa Ana to La Paz — as well as the northern routes from La Paz via San Hilario, San Luis Gonzaga, and Dolores to Ligüí and Loreto, and thence via Comondú to La Purísima and Mulegé to San Ignacio

Pacification of the south and recovery from the revolt required time, and it was not until 1746 that new exploration was ordered by Father Visitor Juan Antonio Balthasar. In that year Father Fernando Consag, missionary at San Ignacio, reinitiated northerly expansion by exploring the gulf to the Colorado River. Five years later, on May 22, 1751, Consag, with Capt. Fernando de Rivera y Moncada, established a visiting station to the north of San Ignacio at the spring of La Piedad, returning to San Ignacio on July 8 after exploring the Bahía de Sebastián Vizcaíno. With the arrival of Father George Retz, La

Piedad became Mission Santa Gertrudis on July 15, 1752, and the road was extended due north from San Ignacio to the new mission.

Further exploration by Consag in June and July of 1753 resulted in the discovery of the spring of Calamajué north of Santa Gertrudis. Five years later Retz, exploring the same area, discovered the spring of Adac, inland from Bahía de los Angeles, between Santa Gertrudis and Calamajué. On

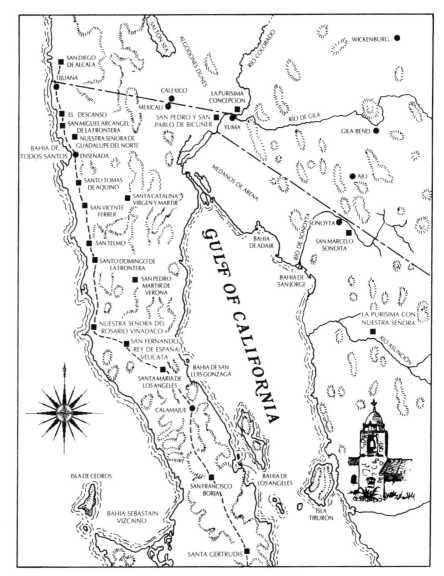

The Old Mission Trail, Central Part

August 27, 1759, Retz founded the visiting station of Adac which, on September 1, 1762, became Mission San Francisco Borja under Father Wenceslaus Linck. To continue the formal designation of routes between missions, in the same year Father Visitor Ignacio Lizasoáin prepared a detailed itinerary, with approximate distances as a part of his report.

The arrival of Father Victoriano Arnés at San Borja in the summer of 1764 enabled Linck to plan additional northward expansion of the mission field. In the spring of 1765 he explored Bahía de los Angeles and Angel de la Guarda Island. In August, employing an astrolabe to take latitude readings, he reconnoitered the gulf coast to the Colorado River. Four years later Linck, with Lt. Blas Fernández de Somera and thirteen soldiers, left San Borja on February 20, 1766, exploring the sites of Yubay, Laguna Chapala, and Cataviñá-Cabujacaamáng. On March 5, the spring of Velicatá was discovered.

In the arroyo there is a stream of water sufficient to irrigate the strips of land which flank its banks. Above the spot where water wells up to form the stream, there are humid plots of soil which some of our escort, experienced in this sort of farming, assure us would easily yield a moderate crop of corn.

Returning to his mission on April 18, Linck relieved Arnés who, with Father Juan José Díez and ten soldiers, journeyed north, extending the road and founding a mission at Calamajué on October 16. Due to the high ferrous oxide content of the water there, Arnés moved to Cabu-

Courtesy The Bancroft Library

Mission Nuestra Señora de Loreto, c. 1855

jacaamáng where, on May 26, 1767, he founded Mission Santa María de los Angeles. With the establishment of this mission the most northerly point of Jesuit expansion had been reached, and the Camino Real extended about five hundred kilometers from San Ignacio.

Political events in Europe led to the crown's expulsion of the Jesuits in 1767 and their replacement in 1768 by missionaries of the Franciscan order, who would later become the new builders of California's great road. As a major part of Spain's North American defense against English and Russian encroachment, Visitor Gen. José de Gálvez had carefully planned the occupation of the Californias through the creation of the Naval Department of San Blas for supply and the preparation of land and sea expeditions to settle the Pacific Coast as far north as Monterey.

Following the expulsion of the Jesuits and the assignment of Franciscan missionaries to the ex-Jesuit missions, Gálvez conferred with Father President Fray Junípero Serra, Capts. Gaspar de Portolá and Fernando de Rivera y Moncada, and Sgt. Pedro Fagés about the march

northward to San Diego and Monterey. On September 30, 1768, Rivera left Loreto and, joined by Fray Juan Crespí at La Purísima, moved supplies and livestock up the Camino Real to Velicatá, base camp for the land expedition. Portolá, with the major contingency, followed from Loreto on March 9, 1769. Nineteen days later Serra proceeded to Velicatá via San Javier, Comondú, Guadalupe, San Ignacio, Santa Gertrudis, and San Borja, joining Portolá and Fray Miguel de la Campa Cos on May 5 at Santa María. On May 13 the Portolá-Serra party reached Velicatá where, the following day, Serra founded Mission San Fernando.

Prior to Serra's arrival on March 24, Crespí, pilot José Cañizares, twenty-five soldiers, and forty Indians began opening the trail to San Diego. Following the route established by Linck in 1766, the expedition traversed the Sierra San Pedro Mártir and finally reached the site of San Telmo on April 14. Proceeding to the coast, they reached San Bernabé (San Vicente) on April 17, Santo Tomás on the 22nd, Ensenada on May 2, San Juan Bautista (San Mi-

Mission San Carlos Borromeo, Carmel, California

guel) on the 9th, San Antonio (El Descanso) the next day, Vallecito de San Pío (Rosarito) on the 11th, and San Pablo (Tijuana) on the 13th. On May 14 they met the sea expeditionaries of the *San Antonio* and *San Carlos* at San Diego Bay.

The route taken by Crespí was followed by Portolá and Serra from Velicatá on May 15. However, due to Serra's badly infected leg, as well as his greater interest in potential mission sites, the party traveled at a slower pace. Noting the abundance of water, trees, and grass, on June 10 Serra explored San Vicente. Proceeding northward, he reached Santo Tomás five days later: "This place has not only water but also plenty of fine pasture, and, dotted with shade trees, room for a good farm." Continuing along the coast the expedition reached Ensenada on June 20, and on the 25th arrived at San Miguel:

> There are fine stretches of land, abundant feed, much water and trees everywhere, and from an enormous lake right in the middle a canal flows to the ocean . . . . A good deal of the ground is covered with rushes and tule reeds, and among the willows you see quantities of grapevines . . . . We all agree that it was a wonderful location for another mission.

After passing through El Descanso the next day, Rosarito the following day, and Tijuana on June 30, Portolá and Serra rendezvoused with the earlier expedition at San Diego on July 1.

With the successful establishment of an overland track from Velicatá to San Diego, the second phase of the expedition to Monterey was now possible. Accompanied by seventy Indians and soldiers, Portolá, Rivera, Fagés, and Frailes Juan Crespí and Francisco Gómez left San Diego two days prior to the founding of the mission on July 14, 1769, and four days later reached San Juan Capistrano (San Luis Rey). On the 23rd Santa María Magdalena (San Juan Capistrano) was explored:

> . . . a very pleasant, green valley, full of willows, alders, live oaks, and other trees not known to us. It has a large arroyo, which at the point where we crossed it carried a good stream of fresh and good water, which, after running a little way, formed in pools in some large patches of tules.

On July 31 the party reached San Miguel Arcángel (San Gabriel). Proceeding northwestward, on August 2 the expedition arrived at the Río de la Porciúncula (Los Angeles) and three days later entered the area of Santa Catalina de Bonomia de los Encinos (San Fernando). From there it proceeded to La Asunción de Nuestra Señora (San Buenaventura) on August 14. The Laguna de la Concepción (Santa Bárbara), "which is near a long point of land running into the sea . . . where . . . there is a spring of good water . . . and . . . many large live oaks," was explored on August 18, and by the 30th the party had reached Santa Rosa (Santa Inés).

Following the coast, Portolá marched inland at La Natividad de

Nuestra Señora (San Luis Obispo) on September 7 and then returned to the coast until he was again forced inland due to steep terrain. Crossing the SanAntonio River on September 24, he soon reached the headwaters of the Salinas River. Fearful of bypassing Monterey, Portolá turned again to the rugged coast. He reached the bay and Carmel River on October 3.

Failing to recognize Monterey from maritime descriptions, Portolá continued northward, and on October 18 named the site of Santa Cruz. Ten days later the expedition arrived at San Simón y Judas (Half Moon Bay), and Punta de las Almejas (San Pedro Point) two days following. From this promontory Portolá recognized Point Reyes. Realizing he had bypassed Monterey Bay, he explored the surrounding area. On November 4 the great bay of San Francisco was discovered. During the next week the southern end of the bay was reconnoitered, until the decision to return to San Diego was finally made. The party reached Monterey Bay on November 27 and, after exploring the Santa Lucía range, erected a cross on December 10, although the site was still not recognized. The successful return of the Portolá expedition to San Diego on January 24, 1770, opened the way for the establishment of missions, and the development of the Camino Real from San Diego to Monterey.

San Carlos Borromeo was founded by Serra at Monterey on June 3, as a result of maritime exploration. The following year San Antonio de Padua was established on July 14 and San Gabriel Arcángel on September 8, at sites discovered by Portolá. Due to the uncertainty of supply by sea, the Camino Real was thus becoming well established as a supply and communications route from Velicatá to Monterey. In 1772 the transference of the peninsular missions to the Dominican Order opened Alta California to further activity, resulting in the founding of a fifth mission, San Luis Obispo, on September 1.

The Old Mission Trail, Northern Part

Although Monterey was considered the principal seat of Spanish administration in Alta California, great interest had arisen in the potential of San Francisco Bay. In 1770 Pedro Fagés, with seven soldiers, had left Monterey on November 21, turned inland to the Santa Clara Valley, and reached the south end of the bay five days later. On November 28 the Golden Gate was sighted. Unable to proceed, Fagés returned to Monterey on December 4. Exploration was continued in 1772 by Fagés, Crespí, and twelve soldiers, who left Monterey on March 20, traversed the southern edge of San Francisco Bay, and reached the site of Oakland a week later. Continuing to Carquinez Strait on March 29, three days were spent exploring the Sacramento River and Diablo Valley. On March 31 the party returned via the Livermore Valley, reaching Monterey on

April 5. Despite these explorations, what would become the most desirable route to San Francisco was established in 1774 by Rivera y Moncada, Fray Francisco Palóu, and sixteen soldiers and Indians. Leaving Monterey on November 23 the expedition entered Santa Clara Valley, proceeded northward through the foothills, and reached the site of San Francisco on December 4, returning along the coast to Monterey eight days later.

Expansion continued at a rapid pace in both Californias. Dominican explorations from Velicatá by Fray Vicente Mora resulted in the founding of Nuestra Señora del Rosario on the coast at Viñadaco in July 1774 and of Santo Domingo on August 30, 1775, thus establishing a coastal route from Velicatá toward San Diego. Similarly, Franciscan expansion to San Francisco was achieved on Oc-

Courtesy The Bancroft Library

Sonoma; Barracks and Mission San Francisco Solano, c. 1846

tober 9, 1776. San Juan Capistrano was founded on November 1 of that year and Alta California's first civil settlement, San José, on the 29th of that month.

Rapid growth continued in the last quarter of the eighteenth century, with Franciscan missions established at Santa Clara de Asís in 1777, San Buenaventura in 1782, Santa Bárbara in 1786, La Purísima Concepción in 1787, Santa Cruz and Nuestra Señora de la Soledad in 1791, San José, San Juan Bautista, San Miguel Arcángel, and San Fernando in 1797, and San Luis Rey in 1798, all at sites explored by Portolá and Crespí in 1769. During the same period, civil-military settlements were founded at Los Angeles in 1781, Santa Bárbara in 1782, and Branciforte (Santa Cruz) in 1797. The Dominicans established Missions San Vicente in 1780 and San Miguel and Santo Tomás in 1785 at sites explored by Crespí and Serra in 1769.

By the opening of the nineteenth century the Camino Real from Cabo San Lucas to San Francisco was well defined. Precise itineraries, with distances in leagues and travel times — as well as descriptions of campsites, waterholes, and terrain — were prepared by missionaries, soldiers, and the 1792 scientific expedition of José Longinos Martínez and Jaime Sensevé. While the primary purpose of the road was supply and communications, it also saw some minor use for the movement of troops and settlers, particularly between the port of Monterey and San Francisco, — as in the case of Juan Bautista Anza's conducting one hundred families to settle San Francisco in 1776.

Nevertheless, the rise of Napoleon in Europe was having its effect in the Californias. Economic, military, and diplomatic pressure on Spain's empire was drawing upon all her resources, even in the most remote areas. As a result, supplies and personnel from San Blas diminished, and the Californias were forced to resort to illegal trade for survival. By far the greatest single asset of the missions were the extensive herds of cattle and the hides and tallow obtained from them, which were traded for manufactured goods from Boston and other ports of the United States. Hides supplied the shoe industry, and tallow became candles to light homes and businesses. Thus the Camino Real became increasingly important as a commercial thoroughfare.

Although the founding of Mission Santa Inés in 1804 created an additional link in the Spanish occupation of California, the United States' acquisition of Louisiana and the subsequent expedition of Meriwether Lewis and William Clark to Oregon in 1805 marked the widening American interest in the Pacific Coast. Furthermore, weakened by the outbreak of the Wars of Independence in Mexico, Spain was virtually powerless to prevent the long-feared encroachment of Russia, symbolized by founding of Fort Ross north of San Francisco by the Russian-American Company in 1812.

Although exchange between foreigners and the missions was not only a reality but a necessity for the survival of the latter, it was, nevertheless, illegal. Thus, in 1817 Frailes Vicente Sarria, Luis Gil, Narciso Durán, and Ramón Abella extended

Spanish control north of San Francisco with the founding of Mission San Rafael Arcángel on December 14. Two years later an expedition under Luis Argüello and Fray Mariano Payeras explored overland to Petaluma, Bodega, and the north bay to Suisún, and plans were formulated for the establishment of further missions and a presidio in the area.

In spite of such plans, funds and personnel were short, and with the approach of Mexican independence in 1821 further expansion in California came to a virtual standstill. This continued until April 1822, when the governor of Alta California, Pablo Vicente Solá, declared allegiance to the Mexican government. Despite political turmoil, expansion to the north of San Francisco was again instituted. In June 1823 an expedition led by José Castro, José Antonio Sánchez, and Fray José Altimira explored the north bay region, and on July 4 Altimira founded Mission San Francisco Solano in the Sonoma Valley.

The establishment of a constitutional republic in Mexico in 1824, and the rise of anticlericalism, brought an increase in civilian settlement and secular control to California. San Francisco Solano had extended the Camino Real to Sonoma, and plans for the movement of settlers along the route from Monterey began in 1825. Nevertheless, political conflict, demands for the removal of Franciscan control of prime lands, and an increasing influx of foreigners served to create a chaotic climate in California.

Attempts at secularization, the conversion of missions to parish churches, and sale of their lands, begun in 1831 under José María Echeandía, was completed in 1833 by presidential decree of Valentín Gómez Farías. Secularization opened new lands for expansion to the north of San Francisco and resulted in the use of the Camino Real as a route for settlement. Used initially by José María Híjar and José María Padrés in 1834, it later served as a military road for the establishment of a garrison at Sonoma by Mariano Guadalupe Vallejo, as well as the focal point for political conflict between the north and south in 1835, 1836, and 1842.

Political instability in Mexico and Manifest Destiny in the United States brought increasing numbers of Anglo Americans to California. The quest for furs and the abundance of cattle attracted such men as Jedediah Smith; James Ohio Pattie, who distributed smallpox vaccine along the Camino Real in 1827; and Ewing Young, who used it to drive stock to Oregon in 1837. At the same time, cheap land and commercial profit brought settlers such as William E. P. Hartnell, Thomas O. Larkin, Abel Stearns, William Goodwin Dana, and John A. Sutter, who in 1846 established a fort in the Sacramento Valley which became a center for fur trappers, adventurers, and immigrants arriving overland from the United States.

As the Anglo-American population grew, California increasingly became the object of U.S. expansion. With the proclamation of the California Republic by William B. Ide at Sonoma on June 14, 1846, the occupation of Monterey on July 2 by

Commodore John D. Sloat, and the declaration of a United States military government by Commodore Robert F. Stockton on July 13, effective Mexican control ended. Occupation, incorporating the forces of John C. Frémont and the Bear Flaggers of the California Republic, was initiated by Stockton with his march to Los Angeles over the Camino Real in August, which he completed with a victory at Cahuenga in January 1847.

The Treaty of Guadalupe Hidalgo of February 1848 ceded Alta California to the United States and thus divided the Camino Real south of San Diego. As former missions and pueblos such as San Diego, Los Angeles, and San Francisco grew into cities, and civilian settlers occupied other ex-mission sites, the Camino Real became the principal north-south artery of the state of California during the last half of the nineteenth century. Baja California's rugged terrain, on the other hand, resisted north-south travel by land. With the collapse of the missions in midcentury, travel between La Paz and the frontier virtually ceased.

The coming of the automobile in the twentieth century radically altered the nature of travel, tourism, and the Camino Real. As early as 1896 California designated it as a state route, and in 1912 it was officially referred to as El Camino. Nine years later, aid from the federal government was obtained for development. Plans for paving the route were approved in 1923, and in 1928 the highway from San Diego to San Francisco became U.S. 101.

Slower development occurred in Baja California, with official designation of the route from La Paz to San José del Cabo and Todos Santos in 1917, from Tijuana to San Quintín and La Paz to Santa Rosalía in 1927, and Santa Rosalía to Ensenada three years later. In 1936 Julio Requelme Inda established the route from San José del Cabo to Tijuana. Although varying from the traditional Camino Real between Loreto to San Ignacio, it followed the routes fixed by the Jesuits in the eighteenth century.

After World War II California converted U.S. 101 to a controlled-access freeway. Paving of Mexico 1 from Tijuana to Cabo San Lucas was completed in 1973. On December 1 President Luis Echeverría Alvarez formally opened the highway from the International Border to the southern tip of Baja California. Finally, after almost three centuries of effort, the Californias were linked by land, and it was possible to travel by automobile from Sonoma, California to Cabo San Lucas in three days.

APACHE AND COMANCHE PLUNDER TRAILS

By Harris Worcester

Two centuries before the heyday of the great cattle trails northward out of Texas, aboriginal Americans began bringing herds of cattle, horses, and mules from northern Mexico into their tribal territories, the areas which later became Arizona, New Mexico, and Texas.

Use of these "cattle trails" reached its peak in the 1840s but continued into the 1880s, by which time thousands of herds had passed over them. The "herders" varied in number from a handful of men on foot to several hundred mounted and armed men traveling with women and children. The distance traversed could range as high as 1,100 miles, from within 300 miles of Mexico City northward to the Arkansas River. One such herd

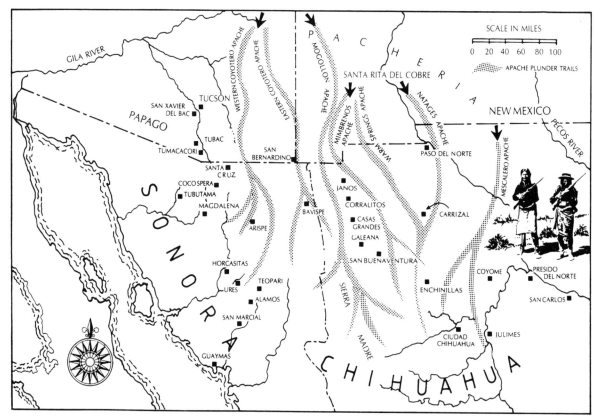

Apache Plunder Trails

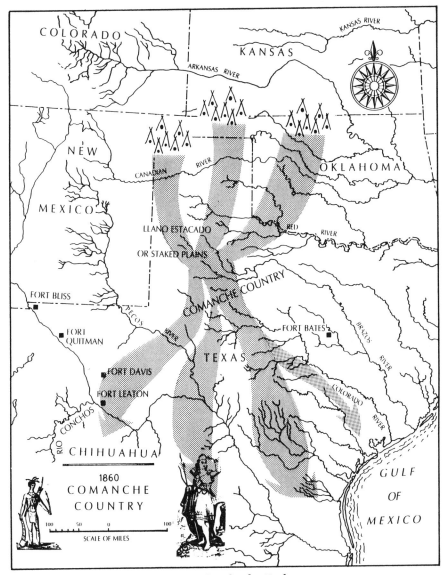

Comanche Plunder Trails

driven out of Coahuila was reported to contain 18,000 head of livestock.

These were not the trails of cowboys and cattlemen. While in operation they brought no benefit to the northern provinces of Mexico, as the Chisholm and western trails brought to Texas. The livestock was stolen. The trails were the raiding and plunder routes of the Apaches, Comanches, and Kiowas, who by the 1840s had made of northern Mexico a *"tierra despoblada."*

From the earliest Spanish excursions into Apachería toward the end of the sixteenth century, Apaches developed a hatred for the Spaniards and a taste for their livestock. A band of Indians identified as *Indios Vaqueros* stole stock from the unauthorized expedition of Gaspar Castaño de Sosa. After Juan de Oñate brought settlers to the Rio Grande Valley in

1598, the Apaches found Spanish livestock an appealing supplement to the meager diet which their harsh environment afforded them. As they did not know how to raise cattle, they ate what they stole. They became dependent on the Spanish herds of horses, mules, and cattle, and they "acquired a lingering taste for horse and mule meat, preferring it to beef or mutton." Subsequent Apache raids soon robbed Spanish settlers of their colonizing zeal, but the viceroy in 1609 refused their petition to withdraw.

Military expeditions against the Apaches were often simple slaving raids, and occasionally the victims were friendly bands. To the close-knit, strongly bonded Apache family, the loss of a member was grievous. By enslaving Apache captives, or by sending them to faraway Mexico City prisons or out of the country entirely — as became the practice later — the Spanish earned the Apaches' undying hatred which contributed significantly to the increasing ferocity of Apache raiding.

By 1650 raiding of northeastern settlements and subsequent depletion of Spanish herds had become serious. Historians theorize that Apaches learned to ride in the 1630s and 1640s, taught by Pueblos who had been trained as herders by their Spanish masters. With the increase in Apache mobility, depredations became more widespread and destructive, rendering travel unsafe by the 1660s and forcing the abandonment of some pueblos by the early 1670s.

During the next two decades the northern provinces of Mexico became acquainted with the evolving style of Apache raiding.

Sonora suffered the increasing severity of Apache raiding in the 1680s; by the 1690s the province had been almost depopulated. The Chiricahuas struck even the more populous areas; with the Gileños they drove the Opatas (allies of the Spanish) out of northern Sonora. The Mescaleros raided northwest into the Rio Grande Valley and southward into Chihuahua. Farther east the Lipans still roamed the South Plains. The Gila Apaches formed an alliance with the Indians to the south (Sumas, Janos, and Jocomes) in western Chihuahua and eastern Sonora. In Sonora a single Apache band was credited with the theft of an estimated one hundred thousand horses.

By this time the Apaches were almost entirely dependent on Spanish plunder. The stealing of large herds, moreover, made it possible for larger groups to assemble, and raiding parties swelled to several hundred warriors and some women. Stealth was no longer important to such sizable forces, and the distinction between raiding and warfare diminished. Relying on force, Apaches attacked settlements and even presidios, destroying what they could, venting built-up enmity for the Spanish. Then they withdrew at a defiantly unhurried pace, challenging the enemy to pursue.

The Apaches' southward push and increased raiding was motivated not only by their increasing dependence on stolen livestock but also by an irresistible force. The much more numerous Comanches were drawn to the area by the availability of Spanish horses, and they swept the Apaches ahead of them. Soon invaders were pushing deep into Mexico in such numbers that Spanish troops were no match for them. Apache and Comanche raiding continued unabated throughout much of the eighteenth century. To cope with the problem, the Spaniards created the Commandancy General of the Interior Provinces, a military organization designed to protect the northern border from the Gulf of Mexico to the Pacific. In the 1780s Viceroy Bernardo de Gálvez devised a new plan for dealing with the Apaches. Those who would live near the presidios and remain peaceful were to be provided with food. Those who refused to accept the Spanish offer were relentlessly pursued by troops.

Military successes and the Gálvez policy bore fruit. By 1793 about two thousand Apaches had made peace and were living in eight *establecimientos de paz* — peace establishments. For the next quarter century the entire northern frontier was relatively peaceful. During Mexico's war for independence, from 1810 to 1821, the northern frontier remained calm.

James Mooney observed that the Kiowas had launched "desultory and ineffective" raids into Mexico in the eighteenth century. After their confederation with the Comanches about 1790, they joined their allies on long expeditions. Raiding became "constant and destructive," lasting until their ultimate subjugation and confinement in the 1870s. Writing in 1898 he observed, "Old men are still living in the tribe who have raided as far south as the city of Durango (which they know by this name) and

southwest through Sonora and Sinaloa to the Gulf of California." Such raiding expeditions, he added, could be two years in duration.

The Mescaleros left the peace establishments some time in the 1820s, taking with them horse and mule herds — and peace. Valverde was abandoned in 1825 after constant attacks by Apaches and Navajos, and the route between there and El Paso again lived up to its name, *Jornada del Muerto* — day's journey for the dead man.

Perhaps owing to neglect by a Mexican government struggling with nationhood, the Apaches abruptly resumed furious, full-scale raiding of northern Mexico. The Gálvez policy of provisioning Indians while at peace had cost the colonial treasury from $18,000 to $30,000 a year. As Donald Worcester has observed, however, "It was always much less expensive for the Spaniards to feed peaceful Apaches than to wage war against them."

When the Apaches resumed raiding, their routes were well etched, in memory and landscape. The westernmost plunder trail was known to white men as "the great stealing road." The path had been chiseled many yards wide by the hoofs of stolen livestock forced to maintain the Apaches' unrelenting rapid pace. Like all such routes, it was littered with the bones of animals unable to keep up. It followed the typical zigzag pattern which allowed the raiders to defend against pursuit. The Coyoteros and Pinaleños left their camps in Arizona's Pinal and White mountains, crossed the Gila bound southward down Arivaipa

Creek, then swung down through San Pedro Valley past the present location of Bisbee, and penetrated Sonora northwest of Fronteras. Thence raiders could swing west to harrass Magdalena mines or ranches along the Alisos River, bear easterly along the Nacozari River, or plunge southward by Arizpe down below Ures and Hermosillo — all three of which housed Sonora's capitol, at different times.

In one day, in October 1846, an expedition led by Henry Smith Turner along the Gila in southern New Mexico crossed several "large trails" leading from the mountains to the north toward Sonora to the south; one showed fresh tracks of horses and mules. The next day they encountered a large trail which appeared to be heavily traveled and which they assumed was the Coyotero route.

A second Western Apache trail farther west led across the Gila and down San Simón Creek, passing through the then-abandoned San Bernardino ranch, and crossed the present-day Mexican border near its junction with the current boundary between Arizona and New Mexico. From there raiding parties of Tontos, Chiricahuas, Mogollones, and Mimbreños — separate or allied into formidable armies — could continue southward into Sonora or strike southeast into western Chihuahua.

Mimbreño and Mogollón bands also patronized the old copper road which connected Santa Rita del Cobre with Janos and continued to Chihuahua City. Raiders could swing west across the Continental Divide at Animas Peak and strike Sonora. Other parties continued southward, leaving the road to skirt Janos, then following the Continental Divide deep into the Sierra Madre, where they established base camps hundreds of miles west of Chihuahua City. From there raiders fanned out in all directions, striking mines, Mexican and Indian villages, and ranches, and making travel unsafe over a wide area.

Another trail left the copper road and skirted Janos to the north and east, then led southeastward to El Chile Cerro, a favorite rendezvous for Apache raiders. There the Mimbreños might be joined by Warm Springs kinsmen who had descended the Mimbres Valley into the Lake Guzmán area. They then proceeded to El Ojo de Apache, where they might be joined by other Eastern Apache raiders who crossed the Rio Grande below El Paso on their way to Chile Cerro. After making their plans the raiders would split into smaller parties and strike ranches and settlements to the east and west of Chihuahua City and beyond to the south.

By the 1830s the Comanches and Kiowas launched regular raids into Mexico to bring back horses. They started south in September, the month they called the Mexican Moon. To the unhappy residents of Texas and northeastern Mexico each full moon became a Comanche Moon. They took over the former trails and crossings of the Lipans and Mescaleros. According to some maps and accounts, a few protracted raiding expeditions might cross the Rio Grande below El Paso at San Elizario and drive deep into southwest Chihuahua, where they established bases in the Sierra Madre. From there they raided as far southwest as the Gulf of California. The Great Trail of the Comanches, however, lay farther to the east. By the 1840s the Río Conchos had become the unofficial demarcation between the raiding activities of the Apaches (who plundered from there westward) and the Comanches and Kiowas (who raided from there to the Gulf of Mexico).

The Texas-Santa Fe expedition of 1841 crossed the Llano Estacado, where members observed at least twenty horse trails cut in limestone and saw the Great Trail, "the largest trail we found on the Plains." When the Comanches began making regular expeditions from their home territory along the Arkansas through Texas into Mexico, they probably used a trail made by buffalo in their southward migration. The Great Trail entered Texas by two forks. One crossed the present state line just east of the contiguous border of Ochiltree and Lipscomb counties in the Panhandle and continued in a southerly direction along and east of the Llano Estacado breaks. The eastern fork crossed the Red River near its confluence with the Pease River and led southwest until it joined the other branch in Kent County, about ten miles north of Clairemont. This main trunk continued southward to Howard County, where it forked near Big Spring. The old buffalo route then continued southeastward into the Edwards plateau region and the buffalos' winter range in the Concho River Valley. The other fork was probably established by the Indians, as it led to the western fords of the Rio Grande and provided a more direct route into Mexico.

Apache rancheria or camp

Although in use for a briefer period, the Comanche Trail resembled the Coyoteros' great stealing road. The Comanches often raided in great numbers, and, unlike the Apaches, they did everything possible on horseback — including raiding. J. Frank Dobie described the trail and its usage thus: "Across the Llano Estacado of Texas, over the arid subplains of the Pecos, by Comanche Springs, where Fort Stockton was established to halt the Cossacks of the Plains, through the mesa-topped hills on south, then through the roughs to the Rio Grande and on into the land of Comanche milk and honey, the main war trail made 'a great chalk line. It was worn deep by the hoofs of countless travelers and was whitened by the bones of abandoned animals.' In September troops of from half a dozen to a hundred Comanches, warrior women among warrior men, joined by Kiowas, Plains Apaches, Utahs from the Rocky Mountains, outlaws from other tribes and renegades from Mexico, strung over it, riding for their carnival south of the Rio Grande . . . . Along in November and December the Great Trail again came to life with herds of cattle, horses and mules from the Mexican supply grounds, with captives laced to their mounts, with hordes of herdsmen and with outriders firing the prairie grass to balk pursuers. Then carrion crows marked the trail from the sky, while dust and smoke signaled it from below."

The Great Trail split into three forks which led to three fords of the Rio Grande, two western and one eastern. The westernmost crossed the Rio Grande at Lajitas, forty miles downriver from the confluence of the Rio Grande and the Río Conchos (Junta de los Ríos) and the troops garrisoned there in the Presido del Norte. Raiders crossing there could swing west and hit the Río Conchos near Chihuahua City. Continuing southward through that valley they could penetrate Durango or drive beyond it into Zacatecas, camping within three hundred miles of the Mexican capital. Turning southeast, raiders crossing at Lajitas could join the middle trail, which crossed at the Vado de Chisos, another forty-odd miles downriver, where the boundary between Chihuahua and Coahuila touches the tip of the river's big bend. This trail continued southward onto the Bolsón de Mapimí, a wild plateau which afforded the Comanches a convenient and hospitable site to establish raiding headquarters, which they might maintain up to nine months of the year.

The eastern route forded at France Way (or Francia Pass), leading through Coahuila into Nuevo León and Tamaulipas. The Comanches were not bound to these routes, of course, and forded elsewhere, as military maps show. After discovering that parties of hundreds of warriors met little or no resistance — much less pursuit — the Comanches developed a more effective (hence devastating) raiding technique: Rather than raiding and retreating by the same route, the Comanches would enter Mexico through a western ford and exit through the eastern, raiding continuously along the route.

The Chihuahuan commander negotiated another treaty with the Mimbreños in 1831, under whose terms western Apachería was divided into three zones, each with a chief designated as "general" and held responsible for maintaining peace. The treaty did not revive the Spanish system of issuing rations, stipulating instead that the Indians must work for their subsistence. Several, but not all, bands signed it; Sonora was excluded. In 1833 Mimbreño Chief Juan José Compá — "general" of the first zone, headquartered at Janos — left the presidio with his people to resume raiding. The Coyotero and Mogollón bands followed his example. That same year Western Apache raiders killed more than two hundred people in Sonora, and the population of that province retreated southward.

Writing in 1835, Ignacio Zúñiga, commander of the northern presidios, observed that there was little left on the northern frontier for the Apaches to take. In the preceding fifteen years, he estimated, five thousand inhabitants had been killed, an equal number forced to flee, and one hundred settlements abandoned. The presidial system had fallen into an ineffectual state. Troops were poorly paid, if at all, and were partially composed of criminals sentenced to military service in these beleagured outposts. Sonora had the least resources to mount a defense, so it suffered most, although Chihuahua attracted more raids. Sonorans managed to field a force in 1834, but with little effect, while Chihuahua was trying to persuade Comanche bands to war against the Apaches. Sonora moved its capital southward

from Arizpe to Ures, as the former's population declined from seven thousand to fifteen hundred from 1838 through the early 1840s.

In the fall of 1835 the Sonora state government, in grim desperation, enacted a scalp bounty law, which offered one hundred pesos (roughly equivalent to dollars) for the scalp of an Apache male, fourteen or older, and permitted the scalper to keep any plunder recovered. The new policy attracted a diverse group of men, including Anglos, runaway slaves led by Seminole John Horse, and Indians — Kirker used Delawares and Shawnees; others, such as Terrazas, used Tarahumaras; and Seminole Chief Coacoochee led a band of his own people who had fled from Indian Territory. There followed a new era of lurid "successes" and villainous "heroes." The grisly trade reached its zenith in sixteen years, although it continued, as did the raiding, until the last hostile bands had surrendered and been confined. The first to attain notoriety was James Johnson, an Anglo trader who had signed a contract with Sonora and had been befriended by Mimbreño Chief Juan José Compá. In April 1837 Johnson visited the chief's band and invited all to a feast. When they had gathered, Johnson fired a concealed cannon, loaded with scrap iron, into their midst. While his men annihilated any survivors, Johnson dispatched his friend with a pistol. Johnson's success was well received in Mexico, stirring the ambition of other adventurers, arousing the jealousy of the military, and prompting Chihuahua to offer its own bounty scale: 100 pesos for a warrior's scalp,

50 for a woman's, and 25 for a child's. The Apaches' hatred of the Mexicans reached a new degree of intensity. Their relationship with Anglos changed from friendship to unrelenting warfare, thanks to Johnson's act and those of other white scalp hunters. The southern Mescalero bands under Chiefs Marco and Gómez, for instance, were friendly to whites until John Joel Glanton's scalpers attacked them in 1849.

The Apaches believed that the appearance of the body at death would be carried into the eternal afterworld. Their grief and anger were intensified if the body of a relative or band member had been scalped or mutilated, since the victim would be bearing those marks when they saw him again in the next world. By their own accounts Apaches originally took scalps only on rare occasions when one was needed for ceremonial use. This changed after they became victims of scalping and other forms of mutilation at the hands of Anglos and Mexicans. According to Eve Ball's remarkable interviews in *Indeh,* for

Courtesy National Archives

Milky Way, Penateka Comanche, 1872

instance, the practice of mutilation increased greatly after the death of Mangas Coloradas, whose killers beheaded him and boiled his head to obtain the skull. This also happened to Massai.

Although scalp hunters put the Apaches on the defensive briefly, and made them more wary generally, they did not stop Apache raiding. On the contrary, the raiders returned with a fury and ferocity greater than before, with the result that in the 1840s death and destruction in northern Mexico were probably greater than in any other decade. Invading Indians increasingly practiced scalping and mutilation in retaliation for the scalp hunters' activities. Despite conclusions drawn from mutilated corpses, the Apaches did not commonly practice torture, although an adult male captive might be turned over by a vengeance party to the female relatives of a slain warrior, who would torture and kill him.

Most infamous of the scalp hunters was a Scotch-Irish adventurer, James Kirker, called Don Santiago (Don Saint James), as well as "king of New Mexico" and, for a time, "king of the Apache nation." After Johnson's brutal exploit, Chief Mangas Coloradas reunited the Copper Mine and Warm Springs Bands, exacted revenge from a party of trappers on the Gila, and cut off the old copper road, eventually forcing the abandonment of Santa Rita del Cobre. A former employee of the mine's owners, Kirker raised a party of twenty-three men and led a surprise attack on an Apache village in the upper Gila Valley. He returned with fifty-five scalps and 400 head of

livestock. His fame spread southward to Chihuahua, whose governor invited Kirker for a visit. In 1839 Kirker received a $5,000 advance on the $100,000 he would receive when he had forced the Apaches into a permanent treaty and had subdued the Comanches. He raised an army of 200 men, paying each a dollar per day and promising half the spoils. The following year Durango also enacted a scalp bounty of ten pesos for the head or scalp of each hostile Indian.

As thousands of eastern American Indians were pushed or relocated west of the Mississippi between 1825 and 1840, and as more Anglos invaded Comanche territory, game became more scarce, while the market for horses and mules increased. In the 1830s Comanche raiding into Mexico became more frequent, extensive, and destructive; by 1840 Comanche raids reached Zacatecas. "The information concerning these depredations is fragmentary and incomplete, but there is extant sufficient evidence to indicate that these raids represent a prolonged and gigantic tragedy, one of the most horrible ever enacted on the North American continent."

In November of 1840 a party of four hundred Gileño Apaches established a base in the Sierra Madre, and from there smaller parties raided Sonora and Chihuahua. From two to four hundred Comanches were thought to be active in Chihuahua at the same time. Daily reports reached Gov. García Conde of thefts, killings, and abductions. An extract of these was published as a weekly column in the government newspaper, and all periodicals contained litanies of personal tragedies, of residents killed and abducted. The Pápago Indians living along the Gila and Sonoita rivers rose in rebellion that same year, killing miners and increasing the chaos and misery. A few Mexican citizens, furthermore, were reported to be masquerading as Indians and plundering their own people.

The Comanches had boasted that they allowed Spaniards to remain in Texas, New Mexico, and northern Mexico only to raise horses for them. Similarly, the Gileños said in 1841 that they had not exterminated the inhabitants of northern Mexico because they raised livestock for them.

In 1841 a Comanche war party descended the western route to San Luis Potosí, then swept through Coahuila to the eastern fork, killing three hundred people, taking scores of captives, and driving eighteen thousand head of stolen livestock. An 1842 raiding party brought back a herd of horses and mules and 150 women and children captives from Coahuila and Chihuahua. The Indians offered to sell the animals to Charles Bent, but he refused, suspecting they would be stolen back.

Despite Bent's reluctance in this case, it should be noted that the Apaches and Comanches had little trouble finding an outlet for their plunder. Towns and settlements in New Mexico reaped the double benefit of peace and profit by maintaining trade with the Indians. Parties such as the one Josiah Gregg encountered leaving Santa Fe in 1840 would meet the Comanches on the Pecos and trade whiskey and guns for horses and mules freshly stolen in Mexico. In New Mexico, these

traders were called *Comancheros*, although the practice was encouraged by civil authorities, including the governor, Gregg said. The Apache band which Kirker surprised outside Taos in 1839 was probably camped there to trade horses. The Comanches also traded in Texas and along the Arkansas, and with Indian tribes that had access to weapons and goods. In 1847, for instance, Comanches traded fifteen hundred mules to the Osages for tobacco, lead, powder, blankets, blue cloth, strouding, and firearms (the smallest item in the trade) which the Osages had obtained from a white trader at their agency. After the treaty of Fort Atkinson, moreover, the Comanches began receiving these items as annuity goods from the U.S. government.

In desperation Mexican governors turned to measures which experience had proven unsuccessful. In 1843 the Chihuahua governor made treaties with the Mimbreños, Mogollones, and Mescaleros under which the state would provide them rations if they would fight the Comanches. While providing some respite to Chihuahua, the treaty and its benefits excluded Sonora. The Gileños continued raiding there and then took refuge in Chihuahua, where they could dispose of their plunder. After raiders from these bands ran off the Fronteras presidio's horse herd, killing twenty-three soldiers, Sonoran forces attacked them at their camps near Janos, killing more than eighty Apaches and ending Chihuahua's separate peace. The latter state then tried to contract with Bajo el Sol and other Comanche chiefs to fight the Apaches for a scalp bounty.

In the mid-1840s Texas Indian agents watched with regretful impotence while Comanche war parties rode off, bound for the lower Rio Grande and beyond. Texans were doubtless aware, as were New Mexicans, that as long as northern Mexico suffered depredations their own territory would remain relatively secure. In the fall of 1844 a Texas agent saw a party of braves ride off for Mexico while elder Comanche chiefs headed for a council with Texas authorities. The war party which killed three Mexicans near San Antonio in February 1845 was probably the same one observed a few days later passing Corpus Christi on its way to Mexico. Led by Santa Anna, this party numbered six hundred warriors.

In May of that year a party of Comanches entered a trading post on the Brazos, representing a band camped nearby which was reported to number one thousand lodges. Embarking on a revenge raid to Mexico, they requested supplies for the trip and a pass to give them safe conduct beyond the Texas settlements. Texas Superintendent of Indian Affairs Thomas G. Western granted their request, instructing Lieutenant Coleman of the Travis County Rangers and agent Robert S. Neighbors to comply with their demands. Another agent reported that the party returned with a large herd of horses in July. Perhaps this was the band of one thousand Indians who raided as far south as Zacatecas, about three hundred miles from Mexico City. That same summer, Buffalo Hump forced

two agents to accompany his band of 730 Penatekas to San Antonio, insisting that a communication he had received from Captain Hays — who commanded the Texas Rangers — indicated that the latter would accompany him on a raid to Mexico. Hays did not, but neither was he able to dissuade the party from its intent.

In October 1845 one Comanche war party was hit twice by different detachments of Mexican troops — once at La Boquilla de San Benito in southeastern Durango, where seventy captive children and one thousand horses were recovered, and again almost two weeks later at La Zarca in northern Durango, where twenty-eight more children were rescued. Between the engagements these Comanches attacked at San Juan del Río, killing sixty-eight and torching thousands of bushels of corn. As usual this band escaped northward, retaining an undetermined number of captive Mexican children.

Buffalo Hump led another raid in 1846, and a trader observed his return with one thousand head of horses and mules and a number of captives, in addition to money and other items of plunder. The following year he led a party of six to eight hundred across the Rio Grande at the mouth of the Pecos (between and roughly equidistant to the western and eastern fords previously mentioned). The Comanches were so familiar with Mexico by this time that they planned their raids well in advance and taught the route to inexperienced members by drawing maps on the ground in day's-journey segments which the young warriors committed to memory, one by one.

With such detailed descriptions of landmarks, water holes, and settlements, the youngest novice could find his way to a base camp hundreds of miles from his home territory. Texas Indian Agent Neighbors heard Buffalo Hump's itinerary before the chief left on a raid intended to avenge a defeat suffered some months previously near Parras in southern Coahuila. His party would strike in Chihuahua, swing eastward to hit Parras and the area around it, then continue eastward into Nuevo León and Tamaulipas before turning northward. Indeed, the agent reported, the warriors returned with horses, mules, and captives.

The defeat which Buffalo Hump avenged, ironically, came at the hands of Missiouri volunteers serving with the U.S. Army, which invaded Mexico after war was declared in 1846. For the next two years the presence of the U.S. military afforded Mexican inhabitants better protection than had been provided by their own troops.

Soldiers and travelers who passed through northern Mexico in 1846 wrote with horror of the conditions existing there and affirmed its designation as *"tierra despoblada"* — depopulated territory. George F. Ruxton, the English traveler-adventurer, came up the trail from Durango through Chihuahua into New Mexico in the fall of that year. Most of the country he traversed was deserted, and the ranches and settlements were in ruins. In those sites still inhabited, people huddled in terror. Of Comanche raiders he wrote:

Every year their incursions extend farther into the interior, as the frontier haciendas become depopulated by their ravages and the villages deserted and laid waste . . . . They are now overrunning the whole department of Durango and Chihuahua, have cut off all communications, and defeated in two pitched battles the regular troops sent against them. Upwards of ten thousand head of horses and mules have already been carried off, and scarcely has a hacienda or rancho on the frontier been unvisited, and everywhere the people have been killed or captured. The roads are impassable, all traffic stopped, the ranchos barricaded, and the inhabitants afraid to venture out of their doors.

That same year Santa Fe trader James Josiah Webb passed by the once-thriving Hacienda de la Zarca in northern Durango. It was by then impoverished, and the people were gathered in terrified anticipation — Comanches had been sighted in the vicinity.

The American troops withdrew from Mexico after the signing of the Treaty of Guadalupe Hidalgo in 1848, in which the United States promised, among other things, to prevent the Apaches and Comanches from raiding across the border. American soldiers were veteran Indian fighters, but they had little experience with the Apaches, who headed back down the trails established by their ancestors, striking even farther and with even greater frequency and destructiveness. Indeed, the U.S. military found it difficult to protect its own interests in New Mexico, where

Apaches and Navajos were credited with the theft of seven thousand horses, more than twelve thousand mules, thirty-one thousand cattle, and four hundred and fifty thousand sheep between August 1846 and October 1850. (In negotiating the Gadsden Purchase five years later, the U.S. abrogated that section of the previous treaty.) The Comanches also resumed raiding, although they more frequently met and fought American troops along their old war trails. In response to Indian complaints, Agent Neighbors could only advise them to find more westerly routes and avoid the troops.

The northern Mexican presidial system had fallen into disrepair, with but few, demoralized troops garrisoned there. All suffered frequent Apache attacks, and stealthy raiders killed about two hundred residents inside the walls of the Fronteras presidio between 1832 and 1849. The Pinaleños captured that strategic outpost in 1848 and held it for two years.

Courtesy The National Archives

Coyotero Apache scout, 1874

Sonora continued to suffer greatly from Apache hostilities. Five hundred people were killed in that state between 1851 and 1853; in one month, July 1853, Apaches destroyed the towns of Santa Cruz and Chinapa and killed 170 Sonorans. Farther east, Comanches continued to raid Chihuahua, Durango, Zacatecas, San Luis Potosí, Coahuila, and Tamaulipas. Nuevo León was the hardest hit, reporting 652 persons killed, wounded, or captured from 1847 through 1857. Thereafter, Comanche and Kiowa raids across the border decreased substantially, becoming "comparatively infrequent" by 1860, a year when one-fifth of the U.S. army was stationed in Texas. As early as 1852 Southern Comanches and Lipans had complained to Indian agents about the troops' presence. An active military operating out of newly established forts — such as Fort Bliss, Fort Stockton, and Camp Verde, which lay along raiding routes — contributed greatly to the decline in raiding. Consequently, the Indians stepped up raids on the north Texas frontier, which had previously been comparatively free from attack. In 1858 and 1859 frontier stockmen suffered serious losses, probably amounting to several thousand horses.

Raids in Mexico continued, nonetheless, until the Comanches and Kiowas submitted to confinement in 1875. Lone Wolf, a Kiowa chief who participated in the outbreak of 1874, had at that time just returned from Mexico. He had gone there to find and bury his son and nephew, who were killed by Mexican troops while accompanying Comanches on a raid. After 1875 the only Comanche involvement in raiding consisted of the few warriors who slipped away from the reservation and joined the band of Victorio, the Warm Springs Apache chief.

Apache raids into Mexico also continued from the 1850s well into the 1870s, primarily as an alternative to starvation. White men were killing or scaring away game as they moved in increasing numbers through Apache lands into New Mexico and Arizona. More important, the U.S. Congress rejected most of the treaties signed in the 1850s. Among those approved, few provided adequate food — whether through no rations, half rations, inadequate "full" rations, or dishonesty in distribution of rations. A variety of ill-conceived or negligent actions by the military also caused Apache bands to flee reservations and resume raiding.

The attitude of Coyotero Chief Francisco was indicative of the longstanding Apache hatred and resolve to war against Mexico. He asked an Apache Pass station agent whether the Apaches would be prohibited from raiding Sonora if the United States took over the state. The agent said yes. Francisco then angrily promised to "fight Sonora" as long as he was alive and led warriors, regardless of American opposition.

Apache raids continued sporadically until the mid-1870s, when most of the Apaches were settled on reservations. Geronimo and a few others remained in the Sierra Madre of Sonora, living by attacks on Mexican towns and ranches. The Chiricahuas and a few White Mountain

Apaches were shipped to Fort Marion in Florida as prisoners of war. Many years later, after they had been transferred to Fort Sill, Oklahoma, most of them were allowed to join the Mescaleros on their reservation in New Mexico. None was ever allowed to return to Arizona.

THE SANTA FE TRAIL
By Valerie Sherer Mathes

Resembling a rope with numerous strands that eventually joined together, the Santa Fe Trail linked the Missouri frontier with the lucrative markets of Spain's northern outposts. This trail, more than eight hundred miles long, traversed western Missouri and Kansas, then dropped south into Oklahoma and on to Santa Fe, New Mexico, or headed north into Colorado along the Mountain Branch and then south to rejoin the main track.

Over this road traveled Indian, fur trader, merchant, soldier, and tourist. So heavy was the traffic that indelible wheel marks still scar the land. Settlements sprang up to meet travelers' demands, military posts were erected for protection, and Indians went on the warpath to defend valuable hunting grounds.

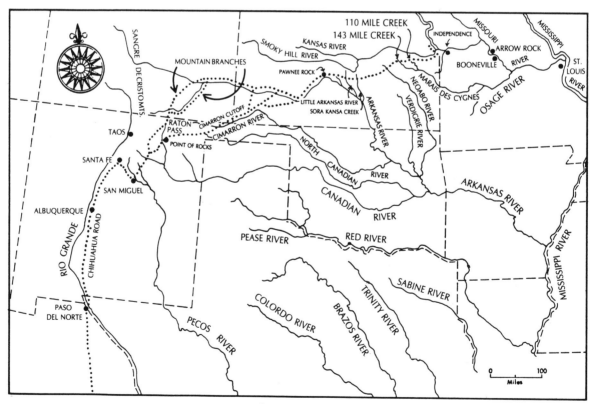

The Sante Fe Trail

The trail initially began at Franklin, Missouri, and followed the Osage Trace to Fort Osage (Fort Clark), built in 1808 by Gen. William Clark, superintendent of Indian Affairs at St. Louis. Apart from protecting the Osage Indians, who were encouraged to settle nearby, the fort also became one of the most successful of the government's twenty-eight trading factories. From there the route proceeded southwesterly to the future site of Independence, Missouri, which in 1827 replaced Franklin as departure point, and which in turn was replaced in the 1840s by West Port Landing (later Kansas City).

Growth in the volume of traffic and the inevitable increase in Indian hostilities prompted the War Department to establish Fort Leavenworth in 1827. This fort, on the west side of the Missouri River and slightly to the north of the road, became yet another strand in the frayed rope of the Santa Fe Trail.

All tracks — usually free of Indian menace and generally over prairie traversed by numerous creeks — converged at Council Grove, Kansas, 150 miles from Independence. The Grove was named by George C. Sibley, former government factor at Fort Osage, who was commissioned to survey the trail and establish peaceful Indian relations. It was the site of his 1825 council with the Osages.

Watered by a branch of the Neosho River, the Grove was a continuous strip of timber and fertile bottomlands. Since this was the last place where hardwood was available, travelers camped, gathered wood, rested teams, and repaired equipment. In final preparation for dangers along the trail ahead, they organized caravans here, established rules, and elected officers.

Beyond Council Grove was an immense prairie. The feeling of this new land was well expressed by Thomas Jefferson Farnham, a young Vermont lawyer on his way west in 1839 for his health: "The eyes ached as we endeavored to embrace the view. A sense of vastness was the single and sole conception of the mind!" Travelers, faced with a lack of firewood, were forced to use buffalo chips as the main source of fuel, as had the Plains tribes for generations and as homesteaders would later. William Hitt, member of the 1829 caravan, wrote:

> The grass was too green to burn, and we were wondering how our fire could be started. . . . One of our number, however, while diligently searching for something to utilize, suddenly discovered scattered all around him a large quantity of buffalo-chips and he soon had an excellent fire under way.

As the route passed campsites at Diamond Spring, Lost Spring, Cottonwood Creek, and Turkey Creek, wagons often became mired in deep mud. These and other stream crossings were difficult because of steep banks. To be lowered, a wagon had to have its rear wheels locked, a yoke or two of oxen hitched to the rear axle, and men frantically tugging as it descended the bank. Sometimes a wagon broke loose, teams became tangled, oxen were run over, or the wagon's contents were spilled in the mud. Surmounting the opposite bank was equally difficult.

Travelers approaching the Little Arkansas were in danger of Indian attacks. Caravans were usually divided into four columns. At the first sign of Indians, teams were whipped up and each column wheeled about to form one side of a hollow square with wheels interlocked. With men and animals safely inside the square, attackers could usually be repelled.

Near the Arkansas River stood a belt of sand hills, and just beyond it was the Great Bend of the river, 270 miles from Independence. Prairie grasses were soon replaced by short grass of the semiarid plains. Following the north bank of the river, the trail crossed Walnut Creek, where in 1864 the government built Fort Zarah for protection against Comanche and Kiowa raiders. Beyond Walnut Creek stood the sandstone pinnacle, Pawnee Rock, where travelers paused to carve their names.

Ahead lay Pawnee Fork, where in 1859 the government constructed Fort Larned on the south bank about five miles from its confluence with the Arkansas. The fort, built at the suggestion of William Bent, Indian agent for the upper Arkansas, provided valuable service to the Kansas section of the trail during and after the Civil War.

Once across the Pawnee River the trail split; the wet route followed the Arkansas, while the shorter route proceeded along the upland divide, rejoining the other trail east of the site of Dodge City. A short distance from the junction the government in 1865 constructed Fort Dodge, which remained active during Indian campaigns of the 1860s and 1870s. Following the north bank the trail passed through the present location of Dodge City and headed toward "the caches," where in 1822 James Baird and Samuel Chambers were snowed in on an island in the Arkansas. Their pack animals wandered off and died. When spring came, the men cached their belongs, made their way to Taos on foot, and returned with more mules. The holes left after the removal of their goods were still visible for nearly a quarter of a century, and the site was known as "the caches" to all who followed the trail.

Two military establishments were erected in the vicinity of the caches. Fort Mann, a government wagon station of four log cabins, was built about 1845 and served as repair depot and rest stop for freighters, travelers, and army caravans. Abandoned and then regarrisoned, it served until Fort Atkinson was established in 1850, one mile distant. Despite a shortage of men, the new fort provided protection for the trail until abandoned in 1854.

West of the caches lay four alternative routes. Three, known as the Cimarron Cutoff, left the Arkansas and headed toward the Cimarron River across Kiowa and Comanche lands. The other, the Mountain Branch, followed the Arkansas to Bent's Fort (near present-day La Junta, Colorado), crossed the river, turned southwest along Timpas Creek, headed over rugged Raton Pass, and intersected the other routes on the upper Canadian River.

Crossing the quicksand in the Arkansas was no easy task. James Josiah Webb, who made eighteen journeys along the trail, wrote in the 1840s: "The current is so rapid and the quicksand so treacherous that a wagon shakes and rattles by the sand washing from under the wheels as much as it would going over the worst cobblestone pavement." Often double-teaming was necessary to pull wagons across the half-mile wide river. If the river was high, the wagon box was caulked and floated across.

Arkansas fords included the Lower Crossing at Mulberry Creek, the Middle Crossing near the site of Cimarron (about twenty miles above Dodge City), and the Upper Crossing at Chouteau's Island. This island was named for Auguste P. Chouteau, who, with his trappers, escaped a large war party of Pawnee by retreating to the island in 1816.

Of the three crossings, the Middle was the most popular because it was on the shortest route. Once below the Arkansas, travelers were in Mexican territory. The trail proceeded through and hills and then entered the Cimarron Desert, known to traders as the Waterscrape and to Mexicans as *La Jornada.* The inhospitable desert was more than fifty miles of waterless wasteland, with no visible trail until after the unusually wet winter of 1834, when the heavily laden wagons left permanent ruts. In 1838 Josiah Gregg, who first followed the trail in 1831 and later became its chronicler in *Commerce of the Prairies,* noted that

> on our passage this time across the 'prairie ocean' which lay before us, we ran no risk of getting bewildered or lost, for there was now a plain wagon trail across the entire stretch of our route . . . and thus a recurrence of those distressing sufferings from thirst, so frequently experienced

by early travelers . . . has been prevented.

Crossing the desert was an ordeal for men and beasts. As they neared Lower Cimarron Spring, thirsty teams often became half-crazed and even stampeded. At the Cimarron the worst was over; the next eighty-five miles of the trail was along the northern bank of the river. Just past Middle Spring it curved into the southeast corner of Colorado and then into the Oklahoma Panhandle. The trail passed Willow Bar, a ridge of sand covered with willow shoots and with the bleached bones of nearly one hundred mules nearby. In 1844 Albert Speyer was overtaken here by a snowstorm. His mules crowded around his fire for warmth, but many died. In later years traders who camped nearby amused themselves

Courtesy Museum of New Mexico
Josiah Gregg

by arranging and rearranging the disjoined skeletons.

Usually the last camp on the Cimarron was at Upper Springs. Just beyond it was Cold Springs, Oklahoma, where in June 1865 Christopher (Kit) Carson established Camp Nichols to protect the trail from raiding Kiowas and Comanches. The fort provided escort service to the Arkansas for traders' caravans returning from New Mexico, but it was abandoned in the fall.

From the Cimarron the trail rose for two-hundred miles into New Mexico, through rocky foothills where dry air loosened spokes and iron tires, requiring frequent stops to tighten them with white oak wedges. Arriving at McNees' Creek, travelers were reminded of the deaths of McNees and his companion Daniel Munroe in 1828. While they slept Indians shot them with their own guns. McNees died immediately —

Munroe, although mortally wounded, was carried forty miles along the trail before he died and was buried in the Valley of the Cimarron.

Passing the twin peaks of Rabbit Ears Mound, the trail led north of Round Mound at more than 6,600 feet. After Point of Rocks, an ancient volcanic outcropping, it intersected the Rio Colorado or Canadian River. Soon after crossing Ocate Creek travelers could see Wagon Mound, a large butte that formed a silhouette of a covered wagon and team, 630 miles from Independence. Beyond Wagon Mound the trail crossed the Mora River and rejoined the Mountain Route. Fort Union, built north of this junction in 1851, was the largest military post on the western plains and had the longest continuous service along the trail. Apart from monotonous patrol duty, the garrison provided a special escort for James S. Calhoun, New Mexico territorial

Courtesy U.S. Army Signal Corps Photo

Fort Union, New Mexico looking south — water tank in center

governor. On his arrival from Santa Fe in ill health in May 1852, Calhoun had the fort's carpenters build him a coffin. His escort carried it as far as Fort Atkinson, where Calhoun died.

From Fort Union the trail continued to the Gallinas River and Las Vegas before descending to San Miguel, which Gregg described as "irregular clusters of mud-wall huts . . . situated in the fertile valley of Rio Pecos, a silvery little river." The ruins of Pecos Pueblo then loomed ahead. In 1846 Susan Magoffin wrote: "It created sad thoughts when I found myself riding almost heedlessly over the work of these once mighty people." At the church her husband pointed out the room where he had spent a night on an earlier trip.

From Pecos travelers climbed Glorieta Pass. As caravans slowly wound down the dozen or so miles to the capital of the Mexican province of Nuevo Mexico, reactions varied. Some were pleased at the sight. In 1821 Thomas James wrote that it

> presented a fine appearance in the distance. It is beautifully situated on a plain on dry and rolling ground, at the foot of a high mountain. . . . The houses were all whitewashed outside and in, and presented a very neat and pleasing sight to the eye to the traveler.

Courtesy Museum of New Mexico

Aerial view of Fort Union, New Mexico, ca 1930

James Josiah Webb disagreed, saying,

> The houses were nearly all old and dilapidated, the streets narrow and filthy, and the people, when in best attire, not half dressed.

Travelers who were worried about crossing the Cimarron Desert used the Mountain route. Beginning at the Upper Crossing of the Arkansas, this alternative climbed slowly for twenty miles to Fort Aubry, named in honor of Francis Xavier Aubry, a trader who made frequent trips along the trail. Built in September 1865 it was abandoned in April 1866.

Still rising, the route passed Bent's New Fort, built by William Bent in 1852-1853 at Big Timbers, a grove of cottonwoods and a favorite Cheyenne and Arapaho campground. Because of a decline in Indian trade this fort was not successful, and Bent leased it to the government in 1860. The discovery of gold in Colorado in 1858 and the subsequent increase in traffic necessitated additional military protection, so Fort Wise was located on the north bank of the Arkansas River, a mile to the southwest. Renamed Fort Lyon I in 1862, it served the Mountain Branch during the Civil War, but because of heavy flooding and unhealthful conditions both Fort Lyon and Bent's New Fort were abandoned in favor of Fort Lyon II, which was built in 1867 twenty miles upstream.

Thirty-eight miles up the Arkansas in southeastern Colorado were the ruins of Bent's Old Fort, built by Bent, St. Vrain and Company about 1835. George Bent, one of William's

sons, reminisced that the fort in its heyday employed over a hundred men. In addition to Indian trade, men from the fort were sent to New Mexico for horses, mules, and silver. "I remember," he wrote,

> when as a boy the wagons come with their loads of bright colored blankets. The Indians prized these blankets with their strips of bright coloring very highly, and a good blanket was traded at the fort for ten buffalo robes.

He also recalled the large camps of Cheyennes, Arapahos, Kiowas, Comanches, and Kiowa Apaches that were often nearby.

> The trade room was full of Indian men and women all day long; others came just to visit and talk, and there were often a circle of chiefs sitting with my father or his partners, smoking and talking.

William's older brother, Charles, had entered the fur trade with John Jacob Astor's American Fur Company but soon became a partner in the Missouri Fur Company. When this partnership was dissolved he bought an outfit for the Santa Fe trade and in 1829 made his first trip west with William. In 1830-1831 Charles and Ceran St. Vrain of Taos formed a partnership and entered Indian trade on the Arkansas the following year. Soon thereafter they completed Fort William, later Bent's Fort.

In 1849 William Bent closed the fort and set fire to the powder magazine; the fur business had declined and the government offer of $12,000 for the property had been too low. The fort was not completely destroyed; it became a stage station after the Civil War.

Six miles west of Bent's Fort travelers crossed the Arkansas River, turned southward along Timpas Creek, and then followed the Purgatoire River to Raton Pass — twenty miles of almost impossible road that often took a week to cross. Susan Magoffin and her party traveled at the rate of half a mile an hour through the pass, with mules unhitched and men pulling the wagons. It took a dozen men to steady one wagon with all wheels locked, "and for one who is some distance off to hear the crash it makes over the stones, is truly alarming," she wrote. One day they traveled a grand total of six hundred to eight hundred yards.

> Out of Raton at last, can it be possible! We have been in it five days, and it seemed that we were never to leave. . . . This morning the pulling has been worse than ever; some very steep, long, rocky hills, but we passed them without an accident save the breaking of some two or three wagon bows — this cannot be considered an accident though — they caught in the trees that reached their giant arms across the road seemingly with that intention.

In 1866 Richen Lacy ("Uncle Dick") Wooton had a crew smooth the road through the pass, built a gate, and charged $1.50 per wagon and five cents per head of loose stock. Once over the pass the trail crossed tributaries of the Canadian and Mora

rivers and then rejoined the main route from the Cimarron Cutoff.

Although Capt. William Becknell is often called the "father of the Santa Fe Trail," it had many parents. The Coronado expedition of 1540-1541 probably covered part of it in search of Gran Quivira. Pierre and Paul Mallett were the first Frenchmen to lead a small party from the Illinois country to Santa Fe, probably traversing part of the trail in Kansas. Arriving in Santa Fe on July 22, 1739, the Malletts remained nine months, engaged in trade, and on their return left two members of the party behind to marry. Other Frenchmen set out in the 1740s and 1750s. Some remained in Santa Fe to marry or ply their trade; others were arrested and sent to Mexico City.

Following defeat by England in the French and Indian War, France ceded Canada to England and her western regions to Spain. Pedro Vial, a Frenchman, arrived in Santa Fe in May 1787 after exploring a route from San Antonio at the request of Spanish authorities. He volunteered to open a trail from Santa Fe to St. Louis and, with two companions, set out in May 1792 down the Canadian to the Arkansas River. They were captured by a band of Kansa, rescued by friends, and reached St. Louis in October. Vial's return trip in June 1793 approximated the later Santa Fe Trail.

One of the earliest Americans to visit Santa Fe was John Peyton, a Virginian who was shipwrecked off the mouth of the Rio Grande in 1773 and taken to Santa Fe as prisoner. He escaped overland to St. Louis, following a route probably very close to that of the trail.

After the Louisiana Purchase, American merchants visualized trade possibilities with the Spanish provinces in the West. In 1804 William Morrison, a Kaskaskia, Illinois, merchant, entrusted French Creole Jean Baptiste La Lande with goods to sell in Santa Fe. Once there, La Lande converted the property to his own benefit and became a prominent New Mexican resident.

The first American official to arrive in Santa Fe was Lt. Zebulon Montgomery Pike. In July 1806 Pike started up the Missouri River from St. Louis, then turned south and west to the Arkansas. He followed the future trail past Pawnee Forks, Pawnee Rock, and Ash Creek. Although arrested by a Spanish detachment, he managed to secrete his journal, which was published in 1810. It clearly showed the possibilities of a profitable commerce between St. Louis and Santa Fe. Because of its isolation and remoteness from Mexico City, the Mexican community was eager for steady trade.

American trading parties soon arrived in Santa Fe, where their members were arrested and imprisoned. Robert McKnight, Samuel Chambers, and James Baird set out with six mule loads of goods, in the mistaken belief that the revolt by Father Miguel Hidalgo had been successful and foreign trade prohibitions had been rescinded. To their surprise they were arrested in July 1812 and imprisoned until the spring of 1820. The trading and trapping party of Julius de Munn and Auguste Pierre Chouteau was sent to Santa Fe in chains in May

1817 and remained almost fifty days in prison before each member was given a horse and ordered to return home. Munn estimated that more than $30,000 in pelts and other goods had been confiscated. The last American imprisoned was David Merriwether, who was taken by Spanish cavalry to Santa Fe in 1819 and accused of being a spy. He was given a mule, gun, and ammunition and then released. Years later Merriwether returned as governor of the United States Territory of New Mexico.

In 1821 Mexico gained independence from Spain, the ban on foreign trade was lifted, and Santa Fe trade was born. In the same year Becknell advertised in the Franklin, Missouri, *Intelligencer* for men to engage in trade for horses and mules and to catch wild animals. In September his party of between twenty and thirty men set out with a packtrain from Arrow Rock, near Franklin, to trade with the Indians of the Rocky Mountain region. Following the left fork of the Arkansas, the men struggled over Raton Pass, rolling aside rocks for their animals to pass. After two days of tedious work they cleared the pass and stumbled upon an encampment of Mexican soldiers. Learning of Mexico's independence, and that American traders were welcome, they headed for Santa Fe. Arriving in mid-November they sold their meager goods of common calico and other supplies for a tidy profit. They returned to Franklin in forty-eight days, possibly pioneering a shorter route along the Cimarron River to avoid snow-clogged Raton Pass.

Other trading parties set out about the same time as Becknell. Thomas

James of St. Louis left in May 1821, hoping to find his brother Robert. Despite an attack by Comanches on the Canadian River, he arrived in Santa Fe two weeks after Becknell. Another party led by Jacob Fowler and Hugh Glenn also set out in 1821 and wintered in the Rockies. In January 1822 Glenn reached Santa Fe and learned of the successful revolution. When the Glenn-Fowler expedition returned to St. Louis, it included Thomas James, John and Robert McKnight, and James Baird, the latter two recently released from Mexican jails. On the way they passed a party led by Col. Benjamin Cooper with his nephews Braxton and Stephen, and on June 29 came upon a track made by Becknell's wagons on his second trip — the trail was becoming crowded.

Becknell's 1822 trip is considered the beginning of the trail, since he carried goods intended for civilians, not merely for the Indian trade. He and twenty-one men set out from Arrow Rock in May with three wagons loaded with $30,000 worth of goods. They followed the Arkansas, soon to be the principal route. About five miles west of present-day Dodge City they left the Arkansas and turned south across the desert toward the Cimarron. Becknell realized the inadvisability of pulling wagons over rugged Raton Pass, but the Cimarron Desert almost proved their undoing. With only canteens of water, and using a pocket compass and stars to guide them, they wandered for two days in search of water, plodding on in blinding heat and beguiling mirages.

Once they arrived in Santa Fe they made a comfortable profit, and Becknell had proved that wagon travel over the plains was possible. Eventually wagons were almost totally used, especially the Murphy wagon. This was manufactured in St. Louis and was usually pulled by ten or twelve mules or three, four, or six yoke of oxen. Three feet wide and sixteen feet long, with rear wheels five feet in diameter encircled by thick iron tires, the wagons were sturdy enough to make the rugged trip. On the way out the wagons carried about five thousand pounds, but on the return trip only one thousand pounds were carried because pastures were poor and teams did not have the strength to haul heavy loads.

Two other ventures of 1822 enjoyed reasonable success. There was only one recorded expedition the following year, led by Maj. Stephen Cooper, who had accompanied his uncle the previous year. Cooper's company had reached the Little Arkansas when Indians ran off all but six of the horses. Cooper headed back to Missouri and returned with fresh stock. Despite such hardships the expedition was a success. The party returned to Missouri in October 1823 with furs, enough money to pay rich dividends, and four hundred mules — which probably began the Missouri mule industry.

The year 1824 brought an increase in traders, the extensive use of wagons, and the beginning of formally organized caravans with constitutions, rules, and elections of officers. The 1824 caravan was composed of eighty-one men, one hundred fifty-six horses and mules, twenty-seven wheeled vehicles, and a field artillery piece. It carried merchandise valued at about $35,000 which was sold for $190,000. This expedition also established the precedent of venturing beyond Santa Fe to Chihuahua and Sonora, which eventually became the primary markets for traders following the trail.

Caravans arriving in Santa Fe were met by Mexican officials who discussed duties. Since these varied at the whim of the governor, each merchant tried to bribe the officials — or to smuggle as much as possible in false wagon bottoms or on packtrains along unguarded mountain trails. From 1822 to 1843 Americans paid an average yearly tariff of between $50,000 and $80,000 in duties and bribes.

As both travel and Indian hostilities along the trail increased, merchants demanded protection against the Indians, as well as a survey of the road. Sen. Thomas Hart Benton of Missouri requested Augustus Storrs, a member of the 1824 caravan and United States consul at Santa Fe, to supply essential information. Storrs suggested that the road from Fort Osage to the Arkansas be surveyed and marked with mounds of earth.

In 1825 Benton sponsored a bill appropriating $20,000 to establish peace with the Osage and Kansa Indians and $10,000 to mark and improve the road. President John Quincy Adams appointed three commissioners to negotiate a treaty with the Indians and to make the survey. One of these was George C. Sibley, former government factor at Fort Osage. The party left the fort on July 17, 1825, and by September 11 reached the Mexican boundary. Tired of waiting for permission from the

Courtesy Museum of New Mexico
Old stagecoach relay station of Santa Fe Trail near Santa Fe, N.M.

Mexican government to enter its territory, two commissioners returned to Missouri on September 22. Sibley and surveyor Joseph C. Brown continued to Santa Fe. Permission to proceed with the survey came in the summer of 1826, but the completed survey did not improve travel along the trail because buffalo herds obliterated the mounds of earth. Treaties with the Osage and Kansa tribes did not solve the Indian threat because the more bellicose tribes lived farther west.

Profits in the early years were substantial, but trade declined as competition grew for the limited Mexican market. Soon merchants looked to markets in Albuquerque, El Paso del Norte, Chihuahua, Sonora, and southern California. During the 1840s Mexico imposed more stringent duties, partially because of the Texas-Santa Fe expedition in 1841. Following independence from Mexico, the Republic of Texas claimed eastern New Mexico, including Santa Fe. In an attempt to open commercial ties with this Mexican capital, a trading expedition was organized in 1841. It failed, but in 1843 several expeditions were sent out with orders to capture Mexican trade caravans along the trail within the boundaries claimed by Texas. One of these expeditions annihilated a party led by Don Antonio José Chávez before Capt. Philip St. George Cooke of the U.S. Dragoons ordered the forces to disband. Angered by the killing of its citizens, the Mexican government closed custom houses in Taos, El Paso del Norte, and Chihuahua, restricting the market to Santa Fe. In September a decree banned from retail business all foreigners except those who were naturalized or married to Mexicans. Following strong protests by Americans, the custom houses were reopened. Santa Fe caravans rolled again in the summer of 1844; in January 1845 it was estimated that trail receipts would exceed $500,000.

In May 1846 the United States declared war on Mexico, and the Santa Fe Trail became a military road. The Army of the West was soon being organized in Missouri, under Col. Stephen Watts Kearny and Col. Alexander W. Doniphan. Kearny planned to march to New Mexico over the trail, assume control, leave part of his command in Santa Fe, and continue on to California. The army left Fort Leavenworth at intervals between May 28 and July 6, 1846, and early in June Kearny began sending unescorted provision trains of twenty-five to thirty wagons to Bent's Fort. Army caravans departed at intervals of three to four days throughout the summer to supply the demands of the invasion force. Before reaching the trail teamsters struggled in a sea of mud in the Kansas heat, and soldiers had to help haul wagons over steep bluffs. Kearny, advised against taking the Cimarron cutoff, marched up the Arkansas to Bent's Fort. Once troops and supplies were assembled there in August, he continued toward Santa Fe.

Grass was inadequate for livestock because of a drought. Temperatures soared to 120 degrees, water was scarce, and blowing sand added to misery. Horses and oxen died, but the troops reached the Purgatoire River, found water, and entered Santa Fe unopposed. Additional reinforcements moved along the trail, including the volunteer Mormon battalion, and soon thirty-five hundred soldiers had marched over the trail. In the spring of 1847 additional volunteer units, accompanied by government supply and trade caravans, arrived from Missouri and Illinois.

The annexation of the Southwest to the United States increased travel along the trail. In the summer of 1848 alone, Col. William Gilpin, commander of Fort Mann, counted approximately three thousand wagons, at least twelve thousand people, and some fifty thousand head of livestock moving west. Increased travel intensified Indian raids, and additional military posts were constructed. To these were added stations to accommodate movement of the U.S. mail to California, which became a state in 1850.

The Civil War brought another era to the trail. Following the secession of Texas in January 1861, secessionist conventions were held in southern New Mexico and Tucson. Both declared for the Confederacy, but northern New Mexico, especially Santa Fe, refused to follow. Confederate troops under Brig. Gen. Henry Hopkins Sibley, former Commandant at Fort Union, invaded New Mexico in the summer of 1861. In February 1862 a large Confederate force left Mesilla, New Mexico, for Fort Craig, routing Union troops at the village of Val Verde. Santa Fe fell in March. Sibley then moved against Fort Union, which had been reinforced by earthen breastworks.

While Confederate forces were marching north, Colorado volunteers commanded by Col. John Slough marched down the trail to Bernal Springs. An advance guard of Colorado volunteers under Maj. John M. Chivington engaged the Confederates in a three-hour battle at Apache Canyon. The Texans were driven from the field, but after dark they moved down the trail through Apache Canyon. Union troops, unaware the enemy was only a mile away, met the retreating Confederates in the six-hour battle of Glorieta Pass, the last Civil War skirmish on the trail and the turning point of the war in the West. The Confederates abandoned plans to take Fort Union and were soon driven from New Mexico. Indian hostilities now posed a new threat, and since the trail was the only direct route between the Union and New Mexico it had to be protected by additional military posts.

Following the war the trail declined in importance, as railroads pushed west. By June 1867 Ellsworth, Kansas, became the departure point for the Santa Fe trade, and former spots such as Council Grove, Diamond Spring, and others were eliminated. By 1871, with completion of the Kansas Pacific, the departure point was Kit Carson, Colorado, and the trail across Kansas was abandoned. Building the Atchison, Topeka and Santa Fe was the final blow. In 1872 its tracks reached Colorado and by 1875 had passed the ruins of Bent's Old Fort. Trade along the trail declined; by 1876 it carried less than half the traffic of 1855. In January 1879 the railroad climbed the slope of Raton and in July reached Las Vegas. In September Raton tunnel was opened, and the trail was reduced to a mere one-hundred miles. On February 16, 1880, the first train entered Santa Fe on a branch line from Lamy, and the sixty-year existence of the trail came to an end.

Travelers over the Santa Fe Trail faced a variety of dangers — including Indian attacks, since much of the trail crossed hunting grounds of the Pawnees, Kiowas, Comanches, Arapahos, and Cheyennes. During the first decade of travel, following Becknell's initial trip, Indian attacks had been rare — probably less than eight persons were killed — but they harassed caravans and often suc-- ceeded in driving off livestock. As travel increased, so did Indian attacks, necessitating the establishment of new military posts, as well as occasional escort service for traders' caravans. The seriousness of Indian hostilities was emphasized by Col. J. C. McFerran in the 1860s when he wrote:

> Both life and property on this route is almost at the mercy of the Indians. Every tribe that frequents the plains is engaged in daily depredations on trains, and immense losses to Government and individuals have occurred, and many lives have already been lost.

Indians did kill numerous travelers, but they were not responsible for the majority of deaths along the trail. The rude grave markers erected by survivors indicated, as Robert Morris Peck discovered, whether or not the victim had died a violent death.

Peck, who served in the cavalry at Fort Leavenworth during the 1850s, was puzzled by the fact that many of the crude crosses marking graves along the trail had slanting crosspieces. Old soldiers informed him that

> when the horizontal piece was slanted it meant, 'died with his boots on,' or a violent death — usually killed by Indians — and that when the cross piece was fastened at right angles to the upright . . . it signified, 'died on the square,' or a natural death.

Many of the square crosspieces were markers for victims of disease, although how "natural" such deaths were is debatable. Malaria was one of the most common maladies of the trail, though many travelers found relief by using Dr. John Sappington's Anti Fever Pills, which contained quinine and were first marketed in the early 1830s. A physician in 1847 with the Army of the West reported 102 cases of malaria among 409 men in the First Regiment of Illinois Volunteers. Typhoid, for which no remedy was known, also struck men down. Although vaccination was known, smallpox occasionally reached epidemic proportions, as did Asiatic cholera. Dysentery and scurvy greatly reduced the pleasures and comforts of travel, although they were seldom fatal.

Mosquitoes made life miserable for man and beast, as Susan Magoffin graphically noted in her journal of 1846-1847. "The winged pestilence unsatisfied with having their greedy thirst only half filled, returned with double force and vigor to the attack." Later she noted, "Millions upon millions were swarming around me, and their knocking against the carriage *reminded me of a hard rain.*" In 1839 Matt Field's party wrapped themselves in blankets and jumped into the waters of Walnut Creek to escape the insects and finally resorted to burning buffalo chips to repel them.

Despite the dangers, travelers made the trek in countless numbers. The majority were merchants or their employees, or military men. Others, such as Josiah Gregg, went to improve failing health. When he began his trip in May 1831 Gregg was confined to a Dearborn carriage, but within two weeks he was strong enough to ride, and he later made other trips along the trail. Some, like Francis Xavier Aubry, were not content with merely one trip a year. In 1848 Aubry stationed relays of saddle horses along the trail and covered the eight-hundred-mile return trip in eight days. Near Pawnee Rock he barely escaped the Indians. When he finally arrived at Independence he had to be assisted from his blood-stained saddle. In September 1848, returning from his third caravan of the year, he covered the distance in five days and sixteen hours, running several horses to death. A more typical return with only partially loaded wagons usually required forty-eight days. One woman traveled in the lap of luxury. Susan Magoffin, accompanied by her husband, had a maid, two servant boys, and a driver. She lived in a small Philadelphia-made tent fitted with a table, a stand for a dressing bureau, and a bed complete with sheets, blankets, and pillows. The floor of her tent was covered with a carpet of sail duck. Despite

these amenities she still faced the normal daily hazards of the trail.

The Santa Fe Trail provided a profitable and welcome outlet for American manufactured goods and a powerful impulse to the development of trading towns such as Franklin, Independence, Westport, and finally Kansas City. It also relieved the ever-present currency shortage of the Mississippi Valley frontier, and it enabled Missouri to become a leading mule-producing center.

Traders using the trail made great profits, although in the long run more came from Chihuahua than from New Mexico. Gregg recorded that between 1822 and 1843 almost $3 million worth of merchandise was carried west. In 1843 alone $450 thousand worth was carried by 350 men in 230 wagons, while in 1858 the value rose to an estimated $3.5 million. The Civil War did not hamper trade, and in 1862 $40 million in goods traversed the trail in three thousand wagons, while in 1866 more than five thousand wagons made the trip.

During the trail's existence of little more than half a century, major changes occurred in the West. Beef cattle spread over the Great Plains, where once only buffalo and Indians roamed; railroad lines crossed the mountains and plains; and sod houses and fenced fields began to appear. Finally, territories and states with Indian or Spanish names joined the Union. The Santa Fe Trail is only a memory now; but in many places left unscathed by the plow, deep ruts carved by thousands of heavily laden wagons are still visible, reminders of a once great roadway.

THE KING'S HIGHWAY: EL CAMINO REAL

By Leon C. Metz

This is the story of a sixteenth century road that ran fifteen hundred miles from Mexico City to Santa Fe, New Mexico.

It and all major highways in colonial Mexico had the title *El Camino Real,* which meant the Royal Road or King's Highway. Modern Ameri-

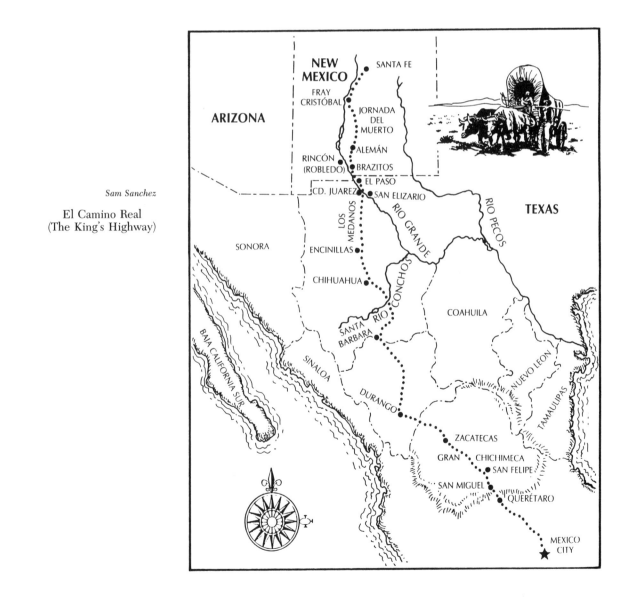

Sam Sanchez

El Camino Real
(The King's Highway)

cans would simply translate it to "Interstate."

Following the conquest of Mexico by Cortez, the Spaniards showed faint interest in the country to the north. It seemed to hold little but savage winds and murderous Indians. Principally the Spanish sought riches. They reasoned that if wealth had existed with the Aztecs it also existed elsewhere. Originally they believed that additional golden cities would be found in the south, since Indians there seemed more settled. Indians to the north wore animal skins and had a propensity for marauding.

For a while that judgment held up. During the next quarter century the Spanish plundered the Mayas in southern Mexico, as well as the Incas in Peru. Wagonloads of treasure left with the conquistadors.

Toward the end of the 1540s the discovery of silver, mixed with small amounts of gold in the northern plateau region, caught Spanish attention. Although the legend of El Dorado fired Spanish imaginations, the European thrust now concentrated on wealth in the ground.

A mining town called Zacatecas arose on that plateau — a bustling, brawling camp four-hundred miles from the capital and containing vast mineral resources locked in its rocky bowels. As silver had to reach Mexico City for minting, a road expanded across that desolate countryside. Locally it became the Zacatecas-Mexico Highway, sometimes known as the Silver Road. Officially, it was never anything but *El Camino Real,* the King's Highway or Royal Road.

The silver flowed south from Zacatecas in one-axeled *carretas.*

These carts rolled on two (although sometimes four) wheels of solid cottonwood, often seven feet in diameter. Made without nails or iron, on a frame lashed together with rawhide, a *carreta* averaged fifteen by six feet. Strong ones carried loads of five thousand pounds. While usually drawn by oxen, the wagons were also pulled by mules. The cargo moved slowly but dependably, even though the intense, high-pitched squeal of wood grinding upon wood produced a numbing effect on the ears.

In those days, the farther one moved from Mexico City the more dangerous the King's Highway became. *Ladrones* (Mexican bandits) operated as far north as Querétaro, roughly 150 miles from the capital. The next stretch of road entered country which even the *ladrones* feared, the dreaded *despoblado,* the unpopulated lands. Actually that was not a correct assessment, since the ferocious Chichimeca Indians lived there. They resented the Spanish intrusion, and they despised the Christian work ethic of enslaving Chichimecas to labor in the silver mines. The Indians rebelled, and for the next forty years very little that was not heavily guarded made its way safely along the length of the King's Highway.

During the early 1550s Mexico established defense towns of San Miguel and San Felipe between Querétaro and Zacatecas, villages that did little more than show the flag. Real protection came only when a caravan parked within the town limits.

After four decades of fighting, Miguel Caldera, soldier, chief justice, and *mestizo* frontiersman, brought peace based on diplomacy and gift giving. To stabilize the countryside he imported a thousand Tlaxcalan Indians from southern Mexico as settlers. By standards of the time, theirs was a voluntary trek north along the *Camino Real*. In early June 1591 a hundred wagons squeaked from Mexico City toward Zacatecas and nearby points.

Spain, meanwhile, had gradually been probing north for three decades. Francisco de Ibarra, a wealthy conquistador, received Spain's blessing to identify sites for future towns and mines in Nueva Vizcaya, a region hazily identified as "lands north of Zacatecas." By 1564 he had explored the center of what is now the state of Chihuahua.

Largely through his efforts, miners poured into a place they called Durango. The King's Highway moved two hundred miles further north to make the connection. By 1575 the road had stretched an additional 250 miles to Santa Bárbara, Chihuahua, another mining town. Here, for the next twenty years, the *Camino Real* paused, 850 miles from Mexico City.

Across this stretch of largely bleak roadway stretched the commerce of empire. Silver and gold comprised most of the cargo going south. Coming north were settlers and administrators, soldiers and prisoners (the latter given a choice between spending life in prison or living on the frontier), and the usual supplies necessary to live and work in these remote regions: pots and pans, muskets, blasting powder, needles and thread, clothes, grain, medicines, and farming implements.

Spain's greatest need in the far north, other than colonists, was men to work the mines. For a variety of reasons Mexico's mines rarely developed into anything other than primitive pits. ("Gopher holes" the Americans would call them in later years.) The owners were interested only in the wealth produced. Such benefits as fair wages, safety, or decent working conditions had no place on their list of priorities. Air, for instance, soured below ground. Torches furnished the only light and consumed the only oxygen. Men grew sluggish and often lost their balance as they climbed ladders ten to eighteen hours a day while lugging enormous baskets of ore on their backs. These ladders were nothing but long, slim tree trunks lowered into the earth and notched for foot and hand holds. Life expectancies dropped to a few years, and there was a natural reluctance among Spaniards and Mexicans to do the work. This left the Indians — because they were plentiful and because they had no choice. Laws protecting Indians were written in Spain, but were seldom enforced in remote Santa Bárbara. Besides, Indians needed to be turned away from hunting and gathering and put to work. They would at least die as Christians.

The trouble was that Indians made themselves scarce around mining centers. So if the Indians would not go to the white man, the white man would go to them. Indians did not yet have horses in large numbers, and most of the natives could be found along natural waterways. Slavers regularly plied the Río Conchos to the Río Grande. A system of trails developed; one was so extensive that it reached from Chihuahua to San Antonio, Texas. It was used by traders, slavers, and *Comancheros* and became widely known as the Chihuahua Road, although it was never a *Camino Real*.

In fairness, there was also a sizable contingent of Spaniards not so much interested in enslaving the Indian as in saving his soul. A classic illustration was the 1581 Rodríguez-Chamuscado expedition, which preached the gospel and searched for gold at the same time. Sgt. Francisco Sánchez, nicknamed Chamuscado (the singed or scorched one), headed the expedition's eight soldiers. With them were three priests, Fathers Agustín Rodríguez, Francisco López, and Juan de Santa María. Included in the caravan were nineteen Indian servants, ninety horses, five hundred head of additional livestock, and plenty of gifts. Like other parties before them, this one followed the Conchos to the Río Grande. It then turned northwest, staying on the south bank of the river until it reached the Frontera crossing, a Spanish ford located about where Sunland Park is now on the outskirts of El Paso, Texas.

The expedition continued north along the Río Grande — in effect blazing, without realizing it, the upper extension of the King's Highway. While the soldiers looked for minerals, the priests scouted for Indians who did not know the white man's God. Eventually, a short distance south of what is now Santa Fe, Father Juan de Santa María decided he had Christianized enough heathens. Ignoring strong military advice he started home. A few days later he was murdered by Indians. New Mexico, and what would become the *Camino Real,* had its first martyr. The remaining two priests announced intentions of staying in New Mexico to preach. They, too, ignored military pleas and were murdered shortly after the soldiers departed. As for the military, all made it home safely except for Chamuscado, who died along the way.

In 1582 Antonio de Espejo, a wealthy Chihuahua rancher wanted by the crown for murder, planned to win a pardon by entering New Mexico and rescuing the priests, or at least learning their fate. He followed substantially the same route as the Chamuscado-Rodríguez expedition but found nothing. He returned home by heading east to the Pecos River, following it south to its junction with the Río Grande, and then ascending the Conchos.

The most audacious trip of all, and the entrada that firmly established the final extension of the King's Highway, took place in early 1598. Juan de Oñate, scion of a wealthy silver-mining family in Zacatecas, led a colonizing expedition into New Mexico, a territory he would conquer, settle, and govern.

Oñate's route differed from that of Chamuscado and Espejo in one major respect: Instead of following the Conchos west to the Río Grande, Oñate boldly struck out to the north across the desert from Santa Bárbara to intercept the Río Grande a few miles east of the present vicinity of El Paso, shortening the trip by at least a hundred miles.

Oñate's train consisted of eighty-three wagons, seven thousand head of livestock, and approximately three hundred men, women, and children. By March the caravan had reached the present vicinity of Chihuahua City (not founded until 1709), crossed the Sacramento River, and marched past what we presently know as Encinillas (live oaks) and El Pinol. By early April the emigrants reached what is now Carrizal and a week later probed the outskirts of the "medanos," the great sand dunes sprawling across 770 square miles of countryside. Today a highway goes right through these dreaded medanos, but in 1598 the sands forced Oñate to circle northeast. He struck the Río Grande at the present site of Clint or Fabens, Texas. Except for the detour, he would have hit El Paso almost precisely.

On April 30, Ascension Day, at a site near San Elizario or Socorro, Texas, Oñate declared lands watered by the Río Grande to be the property of the king of Spain. On May 4 he forded the Río Grande at *El Paso del Río del Norte,* the crossing of the River of the North. On this site would arise two great river metropolises: Paso del Norte (later Ciudad Juárez) and El Paso.

Campsites for the next few weeks would become the historical sites for the future. One was the Paraje de Bracitos, where Doniphan's army would eventually defeat a Mexican force and open up the Southwest to the United States; another was Doña Ana, ten miles north of Las Cruces, New Mexico. On May 20 the colonists passed Robledo Mountain, so named because of a simple journal inscription, "We buried Pedro Robledo."

Photo by Author

Site of the Brazito battlefield where Colonel Alexander Doniphan destroyed a Mexican army on the Camino Real twenty miles north of El Paso. Battle happened in late December, 1846. View is looking toward Interstate 10, not seen.

Near this point the Río Grande flowed through channels too narrow for pack mules and wagons, and the colonists had to trek across a desolate, windswept, waterless countryside for ninety miles before rejoining the river. This was the route that would be known in history as *La Jornada del Muerto*. Most writers have translated that as "The Journey of Death," but a more accurate name would be "The Dead Man's Route." The Spanish never referred to it as *La Jornada del Muerto,* of course, although they buried their share of dead there. Instead, the name is believed to have come from a German trader, Bernard Gruber, whose body was found in the middle of the Jornada about 1670. The site where he died is to this day called *El Alemán,* The German.

The Colonists reemerged near Paraje de Fray Cristóbal and by June 14 had reached the Piro Indian town of Teypana, which Oñate's men christened "Socorro" because of the provisions they received there. After that they camped at Acomilla, La Joya, and Albuquerque. Finally, on July 25, the harsh journey ended with the founding of Santo Domingo in upper New Mexico.

Oñate was the first governor of New Mexico, but he discovered no wealth and fell into disgrace. His successor, Governor Pedro de Peralta, founded Santa Fe in 1609 or 1610. This became the northern terminus of the *Camino Real.* The King's Highway stretched fifteen hundred miles north and south, the longest colonial road in North America.

Half a continent separated the two hubs of empire, Mexico City and Santa Fe, and *El Camino Real* was the artery supplying the blood. Up and down this highway flowed vast caravans of supplies and people. Each train comprised roughly thirty-two wagons, huge conveyances with cloth hoods and four iron wheels. When loaded with fabrics, salt, skins, nuts, mail, agricultural equipment, and whoever happened to be traveling, a wagon required six strong mules to pull it. A normal round trip took a year and a half — six months each way and six months for loading, unloading, and resting. Wagon trains were supposed to leave Mexico City every three years, although in practice it was often five or six years.

Despite its remoteness, Santa Fe survived until 1680, when a disgruntled Pueblo medicine man named Po'pay harangued the various tribes into an organized rebellion. Haciendas and villages were laid waste, and perhaps four hundred Spaniards and Christianized Indians were killed. Surviving Spaniards and their native allies headed south along the *Camino Real*. Winter was coming on. They had little food, clothing, or transportation, and practically no weapons. Not knowing whether the Pueblos would attack again, they streamed three hundred miles to the safety of Paso del Norte — a refuge no one was sure still existed. It was a sad flight, the only large-scale retreat from Indians in North American history.

At Paso del Norte the refugees regrouped and established villages for their Indian allies. They named most of those locations after the New Mexico communities left behind, such as Socorro and Ysleta (the latter for Isleta, near present-day Albuquerque).

Northbound wagon traffic ceased on the *Camino Real,* but squads of soldiers occasionally penetrated short distances to reconnoiter. In 1682 a sizable military unit marched upstream to Isleta and brought back four-hundred Tiguas judged to be converted to Christianity. When Santa Fe was reoccupied in 1693 the *Camino Real* reopened, never to close again.

By 1800 Spain's colonies in New Mexico and California attracted the attention of the United States. Interested in challenging the claims of Europe, the American government sent Lt. Zebulon Montgomery Pike to explore the headwaters of the Red River, but the Spanish suspected his motives and charged him with spying. In 1806 Spanish dragoons escorted Pike down the *Camino Real* to Mexico City. His journal, published in 1810, described the Spanish settlements as ripe for trade; the only obstacle was Spain's refusal to open its doors to foreigners. That obstacle fell in 1821, when Mexico won its independence.

(The republican government of Mexico patriotically changed *Camino Real* to *Camino Constitucional.* In popular usage, however, it continued as the Royal Road and King's Highway until well into the twentieth century.)

Also in 1821 Missouri became a state. It was at the tether's end of the United States, a region whose only claims to fame were fur trappers and St. Louis. Except for trade generated along the Mississippi River, Missouri had practically no commercial or mercantile development.

Santa Fe and Missouri had some similarities. Santa Fe was so far from Mexico City that it was practically forgotten. Wagon trains leaving the capital often sold their goods before completing the trip, and the few trade items that reached New Mexico were of poor quality and high price. Santa Fe faced the dilemma of being forced to depend on an indifferent supplier.

Other potential trading partners were more attentive. By the end of 1821 wagons were highballing down the 800-mile Santa Fe Trail from Franklin, Missouri. During 1824 alone, American traders picked up gross receipts of $190,000.

Santa Fe, however, never had the importance that most historians have accorded it. Max L. Moorhead, in *New Mexico's Royal Road,* called the Santa Fe trade "actually a misnomer." While Santa Fe had many legendary, romantic qualities, in reality it was a tiny village of one-story, flat-roofed huts housing five thousand farmers, practically none of whom had ever handled pocket money. Consequently they wanted much but could pay for little. "After the first two decades," Moorhead said, "most of the merchandise was actually sold in the interior of the country — in Paso del Norte, Chihuahua, Durango, Zacatecas, Aquascalientes," and even Mexico City. Chihuahua City in particular became a primary destination for the Missouri traders, with Santa Fe reduced to a mere port of entry.

Chihuahua City, not Santa Fe, had been the primary destination even of Mexican traders along the

Camino Real. Owing to Santa Fe's poverty and lack of cash, its items for trade were limited: wines, raisins, buffalo and cow hides, nuts, Indian slaves, and various minor goods. Chihuahua City, on the other hand, contained vast silver and gold holdings, as well as a smelter and a mint. Because of its supply of hard currency, the village became an important trading center. Josiah Gregg, chronicler and trader, claimed that between 1822 and 1832 one-fifth of the Santa Fe traders from Missouri actually sold their products in Chihuahua. During the next decade one-half of all American businessmen entering Santa Fe did not even unload. They simply paused before heading south.

This six-hundred-mile stretch of the *Camino Real* between Chihuahua City and Santa Fe became known as the Chihuahua Trail. Wagon masters, traders, and busi-nessmen rarely called it by any other name.

Paso del Norte thus became a way station between Santa Fe and Chihuahua City. In 1827 Ponce de León, prominent businessman and trader of Paso del Norte, took up land on the north bank of Río Grande, where he established a small rancho. His wheat fields once flourished in what is now downtown El Paso.

Because of its location at the river crossing, a half-way point between Chihuahua City and Santa Fe, Ponce's rancho attracted Americans who became Chihuahua traders. The best example was James Wiley Magoffin, an adventurer who left his birthplace in Kentucky for South America before becoming the American consul in Saltillo, Mexico. Next he moved to Chihuahua City, married into an influential family, and actively engaged in the Chihuahua trade. His wagons became familiar

Photo by Author

The Rio Grande not too far from the *La Jornada del Muerto*, the Dead Man's Route sights along the rutted roads between Santa Fe and Chihuahua. By the late 1840s he had migrated to the north bank of the Río Grande across from Paso del Norte, where he established a large hacienda three miles southeast of Ponce's rancho.

In the meantime events took place in Texas that profoundly influenced the Chihuahua Trail. In those days Texas extended only as far west as San Antonio. In 1836 the state won its independence and captured General and President Antonio López de Santa Anna — who promptly signed the Treaty of Velasco, giving Texas territory it had never had before: the Río Grande as a southern and western boundary. As that included Santa Fe, New Mexico (Santa Fe being on the east bank of the river), the treaty made Santa Fe just another Texas community. The treaty also gave Texas title to Ponce's rancho and James Magoffin's hacienda.

Most Texans had never heard of Paso del Norte, Ponce's rancho, or Magoffin's hacienda. But they had heard of Santa Fe, even if nobody knew exactly where it was. The key to jurisdiction was official incorporation, however, so Texas created Santa Fe County, with the village by the same name as the seat. Whether from ignorance or appetite, the county included the Big Bend, the Panhandle, New Mexico east of the Río Grande, half of Oklahoma, and portions of Colorado and Wyoming. Perhaps this is why Texans are still known as people who think big.

In 1841 the Santa Fe Expedition, known also as the Texas-Santa Fe Pioneers, left Austin for Santa Fe. Most historians believe it went primarily to open a trade route, but

Photo by Author

The Camino Real crossed the Rio Grande in front of the white, cone-shaped buildings, creating *El Paso del Rio del Norte* (the Pass across the Big River to the North). Modern El Paso is at the bottom (Interstate 10), and Ciudad Juarez, formerly Paso del Norte is at the top.

there is little doubt that the expedition would have brought Texas political and military blessings to Santa Fe if the opportunity had arisen. At any rate, while the intrusion might have been ostensibly peaceful, Mexico considered it an invasion. Mexican troops met the Texans near what is now Tucumcari, New Mexico, and found them lost, starving, and freezing. They surrendered without resistance, and the Mexicans herded the four-hundred prisoners south along the *Camino Real* toward Mexico City.

By November the caravan had reached the *Jornada del Muerto*, upon which little moved but the prisoners, their captors, and a strong, biting wind. By now most of the Texans were barefoot and ragged. Few had blankets, and all were hungry and weak. Those who could not continue were summarily shot, and their ears were strung on a rawhide cord as evidence that none had escaped. Several had injuries or illnesses so severe that they traded their few possessions for an opportunity to ride a mule or ox. Once they passed a long string of wagons owned by James Magoffin, all driven by "brown, healthy looking Americans." Neither group spoke to the other.

This is not to imply that the Mexicans were warmly dressed. One prisoner's account mentions a group of Mexican soldiers heading north. Their women were dressed so flimsily that all would have frozen had the soldiers not taken special precautions. They ran from one large bush to another, setting them on fire. Each soldier then wrapped his cloak around himself and a woman, sharing with her a moment of warmth.

Magoffin probably knew nothing about the Texans' misery, for he was probably in Chihuahua City, Santa Fe, Independence, or Washington. It is almost certain that he spoke with President James K. Polk during the middle 1840s.

When the United States and Mexico decided in 1846 to settle their differences with cannon fire, Magoffin convinced Gov. Manuel Armijo to surrender Santa Fe without firing a shot. Col. Stephen Watts Kearny and his First Regiment of Mounted Missouri Volunteers walked in and occupied the village.

As Kearny left to conqueror California, a nine-hundred-man contingent under Col. Alexander Doniphan slipped south along the Chihuahua Trail to conquer territory practically unknown to any Americans but Chihuahua traders. Doniphan had his mettle tested at Brazito (near Vado, New Mexico), located on the King's Highway on the east bank of the Río Grande, about twenty-five miles north of El Paso. With most of his troopers out of uniform and partly intoxicated, and his artillery God-knows-where back along the trail, Doniphan faced a thousand Mexican dragoons approaching from Paso del Norte.

After halting half a mile from the American position, the Mexican forces sent a splendidly uniformed officer to negotiate. A small black flag signifying no quarter fluttered from a slender lance. He met with an American interpreter about two-hundred yards from Doniphan's lines.

"Our general orders your commander to come before him," the Mexican officer stated.

"Tell your general that we will meet him halfway."

"No, he must come into our camp."

"If your people want peace, then send your general to our camp."

"Then we will charge and take him [Doniphan]."

"Charge and be damned."

As conflicts go, the Battle of Brazito hardly rates honorable mention in the pantheon of decisive struggles. As the second battle fought on what is now American soil during the Mexican War, however, it had a decisive effect on American history. It gave the United States uncontested control of the Southwest.

The Brazito battle turned into a slaughter. The Mexicans charged and fired too soon. When the horsemen came in close, Doniphan's Farm Boys blew them away with bitter rounds of musketry. The battle ended in minutes. The Americans had seven wounded, none of whom died. The Mexicans lost approximately one hundred. The survivors fled toward Paso del Norte, leaving the battlefield strewn with bodies, weapons, lances, food, and wine.

Two days after Christmas, 1846, the victorious Doniphan and his army followed the Chihuahua Trail down through the pass, across the Río Grande, and peacefully into Paso del Norte. The *Camino Real* from that point north to Santa Fe was now in American hands.

For the next forty-two days this foreign army camped in the Paso del Norte plaza, where the men gambled, argued, and shot each other to

Photo by Author

Site of the Brazito battlefield where Colonel Alexander Doniphan destroyed a Mexican army on the Camino Real twenty miles north of El Paso. Battle happened in late December, 1846. Interstate 10 is in the foreground.

death. On February 28, 1847, the Farm Boys moved out, following the *Camino Real* south toward Chihuahua City, 250 miles away. For the most part the trip was uneventful, except for the lack of sufficient water for animals and men. The final, decisive struggle lay directly ahead on the Plains of Sacramento, fifteen miles from Chihuahua City.

A defensive army greeted the Americans, an army of sixteen hundred by Mexican accounts; American estimates placed it at nearly four thousand. Whatever the number, some were regulars, well dressed and adequately armed. Most were simply vaqueros carrying lances and ropes. To the rear, thousands of women and children lined the hills.

The Mexican soldiers waited behind their artillery for the American charge. Unfortunately for them, however, the Americans did not charge directly into the cannon mouths; they preferred flanking manuevers. This time the battle lasted nearly four hours, but the results were substantially the same as at Brazito. The Mexican army suffered heavy losses. Doniphan's Farm Boys counted one dead and eleven wounded.

With the gates to Chihuahua City forced open, American troops controlled nearly six hundred miles of the *Camino Real*. But the victorious army had no interest in holding the highway, because most of Doniphan's men were reaching the end of their enlistments and wanted to go home. To do so, they walked east across Mexico to the coast, boarded a ship, and returned to Missouri.

In 1848 the United States and Mexico signed the Treaty of Guadalupe Hidalgo, which estimated the international boundary at the Río Grande. The *Camino Real,* the Chihuahua Trail, the King's Highway (all different names for the same road) now belonged to the United States from the point where the road crossed the Río Grande at El Paso, to Santa Fe. Ownership was uncontested and final.

The history of the Southwest changed dramatically as a result of the treaty. Magoffin's hacienda (called Magoffinsville) and Ponce's rancho were now in the United States. Both sites became the core of what was rapidly developing into a brawling border town called El Paso. By 1849 separate roads connected El Paso with Austin and San Antonio, as thousands of Forty-Niners flocked through the pass on their way to California.

Stagecoaches connected El Paso to east Texas. These roads brought a direct decline in the *Camino Real's* importance. Practically all the traffic through El Paso went east and west. Almost nothing went north except an occasional stagecoach. Even the "Post Opposite El Paso," renamed Fort Bliss in 1854, stopped being supplied via the King's Highway during the early 1850s and had its supplies shipped in from the military depot at San Antonio. With its historic ties to New Mexico loosened, El Paso voted to join Texas.

The old Chihuahua Trail still had moments of usefulness. With the Civil War threatening, Fort Bliss surrendered to Texas on February 18, 1861. By July Col. John R. Baylor and three hundred troopers of the Texas Mounted Rifles had marched in from the east and reoccupied the post. On July 25 Baylor dashed north along the trail to Mesilla, New Mexico, forty miles away, and forced Maj. Isaac Lynde at Fort Fillmore to surrender his Union troops. A week later Baylor declared himself military governor of the Territory of Arizona, with Mesilla as the capital. Within weeks, Maj. Henry Hopkins Sibley, an ailing alcoholic, assumed command from Baylor and, with an enlarged force called "The Army of New Mexico," vowed to liberate the entire territory as far north as Santa Fe and as far west as California.

The army surged north along the *Camino Real,* overrunning Valverde, Albuquerque, and Santa Fe. Then the Confederacy crested at the Battle of Glorieta. Sibley won the fight but had his wagon train burned, and he ordered a retreat that quickly became a rout. The fleeing Confederates rushed toward El Paso, abandoning their dead and dying along the Chihuahua Trail. By May 1862 Sibley reentered Fort Bliss, which he burned except for the hospital. Then he turned away from the *Camino Real,* marching back into central Texas, never again threatening the El Paso Southwest.

Meanwhile, Col. James H. Carleton, a man of cold eye and hot temperament, brought his California Column through Arizona and New Mexico, striking the Río Grande and the King's Highway about twenty miles north of Mesilla on July 4. Except for a few skirmishes across his line of march, he never met a formidable foe. He occupied El Paso for the Union, and, for the first time since the outbreak of hostilities, the Stars and Stripes flew over the Chihuahua Trail from El Paso to Santa Fe. Carleton established his headquarters in the latter village.

Carleton did have some worries about the international boundary. President Benito Juárez of Mexico had been pursued out of Mexico City by the French, who installed Maximilian on the throne. In a black coach Juárez fled up the *Camino Real* to Paso del Norte, which became the provisional capital of Mexico. Behind him, in Chihuahua City, the French army stacked its rifles. The European army would remain there, cutting the *Camino Real* in two until driven from the country by Mexican counterattacks. With peace restored, the highway again took second place to east-west traffic.

By the 1880s the Chihuahua Trail was once more the scene of activity, although not in a manner one might expect. The Santa Fe Railroad cut south from Albuquerque in April and followed the King's Highway across the *Jornada,* reaching El Paso on June 11, 1881. While it never became an important route for passengers, it unknowingly followed the three-century-old tradition of the *Camino Real* by hauling immense amounts of trade goods.

South of the Río Grande, the Mexican Central Railroad followed the *Camino Real* almost precisely, from the national capital to Paso del Norte. This track, completed in 1885, still retains the distinction of being the longest rail line in Mexico.

Today a system of concrete and asphalt highways connects the *Camino*

Real from its source in Mexico City to its terminal in Santa Fe. A toll road from Mexico City to Querétaro connects with two-lane Route 57 to San Luis Potosí. From there the highway becomes Route 49 to Jiménez. Route 45 then finishes the journey to Paso del Norte, now the largest city along the Mexican border, with nearly a million people. (El Paso is the second largest, with almost five hundred thousand.) Paso del Norte was renamed Ciudad Juárez in 1888 in honor of Benito Juárez.

At El Paso Interstate 10 chases the Chihuahua Trail to Mesilla and Las Cruces, where it connects with Interstate 25 to Santa Fe. The fifteen-hundred-mile journey that once took between six months and a year can now be made comfortably in four days.

Today the *Camino Real,* Chihuahua Trail, and King's Highway are names forgotten by travelers, recalled only by historical experts or tourists who read the occasional historical markers. It is the rare traveler who realizes that the land he crosses so easily is hallowed ground, a strip soaked with the blood of intrepid pioneers, nourished by dreams, and echoing with the tongues of many languages.

Though its name is largely unknown to the average visitor, the *Camino Real* is still the oldest, most continuously used route in North America. Few of its travelers are famous. Most are ordinary citizens, having many destinations. Regardless of their social status, they are kings all, and traveling on a King's Highway.

Photo by Author

International Boundary Marker #1 which sits alongside the Camino Real at El Paso. The monument identifies the spot where the international boundary leaves the Rio Grande and goes overland for 800 miles to the Pacific. It sets at the junction of Texas, New Mexico and Chihuahua. On the left side of this marker, Pancho Villa and Francisco Madero gathered an insurgent army for the assault upon Juarez, May 1911.

THE OREGON TRAIL
By Kit Collings

"I sat astride my horse and looked down into the valley we had come upon. As far as the eye could see, there were buffalo — thousands and thousands of buffalo. The entire valley moves as one living mass. The size of the herd was beyond description." Such accounts, like this one by Lewis and Clark, started people dreaming of excitement and fortune in the West. But families could not follow the Lewis and Clark trail because they needed wagons to make the trip.

During the 1800s the Oregon Territory (which went from Alaska to California and east into what is now

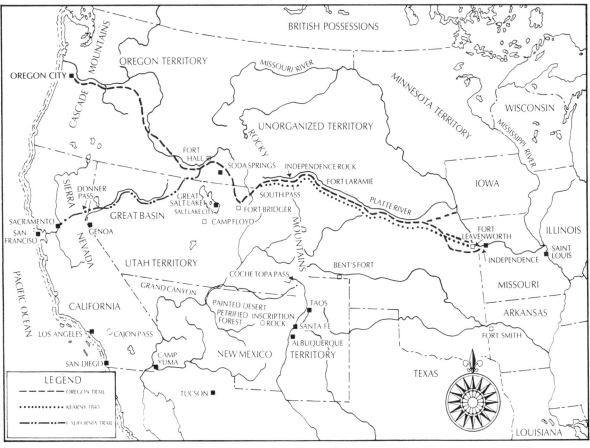

The Oregon Trail

Wyoming) was held jointly by England and the United States. Trouble frequently broke out as the British and American fur companies competed fiercely for furs. In 1811 American Fur Company traders sailed around Cape Horn and up the Pacific Coast to Oregon to set up a trading post on the Columbia River. One of them returned overland to report to company headquarters in New York. He followed Indian trails and discovered that South Pass was an easy way over the Rocky Mountains. His route would become the Oregon Trail. Trouble with the British worsened, and the feeling that Oregon should be American intensified in the United States. Rallies called "Manifest Destiny" meetings were held in many cities.

Missionaries were zealous to Christianize the Indians. In 1836 Dr. Marcus Whitman and the Reverend Henry Spaulding, along with their wives, set out to establish missions among the Indians of Oregon. Mrs. Whitman and Mrs. Spaulding were the first white women to make the difficult trip over South Pass. The wagons overturned repeatedly while trying the navigate the steep mountain trails. "It was a greater wonder that it was not turning somersaults continually," wrote Narcissa Whitman. But because Dr. Whitman wanted to show that wagons could go over the trail, he persevered. When the wagons mired in a creek, he plunged into the icy water to free them. The wagons finally gave out on the lower Snake River. Narcissa rejoiced, for they could make better time without them. But they had gone farther than any wagon had gone before. Her letters made the point to the East — the Oregon trail could be traversed by properly built wagons, and by women!

In 1840, as the fur trade era was ending (owing to a change in styles and the inability to get good furs) Mountain Man Joe Meek built a wagon out of those abandoned by the Whitmans. Meek and another Mountain Man took their Indian wives and the wagon over the Blue Mountains to Oregon, thus completing the traversing of the trail by wagons.

In 1841 the Bidwell-Bartleson party became the first true emigrant train to cross South Pass. Their guide was another former Mountain Man, Thomas ("Broken Hand") Fitzpatrick. Their wagons had to be abandoned along the way, and they proceeded on horses or mules or on foot. The group split up at Soda Springs; some went to Oregon, the others to California. The next year wagons made it all the way to Oregon, and the great migration had started. In all, over 350 thousand persons are estimated to have gone overland with wagons. Land promoters advertised Oregon as the perfect place to live, the land of opportunity, with its fertile soil, clear streams, and snow-capped mountains. A mile square of farmland awaited the family that had the courage to face the unknown obstacles of the trail.

Probably the single most important reason for going to Oregon was to acquire the rich land, for most of the 11,500 people in Oregon by 1848 were from midwestern farming areas. One emigrant admitted going, "because the thing wasn't fenced in and nobody dared to keep me off." Another was tired of Missouri catfish and wanted to try salmon. Others went to enjoy a sunnier climate or to find their fortunes and return. Some went just for the adventure or to keep the British out of land that they believed should belong to the United States.

Some left to escape sickness. Cholera epidemics infested the cities, while fever and ague raged in the Mississippi Valley. Sometimes the emigrants took their diseases on the trail with them. At home one in every forty persons died of cholera. The death rate on the trail was much lower.

The first emigrants hurried past the grasslands of the plains. The area west of the Missouri was designated as Indian land, "forever and ever." Besides, the early plows could not break the tough prairie sod. There was little incentive to stop and homestead.

The Indians called the route "The Big Medicine Trail." Later so many emigrants went over the trail that the Indians called it "The White-topped Wagon Road." But the Oregon Trail was the emigrant's name for the road which started at the Missouri towns of Independence or St. Joseph, or at Council Bluffs, Iowa. During each spring, muddy roads in the states became impassable, so most emigrants took steamboats up the Missouri River to the rendezvous points, the last place to secure supplies before leaving the states. Unfortunately, "every little thing cost three or four times as much here as home," wrote Eleaser Ingalls from St. Joseph in 1850. "The markets are filled with broken-down horses jockeyed up for

the occasion, and unbroken mules which they assure you are as handy as sheep."

Each year emigrants straggled into the rendezvous towns and joined those who had arrived too late to start the previous year. May was considered the best month for departure to assure passage over the mountains before snow fell. Some hauled grain for their animals so they could start on the trail before the grass was up, hoping that by the time the grain was gone the teams could find grass. If the emigrant misjudged the season, his teams gave out. Predictably there were many disagreements about the best starting time. Occasionally recruited oxen (animals rested and fattened) could be purchased from the army or the Mormons. But there was no way fresh animals could be supplied to everyone.

It was about two thousand miles from Independence to Oregon City. Emigrants leaving the several rendezvous points met near Fort Kearny, 325 miles from Independence. When the movement to Oregon began in the early 1840s there were no military posts beyond Fort Leavenworth, but in 1848 the army built Fort Kearny on the Platte near Grand Island to protect travelers from the Pawnees. The following year the government bought the American Fur Company post of Fort Laramie and sent troops to garrison it and to patrol the trail along the Platte. That river was, a farmer noted, too thick to drink and too wet to plow.

On the 335-mile journey from Fort Kearny to Fort Laramie emigrants saw several prominent landmarks. Many men carved their names on

Courthouse Rock, Chimney Rock, or Scott's Bluff. They usually rested a day or two at Fort Laramie to wash clothes and make repairs before heading toward the mountains, where travel was slower and more difficult.

Near Independence Rock the trail met and then followed the Sweetwater River. Here the going got rougher. Alkali in the water poisoned the cattle. The Sweetwater had to be crossed and then recrossed, sometimes several times in one day. South Pass was an unspectacular place except that now the streams flowed westward, and the emigrants realized they had at last crossed the Continental Divide. It was near Fort Hall that the California-bound emigrants and the Mormons left the trail and headed south.

The mountains and valleys of the Snake, Green, and Bear rivers exhausted the teams and broke down many of the wagons. Some emigrants used rafts for the last part of the trip down the Columbia River to Oregon City.

In time the Oregon Trail developed numerous cutoffs, feeders, and outlets. In many places the trail might be fifteen or twenty miles wide, as trains detoured to avoid the ruts and dust of the wagons ahead of them. In other places deep ruts are still visible today where travel was limited to a single-file route through a mountain passage or to a river crossing. Lakes and swamps were skirted, but rivers and steep mountains had to be crossed,

Courtesy USDI National Park Service　　　　　　　　　　　　　*From a Painting by William Henry Jackson*

Crossing the South Platte

and they proved a challenge to the emigrants' courage and ingenuity.

The trip to Oregon by wagon took four or five months. To avoid delays on the trail the welfare of the animals was the major concern. As one traveler expressed it, "Our lives depend on our animals." Forage was the main consideration in selecting campsites. One emigrant told of staying at places without wood (which might mean a cold supper) if forage and water were available. "Our practice is first to look for a good place for the cattle, and then think of our own convenience." A popular expression of the time was, "Care for your draft animals rather than your men, for men can always take care of themselves."

Selecting the proper team to pull the wagon was also difficult. Horses needed grain to have the endurance and stamina required for the long trip, but there was no way to carry enough grain. So, for hauling wagons, the choice was between oxen and mules.

The relative merits of oxen and mules were often disputed. Emigrants became greatly attached to their teams and argued for the animals that brought them through. The main drawback to oxen was their slow, plodding pace; oxteams needed about fifteen more days to make the trip. But most emigrants felt that their stamina and manageability made up for their slowness. Peter Burnett wrote in 1843, "We fully tested the ox and mule teams, and we found the ox teams greatly superior. One ox will pull as much as two mules, and in mud as much as four. They are more easily managed, are not so subject to be lost or broken

down on the way, cost less at the start, and are worth about four times as much here. The ox is the most noble animal, patient, thrifty, durable, gentle, not easily driven off and does not run off. Those who come to this country will be in love with their oxen . . . . The ox will plunge through mud, swim over streams, dive into thickets, climb mountains to get at grass and he will eat almost anything." If one went lame by accident or by wearing down his hoofs (not all were shod) the meat could be eaten. Extra cattle were driven along for replacements for the teams as well as for food. Few families relished the thought of eating mules.

Many of the men who went West were not experienced teamsters and often had trouble with temperamental mules. One company left picket ropes on its mules as a means of catching them whenever they were turned loose to graze, for no one in that party knew how to lasso. Indians often ran off with mules but not cattle, since they did not value oxen. A man on horseback could easily recapture strayed oxen, while mules were more difficult to locate and catch. If a mule got loose near the Missouri border, it might go all the way back to the rendezvous town.

Some men were dedicated to mules even though they cost almost four times as much as oxen. A higher percentage of mules survived the trip. Delanzo Smith remarked in 1853 that he passed the bodies of five thousand oxen along the trail but saw only one dead mule. Except for the few with experience, men usually mismanaged mules. So the slow, gentle oxen were usually chosen to pull the wagons.

Even though slow and cumbersome, the covered wagon was the most successful vehicle for an emigrating family. Anyone who was sick or wounded could ride in the wagon, and the family could continue on the trail. Small children and women, especially pregnant women, found relief from the sun in the wagon. While many of the emigrants rode horses or walked, the wagon could protect them and their cargo from the weather. The wagon provided a mobile home, an ambulance, transportation for young children, and a fortress in case of attack. The covered wagon became a symbol of safety to the American pioneer family moving west.

Huge wagons like the Conestoga and Murphy were too heavy for oxen or mule teams to pull over the mountains, so a family might use two or three smaller wagons. A strong, light, spring wagon was the choice of most travelers. But the emigrants were individualists, and their conveyances were as varied as their dreams. One person even designed a wagon body that could be shortened as provisions were used up. Another tried a wind wagon. Two-wheeled carts were also used — sometimes because it was all the emigrant could afford; sometimes because it was all that remained of a broken-down wagon.

Many travelers, especially young men without families, used pack mules. Everything had to be unpacked when they stopped at night and repacked in the morning, and some articles couldn't be carried on the backs of mules. Additionally, pack mules provided no shelter from the weather.

Missouri newspapers reported the appearance of one man who pushed a wheelbarrow loaded with his supplies. He gripped the handles and had a leather strap over his shoulders. Every day he made twenty-five to thirty miles. From Fort Laramie it was reported that "He left St. Joseph about twenty-five days ago . . . and has out-stripped everything on the road. He appeared in high spirits and felt confident that he would be the first man at the diggings by this route. He . . . pushed on to the tune of YANKEE DOODLE."

Some affluent emigrants rode in coaches while their supplies went in wagons. In 1852 Enoch Conyers observed "a splendid four-horse coach in which four richly dressed young ladies and two young girls aged about 10 and 12 years, and a young man who was handling the lines rode. One of the young ladies was making music on an accordian, another on a guitar, all were singing as they went past, gay as larks."

While new wagons were recommended, in some cases a farmer might use an old one. The light wagons earned the names of "emigrant wagon" and "prairie schooner." Prairie schooner was appropriate, because from a distance the tops looked like the sails of ships. In fact the wagon was like a ship, because it had to contain everything needed for the journey. After leaving the rendezvous towns there were virtually no stores along the way. "See *yourself* that everything you want is procured, do not trust others," advised Joseph Ware's 1849 *Emigrants Guide*. Wise emigrants consulted trail guides, letters, and newspaper articles as they dreamt, planned, and prepared for the trip. They had to be self-sufficient to be successful. Each item was checked not only for utility but also for weight, yet overloading was a common mistake. The load needed to be packed so that it was both accessible and protected from the elements. Supplies and provisions had to last for the duration of the journey.

There was very little known and much misinformation about the land west of the Missouri, for only crude and inaccurate maps were available. During the 1840s a few guidebooks appeared (like the one quoted above), written by men who had already made the trip. Some books ended at Fort Hall near the Snake River, where the hardest part of the trail began. Some drew on the writings of explorers and others, since the writer obviously could not have traveled over all the trails described.

The weather was a problem, since it changed from year to year. A recommended route might be flooded the next year, and waterless stretches were even longer during dry years. The quality and quantity of grass depended on the moisture available, as well as the number of people using the trail.

For a nation unaware of the difficulties of the trip, these guidebooks were extremely helpful. One emigrant recalls, "All went smoothly until we crossed Bear River Mountains, when feeling some confidence in our own judgement, we had grown somewhat careless about consulting our handbook, often selecting our camp without reference to it. One of these camps we had good reason to remember. I had gone ahead to find a camp for noon, which I did on a pretty

stream with abundance of grass for our horses and cattle, which greatly surprised us, as grass had been such a scarce article in many of our camps. Soon after dinner we noticed some of our cattle began to lag, and seem tired, and others began to vomit. We realized with horror that our cattle had been poisoned, so we camped at the first stream we came to, which was Ham's Fork of Bear Creek River, to cure if possible our poor, sick cattle. Here we were 80 miles or a hundred miles from Salt Lake, the nearest settlement, in such a dilemma. We looked about for relief. Bacon and grease were the only antidotes for poison that our stores contained, so we cut slices of bacon and forced it down the throats of the sick oxen, who after once tasting the bacon ate it eagerly, thereby saving their lives, as those that did not eat died the next day. The cows we could spare better than the oxen. None of the horses were sick. Had we consulted our guide book before, instead of after camping at that pretty spot, we would have been spared all this trouble, as it warned travelers of the poison existing here."

Men with frontier experience were in great demand as guides. Such experience could have been gained as a trapper for the fur companies (Mountain Men), in the army during the Mexican War, or on frontier service with explorers like Fremont or Lewis and Clark, or on a previous trip overland. Friendly Indians and the half-breed sons of Mountain Men who had lived all their lives in the West were also sought as guides. Without the help of such men the emigrants would not have known many of the survival skills necessary.

Travelers depended on their guides but were occasionally disappointed. "Our guide, who made a horse trade with Mr. Melville, in which he considered himself cheated, grew indignant and deserted us," wrote James Longmire in 1853, "and we were left in a strange country without a landmark, a compass or guide, nothing to help us." Members of "The Lost Wagon Train of 1853" blamed their guide for misleading them and causing undue hardship when they were on the desert without water. Most of the men who served as guides were reliable, and some became legendary for helping emigrants cope with the dangers and hardships.

While a qualified guide was essential to a wagon train's success, another vital need was organization. There had to be both, for the guide was often away from the train for long periods of time hunting or scouting. The best guide could not lead a ragtag, unorganized group in which there was constant friction among members. Even the most disciplined group could, nevertheless, get lost or find itself in difficulty without the right guidance. At the rendezvous towns emigrants banded together to hire a guide and organize for the trip. Often they traveled a few days to get better acquainted before electing a captain.

"The first thing to do was to organize," wrote William Barlow in 1845. "We called a representative meeting, elected a captain over all, and one little captain over every forty or fifty wagons, each company elected its own captain and he appointed his own lieutenants, etc. The guard was kept up for some time, and we

stopped and started when the captain ordered. He always went on to look out a camping ground, taking into consideration wood, water and grass." Organizing was partly for protection but also to see that the work of herding the animals, preparing the food, and repairing the wagons was properly done. Large herds were not corralled inside the circle of wagons unless there was threat of Indian attack. The animals needed more room to graze. Often the herd was guarded two or three miles away from camp, because that was where the best grass was. Large trains had difficulty finding sufficient grass and water for the animals and fuel for cooking fires.

In 1843 Peter Burnett described his election as train captain. "The candidates stood up in a row before the constituents, and at a given signal, they wheeled about and marched off, while the general mass broke after them 'lickety-split' each man forming in behind his favorite, so that every candidate flourished a sort of tail of his own, and the longest tail was elected." The captain of the train was the most important element in its organization. His decisions were law. He decided which route to take, when to rest, when to leave, where the train stopped and for how long, who stood guard, and whether or not they would observe the Sabbath. Unsound decisions could prove disastrous. Often wagon trains split up because one part of the group refused to follow orders given by the captain. Many men gave their train captains credit for bringing them through safely, but one traveler observed in 1849 that "To be the leader of an emigrant train through the wilderness is one of the most unenviable distinctions."

Also needed for successful organization were rules that all agreed to observe. They were leaving the States for a territory that had no laws. When one man killed another he argued that he had done nothing wrong because there was no law against killing. Those in his wagon train had to agree and ended up by merely ordering him to leave. Below are some of the laws listed in Silas Newcomb's 1850-1851 journal:

> Whereas we are about to leave the frontier and travel over Indian Territory, We consider it necessary to form ourselves into a Company for the purpose of protecting each other and our property during our journey . . . . Therefore resolved that there shall be one selected from the Company, suitable and capable to act as Captain or Leader. Resolved, that we, as men pledge ourselves to assist each other through all the misfortunes that may befall us on our long and dangerous journey. Resolved, that the Christian Sabbath shall be observed, except when absolutely necessary to travel. Resolved, that there shall be a sufficient guard appointed each night regularly, by the Captain. Resolved, that in case of a member's dying, the Company shall give him a decent burial.

Courtesy USDI National Park Service   *From a Painting by William Henry Jackson*

Approaching Chimney Rock

Generally trail life was quite pleasant. The teams were yoked up before dawn, and the train left as soon as it was light. In 1843 Jesse Applegate wrote this excellent account of a well-organized train's start in the morning. "It is four o'clock A.M.; the sentinels on duty have discharged their rifles — the signal that the hours of sleep are over — and every wagon and tent is pouring forth its night tenants, and slow-kindling smokes begin largely to rise and float away in the morning air. Sixty men start from the corral, spreading as they make their way through the vast herd of cattle and horses that make a semicircle around the encampment, the most distant perhaps two miles away.

"The herders pass to the extreme verge and carefully examine for trails beyond, to see that none of the animals have strayed or been stolen during the night. This morning no trails led beyond the outside animals in sight, and by 5 o'clock the herders begin to contract the great moving circle, and the well-trained animals move slowly towards camp, clipping here and there a thistle or a tempting bunch of grass on the way. In about an hour five thousand animals are close up to the encampment, and the teamsters are busy selecting their teams and driving them inside the corral to be yoked.

"The corral is a circle one hundred yards deep, formed with wagons connected strongly with each other; the wagon in the rear being connected with the wagon in front by its tongue and ox chains. It is a strong barrier that the most vicious ox cannot break, and in case of an attack of the Sioux would be no contemptible intrenchment.

"From 6 to 7 o'clock is a busy time; breakfast is to be eaten, the tents struck, the wagons loaded and the teams yoked and brought up in readiness to be attached to their respective wagons. All know when, at 7 o'clock, the signal to march sounds, that those not ready to take their proper places in the line of march must fall into the dusty rear for the day.

"There are sixty wagons. They have been divided into fifteen divisions or platoons of four wagons each, and each platoon is entitled to lead in its turn. The leading platoon today will be the rear one tomorrow, and will bring up the rear unless some teamster, through indolence or negligence, has lost his place in the line and is condemned to that uncomfortable post. It is within ten minutes of seven; the corral . . . barricade is everywhere broken, the teams being attached to the wagons. The women and children have taken their places in them. The Pilot (a borderer who has passed his life on the verge of civilization and has been chosen to the post of leader from his knowledge of the savage and his experience in travel through roadless wastes) stands ready, in the midst of his pioneers and aides to mount and lead the way. Ten or fifteen young men, not today on duty, form another cluster. They are ready to start on a buffalo hunt . . . .

"It is on the stroke of seven; the rush to and fro, the cracking of whips, the loud commands to oxen, and what seemed to be the inextricable confusion of the last ten minutes has ceased. Fortunately every one has been found and every teamster is at his post. The clear notes of a trumpet sound in the front; the pilot and his guards mount their horses; the leading divisions of the wagons move out of the encampment, and take up the line of march; the rest fall into their places with the precision of clock work, until the spot so lately full of life sinks back into that solitude that seems to reign over the broad plain and rushing river as the caravan draws its lazy length towards the distant El Dorado."

As the train moved the children collected rocks, turtles, wild flowers, or other bits of treasure. As their saddlebags filled, the least desirable were discarded. Youngsters played soldier or Indian, or rode on the wagon tongue with a hand resting on the oxen on either side. Children played king of the mountain, explored, and had "snowball" fights with buffalo chips — besides doing their daily chores.

One young traveler described the trip. "This was a real picnic to my nine year old mind and I did enjoy it to the limit. Most of the children rode and slept much of the time, but I was afraid of missing something. I would run ahead of the pokey oxen, not far enough for an Indian to grab me, however, and pick flowers, gather fuel, or whatever came to mind. I seldom walked less than ten or fifteen miles a day. I was thin and tall for my age and if I was tired at night I do not remember it."

The emigrants stopped about eleven o'clock for a break called nooning. This allowed them to eat, as well as to rest the stock during the hottest part of the day. The types of food taken had to be easily prepared. Beans and rice were cooked only when the wagons made an extended stop where there was plenty of fuel. Flour was a main foodstuff and was stored in one-hundred-pound linen sacks. Emigrants took 150 pounds of flour per person, for flour could rarely be obtained along the trail, and if found was of poor quality. Five pounds of salterus (baking powder) was the conventional portion taken. Travelers prepared quick-rising biscuits more commonly than yeast breads. Sea biscuits, hardtack, crackers, and cornmeal were taken for variety. Narcissa Whitman was pleased she could overcome the problems of managing a trail kitchen. "We found it awkward work to bake at first out of doors but we have become so accustomed to it now we do it very easy. Tell Mother I am very good housekeeper in the prairie. I wish she could just take a peep at us while we are sitting at our meals, our table is the ground, our table cloth is an India rubber cloth."

Forty pounds of bacon, ten pounds of jerky per person, and beef driven on the hoof were suggested. Smoked bacon was packed in strong sacks then put in boxes and covered with bran to prevent the fat from melting. Although some pioneers planned on getting all their meat from fishing and hunting along the trail, this was not always possible or desirable. Mrs. E. A. Hadley ate "some hens called sage hens. I have heard say that they were good to eat, some of our company killed some, and I think a skunk preferable, their meat tastes of this abominable mountain sage, which I have got so tired of that I can't bear to smell it. They live wholly upon it and it scents their flesh."

"I cannot urge you too strongly to

be sure to bring plenty of provisions," wrote Jersey Looney after crossing in 1846, "don't depend on the game you might get. You may get some and you may not."

Dried fruits and vegetables were strung from the wagon bows. Thirty or forty pounds per person were carried. Canned foods were available but expensive. Emigrants who could afford them packed the cans in barrels surrounded by flour to lessen the jarring and to maintain a uniform temperature. Pressed vegetable slices were dried in the oven until rock-hard. A small piece, when boiled, swelled to fill a vegetable dish.

Some pioneers drove milk cows or tied them to the backs of wagons. At times cows were used to pull wagons. Narcissa Whitman wrote that their working cow "supplies us with sufficient milk for our tea and coffee."

"Milk is relished upon the plains," stated J. L. Campbell in his 1864 *Emigrants' Guide Overland*. "In case of storm when cooking cannot be done, it serves a tolerable purpose."

Forty pounds of sugar per person was stored in India-rubber sacks to prevent it from getting wet. Many emigrants felt that rice was extremely valuable because of its keeping properties. Other items commonly carried were vinegar, molasses, potatoes, tea, and whiskey. Coffee became the universal drink, since it made alkali-laden water palatable. It disguised the taste of foul water so effectively that one horse preferred coffee to water.

Not all emigrants chose foods wisely. Capt. Randolph Marcy once traveled with a party of New Yorkers who "were perfectly ignorant of ev-erything relating to this kind of campaigning, and had overloaded their wagons with almost everything except the very articles most important and necessary; the consequence was, that they exhausted their teams, and they were obligated to throw away the greater part of the loading. They soon learned that Champagne, East India sweetmeats, olives, etc., etc., were not the most useful articles for a prairie tour." The trail was marked by furniture and other heavy items that had to be abandoned.

Water was sometimes stored in 40-gallon wooden casks. But casks had to be continually soaked and repaired to keep them from shrinking and falling apart in the dry air. A large barrel of water, lashed to the side of the wagon, unbalanced the load, making it difficult to pull. These barrels were often referred to as "ox breakers." Travelers stored water in India-rubber sacks wrapped with wet rags; evaporation cooled the water. As one emigrant recalled, "The question of water was always one of great importance. We had books and maps to help locate the springs. The longest drive we made between water holes was thirty-five miles. We had to travel until midnight to reach the next spring. As we journeyed along we carried water in wooden kegs for drinking purposes. When we traveled along the Platte the water was so muddy that we had to settle it. This was done by allowing the water to stand for several hours in buckets in which had been sprinkled bran and cornmeal."

Cooking utensils consisted of a dutch oven, two or three cast-iron camp kettles, a coffee mill, a graniteware coffee pot, a water pail, silverware, tin plates, and cups. Despite the hardships, many women prepared appetizing meals. One man had supper at a friend's tent near Fort Laramie, and recorded that it consisted of "hot biscuits, fresh butter, honey, rich milk, cream, venison steak, and tea and coffee — and there were fresh peas gathered that day from the wild vines along the trail."

Another housekeeping chore that proved challenging on the trail was keeping the family's clothes clean. The wash was done when the train stopped for repairs, to rest the teams, or to hunt. Esther Hanna wrote in 1852 that we "have to wash without either tub or board but get along very well with a large bucket and pan set on an ox yoke. Still it requires me to stoop considerably. All our work here requires stooping. Not having tables, chairs, or anything, it is very hard on the back."

Overnight stops were often too short to allow clothing to dry. Narcissa Whitman was able to do her laundry only three times during her six-month journey. One father dried his daughter's freshly laundered diapers by holding them over the fire each night. Sarah Sutton describes her 1853 trail washday. "The girls are washing and baking apple and peach pie, stewing beans and rabbit and appear very happy, all are in good health and no trouble. We have eight girls to do all the work. This trip is fun for them.

"About every two weeks it was necessary to have a family wash day. This was quite a chore as all water had to be heated in camp kettles. A good location would be chosen and the fun would begin for us younger ones. We could play a little while in one place for a change. My mother had a new zinc washboard and two wooden tubs at the start. The board she carried through, but the tubs were lost on route. They dried out so in the daytime and when we camped at night the tubs had to be filled the first thing," noted Mary Elizabeth Argo.

Helen Carpenter commented on "women's work" in her 1857 diary: "The plain truth of the matter is we have no time for sociability. From the time we get up in the morning until we are on the road it is hurry-scurry to get breakfast and put away things that necessarily had to be pulled out last night. While under way there is no room in the wagon for a visitor. Nooning is barely long enough to eat a cold bite and at night all the cooking utensils and provisions are to be gotten about the camp fire and cooking enough done to last until the next night. Although there is not much to cook, the difficulty and inconvenience in doing it amounts to a great deal. So by the time one has squatted around the fire and washed the dishes (with no place to drain them), and gotten things ready for an early breakfast, some of the others already have their night caps on. At any rate, it is time to go to bed.

"In respect to the women's work, the days are all very much the same except when we stop for a day. Then there is washing to be done and light bread to make and all kinds of odd jobs. Some women have very little help about the camp, being obliged to get the wood and water (as far as possible), make camp fires, unpack at night and pack up in the morning, and if they are Missourians they have the milking to do if they are fortunate enough to have cows. I am lucky in having a Yankee for husband, so am well waited on."

Wild animals were part of the adventure when going west. Emigrants wrote of the beauty of antelopes racing across the prairie. For the first time the travelers watched prairie dogs, cougars, grizzly bears, jackrabbits, or herds of buffalo. At times the train would drive past the same buffalo herd for days; at other times the ground shook as the buffalo stampeded. "A herd of buffalo was seen this afternoon at a comparatively short distance," noted Helen Carpenter in 1857. "This created general excitement and eight or ten of the company gave chase, some on foot, some on horseback, armed with muskets, revolvers and knives. The train kept right on until the usual camping time (a little before sundown) then halted by a slough. When the oxen were partly unyoked, Reel came in bringing the good news of his success in capturing a big buffalo bull. As it was two miles from camp all haste had to be made in returning the oxen to haul it in, if they made the trip before night set in. Five yoke were taken and there should have been one or two yoke more as it turned out to be a very heavy job. Old Smut and Snarley were the only oxen that could be gotten near enough to the buffalo to hitch on. They did not like the scent of the animal nor the blood.

"They estimate the animals weight at one ton and age any where from 12 to 20 years. The old fellow was grazing apart from the herd when one of the hunters crept up within 60 yards and from behind a little knoll fired a load of buck-shot from his old musket. The buffalo made off and Reel, following on horseback, was soon at close range and being an excellent shot and armed with Sharp's rifle loaded with ounce slugs, the chase was of short duration. A shot in the hip and ranging almost the entire length of the body brought down the game. Yet another was fired through anxiety to have a job well done. The buck-shot merely penetrated the skin and would have caused the animal little or no inconvenience.

"This is the greatest animal show that we have seen. Hale is a large boy for nine years of age and when he stood by the shoulders (the largest part of the body) his head could not be seen from the opposite side."

Prairie storms could change this happy life, for they were more sudden and severe than any the emigrants had ever experienced. The rain changed the dust into deep mud sucking at the wagon wheels. The wind leveled the tents and threatened to blow the wagons over. Sheets of rain soaked clothes and firewood. Lightning stampeded the animals. Hail tore the wagon covers and caused teams to turn and run — but pails filled with hail provided ice water.

The wind blew relentlessly, and wagons could not be closed tight enough to keep out the blowing dust which inflamed eyes and covered everything — clothes, food, beds, and people. Esther Hanna told of the problem, "How can I give you any idea of it? We are almost blinded by it. My eyes are very sore. We are having to wear veils or goggles, some wear handkerchiefs over their faces and with all we are almost choked and blinded. It tries my patience more than anything else."

A forty niner wrote, "The road today has been very disagreeable, dusty, sandy, hilly and crooked. The dust is very annoying being blown into our eyes by a strong S.W. wind and inflaming them so that now although I have washed them in cold water several times I am obliged to keep them partially shaded from the light. I have seen several persons completely blinded by it so that they had to be carried along for several days. Not seeing enough to take care of themselves."

Another storm was described by Helen Carpenter in 1857. "I am wondering just how hard the wind has to blow before it is called a tornado. We were visited last night by the most violent wind storm that we had ever experienced. The wagon was so shaken up that one could not tell which way the vibrations were, backward, forward, side-wise or all three together." A few days later she wrote, "Very black clouds were seen in the west, and from the wind and increasing darkness it was evident that we would soon come face to face with the unwelcome visitor. About four o'clock a terrific storm broke upon us. The wind blew and it rained, hailed, thundered, lightened in a way never before seen even the two years experience in Kansas storms. The cattle refused to obey the drivers or face the storm and turned directly about and had to be well guarded by all the men to keep them from running away. The thunder crashed at our very heads and the guards said the lightening circled around the wagon tires and ran along the chains. The men, although in oilcloth suits, were pretty well drenched."

There were few preventive mea-

From a Painting by William Henry Jackson

Sand Hills of the Platte Valley

sures that could be taken to cope with the storms, so the emigrants overcompensated for real and imagined dangers from Indians or wild animals. Each man had a shotgun or rifle, a pistol, and a belt knife. These weapons were always kept handy, although the men were unused to handling them. One young wife, Lucy Cooke wrote, "Our men are all well armed. William carries a brace of pistols and bowie knife. Ain't that blood-curdling? Hope he won't hurt himself."

Self-inflicted gunshot wounds were the most common accidents on the trail. After seeing a companion shot in the hand while pulling a rifle out of a guard tent, one emigrant noted, "I confess to more fear from careless handling of firearms than from an external foe." Mary Elizabeth Warren narrowly missed death from a gun resting against the wagon. It fired when she jumped on the wagon — and shot off a lock of her hair.

A forty niner from the Granite State Company dropped his rifle, causing it to discharge. The ball struck a pack mule in the knee and severed the artery. The gun's owner "gave up his (riding) horse to be packed by the men having charge of the mule, and walked ever after."

Because of the possibility of accidents or illnesses, emigrants took medicine chests containing blue mass, laudanum, quinine, opium, cathartics, brown sugar to pack cuts, medicinal whiskey, and bandages. Surgery had not been perfected, so if a person suffered from appendicitis little could be done for him either at home or on the trail. The very medicines that could bring relief might also cause

problems, as one child recalled. "I shall never forget that camp. Mother had brought some medicine along. She hung the bag containing the medicine from a nail on the sideboard of the wagon. My playmate, the Currier girl, who was of my own age, and I discovered the bag, and so I decided to taste the medicine. I put a little on my tongue, but it didn't taste good, so I took no more. The Currier girl tasted it, made a wry face, and handed the bottle back. My little sister, Salita Jane, wanted to taste it, but I told her she couldn't have it. She didn't say anything, but as soon as we had gone she got the bottle and drank all of it. Presently she came to the campfire where mother was cooking supper and said she felt awfully sleepy. Mother told her to run away and not bother her so she went to where the beds were spread and lay down. When Mother called her for supper she didn't come. Mother saw she was asleep, so didn't disturb her. When mother tried to awake her later she couldn't arouse her. Lettie had drunk the whole bottle of laudanum. It was too late to save her life. Before we had started father had made some boards of Black walnut that fitted along the side of the wagon. They were grooved so they would fit together, and we used them for a table all the way across the plains. Father took these walnut boards and made a coffin for Salita and we buried her there by the roadside in the desert."

In 1852 Enoch Conyers told of a woman who lost her husband on the trail: "Caught up with a widow woman who had buried her husband back on the Platte. She had four or five little helpless children to care for. All the rest of her company had gone on, leaving her alone with her team and little ones to get over the mountains the best she could She had three yoke of cattle to her wagon. When we overtook her she was driving wooden wedges between the fellows [sic] and the tire of the wagon wheel . . . . The wheels of the wagon had shrunk so much that it required wooden wedges three-quarters of an inch thick driven under the tire all around the wheel to keep the tire on, and then there was no assurance of it lasting until she got down the first hill."

Childbirth was common on the trail. Some went smoothly, some didn't. Diarrhea, caused by the changes in water and by the alkali, was prevalent, but the most dreaded disease was cholera. Many knew that cholera was spread by poor sanitation methods, but most emigrants were not concerned about the way they left campsites, since they would never return to them. They complained, nevertheless, of having to camp in the filth left by others.

After a stop during the heat of the day, the train continued on to the site chosen for the night's camp. As they traveled, the wagons were made picturesque by their covers. One emigrant described the scene along the Platte.

"The drivers stalked limberly and lonesomely by the sides of their ruminating teams, but as the sun beat upon that treeless plain, bathing the sweltering landscape with glimmering heat, the crack of the whip became less frequent and the driver would crowd between the oxen's heels and the wagon wheel and take a sidewise seat on the wagon tongue, and nod-ding, drive. At intervals the driver would wave his long whip and drowsily drawl out, 'Get up thar,' and relapse into silence. There was sort of a rhythmical sequence in these somniferous 'Get ups,' which at regular times welled out from that slow line of dusty teams and sleepy drivers. Like the answering calls of farm yard fowls, when one driver would call out 'Get up,' 'Go along,' each companion would repeat the admonition to his sluggish charges."

A movement on the horizon would bring the lethargic men to instant readiness. Indians? However, the Indians did more harassing than attacking. There is no record of Indians circling the wagons, exchanging arrows for bullets. Until the late 1850s (when the emigrants began settling on the prairie Indian lands), there were few battles with Indians. Until that time Indians worried small parties, stole horses, scattered stock, and frightened emigrants into giving them food, trinkets, horses, and sugar. Indians often assisted at river crossings, and sometimes demanded a toll. If the travelers refused to pay, their stock might be stolen. Indians also helped the emigrants by selling horses (often the emigrants own that had been "lost" the previous day), moccasins, or game. While the Plains Indians were justifiably feared, they caused little trouble.

Helen Carpenter described a meeting with Indians. "Three Pawnee Indians came while we were nooning. They asked for food, but the order was 'don't give them a thing.' It was thought that they would follow and be a nuisance if shown any kindness. I could not eat lunch with those poor wretches watching every mouthful like hungry dogs. Mother found an opportunity to slip something to them, and they did not follow nor give any trouble."

Sarah York wrote of another kind of incident. "We came quite a long ways — we camped, and one night there was five head of horses stolen and we didn't know what had become of them. We traveled along quite a ways and we camped — stopped to get dinner at noon — and there was an Indian came to the camp riding one of the horses that had been stolen, so my father he took the horse and we started on, and in a little while we could see the Indians coming from every direction, all painted up, with their feathers — all ready for war. You could just look in any direction and see Indians coming. They have signs between themselves that they understand — and they come from every direction in such a short time. They just stopped us, but a lot of teams passed us. They let them go by — never disturbed them, but they talked quite a long while, and my father tried to show them that it was his mare, but they wouldn't give in; said they had traded cayuses for that horse. They talked quite awhile. My older brother, Dick, was small — about nine or ten, and he was on the horse and the Indians just walked up and took hold of the bridle and started to lead the horse away with my brother on and my father had to lift my brother off the horse and let the Indians take it. It was the only thing he could do — we didn't dare do anything else. It was the only thing to do."

Aching from the fatiguing work,

dust-covered, with their faces burned from sun and wind, emigrants followed Whitman's advice, which was "Travel, *travel*, TRAVEL; nothing else will take you to the end of your journey; nothing is wise that does not help you along, nothing is good for you that causes a moment's delay." A delay that caused them to be caught in the mountains when snow fell could be fatal.

The emigrants had to invent original solutions to many problems. It took everything in their wagons to survive and to adapt to challenges along the trail. They made do with what they had and went on. When shoes wore out, leather was cut from saddle skirts to repair them. Oxen poisoned by alkali were force-fed bacon and vinegar. A broken wagon tongue was shortened or spliced.

At first emigrants were willing to share what they had with others on the trail, but as supplies ran low, many refused, fearing there would not be enough for their own families. A wagon had to be abandoned when a nut fell off the running gear and no replacement had been packed.

Emigrants who tried to foresee all possible needs and pack for them often overloaded their wagons. A wagon could carry only about two thousand pounds of food, clothes, tools, and prized possessions. Many a cherished chest or spinet piano was carried overland at the price of semi-starvation and a weaker team — or the piano had to be abandoned. "We followed the Snake River for several days," wrote one emigrant. "I do not remember when we left it. We made the trip over the Blue Mountains without mishap. All this time the grass was becoming shorter and scarcer. Our oxen were weak for lack of food. Two of them refused to get up one morning and we had to leave them behind with our heaviest wagon. This was a blow indeed."

Dangers, known and unknown, worried the emigrants. Constant hard work drained energies, food supplies ran short, and many went hungry. Rivers washed away cargoes, valuable stock, and even people. Monotony frayed the nerves of many, and arguments were common. "This much I have learned since we started across the continent," wrote Enoch Conyers in 1852, "that if there is anything in this world that will bring to the surface a man's bad traits, it is a trip across the continent with an ox team."

Despite fatigue and chores, merriment and excitement were revived in a fandango around the night campfire. To break the monotony, the crowd gathered to hear a banjo or fiddle player. Grown-ups talked and smoked their pipes while the children played. In the dusty buffalo grass couples danced and whirled in a reel — shouting, singing, stomping, and clapping as they swatted mosquitoes in time to the music. "There is not room on this river for another mosquito," one man glumly remarked of the Platte.

Smudges were set to discourage the mosquitoes, buffalo gnats, and June bugs. Sarah Sutton also joked about the mosquitoes: "As soon as we stopped we were attacked with the most savage, warlike enemy . . . there were heavy battles fought but no lives taken. On our side there was some bloodshed, it is true, but on the enemy's side hundreds were killed and wounded but none missed. They were of the Mosquito tribe and well known the world over." Buffalo or black gnats swarmed around, getting into eyes, noses, and mouths. June bugs crawled over everything, so numerous that they could be picked up by the handful. But the emigrants continued to sing and dance, sure that Oregon would be all the sweeter because of the hardships they endured.

One pioneer girl remembered the two biggest problems of the trail as having to drink warm milk and climbing onto the moving wagon. While a few remembered only the anxieties and hardships of the trail, most recalled the pleasures. As Lydia Waters remarked, "There were many things to laugh about."

Enoch Conyers recorded in his 1852 diary that "Music, singing and merrymaking can be heard in all directions. At one camp they are dancing after the inspiring strains of a violin. At the adjoining camp they are holding a religious meeting. And still at another many families are seated around a large campfire . . . for a special evening chat. Everyone seemingly happy. No fear of being attacked by Indians in a crowd as this." Gradually the camp became quiet except for the sound of the guards on their rounds or the lonesome howl of a prairie wolf.

When the trip was over the emigrants eagerly faced the task of making homes for their families and getting crops planted. There was general rejoicing that the travel had ended. As Caroline Cook expressed it, "We had been on the road one hundred and eight days, and on the tenth day of August, 1853, we reached the

Willamette Valley. Oh, happy day, when we could go to our beds at night with no dread of the call, 'Drive up, boys!' before we were half rested!"

For those who survived it, the Oregon Trail was an avenue to well-being.

THE SOUTHERN ROUTE
By Harlan Hague

The first trail to California did not run alongside the Platte and Humboldt rivers. Nor was it pioneered by Jedediah Smith in 1826, when he reached the coast after a grueling journey through the deserts of Nevada and southern California. The first non-Indian known to have reached the coastal settlements by an overland route was Juan Bautista de Anza who arrived there in 1774, two years before American pioneers of another sort signed their Declaration of Independence. The first emigrant party to enter California overland was led by Anza the following year,

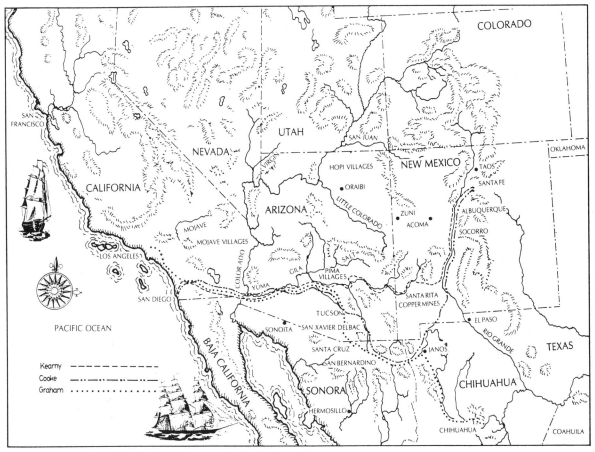

The Southern Route

1775, edging out the Bartleson-Bidwell party of California Trail fame by sixty-two years.

In fact, the first trail-making by other than Indians in what is now the United States was in the present-day Southwest. Long before English settlers began to move cautiously into the timbered fringes of the first English settlement in America, Spanish conquistadores and friars had penetrated deep into the Southwest. Coronado visited the plains of Kansas more than half a century before the founding of Jamestown. Before there was a westward movement in American history there was a northward movement.

Spaniards moved north from Mexico, looking for riches, lost souls, and the Strait of Anián (the fabled water route through the continent) and to thwart assumed foreign designs on Spanish territory. Beginning in the late seventeenth century, settlements were established in New Mexico in the upper Rio Grande Valley in the vicinity of today's Santa Fe and Taos. The trail between these frontier outposts and the interior of Mexico was well-worn by the early part of the eighteenth century.

Westward, missions were established in the frontier regions of Sonora. Father Eusebio Francisco Kino, at his home mission of Dolores, dreamed of an overland route to California. The projected trail was part of an ambitious plan. Kino believed that an overland route from Sonora could be used immediately to succor the Baja California missions operated by his Jesuit brothers. More important, he evisioned Sonora as a hub of Spanish trade in America. It would be possible for the Manila galleon to be provisioned on the Alta California coast directly from northern Sonora, thereby saving the lives of many sailors who died each year en route from The Philippines to Mexico. This would open direct trade between Sonora and the galleon's port. In turn, commerce with the interior of Mexico would increase, trade routes from Sonora to New Mexico would be opened, and eventually trade would be extended overland from there to New France.

Kino died in 1711, before even a fraction of his ambitions had been realized, but he did locate the first segment of the first trail to California. His explorations had taken him northward from Mission Dolores down the Santa Cruz River to its confluence with the Gila, and down the Gila to the Colorado. He had crossed the Colorado, declaring he had located the land route to California. He thereby proved that California was not an island, which was the current belief.

Kino's vision of an overland route to California remained alive, but the task of pioneering it was not taken up again until a half century had passed and a new threat to imperial Spain had materialized. Spain feared that Russia was planning to extend its claim from its foothold in Alaska southward into California. Thus, for reasons of empire and to take the Word to the heathen aborigines, Spain decided to establish a permanent presence in Alta California. Expeditions from Baja California began building a string of missions from San Diego northward along the coast.

It soon became obvious that these

struggling stations could not be provisioned adequately by sea because of the prevailing southerly winds and ocean currents. An overland route from Sonora would have to be opened. The trail finally was established through the joint efforts of soldier and priests — not always a happy partnership on New Spain's frontiers. Father Francisco Garcés, a Franciscan and the resident father at San Xavier del Bac mission near Tucson, was among the last of the great explorer-missionaries who served God and king in New Spain. The soldier was Juan Bautista de Anza, commandant of the Tubac presidio, south of San Xavier. Anza had long sought a commission to search for an overland route to California. Indeed, he had inherited the dream from his father.

The ambitions of Garcés, Anza, viceroy, and king were satisfied in 1774 when a small expedition commanded by Anza reached San Gabriel Mission, the site of present-day Los Angeles, and again in 1776 when a second, larger expedition under Anza established the northernmost Spanish outpost at San Francisco.

The first Anza expedition traveled a known road from Tubac via Sonoita to the Gila near its junction with the Colorado. Beyond the Colorado the expedition was conducted across the dreaded desert by Garcés, who had entered it on a previous journey, and by Sebastián Tarabal, a runaway "mission Indian" who had survived the desert in his flight eastward from San Gabriel. Crossing the San Jacinto Mountains, Anza marched through the Cahuilla Val-

ley and near present-day Riverside en route to San Gabriel. On his return Anza followed the Gila to its confluence with the Santa Cruz, then up that stream to Tubac. The second expedition reversed the order of march — traveling on the westward journey from Tubac down the Santa Cruz and Gila to reach the Colorado, and on the return marching through Sonoita.

Before the new citizens of San Francisco had time to fall on their knees to thank God for their safe arrival, Father Garcés was in the field again, looking for a new trail to California. This time he sought a direct route between the Spanish settlements in New Mexico and California. Kino had announced the advantages of such a link passing through Pimería Alta, Sonora's northern frontier, but Apaches in southeastern Arizona had prevented the opening of the tie in his day. Garcés would bypass the Apaches by exploring a more northerly route.

Garcés had left Anza's second expedition at the Yuma crossing on the westward journey. From there he followed the Colorado River upstream to the vicinity of Needles and thence via the Mojave River and the San Gabriel mission to the California Central Valley. Reaching a point that was a few days' easy travel from Monterey, Garcés turned and crossed the Tehachapi Mountains to follow the Mojave River to the Colorado. He then marched across northern Arizona to reach the mesa villages of the Hopis. Since the Hopis were regularly visited by Spaniards from Zuñi and Santa Fe in New Mexico, Garcés was satisfied that he had proved the feasibility of a direct California-New Mexico route. The trail, however, was not confirmed by authorities or endorsed by use, and it never became a popular travel route.

The tie that Kino had advocated and Garcés had sought was also the object of a search from New Mexico. The very year Garcés was trying to prove his guess, a Spanish expedition from Santa Fe attempted to pioneer a direct trail to Monterey. The leader of the party was Father Atanasio Domínguez, though its chronicler, Father Silvestre Vélez de Escalante, is better known to history.

Moving northward from Santa Fe, the Domínguez-Escalante expedition traveled through western Colorado, then westward to Utah Lake and southward. Their failure to find a pass through the mountains of western Utah — and the cold and snow of an early winter — forced the leaders to abandon their quest. The expedition returned to New Mexico via the Grand Canyon and the Hopi pueblos.

Interest in strengthening the Sonora-California route and locating a New Mexico-California tie remained, but Spain's time had run out. The sun was setting on the Spanish empire in America. During the last quarter of the eighteenth century and the opening years of the nineteenth, Spanish authorities in Mexico City became increasingly preoccupied with a restive Mexican nationalism, and attention was diverted from the northern frontier regions. An uprising by the Yuma Indians closed the road between Sonora and San Gabriel, and other trails in the northern provinces were abandoned.

It was left to the Republic of Mexico to reestablish travel routes and search for better ones. Following the successful revolution in 1821, Mexico was determined to strengthen its hold on its northern frontier. The Colorado road was reopened, though a journey over it remained risky.

Farther north, the long-sought direct link between New Mexico and California was finally opened. While others contributed to the origins of the route, Antonio Armijo, a New Mexico merchant, in 1829-1830 was the first to make the round-trip and to prove the trail's value. He traded New Mexican products for mules. Merchants in New Mexico had not been able to satisfy the insatiable American demand for mules. Now they had found a way to tap a new source in California, where horses and mules were so numerous they were considered pests.

Another expedition, a fur-trapping venture in 1830-1831 led by William Wolfskill, an American, pioneered a path that would largely become the Old Spanish Trail. Proceeding from Santa Fe into southwestern Colorado, the trail skirted Utah's canyon country by running into the central part of that state, thence southwestward to the Colorado River, across the Mojave Desert, and through the mountains at Cajon Pass.

The circuitous Old Spanish Trail was not an easy route, and its course was never marked with wagon tracks. Its virtue was that it lay north of the hostile Indians of southern Arizona. For that reason it was the most heavily traveled route between New Mexico and California — until the gold fever of 1849 made haste paramount and safety secondary. Unfortunately for the argonauts, gold fever, though a communicable malady, was neither contracted nor respected by Apaches.

Armijo and Wolfskill were the first to open a successful route between New Mexico and California, but they were not the first to reach California directly from New Mexico. That distinction belongs to the American Mountain Men who traveled between the two Mexican provinces over various trails in the 1820s. Against Mexican law, which excluded all foreigners from trapping, the Mountain Men ranged throughout New Mexico and Arizona and into the southern portions of Colorado, Utah, and Nevada. Generally, expeditions completed their hunts and returned to New Mexico, where they clandestinely sold their furs.

Some of the westward-ranging trappers, instead of returning to New Mexico, eventually reached the Mexican settlements on the California coast. Richard Campbell probably took a party all the way from New Orleans to California in 1827, narrowly missing the honor of being the first American to enter California by an overland route. Jedediah Smith had reached California the previous year. For want of a chronicler, Campbell's route is not known.

Other California-bound expeditions were better documented. James Ohio Pattie with his father and six others traveled through southwestern New Mexico, where they visited the Santa Rita copper mines, dating from the Spanish era. They trapped down the Gila River and almost perished in the deserts of northern Baja California before reaching San Diego in

1828. Ewing Young took a party, which included Kit Carson, to California the following year. His route ran from Taos through Zuñi to the headwaters of the Salt River in Arizona, down that river to the mouth of the Verde, up the Verde to its source, then westward to the vicinity of the Mojave villages on the Colorado, and finally across the Mojave Desert and the mountains to the coast. He returned to New Mexico in 1831 via Yuma, the Gila River, and the Santa Rita mines.

That same year, Young, newly associated with partners David E. Jackson and David Waldo, sent two expeditions to California. The first, under Jackson, carried seven pack mules of silver coins to buy mules for the American market. The party's trail took them from Santa Fe to the copper mines, San Xavier del Bac mission, Tucson, and the Gila River. The second, a trapping venture under Young's leadership, traveled via Zuñi and the Salt River to the Gila and the Colorado, reaching California in early 1832.

There was another notable expedition in 1841. A party of emigrants under John Rowland and William Workman trekked from New Mexico, probably over the Old Spanish Trail, arriving in Los Angeles in November. If they had left a few days earlier, they, and not the Bartleson-Bidwell party, would be known today as the first expedition of American emigrants to enter California by an overland route. The Bartleson-Bidwell train traveled over the more northerly California Trail and arrived in October.

The Rowland-Workman party

left New Mexico because of feeling against American residents, which had been growing after Texas won its independence in 1836. In 1845 when the United States annexed Texas (which Mexico still claimed) hostility increased and war soon followed. The war in turn would assure that New Mexico and California would be tied even more securely to each other, since the United States coveted both.

During the opening months of the war, two columns of U.S. dragoons marched across the Southwest. The two units were part of the Army of the West, under the command of Brig. Gen. Stephen Watts Kearny, which had taken New Mexico without firing a shot and had witnessed the peaceful establishment of an American civil government. Now, flushed with success, they were bound for California to extend the conquest.

The first expedition, led by Kearny, left Santa Fe in September 1846. Hardly two weeks on the trail, the column met Lt. Kit Carson, who was carrying dispatches to Washington. California had fallen without a blow, Carson told the general, and the war in the West was over. A temporary government had been organized, with Fremont at its head. Since Kearny had been assigned the task of setting up a civil government, this was new cause for haste.

Trimming his unit to an escort force of one hundred men, Kearny quickened the pace. The reduction was unfortunate. Before reaching California the general learned that the Californians had risen, and the conquest was in danger. The army's

route took them by the copper mines, now abandoned because of Apache raids, down the Gila, and across the Colorado at Yuma.

Kearny's small unit became increasingly impatient. Though suffering from fatigue and short rations, the dragoons were eager to reach the coast before the fighting was over. They had been disappointed at Carson's message that the war had ended; this latest news that they might yet enjoy a little "kick-up" with the enemy lifted their spirits considerably.

They were not disappointed. They arrived on the plain of San Pascual, near present-day Escondido, in time to be battered by the Californians. Rescued by sailors and marines sent by Commodore Stockton from San Diego, the column resumed its march and arrived at San Diego in December 1846.

The principal significance of Kearny's trek in the history of pathfinding was that the trail was not a desirable one — at least the portion east of the Pima villages. Kearny's route never became popular.

The march of the Mormon Battalion, the second segment of the Army of the West, under the command of Lt. Col. Philip St. George Cooke, was more successful in a number of ways. General Kearny had hoped to take his wagons through to the Pacific Coast but had abandoned them early. He ordered Cooke to resume the effort to open a wagon road. Cooke and his Mormon volunteers left Santa Fe in October 1846, moving southward along the Rio Grande. The unit left the river near today's Rincon, New Mexico, entered Mexico, and crossed the Continental Divide near Guadalupe Pass.

Now on the western side of the mountains, the battalion marched to the headwaters of the San Pedro River, down that stream, then westward to Tucson. The Mexican garrison had withdrawn but Cooke had little difficulty in convincing the townspeople that the Americans would not harm them.

From Tucson the column marched northward to the Pima villages on the Gila River. From this point the battalion followed Kearny's track to California, arriving in January 1847. Cooke and the Mormon Battalion had taken the first wagons to California over the southern route.

Cooke's trail was shortly improved. At war's end in 1848, a battalion of U.S. dragoons under Maj. Lawrence P. Graham marched from Chihuahua to California. Their route took them through Janos, Guadalupe Pass, the Mexican pre-sidio of Santa Cruz near the headwaters of the Santa Cruz River, and down that stream to Tucson, where the column joined Cooke's road. With the war over, there was no need to avoid Mexican settlements where travelers might find provisions and relaxation.

While Graham's march does not compare in endurance and drama with Kearny's or Cooke's it was important nevertheless. With the completion of Graham's journey the search for a southern route can be considered at an end. Cooke's trail, as modified by Graham's detours through Janos and Santa Cruz, would become the most heavily traveled variation of the southern route.

Cooke's wagon road, as it was most commonly called, was shortly put to the test. Fantastic rumors of a gold discovery in California circulated in the United States during the fall of 1848. When the discovery was confirmed by President Polk in Decem-

Courtesy Kennedy Galleries, New York　　　　　　*Painting by Frederick Remington*

"The Map in the Sand"

ber, would-be millionaires immediately began planning overland journeys, moving toward St. Louis to await spring rains and mild weather. Others booked passage around the Horn. The most impatient argonauts that winter of 1848-1849, however, took the fastest sea passage they could find to south Texas; from there they planned forced marches over the southern route for El Dorado. They were responding to propaganda that enterprising Texans had sent to eastern newspapers. The reports assured prospective travelers that they would find ample grass and water along good roads all the way from the Gulf Coast to the diggings in California — which, furthermore, they would reach in only forty-five days.

As the gold seekers converged at the eastern terminals of the various approaches to the southern route, a new era began. Before considering that story we should reflect on an important aspect of the early development of the route that has not been mentioned: the role of Indians in exploration and trail making. Readers of western history and fiction are well aware that hostile Indians sometimes hindered exploration. It is less well-known that Indians often contributed significantly.

The evidence of assistance in the story of the southern route cannot be ignored. Father Garcés, certainly one of the greatest explorers in all of American history, was enormously successful because of his ability to persuade local Indians to lead him over trails that they knew. An Indian led the first Anza expedition across the Colorado Desert. Armijo had Indian guides, probably all the way to

California. The Patties almost surely would have left their bones in the deserts of Baja California without their Indian guides. Kearny and Cooke had Indian guides — Apaches, in fact. Mojaves sold food to a starving Ewing Young expedition. Crossing the Colorado River would have been extremely hazardous for Spaniards, Mexicans, and Americans alike had the Yumas not volunteered assistance. Had the Yumas chosen to oppose the intruders, the crossing in most cases would have been impossible.

The Pimas best illustrate the point. Spaniards, Mexicans, and Americans traveling to California followed many branches that collectively comprised the southern route, but they almost invariably visited the Pima villages on the Gila River. Why? Because the friendly Pimas, who practiced extensive irrigation successfully, could always be counted on to have ample food stocks to provision an expedition of any size. Without this convenient midway supply point, exploration and travel in the Southwest could have been considerably more difficult.

With the coming of great numbers of Americans, beginning in 1849, the often-amiable relations between Indians and transients largely came to an end. Some Indian peoples, those who had always been malleable, continued to be so. Others, including many who had tolerated, and in some cases even invited, the messengers of alien religions and cultures, began to resist with passion. The Apaches had welcomed American armies as allies against the hated Mexicans. They had a complete change of heart when the U.S. government assigned those same armies to protect the Mexicans, who had become American citizens when the Treaty of Guadalupe Hidalgo ended the Mexican War.

California-bound argonauts, greenhorns typically, found the land as hostile as the Indians. After leaving the comforts of the Texas coastal towns, travelers in early 1849 and thereafter moved without difficulty through the coastal plain, but that was soon crossed. Those who chose San Antonio as their jumping-off place for El Paso followed what was charitably called the Lower Road, established by the U.S. Army in the spring of 1849. It was inhospitable land, largely unpopulated except for Comanches. Arriving in the Mexican oasis of El Paso del Norte, today's Ciudad Juárez, with its vineyards, orchards, and cultivated fields, the Texas gold-rushers met other Americans who had reached New Mexico over the Santa Fe Trail.

After tasting the delights of El Paso, resting and reprovisioning, the gold seekers — or "pilgrims" as they sometimes called themselves — left the Rio Grande and crossed the desert to reach Janos. Other Americans reached Janos after fording the Rio Grande at various points between the coast and the Big Bend country, passing through Monterrey, Chihuahua, and other Mexican cities.

The old Spanish presidio-pueblo of Janos was still a town under siege when the forty-niners saw it. Apaches often visited the settlement, alternately trading and raiding, almost at will. In any event, most Americans did not linger here. At Janos they were only a short march

from the Continental Divide at Guadalupe Pass. Once on the western slope of the mountains, so thought the Argonauts, they would be on the downhill part of their journey, and their impatience grew.

Leaving Janos they soon hit Cooke's wagon road and fell in with other California-bound Americans who had followed Cooke's route all the way from Santa Fe. Spirits rose as they left the arid and treeless plain to enter the foothills of the mountains, where they found ample water, oak groves, and — sweet relief for man and beast — plenty of grass and game.

Now in the heart of Apachería, the argonauts marveled that they had so little trouble with Indians. Apache bands occasionally exchanged shots with the Americans and stole horses and mules from careless parties, but on the whole they tolerated the intruders and even visited and traded with them in their camps. It was the Mexicans they hated, the Apaches said, and they urged the Americans to join with them against their enemy.

While Cooke's trail, like other early western tracks, had been dignified with the title of "road," its transit of the mountains was anything but a highway. Wagons crossed the divide only with the greatest difficulty.

A day or two beyond the pass the argonauts' hard labor was rewarded at the former San Bernardino Ranch, once a prosperous enterprise in a well-watered valley, but now in ruins, abandoned to Apache raiders. Its cattle were still there, however, and were hunted like wild animals to refresh travelers and replenish depleted stores.

Leaving San Bernardino the gold seekers headed through brushy country to the village of Santa Cruz and down the Santa Cruz River to Tucson. Tucson was the last Mexican outpost on the trail to California. Though under constant threat of Apache attack, it provided a respite before tackling the real deserts ahead. Other Americans reached Tucson over the Apache Pass route pioneered in 1849 by Col. John C. Hays.

Hays, hero of the Texas revolution and the Mexican War, Texas Ranger, and recently appointed Indian agent to the Apaches, had been persuaded by a large number of fearful argonauts at El Paso to escort them through Apache country to Tucson. Hays led the party northward along the Rio Grande, planning to strike Cooke's wagon road — a map of which he carried. In the vicinity of today's Las Cruces, the expedition and its eight wagons crossed the Rio Grande and headed due west. Passing the site of Lordsburg and crossing the mountains at Apache Pass, Hays led the expedition into Tucson, opening a wagon road that was more than one hundred miles shorter than Cooke's route.

Leaving Tucson behind, most travelers found the hundred-mile trek to the Gila River as dry and sterile as they had been warned. At the end of the jornada, the hospitable Pimas were always ready to trade. And here the argonauts occasionally were joined by others who had followed Kearny's trail from the Rio Grande, though that was never a heavily traveled route. From the Pima villages the Americans plodded along the Gila, their path marked by discarded, pre-

viously valued belongings and dead and dying stock.

Yuma Indians helped travelers cross the Colorado at its confluence with the Gila. In 1849 the U.S. Army established Ft. Calhoun, the predecessor of Ft. Yuma, and after that the army's ferry assisted the crossing. On the farther side the forty-niners once again stood on American soil. The dreaded Colorado Desert was their final test, and it took its toll in possessions and animals.

Few lingered in the coastal settlements at the end of the trail. More fearful now than ever that the gold would be gone, they hurried northward to the mines in the foothills of the Sierra Nevada, mingling there with the tens of thousands who had arrived in California over other trails. Estimates of the southern route's contribution to this epic migration are difficult to verify, but it seems that approximately sixty thousand people passed over the route during the gold rush.

Most argonauts, whatever their intention might have been when they arrived, stayed in California. They either had not struck it rich and could not afford to leave, or they liked what they found in the Golden State — a gentle land with a moderate climate, fertile soil, and a future. But they were Americans after all, and they wanted to link their new province with the motherland. The new Californians began early in the 1850s to demand permanent ties with the East, arguing first for a regular mail service and later for the transport of freight and passengers.

The best solution seemed to be a railroad. Anticipating the possibility

Harper's Weekly, 1866
Butterfield's Overland Mail Coach starting out from Atchison, Kansas

of a line across the Southwest, the U.S. government, through the Gadsden Purchase, acquired from Mexico the land between the Gila River and the present international boundary that would be needed for right-of-way. The purchase included the additional benefit of placing most of the variations of the southern route on U.S. soil.

There would be no transcontinental railroad built in the stormy 1850s. With friction increasing between North and South, Congress could not agree on an eastern terminus. An overland stage line was then authorized, and bids were invited. In September 1857 the postmaster general, a proslavery Tennesseean, awarded the contract (and a subsidy of $600 thousand annually for semiweekly service) to Butterfield and Company, which had agreed to the route through the Southwest prescribed by the postmaster general. The western terminus was San Francisco, and the eastern was St. Louis, which had rail connections with the largest cities in the East.

Before the Butterfield line entered the field, other companies — the San Antonio-San Diego Stage Line and the Kansas and Stockton Express — provided service of sorts, but they were soon eclipsed by the better organized and capitalized Overland Mail. In spite of myriad problems and considerable opposition to the southward-swinging "oxbow" route, Butterfield succeeded in delivering mail and bone-rattled passengers from terminus to terminus — 2,800 miles — usually safely and in less than the required twenty-five days.

It was all for nothing. The Butterfield Overland Mail was doomed from the start. The simmering hostility between North and South that had given birth to the unlikely oxbow route soon boiled over and terminated it. The South's secession and consequent control over the eastern portion of the route was the final blow in the declining fortunes of the line. Financial problems had plagued the operation. In 1860 Russell, Majors and Waddell had launched the Pony Express over the central route in an effort to win congressional support for a mail subsidy, thereby threatening Butterfield's contract. Finally, in early 1861, an incident between troops and Cochise's people at Apache Pass shattered the friendly relations with Apaches that had permitted Butterfield coaches to roll largely unmolested through Indian country.

In March 1861, with civil war now a certainty, Congress altered Butterfield's contract, requiring that operations be shifted to a central route. That same month the firm formally terminated service over the southern route and began the move northward.

The Civil War had a like effect on long-haul freight. The origins of commercial freighters in the Southwest were similar to those of stagecoaches. Californians in the mid-1850s had called for the construction of transcontinental wagon roads to make the

overland crossing easier for emigrants and freighters. The growing population of the Southwest seconded the call. In response, Congress authorized the building of a road between El Paso (Franklin) and Yuma, the ends of the road tying into existing roads.

By June 1858 the road was completed. It ran along the Rio Grande from El Paso to Mesilla, then westward through El Piloncilo Pass at the New Mexico-Arizona boundary to the San Pedro River. Turning northward the road followed the San Pedro to the mouth of the Arivaypa, a tributary stream, thence westward across the Santa Catarina Mountains to the Gila River and the Pima villages. From there the route was Cooke's and Kearny's.

Initially, commercial freighting was engaged primarily in servicing the mines in the Southwest. Following the opening of mines in 1857 near Tubac, for example, supplies and machinery, including six-thousand-

Courtesy Kennedy Galleries, New York   *Painting by Henry C. Pratt*

View of the Maricopa Mountains, Rio Gila, Arizona, with Maricopa Indian Village.

pound boilers, were brought from Port Lavaca, Texas. Other wagon trains came from Missouri and California. Yuma early became important to freighting, as shallow-draft steamers plied the mouth of the Colorado, ferrying goods between Yuma and the ships which could not enter the river.

Long-haul freighting had hardly been well established when the Civil War interrupted the traffic. At least one unfortunate Arizona-bound wagon train was seized on the road west of San Antonio by Texans at the outbreak of the war. Now both Union and Confederate troops were seen on the southern route. In the early months of the war Confederate forces seized the southern regions of New Mexico and Arizona. The conquered country was organized as the Confederate Territory of Arizona, its northern boundary at the thirty-fourth parallel. This gave the Confederate States of America access to western mines and a corridor to California, whose gold, food, and unblockaded ports could be of inestimable value to the South.

From the Confederate capital at Mesilla, on the banks of the Rio Grande, expeditions were sent westward to strengthen the territory. Col. John Robert Baylor dispatched a small force to reopen the Apache Pass road between Mesilla and Tucson, but without success. Later, in December 1861, Confederate Gen. Henry Hopkins Sibley sent a unit of two hundred men, the Arizona Volunteers, to Tucson. They were welcomed, both as a symbol of Confederate power and for the protection they would provide against Indians,

but their residence was short. They withdrew when they heard that a sizable Union force was approaching from the west.

This was the California Column of 2,350 volunteers under Col. James H. Carleton, which in June 1862 encamped in Tucson. Firmly entrenched there, Carleton sent probes eastward. One of these expeditions was forced to fight a pitched battle at Apache Pass — not with Confederates but with the combined forces of two Apache chieftains, Cochise and Mangas Coloradas. The day was saved for the troops by the new ordnance they carried: breech-loading rifles and howitzers that fired exploding shells. In July 1862 Carleton led the remainder of the California Column over the Apache Pass route to the Rio Grande.

By that time the Confederate Territory of Arizona had vanished. After initial successes against Union forces, General Sibley, learning that Union reinforcements were on the Santa Fe Trail and that the California Column was approaching from the west, bowed to the inevitable. He withdrew his forces to the safety of Texas, and Col. Baylor and the Confederate military government followed. Carleton, now a brigadier general, was appointed commander of the Department of New Mexico. His most urgent task was to control hostile Indians in Arizona and New Mexico.

Relative peace returned to the Southwest. Travel routes disrupted by the Confederate occupation were soon reopened. Freighting increased, particularly to army posts and new mining operations, while war still raged in the East. The roads through

Texas remained closed, but goods moved freely over the Santa Fe Trail to New Mexico. Yuma received merchandise from California and by steamer from ships at the head of the gulf. Freight wagons also reached Tucson from Sonora. These last were mostly transshipments of goods previously landed at Guaymas. Shipments over the entire length of the southern route — from Missouri to California, for example — were rare both before and during the war. Most freighting was either completely within the region or between the region and a point outside the Southwest.

At war's end traffic over the southern route quickened. Texans trailed cattle westward to stock ranches in New Mexico and Arizona and to supply army posts and reservation Indians. Stagecoach service resumed in 1869 and expanded as new mines and towns appeared.

This increased use of the southern route heralded its eventual decline. As settlers took up the land, Indian resistance grew, and the army built more forts. The need for improved communication between the posts, especially to ensure a quicker response to news of Indian attacks, resulted in the construction of telegraph lines. A line from San Diego to Tucson was completed in 1873. Additional lines soon tied all Arizona forts together. In 1877 a line from Santa Fe down the Rio Grande to Mesilla, then westward along the Apache Pass route, completed a transcontinental link — at Santa Fe it tied into the end of the line from St. Louis. Communication along the southern route now was instantaneous.

A transcontinental railroad through the Southwest was not long in coming. The Central Pacific, completed in 1869, had not satisfied the needs of southern California, and the growing population of the Southwest called for rail service. Congress authorized two railroads through the region, along the thirty-second and thirty-fifth parallels, and railroad builders began eyeing the Southwest.

Anxious to preserve their monopoly, the avaricious builders of the first transcontinental railroad moved to forestall a competitor entering California over either of the projected routes. The Big Four — Leland Stanford, Mark Hopkins, Collis P. Huntington, and Charles Crocker — ran the tracks of their California-chartered Southern Pacific Railroad from Los Angeles to Needles, the obvious entry point for the northern line, and to the southern entry point at Yuma, where the first SP train arrived in 1877.

After bribing both the Arizona governor and the legislature to ensure a generous charter, the SP began laying track eastward from Yuma, roughly paralleling Cooke's wagon road alongside the Gila, then turning southward to reach Tucson in 1880. The jubilant town fathers announced the opening of rail service to a long list of dignitaries, including the president of the United States, governors, mayors, congressmen, and the pope.

From Tucson SP track ran eastward through today's Benson and Lordsburg to Deming, where it connected in 1881 with the Atchison, Topeka and Santa Fe Railroad that extended all the way from the Mississippi River. The first transcontinental rail link across the Southwest had been completed.

Neither SP nor AT&SF was finished. The SP continued laying track eastward through El Paso, and by 1882 it had reached the Mississippi River by two routes — by its own line via San Antonio and Houston and by a connection at Sierra Blanca, east of El Paso, with the Texas and Pacific Railroad that ran through Fort Worth. The following year AT&SF completed another transcontinental line when it finished laying track from Albuquerque along the thirty-fifth parallel route to the SP railhead at Needles.

With two rail lines spanning the Southwest, the long haul by wagon over the southern route to California ended. The trails that comprised the route had served their purpose. Some returned to nature. Sagebrush and mesquite invaded the roadways, and wind and water sculpted and shaped the beds until man's handiwork was but a trace on the land. The best of the roads, those that continued to improve the years as travelers found short-cuts and easier grades, changed hardly at all, except that they were straightened, machine-graded, ditched, paved, striped, lighted, and assigned state and interstate highway numbers. The southern route today is still a popular pathway to golden California.

THE MORMON TRAIL

By S. George Ellsworth

Come, come, ye Saints, no toil nor labor fear,
But with joy, wend your way.
Though hard to you this journey may appear,
Grace shall be as your day.
'Tis better far for us to strive
Our useless cares from us to drive;
Do this, and joy your hearts will swell—
All is well! all is well!

Why should we mourn or think our lot is hard?
'Tis not so; all is right.
Why should we think to earn a great reward,
If we now shun the fight?
Gird up your loins; fresh courage take;
Our God will never us forsake;
And soon we'll have this tale to tell—
All is well! all is well!

These lines, penned by William Clayton on the Mormon Trail, April 13, 1846, some 60 days and 110 miles out of Nauvoo, Illinois, came to be an inspiration to fellow-exiled Mormons and thereafter to Mormon and non-Mormon alike — people who find in them something of the universal in man's journey through life. That such should be associated with the Mormon Trail points up the difference between the Mormon experience and that of other westering Americans.

As with other overlanders, the Mormons were both running away from something and toward new opportunities. The Mormons were fleeing the wrath of their Illinois neighbors, and religious persecution in general, in a forced exodus under their own Moses, Brigham Young.

However much the Mormon Trail experience had in common with others, it was unique in several respects. The Mormons had experienced mass migrations before and had built communities only to leave them. It was a shepherded migration from beginning to end — once it got going. All were of one religious faith, united in purpose and common desire, all having shared the common experiences of conversion, of pulling up roots for their religion's sake, leaving loved ones and friends, and emigrating. The overland experience further bonded together this people who would establish hundreds of permanent settlements in the Mountain West and make it Mormon Country. That they shared these experiences and were always among friends, that the companies were well organized and cared for, no doubt made it much easier for them to pass through the traumatic experience of building new homes in wastelands.

The Mormons might never have made their mark in western American history had it not been for their doctrine of the gathering of Israel (they counted themselves spiritual if not literal children of ancient Israel) that impelled them to live as one community. They had gathered about Kirtland, Ohio, and the western borders of Missouri, then in Nauvoo, Illinois. But their sojourn in these places was short-lived, even though they built some of their own cities. Conflicts with their neighbors plagued every moment, it seemed. Events at Nauvoo culminated June 27, 1844, when the Mormon Prophet Joseph Smith and his brother Hyrum were killed in the county jail in Carthage by a mob. Tempers soon cooled, but by the fall of 1845 open hostilities broke out again, and the Mormons determined to leave in the spring "as soon as water runs or grass is green."

To scatter would deny the principle of gathering. To hold thousands of people together under camp conditions would be next to impossible. There was scattering, some never to gather again. But the history-making people remained together, placing their faith and trust in Brigham Young and the Twelve Apostles who, acting upon instructions from Joseph Smith, now looked to the West.

We'll find the place which God for us prepared,
Far away in the West,
Where none shall come to hurt or make afraid;
There the Saints will be blessed.
We'll make the air with music ring,
Shout praises to our God and King;
Above the rest these words we'll tell—
All is well! all is well!

Many places of refuge were considered. Guiding principles dictated that they choose a place no one else wanted, where they would be the first

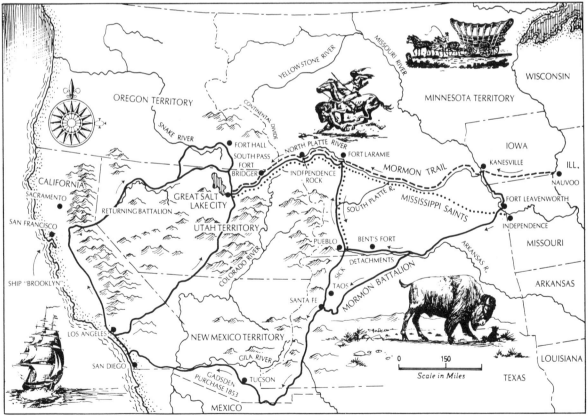

The Mormon Trails

settlers, and where they would have room to expand — conditions they had not known before. While the exact destination was not decided until they got there, it was generally held that they would go "across the Rocky Mountains."

During the fall and winter of 1845-46, Nauvoo was turned into a blacksmith shop. Wagons were built, harnesses made, wagon covers and tents prepared, essential tools and pieces of equipment made or purchased. The Mormons were caught in the price squeeze between supply and demand. The sale of their goods and properties moved slowly, even at ridiculous prices. Unlike the ancient Israelites, these people left behind most of their possessions rather than taking with them the spoils of Egypt.

But the enemy could not wait until spring. Threats and hostile demonstrations continued into the winter. Brigham Young decided that the only way to avoid a rupture was to start at once, in midwinter. The first wagons were ferried across the Mississippi River on Wednesday, February 4, 1846. Others soon followed, landing at Montrose and then making the short haul to Sugar Creek, where these families and subsequent arrivals waited throughout the month of February. The exodus had begun. A steady stream of evacuees followed through the spring and summer.

Orson Pratt, apostle-diarist of the trek, left Nauvoo with his family on February 14. The next day Brigham Young, Willard Richards, and George A. Smith and their families crossed. These beginnings had a tendency to cool enemy hotheads, giving those in Nauvoo a better opportunity to dispose of property, settle business, and otherwise prepare to start. Flatboats were obtained, also some old flat-bottomed barges, and a number of skiffs were kept busy day and night. By the end of February between four and five hundred wagons were at Sugar Creek.

The early evacuee families were ill prepared to live in a winter camp. Besides being exposed to below-freezing temperatures, deep snows, and "cold northwest winds," most of the people left Nauvoo without sufficient provisions to last a fortnight. Those who had supplies were obliged to share with the less fortunate. Many of those chosen to leave early had to leave their families behind, prepare the way ahead, and then return for their families. The planned movement of the camp was delayed by the weather, caring for the poor, frequent trips back to Nauvoo, and the search for needed animals and forage. Men scoured the country for a hundred miles around for horses and cattle. There was no grass; corn had to be purchased to feed the stock.

The food problem was compounded by the trials of camping out in the dead of winter, when temperatures remained below freezing for days. Ice packs on the river impeded the ferries; then the river froze over and wagons crossed on the ice. There were births and deaths, attested to in family records and in the cemetery at Nauvoo.

The historic Mormon Trail developed in two stages: (1) from Sugar Creek across Iowa to Council Bluffs in the winter and spring of 1846, and (2) from Winter Quarters near Council Bluffs to the Rocky Mountains in the summer of 1847. Brigham Young gave initial organization to the people at the Sugar Creek rendezvous. Refinements in the organization of traveling companies were made thereafter from time to time. On March 1 the first wagons set out from Sugar Creek to mark a trail across southern Iowa. The Mormon Trail was begun.

Immediate problems faced the leadership and wagon-bound followers. In finding their way across Iowa they must take advantage of territorial roads, near enough to settlements to make it convenient to purchase food for themselves and corn for their stock (until grass grew) and where they might pick up work in exchange for necessities. Yet they must not be close enough to settlements to cause trouble. Advance parties were instructed to "prepare roads, look out camp grounds, dig wells, when necessary, and ascertain where hay and corn could be purchased for the camp."

The line of march from Sugar Creek was northwestward on a territorial road to Farmington and Bonaparte, where they forded Des Moines River, thence westward. Trails were made through the timbered and generally level countryside, cut by many streams that drained into the Mississippi River. Orson Pratt's daily readings of his thermometer and weather notes showed that sunrise temperatures were always below freezing, and often there was a white blanket of snow covering the muddy wagon wheel traces. There were not enough roads to handle the hundreds of wagons soon on the prairie.

The Mormon migration came to be known for its preparedness, orderliness, discipline, safety, and effective organization, but that was later. The diaries written in those cold wagons during February and March yield a picture of confusion, disorder, and severe hardships. Horse-drawn carriages and heavy wagons drawn by oxen sometimes competed for the road. Delays in camp were frequent. There was a constant movement back and forth between camp and Nauvoo: men visiting their families and concluding business in Nauvoo, churchmen taking care of church business with those left behind to dispose of church properties, men returning to pick up a stove or a table or some other convenience left in their abandoned homes. The "different divisions were so far separated from each other by storms, bad roads and other circumstances, that it was impossible to effect anything like a perfect organization for the first few weeks," wrote George Q. Cannon. Sometimes the advance party, often led by Orson Pratt, was forty-five miles ahead of Brigham Young's group.

Fifty-five miles from Nauvoo, on March 7, Brigham Young's company reached Richardson's Point, a timbered place about a mile northwest of present Lebanon. President Young held a council of the leading churchmen present, then on March 27 issued instructions on a better organization for the moving camps. Able and proven men were named captains of hundreds, of fifties, and of tens. Whether these groups were of wagons or of families is not certain; it varied from one to the other in later years. Brigham Young, whose official position of leadership was as president of the Quorum of Twelve Apostles, was now elected president of the whole Camp of Israel. William Clayton was appointed clerk of the whole company, and other men were appointed clerks to each fifty. A contracting commissary was named to make purchases for each fifty, and a distributing commissary was similarly named for each fifty to distribute goods as needed. This led to a more systematic method of traveling, avoided having one Mormon bid against another for corn and hay, and set a pattern of organization that was to characterize Mormon emigrating companies for the next twenty years.

The trek across Iowa was the most difficult part of the westward movement on the Mormon Trail. Eastern and central Iowa is made up of flat prairie, with deep fertile soil, and scattered woods along the banks of streams. The land in the south is hilly and has fewer trees. While Iowa had been partly settled and there were some roads or wagon traces, the Mormons had to build or repair most of their own roads and bridges. The lands were then being surveyed, and Iowa's initial land rush was underway. The trail led through partly occupied lands and open prairie. At first there was mutual fear between Iowa settlers and Mormons, but Iowa farmers soon found they could sell surplus corn and hay, trade goods for labor, or hire Mormons to split rails, fence fields, build bridges, dig wells, or make other improvements on the new farms.

Notwithstanding the better organization, it would be difficult to exaggerate the hardships of those first weeks on the trail. Sunrise temperatures were almost invariably below freezing until after April 15. Daytime temperatures rose enough to thaw the ground, and the heavily laden wagons became half-sunk in quagmire. Snowstorms continued through March. Rainstorms, sometimes lasting for days, pelted the wagon-dwellers much of April and May. Near Richardson's Point there was "one mud hole, six miles long." Hosea Stout wrote on April 29, "This was an uncommonly wet rainy, muddy, miry disagreeable day. Very wet night last night the ground flooded in water."

In time the men who had been sent ahead to find roads and routes were released to return to Nauvoo for their families, while the main party pressed westward. Brigham Young frequently expressed his intention to cross the Rocky Mountains that summer.

Young's group remained at Richardson's Point eleven days, until the 19th. An encampment was established here, as in several subsequent places, where some facilities were built and improvements made for the benefit of those who followed. From Richardson's Point the trail advanced southward toward the Missouri border. The party reached the Chariton River on March 21, where it remained ten days and refined some points of camp organization.

As Hosea Stout's group moved toward the Chariton they picked up part of the "old Mormon trail," which, he recalled, "we made when I in company with 27 others fled from Far West Mo . . . in 1838 when the saints were expelled from that state." Encampments were formed at the Chariton and the Locust rivers. Near the Iowa-Missouri border the Mormon Trail opened up northwestward. It was now in hilly country with fewer trees. After six days of travel, Young's people rested at Pleasant Point for nearly two weeks, hoping the rains would cease. The season was changing, and spring rains brought swollen streams requiring bridges to be built and muddy roads to be endured. By mid-April grass started to appear, and prospects seemed better, not only for the stock but for the emigrants.

After four days of travel, on April 24, the advance company reached an excellent site for a settlement, which they named Garden Grove. Two weeks before, Brigham Young had sent Orson Pratt and his scouts up the Grand River to select such a farming site so that

> while we were weather and water-bound we could clear and fence one hundred acres, and break them up, and leave such families as were not prepared to proceed farther at present, and when they have raised a crop, let them leave it, and pass on to the Missouri river, where they can winter their stock without grain, then when a company comes on from Nauvoo they will have a resting place, and they can feed from that place to do them through to the Missouri river, and so continue on for years to come until the land is brought into market.

Garden Grove was built for those who would follow. Men were assigned to split rails, make fences, and build houses and bridges. Others

cleared land, plowed, and planted. Some of the poor in the advance companies were assigned land according to their needs.

President Young remained at Garden Grove until May 13. Five days later and forty-five miles northwest, his company reached the middle fork of the Grand River. Here the scouts had formed a site for another farm and way station, which they named Mount Pisgah. The party remained here long enough to build another settlement and establish an additional farm.

On June 2 Brigham Young's company again took to the trail. They were now in Pottawattamie Indian country. The president had obtained official approval from the governor of Iowa Territory to travel and camp on public lands. He now secured approval of the chief of the Pottawattamies to pass through, to make necessary improvements, and to take what game was necessary.

Travel was now much easier. Western Iowa is more elevated and is made up of rolling prairie land. Though new roads had to be broken, the journey was made with comparative ease in favorable weather. Some streams had to be bridged, but this did not cause serious delays. While there were no settlements with which to trade, there were no fences or fields to avoid.

Twelve days from Mount Pisgah, on June 14, Brigham Young and his company camped on the east bank of the Missouri River not far from Council Bluffs. Men set to work at once to build a ferryboat to carry wagons across the river. On the 22nd about five hundred wagons arrived at the Missouri and halted. The first of the Mormon caravans had reached the Missouri River and established the Mormon Trail across Iowa.

That spring, summer, and fall of 1846 witnessed the passage of the Nauvoo exiles — thousands of Mormon families, in hundreds of wagons, accompanied by thousands of head of cattle, horses, and mules, and immense flocks of sheep. On June 28, as Wilford Woodruff left Mount Pisgah, he took in the sight: "I stopped my carriage on the top of a hill in the midst of a rolling prairie where I had an extended view of all about me. I beheld the Saints coming in all directions from hills and dales, groves and prairies with their wagons, flocks, and herds, by the thousands. It looked like the movement of a nation." John Taylor, heading east that summer, estimated that he saw fifteen thousand Saints on the Iowa roads, in three thousand wagons, with thirty thousand head of cattle, great numbers of horses, mules, and oxen, besides "an immense number of sheep." He found the people at Nauvoo leaving as fast as they could. During the week of May 20, four hundred teams crossed the river at three points, about 1,350 souls. The flight continued until September 17, when the anti-Mormons entered Nauvoo and forcibly expelled the lingering poor. Brigham Young sent teams and wagons back to Sugar Creek, and in September and October the refugees were packed up and brought west on the Mormon Trail. The last arrived at the east bank of the Missouri River on November 27.

It had taken the advanced groups three and a half months to go about three hundred miles. From March 1, when the expedition got under way, all or parts of forty days were used in travel. During the first weeks they may have made eight miles a day, but toward the middle and latter parts of the journey they averaged thirteen miles a day. Two-thirds of their 120 days were spent in the encampments at Sugar Creek, Richardson's Point, Chariton River, Pleasant Point, Garden Grove, and Mount Pisgah.

To trace the Mormon Trail across Iowa today one would connect the following communities: Montrose on the Mississippi River, northwest to Farmington and Bonaparte, westward to the Fox River by way of Lebanon to Bloomfield, thence southwest to Genoa near the line, thence northwest to Garden Grove, Leslie, and Murray. Westward and just north of Talmage is the site of Mount Pisgah. From there the trail moved in arcs to Orient, westward south of Bridgewater and on to Lyman and Lewis on the East Nishnabotna River, southwestward to Macedonia on the Nishnabotna, thence west to Council Bluffs. At a later date modifications were made, mainly in a more direct route: from Bloomfield or Drakesville northwestward to near Chariton, thence westward to Leslie, bypassing Garden Grove.

All the while, Brigham Young thought only in terms of passing the mountains in 1846. Crossing Iowa had taken longer than expected and the poor still in Nauvoo needed care, so alternatives surfaced occasionally in council meetings. But the die was cast on June 30 when Army Capt. James Allen appeared at Council Bluffs with an appeal from the United States government for a battalion of from four to five hundred Mormon soldiers to fight in the just-declared war on Mexico. Though the irony of the government's request of its own exiles did not escape the Mormons, the general council of the church voted unanimously to comply. During the next three weeks 549 officers and men were recruited from the camps, and on July 20 the Mormon Battalion marched off to Fort Leavenworth to be inducted. All these factors led Brigham Young to delay the westward expedition that year. The Camp of Israel went into winter quarters.

The Pottawattamie Indians held the lands to the east and the Omaha Indians the lands to the west of the Missouri River. The Mormons established relations with both and obtained permission to remain on their lands temporarily. Winter Quarters were established about six miles north of the new Mormon ferry, on the west bank of the river, in what became the north Omaha suburb of Florence. Ultimately about forty temporary settlements were raised in western Iowa.

At Winter Quarters streets were laid out and lots surveyed. Log cabins and sod houses were erected and dugouts were cut in the banks. Farms and ranches were established on the prairie. That winter between three and four thousand Saints crowded together into several hundred dwellings to try to keep body and soul together on the "Misery Bottoms." Winter Quarters, the lowest point in Mormon fortunes, always had special meanings for those who sang the song of the Mormon Trail:

And should we die before our journey's through,
Happy day! all is well!
We then are free from toil and sorrow, too;
With the just we shall dwell!
But if our lives are spared again
To see the Saints their rest obtain,
O how we'll make this chorus swell—
All is well! all is well!

More than six hundred graves in the cemetery at Winter Quarters tell the grim story of the first winters there. The hardships only heightened Brigham Young's determination to find a refuge for his people during the summer of 1847.

What did the Mormons know about the West in 1846-47? They had lived on the western edge of frontier settlement since 1831. Their newspapers carried articles about Oregon, California, and Texas, and they had Hastings' guide and Fremont's reports. They had good general ideas about the West and some good specific information, too. Still they learned all they could before they leaped. At Winter Quarters they asked visitor Father Pierre-Jean De Smet "a thousand questions." They studied together the reports of John C. Fremont.

Two groups were planned for the 1847 movement: A small exploring party would leave early to find that promised valley; a second party, taking nearly half the population of Winter Quarters, would follow later, prepared to settle.

The second leg of the Mormon Trail began April 5, 1847, when the first wagons moved west out of Winter Quarters to form the nucleus of the exploring Pioneer Company. Others soon followed. By the 15th all had ferried the Elkhorn River, with some difficulty, and were at a rendezvous on the north side of the Platte

River (at the southern outskirts of present Fremont). On Friday, April 16, the company was given its final organization. Stephen Markham and Albert P. Rockwood were elected captains of hundreds, or the two major divisions. Five captains of fifties were then elected, and fourteen captains of tens.

Upon this quasi-Israelite foundation was laid a quasi-military organization, with Brigham Young commanding the whole. Altogether there were 149 persons in the company, including three blacks, three women (wives of Brigham Young, Heber C. Kimball, and Lorenzo Young), and two children. That afternoon the Pioneer Company moved three miles and went into camp. After another day's travel the company rested on Sunday, a custom generally observed by this and subsequent Mormon overland parties. The organization growing out of the Iowa trek was refined during the experience of this Pioneer Company. On Sunday, April 18, Brigham Young laid out the daily routine of the camp:

At five o'clock in the morning the bugle is to be sounded as a signal for every man to arise and attend prayers before he leaves his wagon. Then the people will engage in cooking, eating, feeding teams, etc., until seven o'clock, at which time the train is to move at the sound of the bugle. Each teamster is to keep beside his team with loaded gun in hand or within easy reach, while the extra men, observing the same rule regarding their weapons, are to walk by the side of the particular wagons to which they

belong; and no man may leave his post without the permission of his officers. In case of an attack or any hostile demonstration by Indians, the wagons will travel in double file — the order of encampment to be in a circle, with the mouth of each wagon to the outside and the horses and cattle tied inside the circle. At half past eight each evening the bugles are to be sounded again, upon which signal all will hold prayers in their wagons, and be retired to rest by nine o'clock.

Other rules included a noon rest for the animals. (The travelers were to have their dinner precooked so as to dispose of the necessity of cooking at noon.) At night the wagons were drawn into a circle, and the animals grazed inside it where possible. All persons were to start together and keep together. A guard at the rear saw that nothing was left behind. Of course, even with strict discipline the realization of this ideal fell short at times. When stock had to be staked out at night for feed, extra guards were posted.

The route west to the Rocky Mountains and on to the Pacific Coast was well defined by 1847. However, the Mormon leadership depended upon its own explorations in seeking a route and writing a guide. The leaders chose to remain on the north side of the Platte and North Platte rivers, although they knew they could cross the river and be on the well-established Oregon Trail. They preferred to keep the river between themselves and others and avoid trouble. Making a trail did not prove difficult, and over some terrain they no doubt followed traces left by Indians and Mountain Men. While this route separated them from emigrants on the Oregon Trail, it placed them in closer contact with Indians and moved them through lands charred by the Indian practice of firing the prairie grass to aid new growth.

Orson Pratt kept an excellent diary of the expedition, faithfully recording, from readings of his scientific instruments, the temperature, longitude, latitude, and elevation, besides describing the fauna and flora. William Clayton also kept a faithful diary, besides writing and publishing his detailed *Latter-day Saints' Emigrants' Guide...* (St. Louis, 1848). It was he who suggested that a roadometer be constructed of cogs and attached to a wagon so the revolutions of a wheel would yield an accurate figure for the miles traveled that day. It was done.

The route of the Pioneer Company, after fording the Elkhorn River, followed the north side of the Platte River to near present Columbus, where the Loup Fork flows into the Platte from the west. They followed the Loup Fork to near present Fullerton, a point reached April 23, and crossed it the next day, making use of their "Revenue Cutter," a portable boat for conveying goods across streams. They then followed the Loup Fork a short distance and dropped south to the north side of the Platte River at Grand Island. The company thereafter maintained its place on the north side of the Platte and North Platte rivers across pres-

Engraving by Frederick Piercy

At the Elk Horn River Ferry

ent Nebraska and on to Fort Laramie, passing "Ancient Bluff Ruins" on May 22 and Chimney Rock on the 26th and camping across the river from Fort Laramie on June 1. They clocked 522 miles from Winter Quarters to Fort Laramie in forty-two days, or about twelve miles a day.

Creating the Mormon Trail to Fort Laramie was light work compared to the Iowa experience. Of course streams had to be ferried or forded. Guarding against the sloughs and quicksands of the river was a fairly constant concern, especially during the first days of the trek. The party occasionally crossed blackened prairie. Showers were infrequent. There was a lack of prairie grass for their animals until well into May. Frequent mention is made of the cattle feeding on the bark of trees.

Early in May they became quite excited "at the vast herds of buffalo," and on the 6th it was observed that "The prairie appeared black being covered with immense herds of buffalo." At the outset hunters had been appointed to keep the company supplied with meat; rivalries and friendly contests among the hunters resulted in such an oversupply that Brigham Young on Friday, May 7, "preached in Camp and advised the brethren not to kill any more buffalo or other game until the meat was needed." The company appears to have been well provisioned.

Difficulties with the Indians were greater in anticipation than in realization. On their sixth day out the Mormons encountered Pawnee Indians, and the next two days they passed the burnt remains of the Pawnee Mission House. Though on

their guard, they lost horses by theft and by killing. Approaching Chimney Rock on May 24 they met two Sioux chiefs and thirty-three braves. "They smoked the pipe of peace with us," Brigham Young recorded, and the two groups went their ways.

The routine and comparative ease of the journey led the men to engage in more recreational activities than pleased Young. Three days after passing Chimney Rock, on Saturday, May 29, he "remonstrated with those . . . giving way to trifling, dancing, and card playing."

At Fort Laramie members of the Pioneer Company, though they did not know it then, were halfway to their destination. From this point on, it was decided, they would follow the Oregon Trail. Terrain dictated the decision for the most part. They engaged a flatboat for fifteen dollars and began ferrying their wagons across the river. They stayed at Fort Laramie for three days and on June 4 started up the Oregon Trail, heading west and northwest, gaining in elevation over roads sometimes quite hilly. Ten or twelve men were detached each day to work the road. Orson Pratt observed: "We think that we fully work our road tax" for the improvements made on the road. There was grass, and they could usually camp by springs. Making about 13 miles a day, their journey brought them on June 12 to where the Oregon Trail crossed the North Platte 124 miles from Fort Laramie. Here (at present Casper) the Mormons remained six days, hunting and fishing and building rafts to ferry wagons. Seeing the need of a ferry for Mormon emigrants now on the road,

Engraving by Frederick Piercy

Chimney Rock

Young left ten men to earn a little by ferrying emigrants bound for Oregon, but mainly to wait for and serve the Mormon emigration four to six weeks behind. On the 19th the Pioneer Company left the North Platte and rolled southwestward toward the Sweetwater.

On the third day out the company passed Independence Rock and forded the Sweetwater, camping a quarter of a mile from the upper end of Devils Gate on the south bank. Members of the company closely examined each of these landmarks. Several climbed Independence Rock; others examined Devils Gate, while Orson Pratt measured it precisely and described its formations.

The general spirits of the company had been raised considerably since Fort Laramie. Members liked the country, the taste of the air, and the clear streams with their sandy, gravel, or rocky bottoms. The valley of the Sweetwater and surrounding country was, to Orson Pratt, "certainly very picturesque and beautiful." Stock fared well along the meanderings of the Sweetwater, but much of the plain around was "sandy, barren, sterile," with little vegetation besides the wild sage.

They followed on the south side of the Sweetwater for five days, then on the 26th they crossed the river and camped. The next day, Sunday, they left the Sweetwater, crossed South Pass, and headed southwest toward Fort Bridger. Following streams had its advantages, but this stretch of country streams often led away from a direct path, so they made their camps on or near streams they crossed, streams that flowed ultimately into the Green River. The trail crossed Little Sandy Creek, Big Sandy Creek (at present Farson), Green River, and Muddy Creek (near present Granger). It then turned west to near Church Buttes and south across Blacks Fork River to Fort Bridger, reached on July 7.

If there was still indecision about their destination it had to end here. At Fort Bridger emigrants had a final choice: either go to the northwest and continue on the Oregon Trail (they could later take a branch off to California), or take the trail to the southwest and cross the mountains into Great Salt Lake Valley and, if not satisfied, go on until they found a place to their liking. In 1846 a hundred wagons had taken this latter route — the Hastings Cutoff — from Fort Bridger to California via the Great Salt Lake. The Edwin Bryan party had traded wagon outfits for horses and had made it through nicely. Wagon trains, too, one guided by Lansford Hastings, had made it down the Weber River, through the treacherous last five miles of the narrow, rugged defile, and out into the valley. The last group to take the Hastings Cutoff was the Donner-Reed party, which left Fort Bridger July 31. They, too, could have made it down the Weber in a few days, but, warned by Hastings of the Weber gorge, they avoided it and cut their way south up East Canyon Creek, over Big Mountain, Little Moun-

Engraving by Frederick Piercy

Fort Laramie

tain, and down Emigration Canyon and out into the valley, at a dear cost of labor and precious time.

Brigham Young and his company had received plenty of advice on the trail. Just out of Fort Laramie they had met James H. Grieve and a company of men from whom they "got some information from the Salt Lake country which was flattering." After they crossed South Pass, Mountain Man Moses Harris spent the evening with them and described the country into which they were heading. The next day Jim Bridger, on his way east, stopped and gave them a rambling description of the western country. Two days later Samuel Brannan intercepted the Pioneer Company. He had taken 238 Saints in the chartered ship *Brooklyn* from New York around the Horn to California, arriving in San Francisco Bay during the Bear Flag Rebellion. Brannan had made the overland trip on the California Trail via Fort Hall to Fort Bridger. He was all for California and tried vainly to persuade Young to think of California as the gathering place.

With last-minute blacksmithing completed on wagons and animals at Fort Bridger, the party decided to continue along the Hastings Cutoff. There seems little doubt that Brigham Young had his mind set on the area of the Great Salt Lake as his destination. Two days away from the fort the choice was approved when they met an eastbound party headed by Miles Goodyear, who was well acquainted with the Great Salt Lake area. After the Donner-Reed party had passed through Fort Bridger the year before, Goodyear had gone to the

Great Salt Lake Valley, built a cabin and stockade on the Weber River, and established his man there. A garden had been planted in the spring.

The fourth leg of the Mormon Trail was begun July 9, when Brigham Young headed his company southwest, "taking Mr. Hasting's new route to the Bay of St. Francisco." The traces of the route were "but dimly seen, as only a few wagons passed over it last season." Compared to the well-defined Oregon Trail, the Hastings Cutoff was pathfinding and sometimes road-making. The traces led westward and southwestward, crossing branches of Muddy Fork, touching tributaries of the Bear River, and westward to the head of Red Fork (today's Echo Fork), past Cache Cave, and into Echo Canyon.

Shortly after leaving Fort Bridger, Brigham Young was laid low by "mountain fever." It had begun to strike the camp just before Fort Bridger and now was spreading. Many were down, some quite ill. To avoid delaying the whole party, on July 13 Orson Pratt took 23 wagons and 42 men in search of Reed's route of 1846 across the mountains. While scouts explored ahead, the remaining members traveled slowly and rested when expedient. Even so, they kept within a few days of the advance scouts.

On Friday the 16th Pratt found Reed's route and put men to work clearing it of growth, stumps, and other obstacles. The next day, seeking a better route, he discovered that the Weber gorge was impossible and climbed high for a better view. He could see only "hills piled on hills, and mountains on mountains."

Sunday, July 18, was spent in camp. Pratt and John Brown set out Monday to explore Reed's route all the way. By following East Canyon Creek southward, they found the country closing in on them; one way out was to turn westward and ascend Big Mountain, a gradual incline of about four miles. At the summit they could see a portion of Great Salt Lake Valley. They rode down the southwest side of Big Mountain and "after searching awhile . . . found that the wagon trail ascended quite abruptly for about 1½ miles, and passed over a mountain [Little Mountain], and down into another narrow valley [Emigration Canyon], and thus avoided the kanyon [to the south]; and after making these explorations we returned to our camp."

The scouts were followed closely now by the advance group building road, and Brigham Young's party was close behind. On the 23rd men of the advance group went into the valley, set up camp on City Creek, prayed, and appointed committees. Some men began plowing the ground and building dams across the creek to provide water for irrigation. The next day, Saturday, July 24, Young's company entered the valley and arrived at the encampment on City Creek about noon.

Wilford Woodruff recalled that when Brigham Young first saw the valley from his bed in Woodruff's carriage, he said at once, "This is the right place, drive on!" Members of the company then explored the valley thoroughly, and on Wednesday, July 28, "It was moved and seconded that we should locate in this valley for the present, and lay out a city at this place; which was carried without a dissenting voice." The primary destination of all who would follow along the Mormon Trail had been reached — a land no one else wanted, with room to expand.

While farming, timbering, and blacksmithing went on to help meet needs of a newly born city, explorations of neighboring valleys continued for another month. Satisfied, Brigham Young and others returned over the Mormon Trail to Winter Quarters. On the way they passed the Mormon emigration of the season, which arrived in the valley in various companies between September 19 and October 4. Young would return the next summer, leading another wave of the emigration that was to continue, one way or another, one route or another, for the rest of the century. Between 1847 and 1868 more than two hundred companies of between fifty-three thousand and sixty-eight thousand Mormon emigrants forged a new life for themselves by following the Mormon Trail. The count is imprecise because rosters or partial rosters are extant for only 70 percent of the companies. Even that number is remarkable, but it is also supported by nearly three hundred known and catalogued diaries of persons who traveled over the trail. This does not include the continual pioneering experiences most Mormons of the nineteenth century were put through by the repeated call on many to settle new places — from Canada on the north to Mexico on the south, from Wyoming and Colorado on the east to California on the west. Many of these subsequent moves were far more difficult than their first experiences on the Mormon Trail.

Once the Mormon Trail was established there were the inevitable variations in the route, outfitting places, and ways and means of travel. Mormons frequently obtained government mail contracts to and from the states. From Salt Lake City, Mormon missionaries, going mainly to Great Britain and Europe, made the eastern trip each year and usually served as the agents of the church for companies emigrating to Utah. Salt Lake merchants also traveled regularly, trading in St. Louis, Chicago, and other eastern emporiums. There were varieties of groups going and coming on the trail, although emigrant trains moving westward made up the bulk of that traffic.

The typical experience for the emigrant began when he left his home and assembled with others at Liverpool, England, where Mormon agents chartered vessels to carry the Zion-bound Saints to American ports. New Orleans served as port of entry from 1840 to 1854. Here emigrants transferred to river steamers and went as far as St. Louis before taking smaller craft to a wharf near the outfitting place. After 1855 Mormon emigrant ships docked at New York, Philadelphia, or Boston. The emigrants took the trains as far west as the rails ran, where wagons met and took them to the outfitting place.

At outfitting places the emigrants were equipped, organized into their traveling companies, and prepared for the overland trek. Agents purchased wagons, oxen, tents, and other equipment. Warehouses stored the essential goods. Sometimes emigrants camped out for weeks before undertaking the new task of driving an ox-team. The 1853 outfitting place at Keokuk was described by Samuel Claridge: "About half a mile from the river on the top of a hill, surrounded by wood, and commanding a view of the country for miles around, the Camp of Israel burst to my view. Here were hundreds of tents and wagons with hundreds and thousands of Saints all preparing for a 1300-mile journey across the plains." And when his company of Welsh, English, Germans, and Scandinavians got started, "None of us had ever had experience in driving cattle . . . the cattle had to learn all languages . . . there was a great deal of awkward driving."

Outfitting places needed open space near navigable rivers, and sites along the Missouri River usually were available. While Winter Quarters had served in 1847 and 1848, Kanesville (present Council Bluffs, Iowa) was used from 1849 to 1852. In 1853 the site was shifted to the Mississippi at Keokuk, Iowa, a few miles south of Montrose (across from Nauvoo). These people followed the Mormon Trail of 1846 and 1847 all the way. In 1854 and thereafter, sites were on the Missouri. That year companies were outfitted at Westport (Kansas City area) and in 1855 at Atchison, Kansas, three miles east of Mormon Grove. Companies leaving these sites followed the Oregon trail or its feeder routes along the Platte River and joined the Mormon Trail there.

In 1856 Brigham Young started the unique handcart companies. Since the emigrants generally walked most of the distance and brought only light luggage, why not a simpler way than by heavy wagon? The handcart was simply a box riding on a single axle and two wheels, with an arrangement for one person in front to pull and one behind to push. Usually five wagons (with camping equipment) accompanied a company of sixty or so handcarts. Between 1856 and 1860 nearly three thousand in ten companies took the handcart way. All were successful except the Martin and Willie companies, which started late with handcarts of unseasoned lumber and were caught in the mountains by early snows. About two hundred died of cold and starvation. The route of the handcart companies was due west from Iowa City (terminus of the railroad) about 150 miles (following closely today's Iowa Route 6 as far as Redfield), thence southwestward to Lewis, where the 1846 Mormon Trail was joined.

It was always a task and an expense for Mormon agents to purchase wagons and oxen in the Mississippi Valley for the emigrants, since they often had to compete with other westering Americans for stock, wagons, and supplies. In 1864 Brigham Young called on the Utah settlements to furnish wagons, oxteams, and drivers to go east and meet the emigrants and bring them to Zion. Frequently surplus stock and wagons in Utah were taken east and sold to help defray expenses of the emigration.

From 1864 to 1866 the outfitting place was a small village named Wyoming on the west bank of the Missouri River, seven miles north of Nebraska City and forty miles south of Omaha. Emigrants headed due west to intercept the Mormon Trail

on the north side of the Platte, near Kearney. In 1867 the rails reached North Platte, which became the outfitting place; in 1868 emigrants took the railroad to Laramie and Benton in Wyoming Territory before changing to wagons — the last to take the Mormon Trail.

The transcontinental railroad was completed with the union of the rails at Promontory Summit, Utah Territory, May 10, 1869, and the long overland journey of more than a thousand miles by ox-drawn wagon was no longer necessary. The railroad provided speed, comparative ease, and comfort. In building the line west from Omaha the Union Pacific paid tribute to the Mormon Trail by following its route much of the way along the north side of the Platte River as far as North Platte. Thereafter it struck an independent course westward across southern Wyoming, picking up the trace of the Mormon Trail in southwestern Wyoming and following it down Echo Canyon and the Weber River. At the last canyon, instead of trying to follow the Donner-Reed and Mormon trails the engineers in 1869 cut into the side of the mountain above the riverbed and laid track on an even grade, following the river out of the canyon and on into Ogden, making it the rail center of Utah and the Mountain West.

Highways also paid their respects to the Mormon Trail. West of Omaha U.S. 30 picks up the Mormon Trail and follows it generally to North Platte, where it is forsaken for about seventy miles until U.S. 26 picks it up and follows it to Fort Laramie. Modern roads in Wyoming touch the traces of the trail only in a few places, but Echo Canyon again serves as the entrance into the mountains and Salt Lake City. It should be noted that the famous stretch of the Donner-Reed and Mormon trails from near Henefer south up East Canyon Creek, over Big and Little mountains, and down Emigration Canyon was used for only a few years before Parley P. Pratt found an easier way. He turned south where Echo Creek empties into the Weber, followed the Weber upstream to Coalville, Wanship, and beyond, and then west to Parleys Canyon, which leads into Salt Lake City a few miles south of the mouth of Emigration Canyon. U.S. 40 used part of this road, and today I-80 follows it rather closely.

The Mormon Trail, by following the Donner-Reed Trail those last miles, helped establish the center of the Mormon kingdom at Salt Lake City. At the crossroads of the west the Mormon communities were well situated to provide food, goods, and services to overland travelers and to supply some of the needs of railroaders and miners in the neighboring regions. In turn, the Mormon communities benefited from that location. The cosmopolitan character of the Mormon emigrants who followed the Mormon Trail gave, at least for a generation or two, a unique quality to a large area of the American West — Mormon Country. The far-flung settlements were united by other trails that have their own stories.

Always in the communities at the end of every trail was the memory of those who had first sung the song of the Mormon Trail and saw in it something for their own lives.

Come, come, ye Saints, no toil nor labor fear;
But with joy, wend your way.
Though hard to you this journey may appear,
Grace shall be as your day.

THE COWBOY TRAILS
By Ron Tyler

The cowboy trails northward from Texas have been the subject of folklore, legend, and even serious study by such notable historians as Wayne Gard and Don Worcester. The Shawnee Trail, the Chisholm Trail, the Western Trail, and others are well-known parts of the cowboy story, yet few realize the crucial role the trail actually had in taking an inexperienced youngster, anxious to cut his mother's apron strings by making the long trek northward, and transforming him into a cowboy — or that without the trail drive the Texas cowboy probably would be no better known than his predecessors and counterparts, the Georgia cow hunter and the Mexican *vaquero*.

There were numerous cattle trails — from Texas to Louisiana, from Texas to California, from Oregon to the Midwest — but the trails that attracted most of the attention as well as most of the cattle were those leading northward from Texas to Kansas and Missouri after the Civil War. Returning Texas veterans found millions of cattle running free and unbranded in South Texas and all but worthless unless they could be sold to satisfy the new and increasing national taste for beef. The problem was how to get them to the northern market via the new railroad towns in

Kansas and Missouri, where steers were worth ten times more than they were in depressed and cash-poor Texas. When the first herd of cattle arrived in Abilene, Kansas, in 1867 and sold for a profit, ranchers and unemployed Civil War veterans did not take long to decide that their economic salvation lay in walking their stock north to market.

It was not as heroic a solution to their problem as it might have seemed; cattle had been driven hundreds of miles to market for years. Livestock drovers did not originate in the Southwest. They can be traced to colonial America early in the eighteenth century, when Boston, Philadelphia, and Charleston were market centers. Ohio and Kentucky possessed flourishing ranches while the Texas cattle industry was still in its infancy, and Illinois cattlemen sometimes drove herds to market as far away as Boston. Driving a herd from Texas to Kansas, it is true, was another matter because of the immense desert that had to be crossed, a desert that Col. Stephen H. Long said in 1819 could not be made habitable or easily crossed. The ranchers of Texas felt equal to the task in 1866. These were the same men who had wrenched their independence from Mexico in 1836 and had endured ten years of

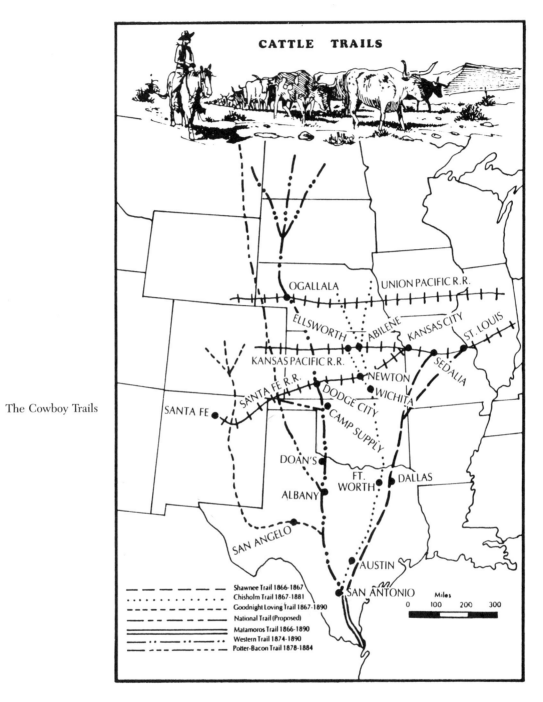

The Cowboy Trails

CATTLE TRAILS

OGALLALA   UNION PACIFIC R.R.

ELLSWORTH   ABILENE   KANSAS CITY   ST. LOUIS

KANSAS PACIFIC R.R.   SEDALIA

SANTA FE R.R.   NEWTON

DODGE CITY   WICHITA

SANTA FE   CAMP SUPPLY

DOAN'S

FT.   DALLAS
WORTH

ALBANY

SAN ANGELO

AUSTIN

Shawnee Trail 1866-1867
Chisholm Trail 1867-1881
Goodnight Loving Trail 1867-1890
National Trail (Proposed)
Matamoros Trail 1866-1890
Western Trail 1874-1890
Potter-Bacon Trail 1878-1884

SAN ANTONIO   Miles
                0   100   200   300

haphazard existence as a republic. They had now survived an even more tragic Civil War and were returning to a style of ranching that was soon recognized as distinctively Texan. The cowpuncher, who over the next thirty years pointed the Longhorn herds north, was a unique combination of skills, techniques, and spirit that could have developed only on the South Texas range. Two cultures, American and Mexican, clashed, 'mixed, and hardened under pressure from a third — the Indian. Heirs to both an aristocratic and a pragmatic tradition, the Texans seemed natural-born leaders, infusing into the cattle trade the same energetic intelligence that is memorialized at San Jacinto and the Alamo. A Galveston Bay rancher, for example, trailed his herd of cattle eastward over the little-publicized Opelousas Trail to Mississippi early in 1838. That same year some ambitious ranchers in South Texas herded several hundred cattle from the Nueces River to "the interior."

Probably the most important element missing from the cattle trade of the 1850s — the element that had prevented it from becoming a nationally significant business — was the daring enterpreneurship that marked other successful ventures of the nineteenth century: trapping for furs, steamboating, railroading. But it was not long in coming.

When cattle-owning Texans realized that their herds might be welcome in gold-rich California, the kind of organization and leadership that promised development of a significant economic force began. T. J. Trimmier of Washington County, Texas, walked five hundred beeves to California in 1848, where he sold them for $100 each. Dozens of drovers were soon on the fifteen-hundred-mile trail to California, a considerable distance farther than the later, more famous, Western, Shawnee, and Chisholm trails that led from Texas to Kansas and Missouri. The California drovers are a relatively unknown part of history, but two cattlemen who left the South Texas region in 1854 kept excellent records. Michael H. Erskine and John James

departed within weeks of each other with large herds of Texas Longhorns for the Los Angeles market. They arrived in November, taking approximately three months longer than it would later take drovers to herd cattle from Texas to Kansas.

Many experiences on the California Trail were similar to events on the later drives on the Chisholm Trail. The cattle tended to stampede early in the drive because they had not yet been trail broken. Cowboys went to sleep and allowed cattle to stray, something that most herders did not want to own up to — and something the code of the trail did not require them to admit, since it was a common and embarrassing occurrence. If possible they blamed a coyote, an Indian, or a kangaroo rat (which James G. Bell, a member of the James outfit, thought would be delicious if properly cooked). Both Erskine and James reported numerous Indian threats but never a direct attack. They resorted to night drives while in the desert to avoid the heat, and they had trouble pushing the cattle through the mountains. Finally, they took their cattle over a trail considerably rougher than those the later drovers would use to get to Missouri and Kansas.

Drives to California were highly speculative because they required such a long time and the cattlemen had no accurate knowledge of the market before they left. But cattle worth $5 to $15 each in Texas were usually priced at $25 to $150 each on the West Coast. That was enough increase in the normal profit for a few adventurous cattlemen to head west every month during the trail-drive season in hopes of improving their profit by selling in the better market.

Despite the lures of California, more conservative Texans sought markets for their stock nearer to home. East Texans had long enjoyed a profitable commercial relationship with Louisiana. Short drives reached the river ports in Louisiana or the Texas Gulf Coast. Small paddleboats carried livestock through the choppy Gulf waters as early as 1848, and from 1850 to 1856 Galveston shippers alone accounted for from three to six thousand animals annually. Central Texans trailed their cattle to Alexandria and then shipped them down the Red River to New Orleans. In 1855 Abel H. ("Shanghai") Pierce, who later became one of the better-known and more colorful ranchers, participated in his first drive from South Texas to New Orleans. In Texas only a year, the twenty-year-old Pierce went to work for $22.50 a month, trailing Tres Palacios Ranch cattle to the Crescent City.

But the cowboy's reputation — and the rancher's fortune — was made with the northern trail drives to Missouri, Kansas, Wyoming, and Montana. By 1850 such drives were plodding through a youthful Dallas toward the shanty towns of the Midwest, where the railroad had momentarily stopped in its transcontinental rush. The Dallas *Herald* editor reported that "several droves of cattle have passed through this place en route to Missouri," where they would either go to furnish teams for emigrants headed for California or be shipped to slaughterhouses farther north. These drovers followed the old Indian and buffalo trail that pioneers had used to enter Texas. It was soon called the Shawnee Trail, although it had gone by less romantic names early in its history: the Kansas Trail, the cattle trail, or just "trail." The Shawnee Trail led from Austin to Waco to Dallas, then crossed the Red River near Preston, in Grayson County, before striking out for Sedalia or Kansas City, Missouri. The *Texas State Gazette* in Austin reported that around fifty thousand cattle left the state via the Shawnee Trail in 1854. It was not called the Shawnee Trail in print until 1874, twenty years after it had been recognized as an important route.

Trouble threatened the newly developed cattle trade and ultimately helped stop the northern trail drives. As early as 1853 Texans en route to Missouri with their herds had been stopped by indignant citizens who protested the entry of Longhorns into their country because they feared Texas fever, a disease carried by ticks. In 1853 no one knew the cause of the disease, and the Texans protested for years that they were not responsible for the death and sickness of midwestern cattle. After all, they reasoned, their own cattle were not sick. The fact is that Texas and southern cattle were immune to the fever, which caused stricken animals to arch their backs, droop their heads and ears, and assume other improbable poses. Other symptoms were glassy eyes and a blind stagger. Some even became delirious and broke their horns against trees or the sides of dwellings. Little wonder that the irate midwesterners protested the coming of thousands of infected but immune beasts that sometimes flattened their fences and crops in a stampede, even when behaving normally.

Despite numerous complaints — and some outright interference from vigilantes — in 1854 Capt. Shapely P. Ross bought a herd in Texas at $13 per head and sold it for $27 per head, making the kind of money that kept the Texans coming. Some drove their cattle farther. Six hundred "fine looking cattle, remarkable for their sleek appearance and long horns" reached Chicago and New York City that same year. Tom Candy Ponting and Washington Malone went to Texas and gathered seven hundred Longhorns. They wintered them in Illinois to put on a little fat, then chose 150 of the best for the New York market. Shipping them at a cost of $17 each, Ponting and Malone hoped the Texas Longhorn would provide New York diners with a new, desirable, and low-cost source of beef. But they were disappointed. The cattle tasted something like venison, observed the writer for the *Tribune,* but were "apt to be a little tough when cooked in the ordinary way." Most gourmets would probably disagree, pointing out that the Longhorn was tough no matter how he was cooked. The writer for the young *New York Times* was even less complimentary, disdainfully reporting after a firsthand look in 1858 that the cattle "were barely able to cast a shadow." Some other observers probably thought that the "long-legged" cattle with "long taper horns and something of a wild look" might be more at home in the zoo than in a good restaurant. Not surprisingly,

New Yorkers did not consume large numbers of Longhorns. The number shipped increased slightly from 1856 to 1859 but decreased to less than one hundred in 1860 and was completely cut off during the Civil War.

The Civil War stifled the expanding Texas cattle trade. Businessmen who had realized the possibilities of the market now turned their efforts to war. Some cattlemen stayed home to provide beef for the Confederacy, but most of the cattle were turned loose while the owners joined the army. Oliver Loving drove a herd across the Mississippi River to the army. When the river was captured by Union forces, cutting Texas off from the rest of the South, even more Texas cattle ran wild, just as they had under the Spaniards and Mexicans. Some were shipped to Mexico, where they were traded for sugar, powder, cloth, and other scarce items. W. A. Peril drove a herd through the rugged Big Bend country into Mexico in 1864, and Richard King, one of the only ranchers who stayed on his South Texas spread after the Union had captured Brownsville and Galveston, engaged in a profitable exchange of cotton and cattle with Mexican merchants and government agents.

After the war, seasoned cowmen realistically appraised problems that they had only sporadically encountered before the war: Indians had become more desperate along the western trails as their homelands gradually decreased and their food supply, the bison, was systematically killed off by the white man; and Missouri and Kansas enforced stricter quarantine laws. Cattlemen returned to their ranches after the war, aware of the opportunities that existed but realizing that something inventive would be required to bypass these serious problems.

Charles Goodnight was one of the first Texas ranchers released from army duty. The thirty-year-old cattleman left the Texas Rangers in 1864 and reentered the cattle business with Charlie Neuhous, getting quite a head start on those cattlemen who did not get out of the army until the following year. Goodnight was unable to take advantage of his early start, however. A drive he planned in 1865 for New Mexico and Colorado was disrupted by Indians, who stampeded the cattle. Neuhous salvaged a little profit by herding the remaining cattle to New Orleans.

Capt. R. H. Williams found a similar situation on his Southwest Texas ranch. The Mexican *vaqueros* there were living "after the manner of their kind," which to Williams meant that his ranch had not been cared for. "Having no one to look after them, these gentry . . . had been taking things easy," he said, "and everything had been neglected. Calves had been left unbranded and horses allowed to stray away on the prairie." "Every man on this cow hunt was a cattle owner just home from the war and . . . out to see what he had left to brand," said Lee Moore, himself a veteran and a cowboy.

Courtesy Amon Carter Museum, Fort Worth, Texas   *Sketched by A. R. Waud, Harper's Weekly, 1867*

A Drove of Texas Cattle Crossing a Stream

Such negligence cost Goodnight more than 80 percent of his herd. Using money Neuhous had gotten in New Orleans, the pair rounded up their cattle in 1866 and found only about a thousand head; the rest had been stolen by his neighbors and the Indians. Goodnight felt that most Texans would go north and fight the farmers over the quarantine laws. He also guessed that western miners had more money to spend on beef than midwesterners, so he decided to head west to Colorado, where Loving had enjoyed such success prior to the war. Relying on the experience he had gained as a ranger, he blazed a trail through the western part of the state. He knew he could graze his cattle on the rich grassland of Colorado and sell them the following year if the miners did not buy at once. Goodnight was doubly fortunate when he met Oliver Loving near Weatherford, Texas, as he prepared for the trek. Loving had planned a western drive, anyway, so he said he would join Goodnight. They combined herds, forming a brief partnership that is commemorated by the Goodnight-Loving Trail, traversed in subsequent years by thousands of drovers.

Young Goodnight and the fifty-four-year-old Loving left for Colorado on June 6, 1866. They traveled the route of the Topographical Engineers until they crossed the Pecos River, then they cut northward through New Mexico to Colorado. Other drovers followed. Captain Williams marched his cattle across part of the Goodnight-Loving Trail before turning south to Mexico. G. T. Reynolds and several others drove their herds along the Concho River to the Pecos, then cut northward into New Mexico. The Goodnight-Loving Trail was soon in constant use.

Correct in their assumption that cattle were worth more money outside Texas, cattle raisers soon opened up other trails to success. H. M. Childress took a herd to Iowa, where he got $35 per head. Monroe Choate and B. A. Borroum followed with eight hundred steers. E. M. ("Bud") Daggett of Fort Worth trailed his cattle to Shreveport, Louisiana in 1865, and K. M. Van Zandt hoped that the farmers of the Mississippi Valley would pay a premium price for his good Texas beef in 1866. Purchasing three hundred cattle on a speculative basis, Van Zandt sent them to the farming regions along the Mississippi, but he found there was no market. Arranging for a Chicago firm to pack the meat in barrels in exchange for the hides, he sold the beef on his next trip to New York. "I had come out about even," he noted in his journal. (Van Zandt was also responsible for one of the more unusual episodes in the history of Nashville's streetcars when he shipped some Longhorns to Tennessee during an epidemic of what he called the "epizootic" that killed numerous horses. Some of his Longhorns were employed to pull the city's streetcars.)

Van Zandt conceded what most drovers already knew: The real market lay to the north — Kansas and Missouri, where the railroad could ship the steers to feeding grounds or to ready market. However, he did not want to battle the quarantine laws that perplexed other cattlemen. At first the Texans tried a direct approach. Col. John J. Myers confronted authorities in Missouri. R. D. Hunter drove his beeves toward Sedalia, where he had more trouble. Halted by a sheriff sporting a coonskin cap, Hunter found himself under arrest. He did not want to lose the herd, so he convinced the sheriff to take him to a nearby town so a friend could post his bond. When they arrived, Hunter managed to get the lawman drunk. Meanwhile Hunter's cowboys had moved the herd beyond the sheriff's legal grasp. Hunter drove his cattle through Kansas, then turned eastward to Missouri, where he sold them for a $6,000 profit.

Still, these were not the circumstances of a profitable business. Cattle trails led in three directions from Texas in 1867, but the most profitable one, and the largest market, clearly lay to the north — a route blocked by a legal haze that prevented the cattlemen from making full use of it.

Although the quarantine laws kept Texas cattle out of certain parts of the state, Kansas had not intended to disrupt the trade completely. Trying to please both farmers and merchants, the state legislature left part of the state open to the Texas beef, hoping the Texas fever would be limited to the less settled portions of the country. Several Kansans acted with more direction. The Topeka Live Stock Company conceived a plan, the outline of which was good. In 1867 the company invited drovers to bring their cattle up an unspecified trail to a soon-to-be-designated depot on the Union Pacific. There the Topekans faltered. The plan was not firmly set up or well publicized.

In Joseph G. McCoy the cattle trade finally found an able businessman willing to promote the industry. McCoy understood both sides of the problem and presented both the Texans and the Kansans a workable proposition. One of three brothers, McCoy was a slender, unpretentious fellow with a thorough knowledge of the cattle business. His brother James operated a large farm in Illinois, where the McCoys ran their own cattle and fed those intended for market. William, the third brother, lived in New York City, where he marketed the stock. The McCoy brothers hoped to make money on their scheme, but it all depended on Joseph, who had to negotiate a delicate three-way deal when he arrived in Kansas in 1867.

He had to work with Kansans, the Texas cattlemen, and the railroad. First he visited with officials in several Kansas towns and found that not all residents of the state wanted to keep Texas cattle out. He selected Abilene as his base of operations. This had two advantages: It was on an already established trail, and it had a railroad depot. "The country was entirely unsettled," he said, "well watered, excellent grass, and nearly the entire area of the country was adapted to holding cattle. And it was the farthest point east at which a good depot for cattle business could have been made." Since Abilene lay within the quarantined section of Kansas, he paid a visit to Gov. Samuel J. Crawford and wangled a "semiofficial" endorsement of his plan. He later got the governor's approval on a map showing how the cattle would reach Abilene. When McCoy returned to Abilene and purchased 250 acres of land outside the city, he knew he had yet to deal with the other faction in Kansas — the aroused local population that would protest the arrival of any Texas cattle.

McCoy was not the first to think of setting aside a designated railhead where Texas cattle could be brought, but he was the first to promote his plan into reality. The Topeka group had never gotten beyond planning. McCoy already had assurances from the Union Pacific Railroad that it would pay him $5 for every carload of cattle he shipped from Abilene; the railroad was tired of returning its cars to eastern terminals empty. McCoy began construction on a barn, an office building, a hotel, livery stables, and a bank. He moved in a large set of scales so no one would have to depend on the traditional range method of "averaging out" the weight of cattle — guessing at their weight.

Having settled the matter with the railroad and the state, McCoy then sent an agent deep into Indian Territory to open negotiations with the third faction, the Texans. At first the cattlemen were suspicious. Having been exposed to border ruffians who stole their cattle and beat up the hands, to Indians who either ran off their stock or extracted a fee for crossing their land, and, finally, to fearful farmers who sought, legally and physically, to block their entry into Kansas, the Texans could hardly be blamed for their apprehension. Still they had little choice but to accept his offer. They knew about the problems of the previous year in Missouri, so they headed their stock toward McCoy's as-yet-unbuilt pens in Abilene.

The first herd belonged to Smith, McCord, and Chandler, a northern firm that had purchased the cattle from Texas drovers in Indian Territory. The cattle arrived before McCoy finished construction of his pens or hotel. The first herd to forge the new trail under one ownership belonged to Col. O. W. Wheeler of California, who had gone to San Antonio with the idea of buying 2,400 steers and driving them to California. When he met McCoy's agent he decided to turn his herd to Abilene.

A momentary crisis arose when local citizens wrote Governor Crawford protesting that Abilene was in the quarantine zone and that Texas cattle could not legally be driven there. "If I mistake not," wrote Will Lamb of nearby Detroit, "there is a State Law prohibiting any person or persons driving Texas cattle inside the limits of civilization on the frontier: If there is such a law why not enforce it; for there is now, and will be still coming, several thousand head of Texas Cattle in this immediate vicinity." But McCoy had laid his plan carefully and solved the problem without further involving the governor. While the governor stalled, McCoy held a meeting in Abilene with irate citizens. With Texas cowboys walking through the group contracting for butter and eggs at huge prices, McCoy promised to pay for all the damages, including dead cattle, caused by Texas fever. The farmers' spokesman seemed convinced by McCoy's offer and announced, "If I can make any money out of this cattle trade I am not afraid of Spanish fever, but if I can't make any money out of this cattle trade then I am damned 'fraid of Spanish fever."

McCoy made little money in 1867 because he started too late in the season. Only the last few herds went to Abilene, amounting to about thirty-five thousand head, of which fewer than twenty thousand were shipped from his pens. But the trend was established, and he shrewdly realized it. The blowout on the night of September 5, when the first shipment left Abilene, was held in a tent within sight of the unfinished hotel.

McCoy realized that for Abilene to become a cow-town metropolis, a new trail was needed. The Shawnee Trail, over which more than a quarter of a million head of cattle had been driven the previous year, was too far east. McCoy promoted a trail that had been in use for several years but was largely unused by the drovers. Known to buffaloes, Indians, a few pioneers, and army troops, it was located about 150 miles west of the Shawnee Trail. Maj. Enoch Steen had marched his six companies of Second Dragoons from Fort Belknap, Texas, to Fort Riley, Kansas, on the trail in 1855. Other soldiers followed in 1861, and by 1864 Indians were using it regularly.

McCoy's trail is perhaps the best-known route of the cattlemen's era. It became known as the Chisholm Trail, named for Jesse Chisholm, a half-breed Cherokee Indian who was living with the Wichita Indians in the fall of 1864. A veteran trader and guide born in Tennessee near the turn of the nineteenth century, Chisholm drove wagons up the trail from his trading post near the mouth of the Little Arkansas River to Fort Leavenworth, Kansas, becoming so identi-fied with the trail that others soon called it by his name.

The Chisholm Trail had gone by other names — the Kansas Trail, the Abilene Trail, the McCoy Trail, or simply the cattle trail — but by the time Jesse Chisholm died in 1868 it was commonly referred to by the more famous name. The name first appeared in print in the May 1870 Eldorado *Daily Commonwealth*.

Combined with other trails, the Chisholm Trail stretched from the southern tip of Texas to Abilene. It ran past the ranching empire of Richard King, past Gonzales, to the state capital at Austin. There it crossed the Colorado River, proceeded to Round Rock (near the spot where the outlaw Sam Bass was killed, soon after helping drive a herd of cattle up the trail), Georgetown, Belton, Comanche Springs, and Fort Worth — itself on the verge of becoming a booming cattle town. The trail crossed the West Fork of the Trinity River there, then continued to Red River Station, which lay on the direct line through Indian Territory to Abilene. It was a more direct route, McCoy advised the Texans. "It has more prairie, less timber, more small streams and fewer large ones, altogether better grass and fewer flies — no civilized Indian tax or wild Indian disturbances — than any other route yet driven over. It is also much shorter because [it is] direct from the Red River to Kansas."

Many old-time cowhands object to the whole length of the trail being called the Chisholm Trail, claiming that it was called either the McCoy or the Eastern Trail throughout the heyday of the drovers. They point out that Jesse Chisholm explored no more than the Oklahoma portion of the trail. But Wayne Gard, author of the most reliable book on the trail, refers to the whole length of the trail as the Chisholm, and that is how the trail is identified in history.

Regardless of what it was called, the trail became an original piece of Americana. In many ways the drives resembled a military expedition, as the boss gathered his crew, rounded up the cattle, and set out for Abilene or Dodge City. The most important member of the crew was the trail boss himself, who was hired first, if he were not a regular member of the ranch crew. Old trail bosses were so numerous in Texas that they formed

a respected social class and reminisced annually at the publicity-bathed Old Trail Drivers Association meetings in San Antonio, long after the last herd had gone up the Chisholm Trail. The trail boss led the herd. He selected the trails and watched for the best camping spot. He scouted several miles ahead of the herd to make sure the route was clear. He usually inspired intense loyalty among his men.

Often an old cowpuncher, who could no longer ride but who longed to stay around the trail, hired on as cook. Well worth the $35 to $55 he was paid per month, the cook got up at 3 A.M. to start the coffee boiling and worked until after dark to feed

Courtesy Amon Carter Museum, Fort Worth, Texas   *Sketched by A. R. Waud, Harper's Weekly, 1880*

Among the Cow-Boys — Breaking Camp

the last of the riders as they came in. He, if anybody, worked longer hours than the trail boss. By tradition, if not temperament, the cook was a determined cuss with his own set of rights and privileges. He was boss around the chuck wagon, which served as social center, hospital, and wardrobe for the cowboy.

The cowboys themselves were seasonal workers who had to ride well, work hard, and eat dust and wrestle cattle every day on the trail. They easily earned their $25 to $40 a month plus grub — but wandering was the inherent right of a puncher, who usually moved on to another range. A cowboy lasted only a few years under such trying circumstances, generally making the drive up the trail only once. Teddy Blue Abbott made it three times, later pointing to the trail and its rigors as the experience that confirmed him as a cowboy.

With the addition of a horse wrangler — sometimes a boy too young to trail-drive but who could tend horses and keep the equipment — the trail crew was complete. The wrangler was in charge of the remuda (as the horse herd is called in the Southwest) or cavvy (in the Northwest), which might contain as many as sixty to one hundred horses. It was his job to see that the horses had the best possible grazing. He usually got up with the cook and put up a rope corral — a rather ingenious device consisting of pegs stuck into the ground to form a circle. He secured them with stake ropes, stretched from peg to peg, making a corral that would hold the horses while the punchers saddled them. It

could be taken down even more quickly than it was put up.

Although departure of the herd was not accompanied by as much heraldry and pomp as the movies usually depict, the hands were excited as they headed out. The drive usually climaxed several grueling weeks of roundup and branding, and the cowboys were ready for a change.

The change was sometimes more than they bargained for. Drovers routinely expected the herd to stampede, and they took extra precautions to prevent it early in the drive. Stampedes were easy to start and difficult to stop. A change in the weather, a rat, a wolf, bad water — almost any excuse was enough to set a herd of high-strung beeves on their destructive path. Sometimes the cowboys could bring the herd under control with relatively little loss; sometimes they could only save their own lives. Arthur Mitchell, who watched hundreds of cattle push and bellow their way over a rimrock, hardly had words to describe the horror he saw: "Mountains of meat — gory from torn flesh. Grotesque shapes with broken necks, broken horns; here and there slight movement indicating that somewhere below were a few not yet smothered. We didn't say much," he recalled, "for we were all thinking that we might have been carried over the bluff if we had been caught in the run."

The trail drive is responsible for much of what is thought of as a cowboy today, for in addition to the hard work and threat of danger there were the campfires after supper, times when the hands could get acquainted — or not get acquainted. One story tells of a puncher who, bored by the usual stories, challenged everyone to add drama to the evening by going around the circle and telling his real name. The campfire was also the source for much of the lore that we now associate with the cowboy, as the men exchanged stories and enriched them with each telling.

Perhaps the most obvious characteristic of the trail was the hard work. By the time they had been on the trail for several weeks most of the hands had mastered the technique of handling cattle. But they had not gotten used to the dust — particularly the drag riders, who had to bring up the rear and be sure no cattle strayed. They ate dust all day. "I have seen them come off herd with the dust half an inch deep on their hats and thick as fur in their eyebrows and mustaches," recalled Teddy Blue, "and if they shook their head or you tapped their cheek it would fall off them in showers." Drag riders usually were young men desperate for a job. "The poorest men," said Teddy Blue. "They would go to the water barrel at the end of the day and rinse their mouths and cough and spit and bring up that black stuff out of their throats. But you couldn't get it up out of your lungs."

The hard work was momentarily forgotten as the drive ended in a much-heralded assault upon decency in such towns as Abilene and Dodge City. "A small, dead place, consisting of about one dozen log huts" when McCoy arrived in 1867, Abilene was the first of the cattle towns cut from the soon-to-be famous mold — a town built almost completely on the cattle trade. Others followed: Ellsworth, Caldwell, Wichita, and Dodge in

Kansas; Cheyene, Wyoming; Kansas City and Sedalia, Missouri. They have inspired reams of literature; superficial, machismo movies; some pretty fair art; and, today, "Old West" towns throughout the Midwest. In reality, the arrival of the punchers in town is another bit of Americana that seems to have been sapped of all its intrinsic interest and embroidered with stories the equal of Parson Weems's fable of George Washington and the cherry tree. We have been deluged by the stereotypical movie scene in which the cowboy strides into the no-man's-land of the saloon to down a drink, the inept marshal warns the trail boss to take his ruffians outside town, or the punchers shoot up the main street and return the following day to pay for the saloon's shattered gilt-edged mirror — proving yet again that fiction is often more interesting than truth.

As it was, McCoy's promotion was quite a success. More than fifty thousand head of cattle arrived in Abilene during 1868, leading the board of directors of the Union Pacific Railroad, usually a cautious bunch, to predict a very large increase in business. McCoy faced a claim of $4,500 from residents of the Abilene area for damage caused by Texas stock during his first year of operation, but he convinced the cattlemen to pay $1,200 of the total.

Several fortunes were in the offing. Men like John W. Iliff and Charles Goodnight proved exceptionally talented; Goodnight earned more than half a million dollars for his financial backer in just five years. Others could hardly wait to get into the cattle business. Literally thousands of cattle walked to market up the trails from Texas.

The trails did not last long, however. The hard winter of 1886-87 greatly hurt northern ranchers; thousands of head of stock starved on the snow-covered range. Then the increasing use of barbed wire (made popular by a De Kalb, Illinois, salesman named Joseph F. Glidden) prepared the doom of the open trail.

Soon there were problems that even Joseph McCoy, the man who had made the trade possible, could not overcome. Wichita, a cow town further south on the Chisholm Trail, cut into Abilene's business, even though it also was located in the quarantined district. Residents became increasingly vocal in their denunciation of the tick-bearing Longhorns. When the Kansas Pacific Railroad voided its contract with him in 1870, McCoy was forced to declare bankruptcy. By 1876 settlements had so enclosed the trail that it was evident that cattlemen needed a new route, one farther west, that would not be molested by civilization.

Answering the need, officials of the Santa Fe Railroad created what was to become the most famous of all cow towns. Moving approximately 175 miles southwest of Abilene, they established their new railhead at Dodge City, a little-known spot fortunately beyond the quarantines. Dodge City was within the Osage Reservation, but that posed no problem. A rider attached to the Indian Appropriation Bill of 1871 provided that the laws relating to townsites could be extended

Courtesy Amon Carter Museum, Fort Worth, Texas   *Drawn by W. J. Palmer, Harper's Weekly, 1875*

Driving Cattle Into A Corral In The Far West

onto Osage land. As the Texans blazed a new trail, railroad officials set to work on new pens. By 1876 the Western Trail was in use. Departing the Chisholm Trail at Belton, in Central Texas, the Western Trail headed north through Fort Griffin in West Texas. It crossed the Red River at Jonathan Doan's store, then proceeded through Indian Territory to Dodge City. By 1877 more cattlemen were using the Western Trail than the Chisholm. Shipments in Wichita dwindled to 4,102 that year, while Dodge City shipped 22,940 carloads of beef. Abilene suffered even more. By 1871 the stockyards' income there had diminished a full 15 percent, with a similar decrease in community revenues. By the spring of 1873, 80 percent of the buildings in Abilene were vacant, and the business community was begging the Texans to return.

But the trade had moved to Dodge City, which proved to be the most famous and the longest-lived of the cattle towns. From the first shipment of beeves, success seemed assured. "The grass is remarkably fine, the water plenty, drinks two for a quarter, and no grangers," boasted a reporter for the Dodge City *Times*. "These facts make Dodge City THE cattle point." Dodge was headquarters for dozens of cattle dealers ready to buy what seemed to be any amount of Texas beef. They mixed with scores of cowboys, behaving as if they had a reputation to uphold. But Dodge was not the only boom town on the Western Trail. Fort Griffin also prospered from the cattle trade, just as Fort Worth on the Chisholm Trail had a few years before.

Even in the midst of prosperity, ex-perienced cattlemen realized that the move from Abilene and Wichita to Dodge City was only a temporary solution to their problem. The primary cattle trail could not be shifted westward every time civilization threatened to enclose it. They had to search for other answers. Railroads had come to Texas, of course, but it was cheaper and easier to trail a herd to Kansas and ship from there than to ship from Fort Worth or San Antonio. Besides, Longhorns, because of their tapered and sharp horns, were difficult to ship, and only a few could be placed in a boxcar. (The later development of shorthorns would ease this problem.)

South Texans thought they had the solution, as ranchers from across the nation gathered in St. Louis in 1884 for the first national cattlemen's meeting. Foremost among their proposals was a recommendation for a National Trail. They wanted a trail under federal control (which would therefore override any state legislation) that would extend from South Texas, through Oklahoma, around Kansas (because of the quarantine), through Colorado, Nebraska, South Dakota, Wyoming, and Montana into Canada. There was considerable support for the resolution, since Texans made up 47 percent of the delegates. Some Kansans favored it, too, because they wanted to see the Texans limited to only one trail.

Texas Sen. Richard Coke and Congressman James F. Miller introduced bills in both houses of Congress in December 1884 outlining the proposal for a National Trail. They asked for a trail six miles wide to be laid out by three commissioners chosen for that purpose by the Secretary of the Interior. Coke and Miller envisioned grazing grounds and quarantine grounds, as well as crossings for local cattle at designated points, where the trail would be no more than two hundred feet wide. All the land for the trail would be withdrawn from the public domain and reserved for that purpose for ten years.

The National Trail concept never really had a chance. Texans supported it because they saw it as the answer to their problem. It would have given them an alternative to paying high railroad fees from Texas or combatting irate citizens in Kansas. But almost no one else supported the plan. Northerners who had plenty of cattle opposed it because they did not want any more competition from the Longhorns. Kansans feared Texas fever, so they opposed it. Ranchmen in Wyoming, Dakota, and Montana grazed their cattle on public domain and did not want to share it with cattle from Texas, so they opposed it.

The northern ranchers might have thrown their support behind the National Trail if the Texans had been willing to compromise. The northerners wanted legislation permitting the public domain to be leased for grazing. Fearful of being evicted from the grassland at any moment, these ranchers would have welcomed a law that guaranteed their grazing rights for several years. But the Texans would not equivocate, thinking that this would prevent them from grazing their cattle on public domain when they were in northern regions, so both measures failed.

With the fencing of the Midwest, the spread of railroads and packing facilities, and no possibility of developing a national trail, the drives came to a close — and with them a unique phase of the cowboy's life. The three-month adventure across the plains, immortalized in the paintings of Frederic Remington, the photographs of Erwin E. Smith, and the writing of Andy Adams, soon became a dominant factor in the cowboy's composite character. Without the danger of stampede, the long trek across Indian country, the freedom (not to say isolation and loneliness), and the final arrival in Dodge City or some other cattle town, the cowboy image today would more closely resemble the hardworking "hand" that William Curry Holden documents so thoroughly in his excellent book on the Spur Ranch.

The trail was an important development that enabled the livestock industry to become one of the important economic factors in Texas, but it also molded, perhaps more than most realize, the contemporary image of the American cowboy.

THE OXBOW ROUTE
By Emmett M. Essin

Sunday, October 10, 1858, was a momentous day for the residents of the Pacific Coast. Early that morning a brightly painted Abbot-Downing Concord Coach drawn by a powerful six-horse team rolled up to the Butterfield Overland Mail office in San Francisco. Only twenty-three days and twenty-three hours earlier the journey had begun when a similar coach left Tipton, Missouri, the railhead of the Pacific Railroad 160 miles west of St. Louis. The once fantastic dream of a letter reaching the West Coast in less than a month had come

true. Almost equally swift was the initial eastbound journey; mail that left San Francisco on September 16 reached St. Louis in twenty-four days and eighteen hours.

Completion of these initial runs received prompt notice. Citizens in San Francisco and St. Louis held noisy celebrations. Newspaper editors throughout the nation — even those from the North, though somewhat reluctantly — gave credit for the amazing accomplishment. The New York *Herald* claimed that "the great Overland Route to India . . . has entirely

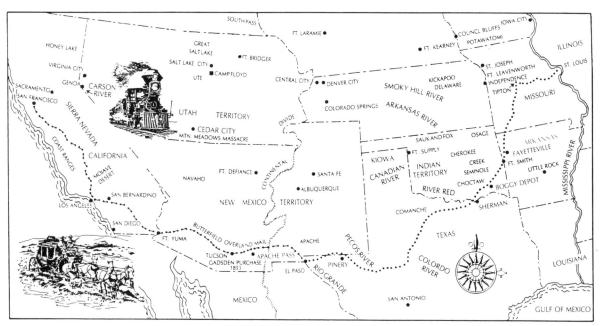

The Oxbow Route

been thrown into the shade by this enterprise." *Harpers Weekly* commented that "California is no longer a colony of the East." President James Buchanan sent John Butterfield a telegram stating that the event was a "glorious triumph for civilization and the union." And from London the *Times* proclaimed that it was "a matter of greatest importance to Europe, inasmuch as it will open up a vast country to European immigration, will be the precursor of the railroads, and will greatly facilitate intercourse with British Columbia."

To westerners, especially, the operation of the Overland Mail stages was a near-dream come true. Since the Mexican cession of 1848 and the gold rush of the following year, Californians and the gold seekers had felt physically isolated from the rest of the country. As soon as California was admitted as a state in 1850 they began efforts to establish semiweekly mail and passenger service between the Mississippi Valley and the Pacific Coast.*

Californians — both then and now — are ambitious, enterprising, and impatient people. They first agitated for the ideal transportation system, a transcontinental railroad. By combining with eastern railroad men and others, they started their campaign. These propagandists knew that private capital could not afford to operate such an expensive enterprise, since railroads made money for their stockholders only in densely popu-

lated regions. Any transcontinental line, therefore, would require massive government subsidies. So they claimed that the road was needed for national defense and was an important matter for the nation's lawmakers. An argument of this kind usually is not ignored in the United States; during the lame duck session in 1853 few congressmen openly objected to appropriating $150,000 from the War Department's budget for "the purpose of conducting various surveys to determine the most feasible route for a transcontinental railroad."

Jefferson Davis, Secretary of War under President Franklin Pierce, acted quickly and decisively. An ardent advocate of a transcontinental railroad, he ramrodded the undertaking. Commanders were chosen for five expeditions. The routes for reconnaissance were to extend from the far North to the far Southwest. The first would begin at St. Paul, Minnesota Territory, and extend to the mouth of the Columbia River between the forty-seventh and forty-ninth parallels. The second would traverse the California Immigrant Trail, and the third was to follow a line between the thirty-eighth and thirty-ninth parallels. The fourth expedition commenced at Fort Smith, Arkansas, and followed the thirty-fifth parallel to Los Angeles. The far southwest route was from Franklin, Texas (El Paso), through the Gadsden Purchase to Yuma along the thirty-second parallel.

The five commanders' reports were ready by 1855 and proved that there were at least five good railroad routes to the coast. In fact, transconti-

*California already had a thirty-day mail service. The Pacific Mail Steamship Company had received a government subsidy to deliver mail. The cost, however, was from twelve to eighty cents an ounce and via Panama. This made the sea route somewhat haphazard.

nental railroad lines were later extended over all these routes. Although Davis claimed that the Franklin-Yuma-Los Angeles road was the best of all possibilities, only southerners agreed with him. The issue of a railroad to the Pacific, as many had earlier predicted, was quickly embroiled in arguments about sectionalism; and these issues would not be settled until southerners rebelled against the Union.

Realizing that their initial plan had been derailed, Californians proposed a less ambitious alternative. In 1856 California Sen. John B. Weller finally succeeded in getting Congress to appropriate funds for building two federal wagon roads to the coast. One would follow the trail through South Pass and the other would follow the thirty-second parallel west of Franklin. Weller's bill for the "improvement of overland transportation" encouraged all those concerned with providing mail and passenger service to the Pacific Coast. Now all that needed to be done was to convince the national lawmakers to provide a financial incentive to a yet-unorganized stagecoach company to provide semiweekly overland service to California. Although several companies had already received mail contracts for portions of the West, a California contract would be different, for many people assumed that a transcontinental railroad would eventually follow a stage line. Thus the sectional issue entered the picture once again.

This time, however, Californians were not to be denied. After the presidential election of 1856 and the unanticipated easy victory of James Buchanan and the Democratic party, Sen. William M. Gwin of California formed an alliance of mutual interest with southern congressmen and senators to insure a mail contract. In February 1857 the interested senators attached a rider to the Post Office Appropriation Bill for a mail contract to be advertised and given to a company that would provide regular mail service. The rider further stipulated that the route followed and the eastern terminus were to be selected by the company receiving the contract. Failing to receive a majority of votes in the upper chamber, this amendment was referred to the Committee of Conference. There Sen. Thomas J. Rusk of Texas sided with committee member Gwin, "slightly" changed the intent of the rider, and successfully lobbied enough members to send back to the floor a distinctly favorable addition to the appropriation bill — one designed to assure Californians of mail service and to advance the ambitions of southerners. According to the terms "worked out in committee," Congress would authorize the postmaster general to contract for an overland mail service from a point on the Mississippi River to San Francisco "as the contractor might select."

On the day before Buchanan's inauguration both houses of Congress, hurriedly preparing for the new administration, passed the bill, along with several others, without debate. That same day it was signed by Franklin Pierce. This was a significant victory for both Californians and southerners. Since it was already known that Aaron V. Brown of Tennessee would be Buchanan's postmaster general and that he, not Congress, would award the contract, southerners suspected that the South would be included in the route selected. Possibly Senator Rusk knew that Texas would not be bypassed.

The terms for mail service to the Pacific were fairly inclusive. The contract stipulated that for a period of six years the government would pay — at the discretion of the postmaster — $300,000 a year for semimonthly service, $450,000 for weekly service, and $600,000 for semiweekly mail deliveries. It also required that the successful contractor complete each run in twenty-five days or less and furnish "good four-horse coaches or spring wagons" that were "suitable" to accommodate passengers and to insure the "safety and security of the mails." The contractor would preempt 320 acres of any land not then disposed of or reserved every ten miles along the route for a station. He had only one year from the date of the contract to get the line into operation.

Presidential preference dominated the awarding of the Overland Mail contract. On April 20, 1857, the postmaster general sent out the required advertisement for competitive bids, but one strongly suspects that a decision had already been reached independently by both President Buchanan and Brown. Nine bids were submitted — three by a syndicate formed by the president of the American Express Company, John Butterfield, and including such other notable New York expressmen as Johnston Livingston and William G. Fargo. Buchanan probably had informed Brown that his good friend John Butterfield would receive the

prize — unwelcome news to his postmaster general, who had already made a committment to Jim Birch, one of the founders of the California Stage Company. Brown acquiesced to the president's command but made sure Birch received a consolation prize, a mail contract for the 1,475-mile San Antonio-El Paso-San Diego mail route. Brown awarded the contract to Birch on June 22, while negotiations continued with Butterfield. For a four-year contract of $149,800 a year, Birch promised semimonthly service starting within thirty days. Dubbed the Jackass Mail — since only mules were used to haul the wagons — it was estimated that the government paid approximately $65 for each letter carried during the years 1857-1861.

The bids submitted by the Butterfield syndicate all cited the shortest "year-round" route from the Mississippi to California, which generally followed the thirty-fifth parallel. This route duplicated most of the railroad survey made by Lt. A. W. Whipple in 1854 and included portions of the Santa Fe Trail. Referred to by some pioneers as the Middle Passage, it was by way of St. Louis or Memphis and Fort Smith, and then along the south bank of the Canadian River to Albuquerque. From there it went westward across the Colorado River, over the Mojave Desert to Tejon Pass, and then through the Tulare and San Joaquin valleys to San Jose and San Francisco. One of the bids was for semiweekly service between St. Louis and San Francisco ($585,000 per year); another was for the same service between Memphis and San Francisco ($590,000 per year). The third bid called for a "bifurcated" route from St. Louis and Memphis ($600,000) which would converge at the most convenient point and follow the thirty-fifth parallel to the West Coast. In submitting the offers, Butterfield stipulated that, in effect, the route chosen was a fairly flexible one, and it could be altered by the postmaster general to expedite the delivery of the mail.

What Butterfield and his associates meant was that the route along the thirty-fifth parallel could be altered. Aaron V. Brown, however, not only deliberately misinterpreted the syndicate's offer but also disregarded the original intent of the law. Turning down the route along the thirty-fifth parallel, he proposed that Butterfield operate lines from St. Louis and Memphis to Little Rock, Arkansas, where the two routes would meet. From there the route would go to Fort Smith, pass through the unorganized Indian Territory, and cross Red River at Preston's Station or some other convenient place. It would then slant southwestward to Franklin, Texas (El Paso); from there it would follow the semideveloped trail to Tucson and Fort Yuma, and finally on to San Francisco via Los Angeles. Brown's proposed alteration meant that the mails would be carried an additional six hundred miles.

Members of the syndicate strenuously objected, but when push came to shove Brown gave very little ground. The only modifications the postmaster general would accept were that Little Rock could be eliminated (the lines would merge at Fort Smith), and that since the Pacific Railroad Company (the Missouri

Pacific) would be completed from St. Louis to Tipton in 1858, the stages could begin there. Brown warned the contractors that if the stage line were moved farther west than Springfield, Missouri, the bifurcated route would end, and the line would operate only from Memphis. Brown's purpose was clear: he was determined to make the overland route a southern and southwestern one. Perhaps he was anticipating a railroad along the same line in the near future?

On September 16, 1857, Butterfield and associates signed the six-year government contract. For an annual subsidy of $600,000, they guaranteed that the new lines would be in operation in one year's time and that their coaches would complete semiweekly runs in twenty-five days. With more than six hundred additional miles to cover, the experienced New York expressmen must have wondered whether they had lost touch with reality. The line now stretched 2,812 miles.

When terms of the contract were made public, many northerners were outraged. The editor of the Chicago *Tribune* proclaimed that the Butterfield Overland Mail Service was "one of the greatest swindles ever perpetrated upon the country by slave-holders" and implied that a central route would be much shorter and more advantageous to the commercial centers of the nation. Others echoed this sentiment and dubbed the new line the "Oxbow Route." The New York expressmen were described as irresponsible speculators. Brown countered by emphasizing that only this southwestern route would be open to year-round travel.

Whether he was correct, and regardless of protests, the contract was an established fact. After the objections subsided, most Americans waited to see whether the Butterfield syndicate would be able to deliver the mail.

Through his organizational abilities, John Butterfield partially silenced his northern detractors. Associated with stagecoaching since his teens, he knew all the ins and outs of the business. His American Express Company had operated successfully in New York and throughout the Mohawk River Valley. An optimist and a man of tremendous energy, he was confident that the overland route would succeed.

The initial task was to survey the exact route of the new line. In areas where existing roads or trails were unknown or obscure, trusted agents investigated and made recommendations. Wherever possible, however, Butterfield ordered that established roads should be used. That would not only save the expense of building new ones but also made it possible to capitalize on the business of established communities. West of Tipton, for example, the line would make use of the Boonville mail road, and from Fort Smith to El Paso it would generally follow the trail mapped by Capt. Randolph B. Marcy in 1849. Butterfield was determined to make a substantial profit. As he received his agents' reports, he sent out construction crews to cut new roads, to repair or rebuild old ones, and to locate and construct stations, dig wells, and build water tanks.

As surveyors were determining the route and test runs were being made, leaders of communities as far as fifty miles off the road were petitioning both Butterfield and Brown to include their towns for mail service. Although most attempts failed, at least one succeeded. Benjamin Franklin Colbert, a Chickasaw Indian, and some leading citizens of Sherman, Texas, a small north-central town in Grayson County established in 1848, were rewarded for their persistent efforts. The original survey had the stages crossing Red River at Preston Crossing, eight miles above Colbert's Ferry Crossing. To divert the line, Colbert agreed to ferry Butterfield stages across the river without charge and to repair portions of the road. The citizens of Sherman agreed to build and maintain a road through Grayson County. These conditions proved too advantageous for Butterfield to refuse.

To organize the Overland Mail Service and facilitate all operations, Butterfield separated the route into eastern and western divisions with El Paso as the dividing line. He subdivided each division into nine departments, with a superintendent in charge of each who had had extensive experience with eastern stage lines. There were five departments in the eastern division and four in the western. The actual departments of the route were: first, San Francisco to Los Angeles; second, Los Angeles to Fort Yuma; third, Fort Yuma to Tucson; fourth, Tucson to El Paso; fifth, El Paso to Fort Chadbourne; sixth, Fort Chadbourne to Colbert's Ferry; seventh, Colbert's Ferry to Fort Smith; eighth, Fort Smith to Tipton; ninth, Tipton to St. Louis. In each department Butterfield established three kinds of stops — terminals, "home stations," and "swing stations."

Dividing the line, establishing separate departments, and designating the different kinds of stations were ideas that had worked well for eastern stagecoach companies. Butterfield had, in fact, transferred an eastern-New York-New England operation to the West. Not only were the superintendents mainly from the East but also many of the drivers and conductors. Following stagecoach tradition, each driver worked a sixty-mile stretch both east and west. He was therefore familiar with the road and usually could compensate for unexpected conditions. Approaching each station, he or the conductor blew a bugle to alert the helpers to get a fresh relay of animals ready. The conductor had total charge of the mail, express packages, passengers, and equipment. At the end of each division he transferred these responsibilities to another conductor and got a receipt. As in the East, coaches carried express packages to bolster the profits from passengers and the mail subsidy. In addition to these employees, Butterfield also recruited stationkeepers, mechanics, blacksmiths, helpers, and even herders from northern New York and especially the Mohawk River Valley. When the line was in full operation he employed approximately two thousand men.

The equipment used on the line was also of eastern origin. Butterfield purchased all harness sets from James B. Hill & Sons of Concord, New Hampshire. He ordered the stageline's coaches from the Abbot-Downing Coach Company of Concord, Goold Coach Company of Al-

bany, and Eaton Gilbert and Company of Troy, New York. Two types of passenger vehicles would cover the route. Those used between Tipton and Springfield and later Fort Smith, and from Los Angeles, were the Concord coaches, sometime referred to as the Southern-style Wagon. These elegant, oval-shaped, full-bodied vehicles weighed three thousand pounds and were capable of transporting four thousand pounds. Built of seasoned hardwoods, lined with russet leather, and with russet leather curtains and thick cushions, these carriages could seat nine passengers inside and several more on the top. All luggage and express packages were placed in the boot. The brightly painted coaches were usually red or "dark bottle" green with "Overland Mail Service" lettered on the top panels of each side. They were the most comfortable, durable, and safe coaches built in the United States. They were swung on thoroughbraces of stitched leather 3½ inches wide; the axles measured 2½ inches in thickness; and the body was reinforced with iron. Most important, the vehicle's base was wide enough to keep it from tipping over in the roughest terrain. Although the Abbot Downing Company built many of the plush coaches for Butterfield, the Goold Coach Company also furnished some of them. In fact, the first westbound coach was built by the Goold Company.

To demonstrate how well made and durable the Concord coaches were, the story is told of the Abbot-Downing Company shipping one of the vehicles to California by sea. In rounding Cape Horn the ship sank. When the vessel was salvaged some three months later, the waterlogged coach was still in good condition. Supposedly it was used for years on California stagelines.

The other type of coaches — those to be used over most of the route — were the Celerity Wagons. The first hundred of these were ordered from James Goold, but later the other two companies also built the wagons. Similar to the Concords, they were built on a smaller frame, were lighter, and could better handle the muddier roads. Sometimes called Mud Wagons, their wheels were smaller and the ride rougher. The top was only a frame structure covered with heavy canvas. One feature of the wagons was that three seats were arranged so that when they were let down they formed a single large bed.

To pull the Concord coaches and Celerity Wagons, company agents purchased powerfully built horses and mules — some 1,800 in all. Mainly bought from suppliers along the route, these animals were usually dark colored, between five and nine years old, and heavily muscled. Depending on terrain and the loads carried, four, five, or six-mule or horse teams would pull the Celerity Wagons. As it turned out, the company used almost as many mule teams as

Harper's Weekly Dec. 11, 1858

Overland stage leaving San Francisco

horse teams. Mules were often used between Springfield and Fort Smith, always throughout Indian Territory, and across wide stretches of Texas. In the Pecos Valley, where some relay or "swing" stations were more than sixty miles apart, herders driving three or four five-mule teams followed the wagons. Every twelve to fifteen miles the herders, driver, and conductor made a "flying change." Toward the end of these trips, the exhausted mules could not keep pace, and one herder remained behind with them. Mules were also used on most stretches between El Paso and Tucson and between Tucson and Fort Yuma. For these districts horses had first been designated, but they presented too much of a temptation for the Indians. Within six months after regular service began, mules were purchased to replace the horses.

Perhaps the company's biggest mistake was that each animal was branded on the left hip with OMC. Whenever station keepers or other employees were empowered to trade worn-out animals for new stock, there was no hiding the fact that these horses and mules had experienced hard times. Smart traders — those with good stock — gave OMC animals a wide berth.

Butterfield and associates spent more than $1 million to get ready for operations during the year stipulated in the contract. Some of the stations in the western division still were not completed when they were ready to start. There were 141 stations in September 1858 and 200 stations by January 1859. By then they had established fares and rules and had worked out a reasonably reliable schedule.

From the terminus of the Pacific Railroad or Memphis to San Francisco the company charged $200. From west to east, however, the fare was only $100. Easterners complained so bitterly over this discrepancy that the Overland Mail changed the rate to a uniform $200 and then reduced it to $150. Throughout its operations the wayfare was ten cents per mile traveled. The price for postage was ten cents a letter. The directors also established the policy that Butterfield stagecoaches would not transport large amounts of money or valuables. The rule was designed not only to discourage highwaymen but also to avoid competing with Wells Fargo and Company, which was affiliated with the Overland Mail Company.

Worked out in advance of the first run, the twenty-five day schedule turned out to be an excellent barometer of the Overland Mail Service. Although a few mails were delayed by flooded streams and sandstorms, most ran on or ahead of schedule. The fastest run was made in only three weeks. Usually the stages averaged 120 miles every 24 hours.

Moving west, Concord coaches left Tipton each Monday and Thursday evening at 6:00 and arrived in Springfield on Wednesday or Saturday morning at 7:45. By early Friday or Monday morning they had reached Fort Smith, and by Sunday and Wednesday at 12:30 A.M., they rolled into Sherman, Texas. By the time Fort Belnap was reached on Monday or Thursday morning at 9:00, a through passenger had been on the stage for one week. And so it continued. By the end of the second week the passenger would be on a Celerity Wagon somewhere between Soldier's Farewell and Tucson. If able to continue he would reach Los Angeles in about twenty-one days.

In advertising the schedule, Butterfield included admonitions he had already given to his employees in greater detail. For prospective customers who read the fine print, Butterfield cautioned that the schedule was "not exact" and that employees were "to use every possible exertion to get the stages through in quick time," even if they were ahead of schedule. Every minute was important to John Butterfield. "If each driver on the route lost fifteen minutes," he warned, "it would make a total loss of time, on the entire route, of twenty-five hours." Although all employees were to be polite to passengers, clearly their first responsibility was to meet or exceed the twenty-five-day mail schedule.

On Thursday, September 16, 1858 — a year to the day that Butterfield had signed the mail contract — a new coach rolled out of Tipton. One day earlier another new vehicle started the run from San Francisco. On the westbound stage rode John Butterfield; his son, who served as the initial driver; Judge B. F. Wheeler, owner of the Fort Smith *Times;* his wife and two children; T. R. Corbin of Washington, D.C.; and a special correspondent from the New York *Herald,* Waterman L. Ormsby, who was the only through traveler. Other passengers, whose names were unrecorded, also rode to the first station. Butterfield and the Wheelers would go as far as Fort Smith.

Ormsby, only twenty-three years old, wrote a series of eight articles for

the *Herald,* for the most part scribbled while en route. He recorded not only the tribulations that passengers encountered but also an excellent description of the topography and of the people he met. The editor of the San Francisco *Daily Evening Bulletin* charged that Ormsby "was especially employed *at the expense of the company,* to go over the route and write it up." Butterfield might have given the reporter a pass, but probably that was all, for Ormsby's descriptions were too frank and critical for him to have been employed by the Overland Mail Company. His honest accounts indicate that he realized he was participating in a historical event, and they also showed that he appreciated the diversity of the scenery along the southern route.

In his articles Ormsby also made repeated references to the animals used to pull the wagon, especially the mule teams. At Park's station on the Cane Hill road — between Fayetteville and Fort Smith — he saw a four-mule team harnessed to the wagon for the "dreaded Ozark range." In this instance his impression of the mules' performance was favorable. Had not the district superintendent provided "a most extraordinary team," Ormsby wrote, "I doubt whether we should have been able to cross in two days. The wiry, light, little animals tugged and pulled as if they would tear themselves to pieces, and our heavy wagon bounded along the crags as if it would be shaken in pieces every minute, and ourselves disembowelled on the spot." The team was used for nineteen miles.

That was the last time, however, that Ormsby wrote favorably of the company's mule stock. By the time the wagon had reached Sherman he was complaining about "wild" mules "which had just been broken, and the process had not fitted them very well for carrying the mail with rapidity." At Diamond's station, twenty miles west of Sherman, he had the first opportunity to witness "harnessing a wild mule." First each animal had to be snubbed to a tree, and then "the harness had to be put on piece by piece, care being taken to avoid his teeth and heels." Ormsby estimated that it took at least half an hour to harness each animal. On the route between Jacksboro and Belnap he described "stubborn and lazy" mules. Across the Staked Plains, when teams were herded behind the wagon, he wrote bitterly of jaded, wild mules. When hitched to the wagon, "the mules reared, pitched, twisted, whirled, wheeled, ran, stood still, and cut all sorts of capers." The wagon "performed so many revolutions" that the scared reporter abandoned it and took to his heels, fully confident that he "could make more progress in a straight line, with much less risk of breaking his neck." By the time the wagon reached Picacho Pass in New Mexico Territory, the tired correspondent could only record, "We changed our horses for another team of those interminable mules and started on a dreary ride." From Tucson to San Francisco Ormsby observed that the line was well stocked and few mules were used. "Were it not for the excellence of the stock and the arrangements of the stations on this end of the line," he concluded, "the first mail could not have come through in time."

In spite of his troubles with mules, Ormsby indicated that he was holding up remarkably well and enjoying the experience. He urged others to tour the southern route. They could travel by comfortable stages, stop along the way to rest, and enjoy "many opportunities for viewing the beautiful, the wonderful, and the sublime products of nature, which are well disposed over the entire distance."

The Butterfield stages rolled day and night over the Oxbow and were never seriously delayed. The line was a conspicuous success and seemed to vindicate James Buchanan, Aaron V. Brown, and John Butterfield and associates. If not for the Civil War, the Overland Mail Company would probably have continued its established operations. But when the war began, through travel became impossible, and the line was switched to the central route through South Pass. The last coach left Tucson on March 6, 1861, and arrived at the railroad terminus on the 21st.

The short-lived existence of the Overland Mail over the Oxbow does not diminish its long-term consequences. Its influence had greatly affected mail delivery all along the route, as it established feeder lines and daily or weekly runs wherever needed. The company also commissioned a steamboat, the *Jennie Whipple,* to facilitate service between Little Rock and Fort Smith. The entire mail and passenger service increased substantially. The mail even operated a semimonthly branch line between Mesilla and Santa Fe, one of the many branch lines operated by the Butterfield syndicate.

Towns and stations along the line grew materially. Sherman, Texas, already one of the few established points on the Preston Road or Texas Trail, became an important distribution center with the coming of the Overland Mail. Within a year not only had it become a meal and timetable station, but its population had doubled. Sherman continued to grow. By 1871 it was the junction of fourteen stage lines and one of the largest towns in Texas. The populations of El Paso, Tucson, and Los Angeles also increased dramatically, and some of the home and swing stations became established towns.

When the Southern Pacific Railroad began construction west of El Paso, it followed large portions of the Butterfield line. In some locations it established the grade in the ruts of the old trail. It also used the wells which had been excavated by Butterfield employees.

For thirty years the Overland Mail line continued to be the main artery of traffic in the Southwest. Texas cattle were herded over the route to Arizona Territory and California. It became the established military highway between Texas and California. Most important, prospectors moving to the goldfields in California and Arizona Territory or pioneers moving west followed the trail, used its water wells, and stopped along the way to populate the old home and swing stations. Although the route in many places followed older trails, the mail line brought together a major thoroughfare from the Mississippi River to California. The establishing of the Oxbow Route was a climax to the work begun generations before by explorers, traders, government surveyors, and freighters.

THE BOZEMAN TRAIL TO MONTANA
By Michael J. Stephen

The year was 1863. Gold strikes in Montana had brought a small stream of miners to the territory after 1852, but for ten years none had struck it rich. In July 1862 John White and other prospectors discovered rich deposits on Grasshopper Creek, and the rush to the Montana diggings began. Bannack City, a collection of miners' shacks and a few stores, quickly arose on the banks of Grasshopper Creek. Separated from the Oregon Trail by mountain and desert that made hard going for freight wagons, the new mining town was extremely difficult to supply.

One possible route for supplies was by way of the Missouri River and Fort Benton, but in 1861 not a single riverboat reached the fort. Hard-

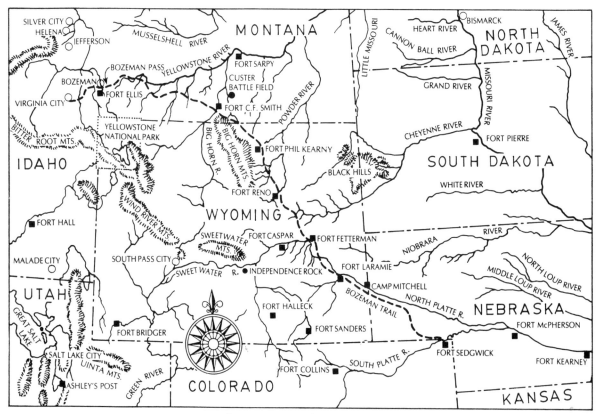

The Bozeman Trail to Montana

pressed for supplies of all kinds, the growing number of Montana miners were desperate. Two men were determined to find a shorter and easier wagon route from the Oregon Trail in hope of profiting by guiding wagon trains over it.

One of these was twenty-five-year-old John Merin Bozeman of Georgia who, like many others, had left wife and family for the lure of gold. And, like many, he never saw his family again. His partner was Mountain Man John Jacobs, who knew the lay of the land, the rivers, waterholes, and mountains. By combining their skills they hoped to gain the wealth that had eluded them in the diggings. Young Bozeman, with only four years' experience in the West, would be the promoter.

Late in April 1863 Bozeman, Jacobs, and Jacobs' half-Indian daughter rode out of Bannack City eastward toward the Yellowstone River. Their trip proved more eventful than expected. An Indian war party captured them and seized their possessions. They scolded Jacobs' daughter for traveling with white men, then took the party's fresh horses, leaving three broken-down Indian ponies in exchange. Bozeman and his companions continued, arriving on the Oregon Trail half-starved.

After resting and gathering supplies for several weeks the party was ready to guide the first wagon train north over the Bozeman Trail. Bozeman and Jacobs were unaware that while they had been preparing for the return trip a large gold strike had been made at Alder Gulch. Now their road was needed more than ever.

The first arrivals at the Grasshopper diggings near Bannack had come a great distance and endured many hardships. They had traveled along the Oregon Trail across Nebraska and Wyoming, then followed the

Bozeman Trail, Crossing the Bighorn River Near Fort C. F. Smith.

Platte River to Fort Caspar. The route continued west through South Pass over the Continental Divide and then southwest to Fort Bridger. They crossed more mountains and deserts before turning northwest to reach Fort Hall. From there they left the Oregon Trail and headed north, crossing the Great Divide again at Monida Pass and finally reaching the Grasshopper Creek goldfields. The proposed Bozeman Trail avoided most of the mountain and desert travel, was four hundred miles shorter, and eliminated six weeks of unnecessary hardships. The new road also offered a less-traveled route, which meant that more grass and water were available for the livestock, and more wild game and firewood were available for the people. The only drawback was danger from Indians, but Bozeman and Jacobs were convinced that a large wagon train could defend itself.

After several weeks of promoting their shorter route and discounting its dangers, the pair convinced a group of emigrants to try the new trail. On July 6, 1863, forty-six wagons with eighty-nine men, ten women, and several children set out toward the goldfields of Montana. The starting point was Deer Creek Station on the Oregon Trail between Fort Laramie and Fort Caspar. The country was rough, but grass and water were plentiful. The first few days they averaged ten to fourteen miles a day. By July 12, however, there was little good water. The creeks tasted salty, and the cattle weakened.

On July 20, as they neared the Big Horn Mountains, about 150 Cheyenne and Sioux warriors approached the corraled wagons. Bozeman and Jacobs met with the Indian leaders, who warned them, "go back or we'll kill you." The startled emigrants discussed the risks of ignoring the warning and weighed the alternatives. For eleven days they argued, hoping that another wagon train or a military escort would join them. The Sioux and Cheyenne warriors grimly waited, ready to carry out their threat. Finally, on July 31, the settlers, guided by Jacobs and two scouts, reluctantly turned their wagons back toward the Oregon Trail.

John Bozeman and nine of the men meanwhile rode north over the Bozeman Trail. They had only one horse packed with grub, and they traveled at night to avoid the Indians. For twenty-one days they toiled along with little food, crossing the mountains and long stretches without water or game. The final three days they had neither water nor food. On the third day they reached Stinking Water, a tributary of the Clark's Fork of the Yellowstone. They slaked their thirst, then proceeded on into the Big Horn Basin, where both water and wild game were plentiful.

Bozeman's party made the entire trip without losing man or horse, but they had spent considerable time avoiding numerous Indian war parties. From the Big Horn Basin they moved on toward the Belt Mountains and through a narrow pass which scout Irvin named Bozeman Pass in honor of his leader. From Bozeman Pass they entered Gallatin Valley and learned of the gold discovery at Alder Gulch. They also learned that people were leaving Bannack City to try their luck in the new towns of Nevada and Virginia City on Alder Creek.

In the meantime the wagons that turned back on the Bozeman Trail continued westward on the Oregon Trail. They reached Bannack on September 29, where they learned of the new diggins farther east at Alder Gulch. Some of the men struck out for the new area, arriving in Virginia City on October 3.

In 1864 John Bozeman returned to the Oregon Trail to try again to guide an emigrant train over his trail. This time he succeeded, following a course east and north of the Big Horn Mountains, and then up the Yellowstone River through Clark's Pass into Gallatin Valley.

The many camps of Bannack and Virginia City and Nevada City were bustling with activity, but there were no government officials nearer than the capital of Idaho Territory, far to the west of Bannack. The miners, eager to establish their own government, sent former Congressman Sidney Edgerton to Washington in hope of convincing President Lincoln that a new territory was needed. Edgerton met with Lincoln and many congressmen, promoting the name "Montana." Congress acted quickly; the Union needed financial support, and gold from Montana was welcome. Lincoln signed the Organic Act of May 26, 1864, and named Edgerton as the first governor of Montana Territory. Edgerton selected Bannack as the first capital because he lived there.

While the Bozeman Trail was much shorter than other routes to the goldfields of Montana, Indian hostility made it more dangerous. Jim Bridger guided two trains up the west side of the Big Horn Mountains in the summer of 1864. The first train of 62 wagons and 300 persons contained the Reverend L. B. Stateler, a Methodist Episcopal preacher. Bridger's new route differed from the Bozeman Trail by going west of the Big Horn Mountains and then through Big Horn Basin. This area appeared to be ignored by the Sioux, but the loaded wagons had difficulty because of the rough terrain. Only one Indian confrontation took place during the first trip, and the group arrived at the Madison River on July 8. Stateler eventually settled in Jefferson Valley and preached throughout the new territory.

Bridger's second trip started near

Courtesy Montana Historical Society, Helena
John M. Bozeman

Red Butte on September 18, and his party contained about twenty-five men, including John Owen. In the early 1850s Owen had purchased St. Mary's Mission from the Jesuits and transformed it into Fort Owen. Because of the late start, Bridger's party immediately ran into bad weather. The trail was difficult for the heavy wagons, and many overturned. Some days the train advanced but two miles. The oxen were plagued by poor water or none, yet the grass at times was good. On October 23 twelve yoke of oxen disappeared, probably run off by Indians. Bridger's route, unlike the Bozeman Trail, was relatively free of hostile Indians, but it crossed more rugged terrain and lacked good grazing and potable water.

One train that followed the Bozeman Trail in 1864 was that of A. A. Townsend. On June 29 he led 150 wagons, 467 persons, and 919 head of livestock from the Oregon Trail toward Montana Territory. Within a few days the Indians started to demand food and other items. On the Bozeman Trail Townsend lost four men and at one time was confronted by six hundred Crows demanding provisions. After Townsend's train arrived in Bozeman City many emigrants went on to Virginia City in search of gold.

John Jacobs also piloted a wagon train to Montana Territory in the summer of 1864, this time using Bridger's new road. Jacobs was in business to make money and was willing to escort people for pay over any route they wished to take.

In the summer of 1864 many other wagon trains ventured north to Mon-

tana. Indians continued to be the major obstacle, for they continually tried to force the emigrants to turn back. Wherever whites had traveled, buffalo became scarce; this was the last good hunting ground of the Sioux and Cheyennes, and they were growing desperate. Still the emigrants continued to flock to the goldfields of Montana. Bridger's road proved much too difficult to be used regularly, and after 1864 it was abandoned.

During the Civil War the regular troops were sent East from Fort Laramie and other western posts and replaced by untrained volunteers, who were eager to fight Indians. In 1864 the Sand Creek massacre of Cheyennes and Arapahos "set the prairie on fire"; the Brulé and Oglala Sioux joined the Cheyennes and Arapahos in a determined effort to rid their lands of whites. After burning stage stations along the Platte road and sacking Julesburg, most of them withdrew to the Powder River country, where buffalo were still plentiful. The Bozeman Trail ran through the heart of the last rich hunting grounds of the Sioux and their allies, and they were determined to keep whites out at all costs.

The driving factor pushing everyone toward Montana was, of course, gold. The federal government was also interested. After four years of civil war the U.S. Treasury desperately needed gold to offset the national debt. One way to obtain gold was to encourage more settlers and prospectors to journey west, and Congress appropriated money to survey a direct route from Sioux City to Montana by way of the Niobrara River. Col. James A. Sawyer led the survey expedition of about 100 men and 250 wagons. The party included professional engineers and prospectors and was escorted by two companies of former Confederate soldiers. Sawyer met such strong Indian resistance that he was forced to alter his route; he finally reached Virginia City by the Bozeman Trail. His report to Congress in March 1866 received considerable publicity and emphasized the need of protection for travelers on the road to Montana.

In 1865 Gen. Patrick E. Conner led an expedition to the Powder River country in an attempt to subdue the Sioux and Cheyennes. The expedition was a complete failure and only made the Indians bolder.

During this same period the government was negotiating treaties with bands of Sioux, Cheyennes, and Arapahos, guaranteeing Indian tribal rights to territory lying between the Black Hills, the Big Horn Mountains, and the Yellowstone. These rights, which had been gained by possession, were upheld only in exchange for safe passage for whites through the Powder River country. The treaty commissioners, however, overlooked the fact that most of the signers were peaceful Indians who had settled near the forts and who had no authority to speak for the hostiles. Red Cloud continued to raid emigrant trains along the Powder River, and there was still no safe route between Fort Laramie and Virginia City.

In the spring of 1866 the government sent a second treaty commission to Fort Laramie to offer new terms. At the same time, the War Department was reacting to pressure to protect travelers on the Montana Road. Maj. General John Pope, one of President Lincoln's unsuccessful Civil War commanders, was in charge of the Department of the Missouri, which included the Powder River country. On March 10, 1866, Pope ordered the Second Battalion, Eighteenth U.S. Infantry, to garrison Fort Reno on the Powder River and to build two new posts on the route to Virginia City in Montana. Four companies were to go to each of the other posts. They were commanded by Col. Henry B. Carrington.

Carrington was not a West Pointer; he graduated from Yale in 1845. His military accomplishments were few, for his duties had been administrative. Carrington had never heard a shot fired in combat and never commanded a unit on the field of battle. His recruiting and administrative assignments had, however, enabled him to make friends with men of considerable political influence in Washington. In the spring of 1866 Carrington placed himself in a position to be chosen to command the infantry battalion sent into the Powder River country. Because of public criticism of the army's excesses against the Indians, Carrington was not expected to be an Indian fighter.

Earlier, the tribes had permitted settlers and prospectors to move across the lands, believing they would not stay. But when the newcomers built forts and laid out overland stage routes, the buffalo herds rapidly declined, and the Indians began to raid. To protect the westward migrating citizens, and to compensate the Indians, the government had met with tribal leaders at Fort

Laramie in 1851. Treaties were signed with various tribes (Sioux, Cheyenne, Arapaho, and Crow) giving the government the right to maintain routes of travel and forts across the plains, while reserving tribal hunting rights for the Indians. For fifteen years the Indians saw endless numbers of whites encroaching on their lands, while the buffalo herds declined drastically. Conflicts occurred with increased intensity as the treaty agreements were continually broken. By 1865 the Plains Indians had finally reached a conclusion concerning the white man's intentions and worthless treaties. It was time to fight.

Carrington's initial plan called for picking up supplies and troops at Fort Kearny, Nebraska, and proceeding to Fort Reno, formerly Fort Conner. From Fort Reno they were to move north and build two new forts. Carrington built Fort Phil Kearny at Big Piney Creek and Fort C. F. Smith farther north on the Big Horn.

Carrington had only enough troops to defend the forts, which were constantly surrounded by hostile Sioux and Cheyennes. Since he couldn't provide escorts for wagon trains, Carrington refused to let them travel over the Bozeman Trail unless they were large enough to protect themselves. Few of them were, so travel virtually ceased. One of the men who traveled north along the Bozeman Trail, over Carrington's objection, was Nelson Story, a former freighter who had joined the rush to Virginia City. Story decided supplying miners was more profitable than panning gold. In 1866 he rode to

North Texas, where he bought one thousand cattle, mostly cows with the calves thrown in.

With twenty-five well-armed men, Story drove his herd north. When he finally reached Fort Phil Kearny, Carrington warned him to go no farther, for Red Cloud and his warriors barred the way.

Story had come too far to turn back; he continued the drive at night. He made it through to Bozeman with the loss of only one man, and he became one of the pioneer cattlemen of Montana.

For the troops at Fort Phil Kearny the winter of 1866 was a time of frustration. Some of the young officers at the fort fretted over the obstacles that had so far prevented them from achieving glory by killing Indians. Colonel Carrington knew full well that each fort was vulnerable. Even at full strength (and none of the forts were) the forces were inadequate to meet hostile Indians. Carrington was prudent and cautious, providing

Courtesy Montana Historical Socity, Helena
Nelson Story

guards to protect the women and children of the fort as well as any small body leaving the fort for special duty. Because his was not a fighting assignment, he tried to avoid clashes with the Indians. Carrington's caution and prudence were irritating to some of the hot-headed young officers, particularly those with no training or experience in Indian warfare who were eager to show the world how to fight Indians.

Colonel Carrington had orders to protect those traveling along the Bozeman Trail, but he had no troops to spare for escort duty. General Cooke, Carrington's superior, wanted the Indian warfare brought to end by battling the Indians throughout the winter. With barely enough men to hold the forts, Colonel Carrington was still waiting long-promised reinforcements. While he waited, some of the young officers became increasingly impatient and critical.

Capt. William J. Fetterman demanded an opportunity for action. He arrived at Fort Kearny in November 1866 and after a month joined the most restless and impatient officers — Capt. Fredric H. Brown, Lt. George W. Grummond, and Lt. J. S. Bingham. All were critical of Carrington for his refusal to risk his troops in unequal battles.

On the morning of December 6, 1866, Captain Fetterman first encountered an Indian force. The wood train had signaled from Pilot Hill that it was surrounded and needed help. Captain Fetterman and some mounted infantry were sent with Lieutenant Bingham to drive the Indians back over the ridge, while Colonel Carrington and Lieutenant Grummond with thirty men crossed Big Piney Creek to intercept the Indian force. In the midst of the battle against three hundred Indians, Lieutenant Bingham suddenly left the area with fifteen men, and Fetterman was on his own. Colonel Carrington pushed forward to reinforce Fetterman. Efforts to recall Bingham went unanswered, and, after an hour of searching, his body was found along with several others from his party.

Fetterman had served in the Civil War, but he had no experience on the frontier. He was reported to have said once that "A single company of regulars could whip the entire array of hostile tribes." Captain Fetterman continued to protest because the Indians were not punished, stating that with eighty men he could ride through the Sioux nation. He was soon to have his wish.

On the morning of December 21, 1866, a long wood train moved from Fort Kearny toward the pinery. It had gone less than two miles when the picket on Pilot Hill signaled that there were threatening Indians on Sullivant Hill. Carrington ordered a relief column readied, which was soon organized by Maj. J. W. Powell. On the insistent request of Captain Fetterman, Colonel Carrington allowed him to command the column. He warned Fetterman of the danger he faced and gave him explicit instructions: Support the wood train, relieve it, and report to me. Do not engage or pursue the Indians. Under no circumstances pursue them over Lodge Trail Ridge.

Fetterman rode toward the wood train, and within half an hour the picket on Pilot Hill signaled that the train was proceeding toward the pinery. There was no report, however, from the detachment of eighty-one officers and soldiers and two civilians. Within another half hour came the sound of rifle fire toward Peno Creek, beyond Lodge Trail Ridge. First, only a few scattered shots were heard, then intense, rapid fire was followed by a few volleys — after that, silence.

Capt. Tenedore Ten Eyck was dispatched immediately from the fort with a small force including two wagons, ambulances, and two doctors. He reached the hillside overlooking the battlefield and was immediately challenged by a large group of dancing, yelling Indians. Captain Fetterman's party was nowhere in sight. Captain Ten Eyck moved cautiously forward with his men and wagons. The battlefield soon came into view — there was not a living soldier, horse, or civilian to be seen, only the Indians retreating on the far side, still challenging and warwhooping.

The bodies of Fetterman and forty-eight others were loaded onto the wagons, which moved slowly back to the fort. The wood train had returned earlier to Fort Kearny, having neither seen nor heard Captain Fetterman's party.

The following day Colonel Carrington ordered a search for the remaining bodies beyond Lodge Trail Ridge. He was concerned about the safety of Fort Kearny, since the garrison was badly outnumbered. Arriving at the crest of Lodge Trail Ridge, Carrington observed the scene of action. There were thirty-two bodies, stripped naked and riddled with arrows, sticks, and spearheads. They were loaded into wagons, and the

party went back to the fort without seeing an Indian. The bodies were placed in the fort hospital and surrounding tents. The dead were dressed in uniforms and buried, after five days of digging graves in twenty-below-zero temperatures.

On the eve of the Fetterman fight Carrington sent John ("Portagee") Phillips to alert Fort Laramie, 236 miles to the southeast. Riding Colonel Carrington's thoroughbred horse and traveling only at night in subzero weather, Phillips reached the Horseshoe telegraph station at ten o'clock Christmas morning. He sent telegrams to the department commander at Omaha and the post commander at Fort Laramie. Not satisfield that the messages would get through, Phillips continued his journey to Fort Laramie, arriving about midnight the same day, where Carrington's horse died.

Reinforcements were immediately sent north from Fort Laramie under the command of Gen. H. W. Wessels. The trip was difficult and dangerous. Many soldiers suffered from frostbite as the mercury plunged to forty degrees below zero. Snow was waist deep.

With the arrival of General Wessels came an order relieving Colonel Carrington of command at Fort Phil Kearny. He was instructed to report to Fort Caspar. He and his family and the widow of Lieutenant Grummond left immediately.

Carrington knew how the public regarded the Indian campaign in the Powder River country. Sympathy was not with the soldiers and emigrants but with the Indians whose lands were being invaded. No one in the East could perceive the actual conditions on the Bozeman Trail. Yet a tragedy had occurred, and someone must be held responsible. The War Department was at last convinced that the Indians were a formidable opponent and not to be taken lightly.

General Wessells insisted on a sizable sentry guard at all times. The weather remained severe, and, with the increased guard and the task of cutting wood, many men came down with scurvy. When spring came the bull trains began to leave Fort Laramie for Montana, and Red Cloud's warriors attacked every wagon train that passed over the Bozeman Trail.

During the month of June a bull train owned by Gilmore and Porter arrived at Fort Kearny with wagons loaded with rations, forage, and arms. Among the weapons were seven hundred new breech-loading Springfield rifles to replace old muzzle-loaders.

Gilmore and Porter remained all summer, as they had previously negotiated a contract to provide logs and firewood to the fort. Obtaining good wood was becoming increasingly difficult, and the contractors constructed a corral six miles west of the fort on an open plain. They removed the boxes from fourteen wagons and formed them into an oval corral into which their stock was driven each night. Tents were pitched nearby, and seven thousand rounds of ammunitions were stored inside the corral.

A company of soldiers was assigned to provide security for the woodcutters in the pinery and to and from the fort. Few Indians were seen in July, but on August 1 several of the sentries suspected that Indians were near. On August 2 one group of wag-

ons left the wagon-box corral for the fort with a load of logs, and a second train departed for the lower pinery.

Suddenly seven Indians were sighted riding toward the Little Piney from the west. About the time the first shot was fired more Indians were observed in the foothills to the north. In a matter of minutes the small force had made it back to the wagon-box corral and assembled under the command of Captain Powell. Unknown to the Indians, each soldier was armed with a new breech-loading, fifty-caliber Springfield rifle.

When the Indians advanced from the north, troops began firing the new rifles at the mounted warriors. The corral was surrounded by painted warriors armed with guns, arrows, and spears. Some Indians ventured close enough to throw war clubs or to strike the wagons with coup sticks. In the open the Indians were exposed to rifle fire, and the new rifles could be reloaded and fired much more rapidly than the old muzzle-loaders.

The corral was some distance from any cover except to the northwest, where the Indians could hide behind a slope about seventy-five yards away. Here the Indians massed to charge the wagons, but they suffered heavy losses.

The fight continued into the afternoon; the day was hot and the water supply was low. A second charge came from the west end, as the Indians assembled from the east, south, and southwest to charge under the partial concealment of the tents pitched on the west perimeter. Again the Indians were beaten off with many casualties. The Springfield rifles were fired so rapidly the breechblocks had to be opened to cool the barrels.

In midafternoon the Indians withdrew from sight. The main body was situated to the east, where Red Cloud could easily observe the activities. Only a few scattered groups could be seen circling about, but the men behind the wagon boxes heard a humming, chanting sound that steadily grew louder. Suddenly from the west a horde of naked warriors swarmed out of the ravine and charged the corral. Hundreds and hundreds of Indians, all on foot, dashed toward the soldiers. The troops opened fire, cutting down those in front, whose places were immediately taken by those behind. The swarm of Indians got closer to the corral as the fire from the soldiers grew more intense. When it looked like all was lost the Indians suddenly broke and fled. Moments later the big boom of the post howitzer signaled that a relief party from Fort Kearny was approaching, and the Indians scattered. Captain Powell ordered the casualties loaded into the ambulances, and the entire force returned to the fort. Estimates of the Indian losses vary, but they probably were not nearly as heavy as some suggest.

During the summer of 1867 Sioux and Cheyenne warriors assembled on a stream about fifteen miles east of Fort Reno. Several thousand Indians planned to combine forces and destroy all the military posts along the Bozeman Trail.

Disregarding numerous warnings by friendly Crow scouts, soldiers at Fort Reno did not believe the tales of a gathering of more warriors than the Crows could count. Military operations continued as usual.

On July 31 the large Indian force split up, some staying in the immediate vicinity while others rode toward Fort Phil Kearny, ninety-five miles to the north. The remaining Indians waited a day and then attacked laborers in a hayfield who were cutting and curing hay for the winter. The hayfield corral was one hundred feet square and was constructed of logs laid on the ground and supported by posts. The field had been fortified earlier to protect the livestock.

Nineteen soldiers and civilians were at work the morning the Indians attacked. The soldiers were equipped with new Springfield rifles, while the civilians were armed with repeating rifles. Under the command of Capt. D. A. Colvin the small group fought from behind the log barricade.

Colvin, an excellent marksman, was armed with a sixteen-shot repeating rifle. He fired more than three hundred rounds during the day and estimated that he killed nearly 150 Indians. The Indians charged the hayfield defenders on foot and horseback, firing burning arrows into the barricade. The fighting continued all afternoon, while the small force anxiously awaited a relief party from the fort. After the fighting had subsided the post commander sent three companies of soldiers to relieve the hay cutters and troops. During the day he had sealed off the fort and was reluctant to send a relief force to the field, where the laborers were badly outnumbered. The defenders' casualties were three dead and four wounded, with the added loss of thirty mules. The Indians suffered heavily; several burial sites nearby contained more than fifty bodies each.

After the hayfield and wagon box fights of early August 1867, the federal government was again in a dilemma. The Indians were demanding better hunting guns from the Indian Department, while the War Department was furnishing guns to the whites to defend themselves.

In 1867 the Union Pacific Railroad forged through Wyoming, driving the Indians away from the railroad-stage routes to the northern part of the Bozeman Trail. A peace conference at Fort Laramie in late fall of 1867 produced no satisfactory results. Red Cloud refused to participate, and he vowed to defend the Powder River country, "the only hunting ground left to his nation." In the spring of 1868, however, he agreed to meet with peace commissioners at Fort Laramie. Finally, on November 6, 1868, Red Cloud signed the treaty, in which the United States agreed to abandon the three forts on the Bozeman Trail. When the troops withdrew, Red Cloud's warriors moved in and burned the buildings. The Bozeman Trail was closed.

It would be many years before the northern portion of the Bozeman Trail would become safe for travelers. The abandonment of the trail was regarded by many as a serious mistake, since much time and energy had been spent trying to settle the Powder River country. Yet the dangers along the Bozeman Trail in the late sixties and early seventies were just as great as before. The treaty of 1868, furthermore, set aside the country north of the North Platte River and east of the Big Horn Mountain summit as Indian Territory. Over the years both parties violated the agreement.

On April 17, 1867, John Bozeman and Tom Coover were en route south along the Yellowstone River to Fort C. F. Smith. They were camped along the river when a small group of Indians made off with a number of their horses.

The next day, while eating their noon meal, Bozeman and Coover saw five Indians approaching with the stolen horses. Bozeman, believing them to be friendly, offered them food. Without warning they shot him, while Coover fled. The Indians took the remaining horses and supplies. Coover learned later that the Indians were fugitive Blackfeet living with the Crows. Bozeman's body was recovered and laid to rest in a cemetery in the town named after him. He was thirty-two at the time of his death.

Indians remained in the vicinity of the Bozeman Trail, particularly in the north where the Crow Reservation is today. Much of the land is a cattle range, with the valleys used for cutting wild hay or alfalfa. In 1879 Buffalo, Wyoming, was founded on Clear Creek; Big Horn and Dayton were built in the early eighties. The entire area north of the Platte is generally an agricultural area and sparsely settled. Little remains to recall the sacrifice of the men who attempted to conquer and possess the Powder River country. Also largely forgotten were the desperate efforts of the Sioux and Cheyennes to retain their last buffalo range along the Bozeman Trail.

THE ALASKA GOLD TRAILS
By Robin May

"We are on the threshold of the greatest gold discovery ever made," proclaimed the San Francisco *Call* on July 20, 1897, quoting a Canadian official. As if to prove it, a whole boatload of Bonanza and Eldorado kings from the Klondike were in the city. They had landed five days ear-lier to the roars of thousands on the waterfront: "Show us the gold!"

As it turned out, the Klondike strike was not one of the biggest, yet its fame remains unimpaired. Other strikes followed, notably at Nome and Fairbanks, and many disappointed Klondike Stampede veterans

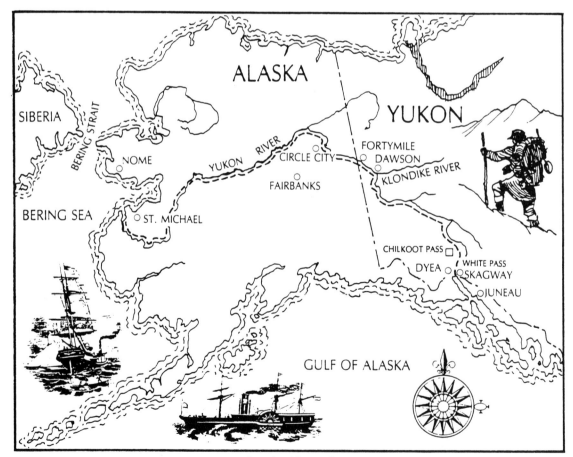

The Klondike Trail

headed out of Canadian territory into Alaska. Yet the Klondike remains fabulous — in history, legend, and literature — and the Americans, Canadians, Britons, and others who went there will dominate this chapter.

Part of its fame is due, of course, to the power of photography. The endless line of climbers on the four-mile trek to the summit of the Chilkoot Pass has caught the imagination of successive generations, the pictures symbolizing the unique quality of the rush to the Klondike, a remote, spectacularly rugged land. It is a land where hot summers give way to cruelly cold winters, a land that was invaded by ill-prepared thousands within living memory.

The Yukon River dominated this last frontier. More than 2,000 miles long and rising a mere 15 miles from the Pacific — or, more exactly, the Gulf of Alaska — it flows through Canadian, then American, territory to the Bering Strait. The Throndiuck, mispronounced "Klondike" by miners, was a tributary of the Yukon. The strike near the stream gave the world a new disease, Klondicitis.

Alaska was discovered by whites in 1741 during a Russian expedition led by Vitus Bering. Thanks to William H. Seward, it was bought by the United States in 1867 and promptly christened "Seward's Folly," "Seward's Icebox," "Icebergia," and so on.

Some gold had been found before the historic sale, but the Russians, ruling from the island of Sitka, were interested only in the fur trade. Meanwhile, Hudson's Bay traders, whose Fort Yukon was suddenly deep in American territory without their knowing it, were aware of golden possibilities but were not greatly concerned.

Gradually, Americans entered Alaska, some of them veterans of the California rush. Almost all were experienced miners, not greenhorns, and after 1880 modest amounts of gold were found.

The miners, mostly American, also struck gold over the ill-defined Canadian border, and two "towns" sprang up — Circle City in Alaska and Fortymile just across the Canadian border. The Canadian government, anxious not to allow the area to become American merely because Americans were there, sent a 20-strong detachment of Northwest Mounted Police under Inspector Constantine to Fortymile. It was now 1894.

The region, with its few hundred prospectors, was hardly even a frontier. There was little crime in Circle City, and the most industrious citizen seems to have been "Old Man Hunker" from Germany, who was busily devouring Gibbon's *Decline and Fall of the Roman Empire.* "Take 'em everywhere, and read 'em every night when I get time," he told a visitor to his grubby cabin. "I'll bet I know more about Caesar, Hadrian, Attila, Belisarius, and all the others than you do — or most anyone else."

One mining improvement helped counteract the effects of the long winter. In the late 1880s the system of "fire-setting" or "drifting" caught on after one miner decided to build a fire on the bottom of his frozen creek claim. Ground was thawed every night and day until bedrock was reach. This might be down ten or fifteen feet, in the sub-Arctic Yukon region. Drifting allowed a miner to work along the "pay streak" right through winter in his burnt-out shaft. In *Two Years in the Klondike and Alaskan Goldfields,* W. B. Haskell wrote: "By morning, if the amount of fuel has been properly gauged, nothing remains but the dying embers and the hot ashes; the smoke and gasses have all escaped." Pay dirt was piled in a mound, and in the spring the mounds, known locally as dumps, were tested in the traditional pan, rocker, and sluice box.

Only the extreme remoteness explains why it took so long for the Klondike Stampede to occur. Back in 1804, Alexander Baranov, the self-made genius who ran Russia's Alaskan territory from Sitka, saw a hunter take gold nuggets from his pocket. According to Jack London, writing in the *Atlantic Monthly Magazine* in July 1903, Baranov uttered these striking words:

> Ivan, I forbid you to go farther in this undertaking. Not a word about this, or we are all undone. Let the Americans and the English know that we have gold in these mountains, then we are all ruined. They will rush in on us in their thousands, and crowd us to the wall — to the death.

In any event, it was not until 1896, long after the Russians had gone, that the historic find was made by two Indians and a white man. As a result, "sturdy, indomitable gold-hunters of Anglo-Saxon stock," as Jack London dubbed them, set out for a place about which few of them knew anything.

Some, including the unlucky miner himself, claimed that the true hero of the Klondike strike was a dour Nova Scotian of Scottish descent, Robert Henderson. Grubstaked by a shopkeeper named Ladue, he started on a journey dogged by bad luck, until he reached a mountain from which he gazed in wonder at the majestic peaks around him. Below were some of the richest gold-bearing creeks on earth. He panned eight cents worth from one creek, which he hopefully called Gold Bottom. He moved on to where about twenty miners were working, persuading three of them to join him at his claim.

It was now July 1896, and by the end of the month the four had extracted $750 worth of gold. Being short of food, Henderson returned to Ladue's trading post at Sixtymile on the Yukon, passing on news of his strike to everyone he met. Soon all but Ladue were heading for the spot.

The Indian River down which he had come was now shallow in high summer, so, with new supplies, Henderson started down the Yukon. He was certain that his creek was a tributary of the Klondike, as it was already being called. The Indian "Thron-diuck" meant "hammer-water" because the local Indians hammered stakes across its mouth over which they spread nets to catch the teeming salmon. The swampy northern bank was covered with scrub timber, and it was here that the famous city of Dawson was to arise.

That day Henderson could see nothing but a solitary white man fishing. He decided to pass on the good news to the man, whose name was George Washington Carmack. The fisherman was a Californian, now married to an Indian woman named Kate, daughter of a Siwash chief. Carmack's sole ambition was to become a chief himself. Unlike most whites in the area, he genuinely liked Indians and liked to be called Siwash George. He also liked to read scientific journals and poetry — and to play the organ in his cabin.

Before Henderson reached shore, Carmack was joined by Skookum Jim, tall, handsome, and a renowned hunter; another Indian, Tagish Charley; and Kate and their daughter. They listened to Henderson's news, then the Nova Scotian made a fatal mistake. His exact words are disputed, but he probably said: "There's a chance for you, George, but I don't want any damn Siwashes staking on that creek." Then he pushed his boat out and left.

Carmack resented Henderson's words. Skookum Jim (Skookum means "strong") was furious. Carmack calmed him down and suggested that the three of them look for their own creek. They set out, without haste, toward Gold Bottom. On the way they panned a little in Rabbit Creek, which emptied opposite the future site of Dawson. The creek yielded a little color but not enough to excite them.

They called on Henderson at Gold Bottom and, unimpressed, headed into the hills. They then went back to Rabbit Creek.

It was soon to be known as Bonanza Creek.

An important misunderstanding had occurred during the second meeting with Henderson. According to Carmack, he told Henderson to come over to Rabbit Creek and stake a claim. Henderson later swore that it was he who urged Carmack to prospect Rabbit Creek. Whatever the truth, it seems that Carmack did promise to let Henderson know if anything worthwhile occurred at Rabbit Creek. But the anti-Indian Henderson ruined his chances again; when the Indians tried to buy tobacco from him he refused them.

On August 16, half a mile from the junction of Rabbit Creek with Eldorado Creek, the trio made history. Carmack always claimed that he found a protruding rim of bedrock and extracted from it a chunk of gold the size of a thumb. The Indians' version, probably correct, was that, while Carmack was sleeping, Jim was cleaning his pan in the creek and found the gold.

Gold there undeniably was, sandwiched between slabs of rock. One pan produced a quarter of an ounce, worth four dollars. This was a major find in the Yukon, where miners celebrated at ten cents worth.

The trio performed a war dance, described by Carmack as a combination of Scottish hornpipe, Indian fox trot, syncopated Irish jig, and Siwash hula. Then they rested and started work again. By the time the wonderful day had ended, Siwash George had been transformed into George Carmack, would-be gentleman of means. He would return to the white man's ways.

The next day they staked four claims — two for Carmack as the discoverer, as Canadian law allowed.

Jim later said this was agreed because, as an Indian, his claim to be the discoverer would not have been recognized. Meanwhile, Carmack cut away some bark from a spruce and wrote in pencil:

TO WHOM
IT MAY CONCERN
I do, this day, locate and claim, by right of discovery, five hundred feet, running up stream from this notice. Located this 17th day of August, 1896.

G. W. Carmack

Recording their claim at Fort Cudahy on the Yukon, they went on to Fortymile, telling everyone they met. They sent no message to Henderson, however. The sight of the gold transformed any doubters, and Bonanza Creek was rapidly staked out. Many veterans, especially at Circle City, were still suspicious of the worth of the finds, but reports of a $65 pan, then one of $212, caused a stampede. Since this happened in midwinter, it was rugged in the extreme.

As soon as Joseph Ladue heard the news, he laid out the townsite of Dawson, naming it after a government geologist. The wretched Henderson heard nothing until early September, when some miners told him of gold at Bonanza Creek, a name new to him. When its direction was pointed out, and when he heard the name of the finders, he flung his shovel down in despair. Reaching Bonanza Creek, he could only obtain claims of slight value, yet one of them — after he had sold it — proved fabulous. Returning to Seattle in 1897, all he had made was stolen. Canadians and British regard him as the true finder

of Klondike gold; Americans support Carmack. Many years later Henderson was given a $200 pension, but he never found the bonanza he endlessly sought. He died in 1933, and his son took up the quest. Like his father, he hoped to find the mother lode of the Klondike, which was probably destroyed long ago by glaciation and erosion, and, like his father, he died frustrated.

The other three were more fortunate. Tagish Charley was granted Canadian citizenship and, after selling out in 1901, became a successful hotel owner. As an honorary white man he was allowed to indulge in too much drink. Finally, popular and genial Charley fell off a bridge when drunk and drowned. Skookum Joe was made of sterner stuff. Despite getting $90,000 a year from his mine, the lure of prospecting never left him. He sought endlessly for a quartz lode and died of sheer exhaustion in 1916.

Carmack, rich beyond his wildest dreams, visited the U.S. Pacific Coast, taking his Kate with him. They used to toss money out of their hotel windows in Seattle and San Francisco just to enjoy watching the excitement below. But Kate was never really happy. She went home with her children and lived on her government pension until her death in 1917. George married Marguerite Laimee who had served the needs of miners in South Africa, Australia, and the Yukon, where she ran a cigar store and panned about $30 worth of gold dust a day from the sawdust on the floor. The happy couple made their home in Vancouver, British Columbia, where George died in 1922 and

Marguerite, his very wealthy widow, in 1949.

The outside world knew nothing of the Klondike that first winter of 1896-97. There was some tension at first at Bonanza Creek because the original staking had been inefficient. Disputes arose, and sometimes claimants slugged it out. But in January, William Ogilvie, a government surveyor, reached the Klondike and untangled the confusion, first insisting that his decisions must be considered final. Since a man stood to gain or lose a fortune over a few feet, it speaks vol-

umes for him that his rulings were accepted. And from the start the Mounties enforced the laws. The richest spot in the world that winter was governed by two men, Ogilvie and Inspector Constantine. Neither of them made a cent from the strike, although Constantine allowed his men to stake claims and some were lucky.

Every inch of the creek became important. Incredible riches were found where Bonanza and Eldorado creeks met. One pan yielded $1,000 worth of gold. On the next claim, owned by Dick Lowe, who had mined

Klondike Stampeders at Lake Bennett 1897–8, waiting for the ice to break before going downstream to Dawson. Note the boat-building.

in the Black Hills of Dakota, nuggets on the stream bed could be seen from twenty feet away.

The long winter wore on, and the Klondike's first Bonanza king appeared. He was Big Alex McDonald, who had mined in Colorado and now decided to buy property instead of dig. The King of the Klondike held interests in twenty-eight claims by late 1897 and was probably worth millions.

As news of the strike spread slowly over Alaska, miners headed for Dawson. The first of thousands climbed the Chilkoot Pass and built boats beside Lake Bennett, waiting for the ice to crack so they could sail down the Yukon, which rose in the lake. Many aiming for Circle City, knew nothing of the Klondike. When the ice broke in May and they sailed downriver they were amazed to see two new towns facing each other across the stream. Dawson's rival was Klondike City, and two of its saloonkeepers hoped to make it the main center. Ogilvie, who had a nice sense of humor, infuriated them when he tied down the steam whistle on Ladue's sawmill. This acted as a siren's song to the small boats coming down the river, and most of them berthed at Dawson. By the end of the summer the boomtown of Dawson boasted ten saloons, with transactions mainly in gold.

Even floors were panned for gold. In Big Harry Ash's Northern Saloon, the boss paid a boy $25 for all he could extract from the sawdust in front of the bar. The result was $278 worth. It came in fine dust which sifted through the little bags called pokes, in which miners carried their gold and which they slapped down on the bar.

The small sternwheeler *Alice* was the first steamboat to dock at Dawson, after a 1,700 mile journey up the Yukon. She brought food and drink in equal proportions. Two days later the *Portus B. Weare* docked. Those who had struck it rich were particularly pleased that vessels were arriving. They wanted to get to the outside world as soon as possible — some to enjoy life as never before and then return, others to live securely off what they already had. Eighty Bonanza and Eldorado kings, their professions ranging from blacksmith to bookseller, set off aboard the two ships, their gold in boxes, cases, jam jars, blankets, bottles, and pockets. Both ships groaned under their golden loads, but both were short of food. That came at St. Michael, where the travelers transferred either to the Seattle-bound *Portland* or to the *Excelsior,* which sailed towards the city that had seen it all before, San Francisco. Yet even San Francisco had never greeted a whole boatload of Bonanza and Eldorado kings.

Everything conspired to make the arrival of the ships a sensation. America, with its population explosion, was running short of gold that summer of '97, while the Pacific Northwest was experiencing a slump. The nineties were reaching their frenzied climax of feverish revelry and considerable misery, in an age when millionaire often meant robber baron. Gold was as emotional a word as ever. Communications were infinitely more rapid, so that Britain in the high noon of imperialism would hear news of the Klondike when America did, and her young men would join the call of the wild and exult that it had happened in part of the Empire. As noted earlier, the Klondike, in terms of gold extracted, was one of the lesser rushes, yet its fame was and is colossal. The world was ready for a sensation — the Spanish-American War and the Boer War had not yet occurred — and there was a sensational press to increase the fever. In terms of impact, the Klondike was the most internationally stirring rush of them all.

The *Excelsior* docked at San Francisco on July 15, her decks crammed with mud-stained working men who had made fortunes. The welcome they received was ecstatic, and two days later the same thing happened in Seattle. Some of the kings became almost crazed by it all; others were prostrated with exhaustion.

Rumor soon multiplied the finds. The Seattle Chamber of Commerce rose to the occasion, seeing to it that their city became the center of the gold-rush trade, though it was to be denuded of people in the way San Francisco had been so many years before.

Only a small percentage of those who joined the stampede were miners, and the number of greenhorns on the trail reached record proportions. Many were totally unfit for the rigors of the Klondike, about which they knew next to nothing. Shopkeepers did their dishonest best to supply their wants. The majority of the stampeders were American and Canadian, but every part of the British Empire where gold had been found supplied its quota, as did the Mother Country. Many South Americans, too, headed north.

The sophisticated bought evaporated food — eggs, soup, etc. — which was all the rage, along with milk tablets, saccharine, and other novelties. Meanwhile, the world gradually discovered roughly where the Klondike was, though how to get there remained a puzzle. A Londoner asked an old Alaska hand if one could bicycle over the Chilkoot, while at least one would-be prospector asked the Seattle stationmaster which train he should catch. Publishers rushed out books and pamphlets about the Klondike, full of misinformation but not the deliberate rubbish which accompanied the Pike's Peak rush. A few dismal voices urged caution, but no one wished to listen. Louis Sloss of the Alaska Commercial Company criticized transportation companies for encouraging men to go to the Yukon and prophecied disaster, starvation, and crime in Dawson that winter. Thanks to the Mounties there was to be no crime or starvation, but otherwise his predictions were all too correct.

Warnings were issued that anyone starting after September would not reach the Klondike until the following summer. But nine thousand tardy adventurers were already on their way. Then another gold filled boat reached San Francisco; this event, plus the clamor from newspapers and vested interests, destroyed any chance of holding back the horde until the spring of 1898. Merchants in all cities south of Victoria scrambled for gold-rush business; competition was made even more intense by the trade rivalry between Canada and the United States.

There were four main routes to the

Klondike. The two most used were the long journey up the Yukon and the shorter but terrible trek over adjacent Chilkoot or White passes. The others were the Ashcroft Trail north through British Columbia, a nightmare, and the Edmonton trip, which was a killer.

The Ashcroft Trail began from a town of the same name 125 miles northeast of Vancouver. It headed through a wilderness of bogs, forests, rivers, and rain, with horses and men being constantly attacked by flies and mosquitoes. By mid '98 the trail had been denuded of fodder, and horses died by the score. Many gave up, others continued their hellish thousand-mile trek, linking up at Glenora with other unfortunates who had fought their way up the slush and ice of Stikine River, a route that had been publicized by the British Columbia Board of Trade. Many had suffered at the hands of "Soapy" Smith's gang, which had already spread from its headquarters at Skagway to Wrangell at the river's mouth. Some 1,500 stampeders tried these routes in 1897-98, but only a handful reached Dawson.

The trip from Edmonton was far worse. The city promoted its route as the perfect one, a ninety-day journey if properly equipped with horses, canoes, and Hudson's Bay Company supplies. The truth was that either the 2,500-mile trip along the Mackenzie river (almost to the Arctic Circle) or the shorter 1,700-mile route along the Peace River was extremely difficult for frontiersmen — and akin to a death sentence for the majority, who were rank amateurs. Of the 2,000 who set out from Edmonton, at

least 500 died. Perhaps 100 reached Dawson by late 1899, and some of them had been on the trail for two years. By then the gold rush was over. Behind them was the stench of dead horses, a smell that permeated all trails to the Klondike.

Meanwhile, the vast majority had taken saner, if hardly more comfortable, routes. There was a serious shortage of ships, with vessels called into service that could just float and were grossly ill-suited to the conditions they would meet. Many captains had never sailed on an ocean, and crews were often inexperienced. Overcrowding was inevitable. Typical was the *Amur,* a "floating bedlam, pandemonium let loose, the Black Hole of Calcutta in an Arctic setting." Instead of the normal capacity of 100 passengers there were 500 aboard, plus an army of big dogs — which would prove useless in the Klondike. Passengers, who included 50 prostitutes, were 10 to a cabin, though tickets promised them a cabin each. Meals took a full seven hours to serve.

It was 1,700 miles upstream to the goldfields, but the great river was frozen by late September. Many wintered at Fort Yukon or Circle City, where they were joined by others from Dawson who had reached the Klondike in the autumn to find food in short supply. That they left Dawson was a stroke of fortune for newcomers and old-timers alike, for though starvation loomed that winter, the worst never happened.

Along the Yukon despair turned to rage, as bitter, hungry men, having failed to reach their goal, sometimes became violent in remote places totally without organized law and order. Crime was almost inevitable. Skagway, gateway to the Chilkoot and White passes, was gripped by crime on a spectacular scale.

It was a 600-mile journey from Skagway to Dawson. The first gruelling obstacles were the passes. White Pass, 600 feet lower than the Chilkoot, was a more roundabout route to Lake Bennett, headwaters of the Yukon River. Few of the 5,000 people who crossed the pass in 1897 reached the river before it froze over for the winter. Along the way they faced challenges ranging from swamps to a path on Devil's Hill that was only 2 feet wide, alongside a sheer drop of 500 feet — and Summit Hill, down which poured rivers of mud.

White Pass is chiefly remembered for the fate of the horses. Many had been bought in Victoria and Seattle for stiff prices, though only fit for a glue factory. Some were unbroken. Most were overloaded by men who knew nothing about horses. Jack London wrote that "The horses died like mosquitoes in the first frost and from Skagway to Bennett they rotted in heaps." The tragedy shamed the Klondike Stampede, but not enough to tarnish the courage and determination of the men and women who went over the Chilkoot that winter when the White Pass ceased to function — an incredible twenty-two thousand.

Chilkoot Pass, with its notorious four-mile climb, was a shortcut to Lake Bennett. It was too steep for horses, so an endless human chain, backs bent double under heavy loads, toiled toward the summit. The threat

of starvation in the Klondike caused the Mounties to patrol the head of the pass, demanding that each miner take in a year's supply of food and such essentials as a tent and tools. This meant repeated trips up the mountain for the stampeders.

Not only did the gold seekers struggle against nature, but they were at the mercy of Soapy Smith, a remarkable scoundrel who, with his gang, controlled organized crime in Skagway and along the Chilkoot Trail as far as the summit. Much to Soapy's disappointment he never succeeded in getting any of his men past the Mounties at the top.

Smith had reached Skagway in the fall of '97. It was already notably wicked, as a British visitor, Alexander Macdonald, noted when he reached it soon afterwards. In his *In Search of Eldorado* he wrote:

I have stumbled upon a few tough corners of the globe . . . but I think the most outrageously lawless quarter I ever struck was Skagway . . . . It seemed as if the scum of the earth had hastened here to fleece and rob or . . . to murder . . . . There was no law whatsoever; might was right, the dead shot only was immune to danger.

Soapy did not look like scum. One of his men, "Reverend" Bowers (said to exude piety from every pore), appeared even more respectable.

Smith got his nickname while he was a con man in Denver. His most famous trick was to con miners into believing that the soap he sold on the street for $5 a cake might have money under the wrappers. The first cake had $100 around it (the crowd watched the soap being wrapped, and Soapy made sure they saw the bill), but nearly all the others were nothing but soap.

Soapy became king of Denver's underworld with an army of con men. He improved his act, gave money to charity, but was finally forced to move to Creede. When the going got too hot there, he and his gang headed for the last frontier. Skagway was his masterpiece.

He increased his gang from seven to a hundred, and it became virtually impossible for a stampeder to get through Skagway without falling into his clutches. It helped that he chose so many underlings who looked respectable. Reverend Bowers was one of his finest assistants, having a genius for warning a newcomer about the temptations of the wicked city, then leading him, if he was determined to gamble, to men he could really trust. In a few weeks Soapy owned Skagway.

He set up a number of sham enterprises, including a Telegraph Office, a Cut Rate Ticket Office, and A Reliable Packers firm. At each of these establishments prospectors were told that a small deposit was required to

Courtesy The Public Archives of Canada   *Robin May Collection*

Up the Chilkoot Pass, 1897–8

ensure that his business would not be taken elsewhere. This was a scheme to get a glimpse of the customer's wallet. If it was loaded, this touched off a well-rehearsed bedlam. One gang member grabbed the wallet; other gang members, divided between good guys and bad guys, engaged in a brawl — during which the thief and the wallet disappeared. The only man ever known to have recovered his money was the pioneer prelate of Alaska, Bishop Rowe. When the robber found out who his victim was, he returned the wallet, explaining he was a member of the congregation. One of the reasons Soapy lasted so long was that he kept on the right side of the townspeople.

A surveyor named Frank Reid ended Soapy's reign. Skagway's reputation was becoming so evil that responsible citizens, well aware that the town was the obvious shipping point from the goldfields, saw the folly of having bandits in control. A vigilante committee was formed, masterminded by Reid — one of only two men in the Yukon that Soapy feared. The other was Sam Steele, who had taken over the Mounties in Dawson in June, replacing Inspector Constantine. Soapy said of Steele: "It's men like him that make it a bum place to live."

Even Reid liked Soapy personally, but that did not stop him from killing him in a gunfight in which Reid himself received a mortal wound. The date was July 8, 1898, and that was the end of the gang. Some were imprisoned in Sitka, the rest were put on a Seattle-bound boat.

A month before Soapy's downfall, the mass of stampeders reached Dawson, having waited along Lakes Lindermann and Bennett for the ice on the Yukon to break. Most had come across the Chilkoot.

The trail over Chilkoot began at Dyea, three miles beyond Skagway. From Dyea to Lake Lindermann was less than 30 miles and was easy enough at first. Gradually the sides of the route were seen to be littered with discarded baggage and the going got worse, until the base of the pass was reached at Sheep Camp. Now the stampeder could see the grim four-mile climb ahead of him and the endless line of men heading for the summit.

Sheep Camp was mostly populated by packers, but women were available for $5. A plate of bacon and beans, plus tea, cost half as much. It was here that the unfortunate horses were abandoned. Most were shot. On the four-mile climb, which reached nearly thirty-five degrees, men did "The Chilkoot Lockstep" as they moved ever upward. There was nothing to frighten an experienced climber on the Chilkoot, but few qualified — most were undernourished or sick or both, and all were utterly exhausted. In their overheavy furs and woolen garments they either froze or roasted, while mountain winds often turned into blizzards that halted all progress. The climbers stank because they lived in their clothes. Most were too poor to hire carriers; getting a ton of goods across the pass meant journey after journey. The average climber was only able to manage a fifty-pound pack at a time. It could take up to three months of shuttling back and forth, perhaps forty climbs.

The last 150 feet were the worst.

Steps had been hacked out by enterprising climbers, who then charged others for their use. There were even resting places, but anybody using one might need a day to get back into the lockstep. Naturally, the packers were fit. One Indian reached the summit with a 350-pound barrel on his back, while pianos and sections of steamboats went up at one time or another. The ton of supplies had to be assembled in dumps marked with poles. After each trip stampeders usually descended on their backsides for the next load. However, in the spring of '98 a clever aerial tramway was installed which could move goods in 300-pound carloads at a rate of a load a minute.

Most of the horde climbed the Chilkoot the hard way, before the tramway was built. Some died in avalanches. On this grimmest of journeys the thought of gold no doubt sustained most, but others kept going because they had set themselves a task and would not be beaten.

At the top was a freight city, plus the Mounties with a sentry on duty at a Maxim gun and a Union Jack flying. They checked the twenty-two thousand through: Americans, Britons from all over the Empire, people of nearly every nation, Dawson-bound dancing girls, wives, even an old German woman of seventy, plus an English nobleman with a valet. Many were going not for gold but to start a business. And there were Soapy's men, selling seats for the weary or places by a fire, and starting con games which drew players eager for a break. But the gang never got past the Mounties.

The Chilkoot trail ended at Lake Lindermann, where thousands started building boats. The majority pressed on to larger Lake Bennett, where those who had once come over White Pass were building their boats. Others were at Lake Tagish, still farther forward, but Lake Bennett's tent city was the biggest, with tents surrounding the entire lake.

The long months beside the lakes went smoothly because of the presence of Superintendent Sam Steele and his men. Steele, soon to be known as "The Lion of the Yukon," ruled the Klondike along military lines, but with humanity and understanding. It was sober truth that a sack of nuggets left on the trail for two weeks would be there when its owner returned. He saw to it that every stampeder had a year's supplies, checked every boat and its occupants, and organized a search if one failed to appear when the move downstream began.

The ice cracked on May 29, 1898, and two days later 7,124 craft set out, everything from true boats to — literally — floating coffins. Oxen, horses, and dogs sailed, too, in the mighty armada. The one terrible gauntlet was Miles Canyon, a 50-mile stretch of rapids 100 feet wide and 50 feet deep, plus a whirlpool. During the first days 150 craft were destroyed and 10 lives lost. A panic ensued, causing a total bottleneck. Then Steele appeared, calmed the mob, and ordered that no boat shoot the rapids unless first checked by his expert, Corporal Dixon. All women and children walked past the rapids, and the boats were steered by competent men. Hardly another boat was lost.

Some had already reached Dawson across the ice, including one smart operator who arrived with 2,400 eggs, which he sold for $3,600. On June 8 the armada was sighted, and within a matter of days Dawson was a booming gold-rush town. Boats had at last managed to sail up the Yukon, and small steamers sailed down to Dawson after being taken over the Chilkoot piece by piece and reconstructed.

Dawson's population figures are uncertain. From about five thousand in 1897 it rose to between twenty-five and forty thousand the following year. It soon became clear that the horde of 1898 had arrived too late; the best claims had already been staked. Some men chased every wild rumor of a new strike, but others were crushed and wandered around overcome by inertia.

Many were happy enough that they had reached Eldorado. Simply to have got there was a matter of pride. Men wore their Chilkoot clothes like uniforms that hot summer and kept their shaggy beards. Many sold or tried to sell enough of their statutory ton of goods to pay for the journey home, so Dawson looked like a giant street market by day. By night it was like any other mining town, but with one unique quality. In the whole fabulous year of '98 there was not a single murder. Men could even leave their homes unlocked with their gold inside.

Superintendent Steele was no killjoy. He drew the line at obscenity, cheating, and disorderly conduct, but he saw no harm in saloons, gambling halls, and brothels as long as public order was not threatened. Firearms were forbidden. Offenders were expelled or sentenced to saw wood to heat government buildings — a very

unpopular punishment because it had to be cut to fit the stoves. Sundays were peaceful, though some theater owners managed to stage "sacred concerts" of tableaux from the scriptures. One evening was anything but sacred. A dance hall queen named Caprice topped the bill stark naked except for tights, slippers, and a huge cross which she clasped to herself most suggestively.

The year saw one new technique for the minority who were actually mining. Thawing ground by "burning" was a slow process, and C. J. Berry from California, who became a Klondike millionaire, found a better method. He noted that steam escap-

Courtesy Public Archives of Canada   *Robin May Collection*
"Snake-Hips" Lulu of Dawson

ing from an engine exhaust had thawed a hole, and he began to experiment with a rubber hose. This led to his "steam point." From a boiler on the surface, steam was sent through a hose to an iron pipe five or six feet long. The pipe, pointed at its lower end, had an opening for steam to be applied to the ground and, once in the frozen gravel, it was pushed forward by gentle hammer taps. In summer, burning had not been completely effective because of wet ground, and Berry's method, soon improved, was much faster and more efficient.

By mid-1899 companies were buying claims, mechanization was taking over, and the "poor man's rush" was at an end.

It is difficult to estimate how much gold was extracted from the Klondike. The Canadian government's 10 percent royalty on gross output must have caused gains to be concealed, even with a $2,500 annual allowance for the cost of extraction. Production peaked in 1900, when most miners had gone home or headed for Nome; 1,350,000 fine ounces of gold worth $22,250,000 were extracted that year. It is estimated that between 1897 and 1905 the total value of gold was $100 million. Mining still continues, but Dawson, the last truly fabulous gold boomtown, has less than a thousand residents today. Trains now go through White Pass, but the Chilkoot is majestically silent.

Financially speaking the Klondike was not one of the greatest rushes, yet in terms of the human spirit it was arguably the finest of all. Its practical results were considerable. It opened Alaska and paved the way for the rushes that followed. The cities of Seattle, Edmonton, and Vancouver received major benefits, and there was no longer talk of a slump in America's Pacific Northwest. As for the stampeders, an extraordinary number, fine-tuned by their ordeal, succeeded in Canada and the United States in every field from politics to the battlefield. The most decorated unit in the Canadian Army in World War One was a machine-gun battalion of Klondike pioneers.

The epic of the Klondike dwarfed all other rushes that took place later in the huge area beside and beyond the Yukon basin. Alaska's capital, Fairbanks, grew out of a strike along the Tanana River in 1902. The prospector was an Italian, Felix Pedro. Fairbanks was not a "poor man's diggings." It was a place for capital expenditure, with steam-pointing the best method of getting out the pay dirt. From 1906-09 it produced some half a million ounces a year. Times were changing in the Yukon: The day of the old-time miner, the sourdough of legend, was fast drawing to a close.

The last gaudy heyday of the oldtimers happened at Nome, a mere 200 miles from Siberia. It was a genuine poor man's diggings, the finest of them all, for the sands were so impregnated with gold that all a miner needed was a bit of effort with a shovel and a pan or a rocker. Assuming he could get on the beach!

The golden sands were not discovered until the summer of 1899, although modest finds in the area were made in 1897 on Golovnin Bay at the mouth of the Fish River. On September 22, 1898, three Swedes, Jafet Lindeberg, John Brynteson, and Erik

Lindblom, panned about $50 worth of gold three miles inland at Anvil Creek. They went through the correct legal processes of organizing a mining district, staking forty-three claims for themselves and forty-seven for friends and acquaintances. Inevitably the secret leaked out, and by winter the rush had started.

It came at a time when thousands had reached Dawson only to find they were too late. Others resented the royalty demanded by the Canadian government. Many headed for Cape Nome, along with miners from all over Alaska and elsewhere. Wyatt Earp was one of the more notorious arrivals. He ran a saloon for two years, until news of a gold strike at Tonopah, Nevada, sent him south again.

The beach had already become a tent town by early 1899, before the discovery of the golden sands. It had a population of two thousand by midsummer. Many resented that the best ground had been grabbed, and the angry newcomers were hostile to the Swedes who, being aliens, were entitled to hold down claims only if they swore to become citizens in front of a commissioner — an official conspicuous by his absence in Nome. Plans were made to hold a meeting and then jump the Swedes' claims at Anvil Creek, but the miners were frustrated by Lt. Oliver Spaulding and a small detachment of men whose bayonets they were not prepared to face.

Then a miracle occurred, or so it must have seemed. Two weeks after the showdown with the military, John Hummell, aged and infirm, decided to pan down by the water's edge. He scooped up some of Nome's

black sand and found gold. The beach rapidly filled with diggers. That summer two thousand of them extracted well over $1 million from the forty-two miles of sand, while several hundred thousand dollars worth of gold was found in the creeks behind town on a handful of lucrative claims. By the summer of 1900 there were twenty thousand miners on the beaches — though many found no free ground and moved on.

Beach mining created strange problems and events. Claims covered only about twenty square feet, compared with twenty acres allowed on creeks. Tides constantly washed over the claims, removing markings. Miners were in a constant, and thus far successful, struggle against business companies claiming that their property lines extended to the water's edge. Hordes of claim jumpers were a more serious menace. "One hundred beachcombers to one claim owner," wrote one sufferer.

It was easy to steal property in the tent town along the beach. There was not even a hanging tree — Nome was treeless. Sewers could not be built because of the cold. Garbage was carried out onto the ice so it would be taken to sea when the ice broke in the spring.

The miners' candidate won when a town government was set up in 1899, but the main flood of prospectors arrived in 1900. Nome, complete with one hundred saloons, became a paradise for criminals. The most brazen was a political boss from North Dakota named Alexander McKenzie, a former lawman who had put suspected killers in a coffin before questioning them. A power in Republican circles in Washington, he fell in with a Nome lawyer whose firm aimed at dispossessing claim holders, including Lindeberg, one of the lucky Swedes. What could be better than to persuade Congress to remove a clause from a new bill that allowed aliens to acquire and hold land?

All went as planned. McKenzie's friend, President McKinley, helped him secure both a tame judge and a federal district attorney, and McKenzie himself organized the Alaska Gold Mining Company. Then the trio descended on Nome like birds of prey, arriving July 19, 1900. Soon McKenzie was receiver of a number of mines, the richest in the area, and was boasting: "Give me a barnyard of Swedes and I'll drive them like sheep!" Happily, the wronged claim-holders got an appeal off to San Francisco before the ice closed in, and an honest judge declared in their favor. McKenzie was shipped out on the last boat of the season and was sentenced to a year in prison. But his friend, President McKinley, pitying him for alleged ill health, had him released after a mere three months. McKenzie returned to politics, dishonored only in distant Alaska.

Meanwhile, other creeks and beaches were yielding gold, but Nome was now depending more and more on the tundra behind the beaches. Six million dollars worth was produced from the claims in 1906, but a decade later Nome's population was a mere one thousand. While equipment rusted in a fading town, the once fabulous beach was abandoned.

It was over. From Sutter's Mill to the Bering Strait, via legendary spots in America, Australia, New Zealand, South Africa and Canada. There were forty-niners in the Klondike, in Australia and New Zealand; there were Australians in California. They were a restless, mighty portion of humanity on the move, but now it had ended. The best of them had been — like Tennyson's Ulysses and his men — "strong in will, to strive, to seek, to find, and not to yield."

THE CHEYENNE-DEADWOOD TRAIL
By Mae Urbanek

Gold in the Black Hills, Dakota Territory! Gold!

The Black Hills were pledged to Sioux Indians "so long as grass shall grow and water flow" in treaties signed at Fort Laramie, Wyoming, in 1851 and 1868. Then the United States government sent Gen. George A. Custer with 110 wagons and the Seventh Cavalry of about four hun-

dred men to map the hills in 1874. Soldier Horatio N. Ross discovered gold on French Creek near the present town of Custer. Scout Charley Reynolds immediately carried the news to Fort Laramie. It was telegraphed to the world in August 1874.

Newspapers screamed: "Gold! Land of promise! Glittering treasure found — precious dust under horses'

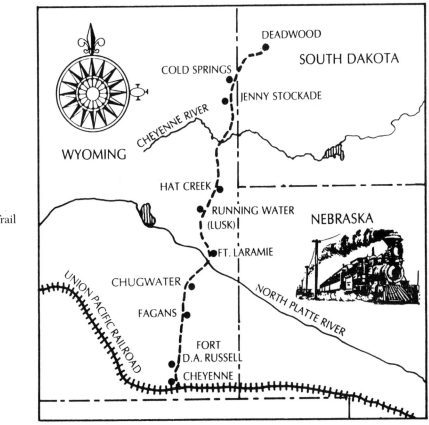

The Cheyenne-Deadwood Trail

feet." It was a time of depression and unemployment. Prospectors swarmed to the hills. The government tried to keep gold seekers out of this land pledged to the Sioux. It was an impossible task. Congress in the treaty of 1876, finally forced the Sioux to relinquish the hills and live on a reservation.

Late in 1875 prospector James Pearson was camped in a gulch filled with dead trees north of French Creek. There he discovered gold-bearing sand in surprising amounts. He couldn't keep his secret forever, and in March 1876 the rush from French Creek to Dead Tree Gulch was on. Deadwood, as it became known, burgeoned from a camp to a town of twenty-five thousand or more. Custer City was a ghost town of empty cabins on French Creek.

Cheyenne, Wyoming, the closest railroad town, became the starting point for the 350-mile trip to the gold-fields. The first stagecoach left Cheyenne on March 8, 1875, carrying three gold prospectors. This stage ran every Monday and Thursday, returning on Tuesday and Saturday.

Gilmer, Salisbury, and Patrick bought and greatly improved the stage line, calling it the Cheyenne-Deadwood Stage and Express Company. Their first daily stage left Cheyenne February 1, 1876. By 1877 superintendent Luke Voorhees was using six hundred horses and thirty Concord coaches. (The coaches were drawn by six-horse teams.) Passengers and express rode to the hills; gold bars were brought back to the railroad. In addition to the stage, more than twenty firms ran regular freight wagons from Cheyenne to Deadwood, and there were also many individual freighters. A telegraph line was completed to the Black Hills.

Freighters used oxteams, mules, and horses. Mud and snow often

Courtesy Wyoming Archives & Historical Dept.

Concord coach on Cheyenne-Deadwood Trail

made the roads impassable for the overloaded freight wagons. "Struggling along" was all in a day's work for "bullwhackers" and "mule skinners," as the drivers were known. In 1877 William Randolph Hearst and partners, who were developing the gold mine at Deadwood, brought a huge stamp mill from Cheyenne by oxteam at the cost of $30,000. Hearst made his original fortune in Deadwood.

Concord coaches for the stage line were built in Concord, New Hampshire, then shipped to Omaha, Nebraska, and brought overland to Cheyenne. Each coach weighed about twenty-five hundred pounds and swung on thoroughbraces of leather for springs. Nine passengers could ride inside on padded leather seats. More could perch on two top seats with the luggage. There was a boot, or storage box, on the back of the stage. An armed guard rode beside the driver, hence the term "ride shotgun." The coaches were painted bright red; the undercarriage was yellow.

Scott Davis, known as "Quick Shot," was captain of the shotgun messengers who protected the stage. In territory infested with Indians and road agents (robbers), shotgun messengers rode on top of the stage or on horseback. It took nerve to drive a stage loaded with passengers through the vast, unsettled country north from Fort Laramie and then bring back gold bars from Deadwood.

First-class tickets, Cheyenne to Deadwood, cost $20. Third-class was $10, but these passengers sometimes had to walk up steep hills or push when the stage mired down in wet gumbo or snow. The route was roughly spaced into forty-mile stretches, with an average speed of eight miles per hour. The last stage left Cheyenne February 19, 1887, with George Lathrop, its most famous driver, holding the ribbons (reins).

The run from Cheyenne to Deadwood usually took forty-eight hours in dry weather, but as much as seventy-two hours in rain, mud, or snow. One winter, coaches ran on sled runners from Deadwood to Jenney Stockade on the edge of the hills. Passengers placed buffalo robes over their laps in winter. Hot bricks or stones, wrapped in gunnysacks, kept their feet warm.

The Cheyenne-Deadwood Trail was one of the famous thoroughfares of the West. It had all the ingredients of romance — gold, soldiers, miners, gamblers, ladies of fortune, stage robbers, shotgun messengers, and angry Indians.

Wild Bill Hickok, gunman and gambler, sometimes rode the stage to Deadwood, then his headquarters. On August 2, 1876, he made the mistake of sitting with his back to the door at a poker game in a Deadwood saloon. He was shot in the head by Jack McCall to settle a grudge. The cards that slipped from his hand were aces and eights. They became known as the "dead man's hand."

Calamity Jane, clad in men's buckskin garments, sometimes worked as a teamster with freighting outfits. On one occasion, when stage driver Jack McCall was wounded by a road agent, she took the reins and drove to the next stop. Jane was popular with men, a soother of pain, and an angel in disguise. During the Deadwood smallpox epidemic of 1878, she and one doctor cared for the sick. She loved Wild Bill, but he hated her. She died in 1903, and at her request she and Hickok are buried side by side in a Deadwood cemetery.

The dance hall girls of Deadwood needed pets — not men, but cats. In 1877 Phatty Thompson, independent freighter, bought cats in Cheyenne for twenty-five cents apiece, put them in a huge crate, and started for Deadwood. When his wagon tipped over the crate broke, and the cats scattered over the prairie. Using tasty morsels for bait, Phatty rounded up his cargo. When he finally reached Deadwood, he sold his cats for $10 to $25 each.

Cheyenne, stage headquarters, was a whooping tent town when, on July 4, 1867, Gen. G. M. Dodge, chief engineer of the Union Pacific Railroad, named it for the Cheyenne Indians. This "Magic City of the Plains" was the first in the nation to have electric lights and first in the world to have a free library.

Pole Creek ranch, eighteen miles north of Cheyenne, was the first regular stop for stagecoaches. It boasted a two-story hotel that served meals at all hours. The second stop, another ten miles, was Horse Creek or Fagan's ranch, where the accommodations included a "ladies parlor." During the 1876 blizzard, 250 travelers stayed here for two days.

Little Bear Station was on Bear Springs Creek. Owner Isaac Bard referred to the travelers as "Black Hillers." The trail continued north over open plains to the timbered Chugwater ranch of John Portugee Phillips. Near here was the ranch of H. B. Kelly, who irrigated his hay meadows and ran blooded Shorthorn bulls with his 1,500 cows. In 1884 he sold the ranch to Swan Land and Cattle Company, which became one of the most famous of Wyoming ranches. In 1964 it was made a national historic landmark.

Up Chugwater Creek was the John Hunton ranch, a relay station.

Freight wagons, Cheyenne-Deadwood Trail

Chugwater was so named because Indians once stampeded buffalo over high cliffs near there. The falling buffalo went "chug," "chug" when they hit the rocks and creek below. The wounded buffalo were then killed and skinned by the Indians for their hides and meat. Whites adopted the Indian name. Only sagebrush now marks the place where the Chug Springs Station once stood.

Seven miles north the route passed tall, sandstone cliffs where eagles nested. Here was Eagle's Nest Station. Travelers carved their names and dates on the cliffs; the earliest date, 1834, was probably carved there by a trapper. Two outlaws once stopped the northbound stage here at night. They forced the passengers out and had them hold their hands over their heads. One robber stood guard with a gun while the other searched the victims by candlelight. He got $24

from five men. Then he came to Mrs. King, the only woman passenger. On the first search he found no money, but when he demanded that she take her hair down, a roll of bills fell out.

Six-mile ranch, six miles south of Fort Laramie, was a "hog ranch," where soldiers came to have fun. Seven men met death here in drunken brawls. There was another "hog ranch" three miles west of Fort Laramie.

North from Fort Laramie travelers on the Cheyenne-Deadwood stage had an easy crossing of Platte River on a new steel bridge built in 1875 by the government. Northward, across open plains, the trail raveled out like an old rope, seeking many routes to avoid snow-packed canyons, bad river crossings, and ambush spots used by road agents or Indians. The main route was north to Ten Mile, and four miles more to the Govern-

Photo by Mae Urbanek

Hog Ranch, now chicken house near Fort Laramie

ment Farm Station. Log buildings were erected here in the 1860s by soldiers from Fort Laramie. The land was subirrigated, and soldiers carried on experiments in raising grain and vegetables. Abandoned in 1872, John Montgomery rejuvenated the place for a stage station in 1876.

Rawhide Buttes Station

Twelve miles north of the Government Farm was Rawhide Buttes Station, at the site of a fine spring on Rawhide Creek. Sheltered by hills and trees, the place had long been a favorite campground for Indians and trappers. Here in the late 1800s white men bargained with Indians for beaver pelts and buffalo hides, which were salted and pressed into packs with fur presses. The hides were taken by packhorse to load on boats that floated down Rawhide Creek, then the Platte and Missouri rivers to market in St. Louis. Because of this trade the three buttes near the station were called Rawhide Buttes. There is also a legend that Indians once skinned a white man alive here, after he had shot an Indian maiden.

J. W. Dear, a trader, built the first house here in 1876, but Sioux Indians soon burned it down. In August 1877 the Rawhide Stage Station was built and opened. On May 15, 1883, Russell Thorp, Sr., bought the Cheyenne-Deadwood Stage Line and made Rawhide the home station. There was a store, post office, blacksmith shop, and telegraph station. The station and ranchsite were bought by John Agnew and Robert Ord in 1902 and were owned and operated by these families for seventy years.

Mother Featherlegs

On Demmon Hill, five miles north of Rawhide Buttes Station, was the dugout home of Madam Shepard, or "Mother Featherlegs." While all other women still rode sidesaddle, she found liberation by tucking her skirts into long, red, beruffled pantalets and riding astride, her red hair aflutter. Once as she galloped past a cowboy he remarked: "Those red pants make the old girl look like a featherlegged chicken in a high wind." So the madam with the scarlet reputation became widely known as Mother Featherlegs.

Madam Shepard came to Wyoming in 1876 from the swamps of Louisiana, where she had been a member of an outlaw gang that plagued the South after the Civil War. When her sons, Tom and Bill, were hung by vigilantes, she fled north. She opened an underground roadhouse with a rock chimney near the stage route. Business was good, and she kept her money hidden in the cave. In about a year she was joined by Dick Davis, the "Terrapin," an old pal from Louisiana.

There were few women living on Wyoming prairies in 1879. One day Mrs. O. J. Demmon, her loneliness overcoming discrimination, rode over to see her neighbor. She found Mother Featherlegs sprawled near her dugout, face down, her back perforated with bullet holes. Dangerous Dick, the Terrapin, was gone, and so was the cash from the cave. Mother Featherlegs was buried near her dugout. She soon had company: George McFadden, a murdered man, was buried on one side of her, and Ike Diapert, a suicide, was buried on the other.

A monument, a 3,500-pound slab of Rawhide granite, was placed about 100 yards from the site of the dugout on May 17, 1964. Lewis E. Bates, a Cheyenne editor, speaking at the ceremony, remarked that "Pioneers are those who prepare the way for others . . . including the accumulators and despoilers, as well as the builders . . . even the type of person whom this granite shaft honors, a practitioner of the world's oldest profession."

Running Water, Silver Cliff, or Lusk

About fifteen miles north of Rawhide Buttes Station was Running Water, located on Running Water or Niobrara River, English version of the Omaha Indian name *Ni* (water) and *obthatha* (spreading). J. W. Dear built a station here in 1876, but Indians burned it. Then Jack Madden built a large stone barn with eight-foot walls, covered with a pole and dirt roof.

In 1880 a prospector named McHenry became interested in the large hill south of Running Water Station. Hiring miners, who lived in tents, McHenry started mining the hill for silver, gold, and copper. The hill and tent town became known as Silver Cliff. By 1885 a large stamp mill had been constructed by Great Western Mining and Milling Company. It was called the Rochelle Mine for Albert Rochelle, and the tent town became known as New Rochelle.

A New York Company financed the mine. When their paychecks proved worthless, the miners became angry and hanged the owner in effigy. The mining ended. In 1898 the machinery was torn down and shipped to New Mexico. Prospectors continued to dig in the abandoned shafts, and the first uranium in Wyo-

Courtesy Wyoming Archives & Historical Dept.

Stage at stone barn, Silver Cliff or Lusk

ming was found here in 1918. Madame Curie is reported to have used this uranium for some of her experiments.

When the Fremont, Elkhorn and Missouri Valley Railroad, now the Chicago and Northwestern, arrived in July 1886, homesteader Frank Lusk donated land east of the mine for a townsite, Railroad officials named the town Lusk. Everyone in Silver Cliff quickly moved to Lusk.

The Stagecoach Museum in Lusk now houses one of the stagecoaches used on the Cheyenne-Deadwood Trail, the gift of Russell Thorp, Jr. A mile west of Lusk on Highway 20 is the grave of and monument to George Lathrop, who was an expert horseman and stage driver. He had the honor of holding the ribbons on the last stage from Cheyenne to Deadwood in February 1887.

Hat Creek

After gold was discovered in the Black Hills in 1874, Capt. James Egan and a force of cavalry were sent from Fort Laramie to establish a fort on Hat Creek in Nebraska. Wandering in unmarked wilderness, they came to Sage Creek in Wyoming in 1875 and, thinking it to be Hat Creek, built an L-shaped log barracks. A tunnel, roofed with logs, was built from the barracks down to Sage Creek so water would be available in case of siege by Indians. A horse corral was part of the L-shaped building.

John Bowman started a stage station at Hat Creek in 1876 and next year advertised that he would "furnish accommodations to the traveling public at reasonable prices at his hotel." There was a brewery, a bakery, a butcher shop, and a blacksmith shop. A number of buffaloes were killed along Sage Creek as late as the summer of 1878. It is not definitely known what became of the old barracks, although they probably were burned.

Early in the 1880s John Storrie and Tom Swan erected a two-story log store here that is still standing. Their roadhouse was popular with cowboys as well as with travelers. A historic sign on Highway 85, fifteen miles north of Lusk, tells the history of Fort Hat Creek. The old store is two miles east and a mile south of the sign.

At first the stage route led east from Hat Creek into Indian Creek country, where the Sioux were numerous, but in June 1877 the route was shortened to run almost directly north from Hat Creek. This way was still dangerous because of road agents and Indians. The first station was on Old Woman's Creek, so named because the ghost of an Indian woman had been seen dancing on the rimrocks above the creek. Here on September 13, 1878, six men stopped a southbound stage. Shotgun messengers killed one robber, and the others fled.

Robber's Roost

Twenty-eight miles north of Hat Creek was Jim May's ranch on Lance Creek. Next was Robber's Roost Station on the Cheyenne River, where Jim's brother, D. Boone May, was in charge. Here the bridge across the river slowed the coaches to a crawl. Steep riverbanks, covered with brush and timber, gave cover to road agents, who could watch the

Photo by Beryl Williams

Hat Creek Store, 100 years old, still standing

stages approaching. The station was built in 1877 south of the river bridge and was burned by Indians in 1886. It was never rebuilt and is locally known as "Burnt Station." Near the site of the station, about fifty miles north of Lusk, is a historical marker dedicated to Robber's Roost by the Niobrara Historical Society.

Space allows for the telling of only one of the many holdups that took place at Robber's Roost. Once a road

Wyoming Travel Commission

Stage at Old Fork, Hat Creek

agent stopped the stage and made the driver unhitch his team. The bandit then dynamited the safe but obtained only one gold brick. He fled on horseback. When the stage finally got to the first crossing of Lance Creek farther south, the driver, seeing the bandit watering his horse, shot and killed him. The gold brick was never found; it must have been buried somewhere between the two crossings.

Jenney Stockade

The Black Hills were explored for mineral wealth as early as 1857. Lt. G. K. Warren and Dr. F. V. Hayden camped on the banks of Beaver Creek and built a log corral. In June 1875 Professor Walter P. Jenney, with 75 geologists and miners and 432 soldiers from Fort Laramie, came to this old campsite and built a log fort called Camp Jenney. It served as a supply center for a government surveying team during the summer. The soldiers returned to Fort Laramie in the fall, and gold miners used the stockade during the winter.

Jenney Stockade became a regular stage stop on the Cheyenne-Deadwood Trail in 1877. Stages brought passengers, fruit, and vegetables to the Black Hills from Cheyenne, and returned with cargoes of gold. Runs were made at night with armed escorts. Luke Voorhees used salamander safes of chilled steel with Yale locks for gold shipments, but even then the gold was not always safe.

The LAK Cattle Company bought the land on which Jenney Stockade was located in June 1877 and for fifty years used the stockade as a house and blacksmith shop.

When LAK built modern buildings, one cabin of the old stockade was given to the Newcastle Twentieth Century Club in 1928. Logs were numbered, and the cabin was reconstructed on the courthouse lawn in Newcastle. This oldest building in the hills is now the Chamber of Commerce office. It still has the original portholes.

The site of the Jenney Stockade on the ranch was enrolled in the National Register of Historic Sites in 1969. The LAK ranch is five and a half miles southeast of Newcastle.

Cold Springs Robbery

Canyon Springs Stage Station was in timbered country on Beaver Creek, about twenty miles north of Jenney Stockade and about thirty-seven miles south of Deadwood. It was only a relay station for changing horses and was not as well known as the Cold Springs ranch. It was the last station in Wyoming, two miles up what is now known as Mallo Canyon. The biggest holdup of the Cheyenne-Deadwood stage occurred at Canyon Springs, but it is generally known as the Cold Springs robbery.

There are several versions of this daring holdup. On September 26, 1878, four road agents tied up the two station tenders at Canyon Springs and greeted the southbound stage with a hail of bullets, killing the only passenger, Hugh O. Campbell. Shotgun guards and the stage driver fought back, killing one bandit and wounding another. Scott Davis, a guard, escaped into the timber and although wounded, walked for help. The bandits tied up the other men, opened the locked box with a sledgehammer, and escaped with about $37,000 in gold dust, gold bricks, and jewelry.

Using an old spring wagon, the bandits hauled their booty eastward, making a wide circle around Rapid City. The stage company offered a $2,500 reward for the capture of the bandits and the return of the gold and valuables. Search parties struck out in all directions. Those on the trail to Pierre, South Dakota, found where the bandits had camped and buried one of the gang who had died of his wounds. Dr. Whitfield, kicking in the campfire ashes, found a gold brick valued at $3,200. He received $1,100 for returning it to the stage company. Part of the loot also was recovered in Atlantic, Iowa, but the bandits escaped.

After the robbery the stage route was changed to more open country for the few remaining months of its existence. Today no trace remains of either Canyon Springs Station or Cold Springs ranch. Old maps place

them a short distance southeast of present Four Corners on Highway 85 north of Newcastle.

On March 26, 1876, a northbound coach was stopped farther north along the trail in South Dakota. The thieves had learned that a new bank would soon open in Deadwood. They found no money on the coach, but they killed the driver, Johnny Slaughter.

A day later Mrs. Thomas Durbin, her baby, and her brother-in-law (the new banker-to-be) traveled to Deadwood from Cheyenne. In the bottom of a basket, where she kept the baby bottles, a package was wrapped in a blanket. South of Deadwood a log lay across the road. As passengers quickly rolled the log away, they spotted a man hiding in the trees. The driver cracked his whip and the coach rolled safely on to Deadwood. In the blanket among the baby bottles was $10,000 in currency to start the new bank.

THE MULLAN ROAD
By Rex C. Myers

Lt. John Mullan dismounted. He straddled the Continental Divide on a grassy ridge sandwiched between towering, snow-covered peaks. Handing his reins to the soldier beside him, Mullan looked up at the Flathead Indian half-breed on his pony.

"Does this pass have a name, Gabriel?" the lieutenant asked, studying the gradual approaches from both sides. "What do your people call it?"

"Indian live with mountains. Not name them. White men name them. I give you this pass. It can be Mullan's Pass." Gabriel Prudhomme smiled at the thought of his own suggestion. The officer nodded an acknowledg-

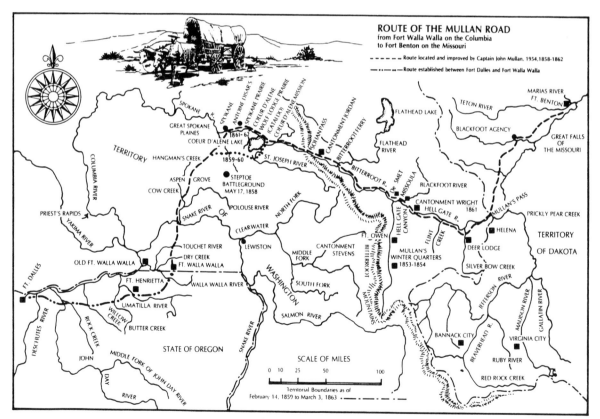

The Mullan Road

ment but seemed lost in his own thoughts.

With an engineer's eye he surveyed the slopes. A wagon could climb either side without double-teaming, he guessed. No. It was not a guess. He knew this pass was the most gradual he'd seen during the last six months. Certainly a loaded wagon could traverse the Continental Divide at this point — connecting the Missouri and Columbia river watersheds. If a wagon could make it, then in time a railroad could follow. Wagons and locomotives across Mullan's Pass — he closed his eyes and formed the pictures in his mind. Teamsters pushing oxen and mules toward the Pacific; smoke-belching engines hurrying Oriental spices and silks to the Atlantic. The idea of this transcontinental highway of commerce excited Mullan, and he knew his commander would share his enthusiasm. Suddenly he could not wait to share the discovery.

"Pearson," he called. The grizzled expressman spurred his mount gently and reined in beside the officer. Out of habit he removed his stained felt hat before addressing the lieutenant.

"Sir."

"Pearson, I want you to deliver a message to Governor Isaac Stevens, Olympia, Washington Territory. Tell the governor I've found the low pass needed for road and railroad transportation to the Pacific. Tell him that, with some timber cutting and grading, a loaded wagon can cross this pass without double-teaming. Tell him details will follow in my official report. Got all that?"

"Sir? Should I write it down?" Mullan saw puzzled frustration in

the man's eyes, then remembered the expressman could not write. Stepping to his saddlebags he untied the flap, withdrew his bound journal, and tore a page from the back. Quickly he wrote and signed the message. Folding the paper he handed it to Pearson.

"Make sure this gets there. Any questions?" Mullan's eyes met those of his expressman to impress the importance of the message.

"Yes, sir!" Pearson jerked the reins to one side, turned his horse, and started down toward the meadow which marked the headwaters of the Little Blackfoot River — a tributary of the Columbia carrying water bound for the Pacific.

As the young lieutenant watched, he reached up and removed his slouch campaign hat. Habitually, he slapped it against his uniform as if to remove trail dust. His eyes caught the white of snowdrifts crouching in the surrounding timber and extending to the tops of the mountains. He remembered there was no dust. It was March. March 10, 1854, to be exact. He felt a bit embarrassed at this action.

Behind him the Flathead half-breed smiled his broken grin. The bluecoat had much to learn, but he admired the youthful enthusiasm and dedication. Second Lieutenant Mullan had his first command. Assisting with the 1853 Stevens survey of the northern route for a transcontinental railroad, Mullan rose in the esteem of his commander — rose to the point that Stevens entrusted him with the expedition's most important work. During the summer Mullan met with Flathead Indians on their buffalo hunt and convinced them to sign treaties of peace and friendship with the United States government. In October the governor concluded the initial phase of his survey and departed for new duties as chief executive of Washington Territory. Deep in the heart of the northern Rockies he left the twenty-three-year-old Irish, West Point graduate and a small command of thirteen men. Mullan's orders: Explore all major mountain passes and valleys in the region; determine their suitability for road and railroad construction; compile meteorological data on the severity of the winter and the nature of the climate.

Mullan moved his men upstream along the Bitterroot River to a point ten miles above John Owen's fur post. His men constructed three log barracks and a storehouse, which, together with a corral for the horses, they dubbed Cantonment Stevens in the governor's honor. Before deep mountain snows closed travel, Mullan explored the upper reaches of the Bitterroot, journeyed to Fort Hall, and on his return explored the Beaverhead, Jefferson, Gallatin, and Madison tributaries of the Missouri River. During winter seclusion at the cantonment, Gabriel informed Mullan of a low pass across the crest of the Rocky Mountains. The Flatheads used it often as they moved back and forth between their mountain home and buffalo hunting grounds in the Great Plains.

Now the half-breed smiled again, thinking of his own importance and the lieutenant's obvious approval. Mullan's Pass it would be. The officer replaced his hat. He turned, walking back to where Prudhomme and the other members of the party waited on their horses. Mullan looked like a soldier. Short and stocky, his body had spare lines and strong features. His dark, thick hair extended out from under his hat, framing a straight nose, square-cut face, and long sideburns. His deep blue eyes sparkled with excitement as he reached for the reins to his horse, planted his left foot in the stirrup, and swung himself up into the saddle. With a military wave of his hand he signaled the group to start the advance down the eastern side of the ridge into the Prickly Pear drainage and on toward Fort Benton. Stevens had left a wagon there the previous fall, and within two weeks Mullan would demonstrate that one could, in fact, move a vehicle across his pass with remarkable ease.

By September 1854 Mullan completed his assignment. Stevens ordered him to abandon his cantonment and bring his men to Fort Vancouver. As Mullan reviewed his field notes he became more and more convinced that a road and later a railroad were possible across the mountains of the northwest. The route began to take specific form in his mind. From the Missouri River near the American Fur Company post at Fort Benton; south and west across the high prairie land to the Sun and Dearborn rivers; into the mountains through the canyons of the Prickly Pear; to the crest of the Continental Divide at Mullan Pass — that section Mullan knew could be constructed with ease, using existing trails in several places. From the pass the route should follow the Little Blackfoot to its junction with the Hell Gate; down the canyon to the Bitterroot; westward along that river until it met the St. Regis de Borgia. Mullan knew this segment of the road would require frequent river and stream crossings and some side cutting through mountain spurs and narrow canyons. Toward the St. Regis timber became heavier, and axmen would be needed to clear the route.

Where the Bitterroot turned north to join the Flathead and become the Clark Fork River, Mullan decided the route would press almost due west, following the St. Regis de Borgia. True, by following the Bitterroot and Clark Fork he could achieve a water-level route to the Coeur d' Alene mission, but heavy spring runoff along this route suggested it might be hard to maintain. Aeneas, an old Iroquois trapper for the Hudson's Bay Company who had long resided in the Bitterroot, told Mullan of a narrow pass through the Coeur d' Alene mountains at the head of the St. Regis. In June, Bassille, a Coeur d' Alene Indian, led Mullan through the pass, convincing him of its suitability. So the road should continue up the St. Regis de Borgia, over the pass, and on to the mission.

From the Coeur d' Alene mission, Mullan recommended a southern route to skirt the bottom of Coeur d' Alene Lake along the St. Joe River. Once out on the Great Spokane Plains, an easy road could be built due south across the Snake River to Fort Walla Walla. Established routes connected this point with the Columbia River and the Pacific, completing an east-to-west/west-to-east traverse of the Rocky Mountains. "In connection with the proper location and construction of a railroad, one of the most essential aids in advance is a good wagon-road line." Mullan felt Governor Stevens would agree.

Isaac Stevens more than shared Mullan's belief that a road from Fort Benton to Walla Walla was possible. For Washington Territory to grow and thrive, such a road was essential. He'd already said so in communiques to Congress and his War Department superiors back east. Stevens dispatched Mullan to the nation's capital in January 1855 with reports for the War Department and resolutions from the legislative assembly of Washington Territory recommending road work begin immediately. On his arrival at the capital, Mullan learned Congress had already appropriated $30,000 for a military road westward from the Missouri River, through Nebraska Territory, and on to Walla Walla — Stevens' initial reports of Mullan's findings had borne fruit. But $30,000 would not begin to finance the work. While in Washington, Mullan also learned that Indian hostilities had broken out in the eastern portion of Washington Territory. The War Department had more pressing concerns now — road construction would have to wait.

Frustrated, the young lieutenant received a change of assignment. For the next year he served in Florida fighting Seminole Indians, receiving a promotion to first lieutenant for his efforts. Returning north, he completed work on a master's degree at St. John's College and then received a transfer to frontier duty at Fort Leavenworth. His dream of a road seemed as far away as Washington Territory itself.

Isaac Stevens had not forgotten the

road, however. In 1857 he resigned as governor and was elected territorial delegate to Congress. In the nation's capital Stevens set to work immediately cutting through military red tape and reviving consideration of a northern military road connecting the Missouri and the Columbia. His position was strengthened when the Mormon War erupted that year, effectively disrupting the traditional route to the Pacific along the Oregon Trail.

On March 15, 1858, the orders Mullan had waited for so long arrived. The Office of Explorations and Surveys secured a special assignment for him: Proceed immediately to Fort Dalles on the Columbia River; procure supplies, surveyors, and laborers; negotiate for a military escort at Fort Walla Walla; and commence work. Charles P. Chouteau, of the St. Louis fur trading family, promised to push one of his riverboats as far up the Missouri as possible that spring — perhaps to Fort Benton.

In mid-May Mullan arrived at Fort Dalles after a six-week trip by way of the Isthmus of Panama. Quickly he assembled a construction party and made arrangements for a sixty-man military escort at Walla Walla. The work crew had advanced only as far as Five Mile Creek when a courier brought word of Lt. Col. Edward J. Steptoe's defeat on the Spokane Plains. Mullan queried Steptoe on the advisability of continuing road construction through the area, anticipating a negative reply even before it arrived on May 30. He had no choice. Marching his men back to The Dalles, he discharged them. Lest the entire summer be wasted, Mullan requested assignment to the punitive expedition against the Indians. The commander, Col. George Wright, had been Mullan's superior at Fort Leavenworth, and he welcomed the lieutenant as his topographical officer. Mullan assisted in the campaign during the summer of 1858 and in several instances distinguished himself in combat. More importantly, however, he used the opportunity to run preliminary surveys through the area, including the primary westward approaches to the rugged Bitterroot Mountains. The more he saw, the more Mullan realized the immensity of such a road construction project.

At the conclusion of Wright's successful campaign, Mullan returned to Fort Vancouver. He relaxed and played cards with other officers stationed there, including Capt. William T. Sherman and Lt. U. S. Grant. In a single game Mullan won $300 from Grant, but the money which concerned him most was the amount necessary to fund a construction force large enough to build the road from Walla Walla to Fort Benton. Impatient and frustrated with waiting, Mullan left Fort Vancouver during the winter and went to Washington, D.C., to argue his cause. Isaac Stevens assisted in lobbying for the road, and in March 1859 Congress allocated $100,000 for the project.

Again Mullan hurried to The Dalles and Walla Walla via Panama. He assembled his forces, hiring ninety civilians, including members of the abortive 1858 expedition such as topographers Gustavus Sohon (a guide and interpreter for Mullan in 1853-54) and Theodore Kalecki.

P. W. Engle of the Topographical Engineers joined the other two surveyors, as did W. W. Johnson, Conway R. Howard and W. W. DeLacy — civilian engineers with eastern railroad experience. Under the command of Lts. James L. White, H. B. Lyon, and James Howard, 100 men from the Third Artillery provided a military escort and additional manpower. Another 30 men supported the escort troops, bringing Mullan's total command to 230, which was enough to repel any hostile Indian attack and to complete the initial phase of road construction between Walla Walla and the Bitterroot River before winter set in. Mullan dispatched Sohon to explore the Palouse River and Engle to investigate the Snake to the mouth of the Clearwater and beyond, to determine whether either route would be suitable. The main party departed from Walla Walla on July 1. Construction of the northern military road had begun — Mullan's Road.

The expedition's first days provided an opportunity to organize the party. Still apprehensive about possible Indian attack, Mullan stationed soldiers as perimeter guards day and night. Civilians carried their own weapons, loaded and capped at all times. Furthermore, employees pulled two-hour shifts each night, riding guard over horse, mule, and cattle herds. No actual attack ever tested the double ring of security, but throughout the summer on the Spokane Plains the party stayed alert.

Each of Mullan's topographers and engineers kept meticulous journals, as did Mullan himself. Sohon and Engle rejoined the main party during the first week of July, reporting impassable terrain along both the Palouse and Snake rivers. Even crossing the Snake presented problems; soldiers and civilians worked sixteen hours on July 3 swimming stock across and ferrying supplies on rafts. One raft broke loose, carrying a civilian into some rapids where he drowned. After Sohon's and Engle's reconnaissance, Mullan chose to continue north and east toward Coeur d'Alene Lake and the St. Joe River, a route he had explored in 1854 and again in 1858. Work across the rolling prairie progressed rapidly. "Road excellent; camps good, with fine water; hill-sides bowed down in beauty under their loads of the most excellent and nutritious grasses," Mullan noted in his journal.

Separate topographical parties preceded the main contingent. Bridge crews worked at the Touchet River, Dry Creek, and elsewhere as needed. Pick-and-shovel brigades followed to cut the road into hillsides, or grade approaches at stream fords. To mark the route, Mullan recalled reading about Roman roads and their mileposts. He had mileposts sunk along the way, and on each his men branded "M.R." (military road) and enscribed the appropriate mileage from Fort Walla Walla.

Mullan remembered the St. Joe River Valley as a beautiful gem, embedded in a noble range of mountains. Here, however, he encountered the first real obstacles. Where the outlet to Poun Lake joined the St. Joe, crews worked eight days completing a timber bridge sixty feet long. Rocky abutments on either side of the bridge required extensive excavation before the entire party could cross. Soft ground along the river mired horse and wagon travel, making corduroying necessary. Axmen felled trees, dragged them to the roadway, then laid them crosswise for almost four hundred feet, providing a more stable surface.

Beautiful as the St. Joe was, it proved too wide for a bridge, so a ferry had to be constructed. Sawyers set to work cutting lumber; others burned tar for caulking. Carpenters built two flatboats, each forty-two feet long, twelve feet wide, and two feet deep. The first boat was placed in service across the St. Joe, ferrying their wagons to the opposite side. Mullan dispatched the second with a small crew across Coeur d'Alene Lake and up the river of the same name to a point where surveyors determined another ferry would be needed.

Mullan divided his men into parties. One group of surveyors laid out the twelve-mile route between the St. Joe and the Coeur d'Alene, a second explored and mapped the St. Joe to its headwaters, and a third mapped the outline of Coeur d'Alene Lake and sounded its depths. Other men laid additional corduroy roads, cut through timber, excavated sidehills, and built three bridges. By August 5 the main body reached the Coeur d'Alene River and, in another four days, completed a road along its bank to the point where the second ferry waited. Mullan devoted August 10 to crossing the river. The next six days were used to open the road as far as the Coeur d'Alene mission, requiring 1,200 feet of excavation through a rocky spur which abutted the river, three miles of ax work through heavy

timber, and three more bridges. All elements of the expedition arrived at the mission — two hundred miles and six weeks from Walla Walla — on August 16, 1859.

Father Anthony Ravalli and other missionaries welcomed the crew as best they could. Rest was short, however, for Mullan worried about the lateness of the season and the one hundred miles of rugged terrain which lay between the mission and the mouth of St. Regis de Borgia River, where he hoped to establish winter quarters. Some good news tempered his pessimism. Chouteau's Missouri River steamboat *Chippewa* had reached the Fort Benton vicinity during early summer with twenty-four thousand rations and additional construction supplies. The voyage indicated that the Missouri was truly navigable to the point where Mullan proposed ending his road.

Like the construction workers, P. M. Engle and Gustavus Sohon rested only a day with the Jesuit brothers. Engle and several Indian guides set out to explore the Clark Fork River, reaffirming Mullan's 1854 observations that narrow canyons would frustrate construction work. Sohon also used Indian guides to assist him in plotting and marking a general route from the Coeur d'Alene mission over what became Sohon Pass, then down the St. Regis and Bitterroot rivers to Hell Gate Valley. Other surveyors worked in advance of the axmen, marking a path approximately twenty-five feet wide through one hundred miles of dense timber.

Day by day, construction camps advanced. Each evening Mullan tried to update his journals. "The standing timber was dense, and the fallen timber that had accumulated for ages formed an intricate jungle well calculated to impress one with the character of impracticability," he noted in late August. Each night and frequently several times during the day, shovels, picks and axes had to be resharpened. Few men complained, however. In time, even Mullan had to admit the task was more than he had envisioned. Only the industry and fortitude of the men made it possible to press on.

Terrain between the mission and the crest of the Bitterroots contained more than trees and rocks. A Flathead Indian named Moise, who served as a herder, came to Mullan one day with a small pouch containing gold that he had discovered along a stream as he watered stock. Mullan examined the nuggets, determined that they were indeed gold, then convinced the herder to keep the discovery a secret. Had his workmen realized the potential mineral wealth at their feet, Mullan feared they would abandon the work. At least twice more, along the Bitterroot and again near the junction of the Hell Gate and Little Bitterroot, individuals discovered gold. In each instance Mullan recorded the find in his journals but worked to keep his men from spreading the knowledge and jeopardizing the entire venture.

August became September, and the weather held. October turned cold. Water froze in buckets, and ice often lined stream banks as crews graded hundreds of fords. Still there were countless trees to be cut, thou-

Cantonment Stevens; Mullan's winter quarters, 1853–54

sands of cuts and spurs to be graded, and small bridges to be built. The first light blankets of snow covered the ground. Stock had to dig for forage. By November, Mullan admitted in his journals that the task was far greater than he or his surveyors had estimated. Snow at Sohon Pass accumulated to nearly eighteen inches by November 6, and two days later the thermometer dropped to below zero and held. Fatigue began to overtake men and animals. Two men were cut with axes, another accidentally shot, and a fourth hurt by a falling tree. Weaker animals began to die. The possibility of even more snow and cold preyed on Mullan's mind. His position teetered precariously close to disaster.

About Thanksgiving, Mullan decided he would not reach the junction of the St. Regis and the Bitterroot. He selected a spot for his winter quarters in dense timber along the St. Regis, fifteen miles east of the pass and another fifteen miles short of his goal. Wagons became sleds as men worked to get themselves, their stock, and their supplies down off the pass. By December 4 a preliminary road had been completed, and Mullan designated the point Cantonment Jordan. Temperatures hovered near forty below zero the next day as men worked to build winter quarters. Mullan ordered all remaining cattle butchered to provide food. Split carcasses soon froze solid and lasted until March. To preserve what mules and horses remained, Mullan had them driven one hundred miles farther east to the protection of the upper Bitterroot near Fort Owen. Few survived the trip. Hundreds died along the St.

Regis de Borgia, littering the ground with bodies. Birds of prey, wolves, coyotes, and mountain lions feasted on the carrion, oblivious to the activities of the men nearby.

Surveyors and members of the scientific corps used the seclusion of winter to compile field notes, prepare official reports, and write memoirs. Soldiers and laborers kept fires going and pulled guard duty, "merely to preserve discipline" Mullan admitted. For everyone, work hours began at 10 A.M. each day, continued to 3 P.M., then resumed from 6 to 9 P.M. Once a month expressman P. E. Toohill or Pend d'Oreille half-breed Spokane Garry brought in mail from Fort Walla Walla. As snow depths approached five feet near Cantonment Jordan and nine or more feet at Sohon Pass, Spokane Garry changed his route and followed the Clark Fork and Bitterroot rivers. He told Mullan that no Indians ever cross the pass during winter. Although much longer, the river route had little snow. Mullan sent out parties on foot to investigate, and he learned that along these rivers — less than twenty miles from his encampment — some ground lay bare, and snow rarely accumulated to more than six to eighteen inches in depth. Again the lieutenant felt compelled to admit he had erred in his initial route projections. His 1854 experience with heavy spring runoff along the Clark Fork had resulted in a hasty decision not to follow that course.

Before Christmas Mullan dispatched Engle to proceed with a preliminary survey along the Bitterroot and Hell Gate rivers to Mullan Pass and then on to Fort Benton. He used these reports the next spring to facilitate planning for a more definite route. In January W. W. Johnson left Cantonment Jordan for Washington, D.C., with letters from Mullan to the secretary of war, the quartermaster general, the chief topographical engineer, and Delegate Stevens. In each, the lieutenant outlined a plan to move a military train from the headwaters of the Missouri to the headwaters of the Columbia during the summer of 1860. Mullan was due at Fort Benton in August. At that point he would have a substantial wagon train. To get it back to Walla Walla he would have to hire teamsters. The U.S. Army in Washington and Oregon desperately needed new recruits. If the army shipped three hundred soldiers to Fort Benton, these men could return the wagon train (saving approximately $30,000), fill vacancies, and demonstrate the applicability of Mullan's road. The army set to work implementing the plan.

Before winter broke, Mullan faced other problems. His brother, James, a physician with the expedition, diagnosed more than twenty-five cases of scurvy among the men — a result of the straight beef diet at Cantonment Jordan. Mullan traveled to the Pend d'Oreille mission to purchase fresh vegetables and vinegar from the priests.

When and if spring ever came, Mullan also realized his work force lay stranded because of livestock losses. In March he journeyed to Fort Owen and negotiated with the Flathead Indians for 117 animals. He told the Indians of his condition along the St. Regis and pointed out that he could not get the supplies waiting at Fort Benton without their help. Chief Ambrose asked for a day to consider the matter, promising to send Mullan as many sticks as he had men and animals to offer. The next morning a brave arrived at Mullan's quarters with 137 sticks — 117 animals and 20 men at his disposal. "Such nobleness of character as is found among some of the Flatheads is seldom seen among Indians; they always treated myself and my parties with a frank generosity and a continuous friendship," Mullan recorded.

Gustavus Sohon headed to Fort Benton with half of the horses and Indians; Mullan led the remainder toward Cantonment Jordan. The lieutenant did not wait for snow to melt along the St. Regis. He ordered his men to leapfrog over the remaining fifteen miles to the Bitterroot and begin construction from that point forward. In late April a contingent returned to complete cutting and grading over the gap.

Crews followed the north bank of the Bitterroot for thirty miles when they encountered Big Mountain with a spur six miles wide which could not be bypassed. On May 10 Mullan massed 150 men for the work of cutting and blasting through the mountain. They labored for six weeks to complete the hardest and longest cut on the entire route. During blasting one man was blinded and another stunned in premature explosions.

From Big Mountain, construction progressed rapidly through broken timber along the Bitterroot. By June 28 the entire party entered Hell Gate ronde, 105 miles from Cantonment Jordan. All rested for two days. De

Lacy took boats and floated down the Bitterroot to map its entire length. July 1, 1860, Mullan pushed the rest of his men eastward along the Hell Gate for three miles. He spent the remainder of that day and all the next ferrying across the Big Blackfoot River. Conway Howard and Kalecki broke off from the main party to explore the length of the large stream and rejoin the construction force near Dearborn River on the eastern slope of the Continental Divide.

The winding nature of the Hell Gate River necessitated eleven crossings and frequent grading, but timber was light and work went quickly for sixty miles. Mullan received word that Maj. George Blake and the three hundred recruits had arrived at Fort Benton. Anxious not to keep his superior waiting, he pushed his men eastward along the Little Blackfoot. Some corduroying made low ground passable, and all in all the section involved only light work. July 17 the party reached the summit of the divide — the pass Mullan had first crossed six years earlier. The same morning a solar eclipse occurred, halting work briefly.

Grading and bridging went well through the Prickly Pear drainage and then north to the Dearborn and Sun rivers. All parties assembled at the old Blackfoot Indian agency along the Sun on July 29. From there to Fort Benton the existing road was quite suitable. Mullan received word there that Congress had continued funding for his work with an additional $100,000. Relieved, Mullan divided his party for a final time. Four contingents under separate surveyors examined the broad country between the Sun River and Fort Benton. August 1, as promised, all elements converged on the Missouri River port. Lieutenant Mullan reported to Major Blake, turning over all wagons and supplies. Mission accomplished.

Blake had been cooped up at Fort Benton with three hundred recruits for nearly two months and was anxious to begin his westward march. He dismissed from the Mullan expedition all civilians and military personnel whose contracts or enlistments had expired. Gustavus Sohon stayed on as a guide along the newly completed road. Mullan and twenty-five men, with a packtrain, preceded the major's column by a day to clear any remaining obstacles and locate suitable campsites. Mullan left Fort Benton on August 5, and Blake followed the next day.

Some small bridges had washed out, a few fords had to be regraded, and en route Mullan decided to relocate the road near the junction of the Little Blackfoot and Hell Gate. By turning south into the Deer Lodge Valley for three miles he avoided several troublesome river crossings.

October 8, 1860, Blake marched into Fort Walla Walla: six hundred miles and fifty-seven days from Fort Benton. His glowing reports of the road and Mullan's work justified the expense and effort. Mullan broke up his remaining crew and moved down the Columbia to Fort Vancouver. There he drafted plans for the second phase of work on the road under the authorization and funding Congress had already provided. He planned to relocate the western segment around the northern shore of Coeur d'Alene Lake, avoiding the troublesome St.

Joe River Valley. From the mission east he proposed construction of eighty bridges, eliminating fords and ferry points.

As Congress debated this plan, Mullan conceived an even grander idea. He proposed outfitting his 1861 party at Fort Leavenworth rather than Walla Walla. From there the expedition could march overland to Fort Laramie and then into the Deer Lodge Valley for the winter of 1861-1862. During the 1862 construction season Mullan would improve the existing road westward to Walla Walla. Mullan's idea foreshadowed John Bozeman's 1864 work along the trail which bore his name, as well as post-Civil War construction of the Powder River Road. Mullan hurried to Washington with his new suggestion, only to discover that Congress had approved the original plan. Caught up in the confusion of Abraham Lincoln's inauguration and the pending breakup of the Union, Mullan's new proposal fell on deaf ears. Hastily the lieutenant returned west, intercepting his orders at Walla Walla.

By May 13, 1861, Mullan had assembled sixty civilians for his work force, drawing principally from veterans of the previous two years. One hundred soldiers from Fort Walla Walla and Fort Colville joined the party. Mullan followed his previous route as far as the Snake River crossing. Earlier construction withstood the seasons, and the road's condition pleased everyone. From the Snake he struck out almost due north toward the Spokane River. Mullan wanted his new road to cross the Spokane River, using a ferry operated by An-

toine Plante under a charter from Washington Territory. Mullan dispatched several men to the St. Joe's ferry with orders to row the craft across Coeur d'Alene Lake to the first crossing of the Coeur d'Alene River.

Antoine Plante welcomed the party of road builders and the idea that a military highway would bring business. Just over fifty, the French-Gros Ventre half-breed had lived along the Spokane for sixteen years. His vegetable garden, fat animals, smiling Flathead wife, and happy children spoke of good living; but his new house reminded Mullan of his last visit to the site. During the 1858 Indian campaigns, hostile warriors had burned the Plante residence. Meticulously he'd hewn and dovetailed new logs for an enlarged structure — complete with veranda and windows, neatly glazed and painted. The river at this point was three hundred feet wide and eight feet deep. Plante had constructed a forty-foot-long cable ferry, capable of carrying a loaded wagon and teams. Although the Spokane was fordable only six miles upstream, Mullan liked the amiable Plante and agreed with Isaac Stevens' suggestion to use the ferry.

Mullan lingered at the Spokane only long enough for men and equipment to cross. He moved east June 3 and entered a band of timber nearly thirty miles across. The forest proved far heavier than south of the lake. Mullan divided his force into two detachments — first axmen, then graders. Work progressed at painstakingly slow pace, often two miles a day or less. To make matters worse, constant hordes of mosquitoes swarmed about. Workmen who removed their shirts during the heat of the day soon found their bodies riddled by the hungry insects. Again the lieutenant admitted he had misjudged the nature of the terrain and the immensity of the task.

June became July as the men chopped through the timber, grubbed out the stumps, shoveled and blasted the road eastward. On July 4, while crossing the divide between Coeur d'Alene Lake and the Coeur d'Alene mission, party members caught the holiday spirit and set off several black powder blasts to celebrate. Others fired rifles into the air, adding to the din and causing nearby Indians to assume the white men had gone "kultus." They fled to the mission for refuge. That same day, just below the summit, axmen came to an unusually large white pine. They removed the bark on one side and engraved "M. R., July 4, 1861" to mark the occasion. By afternoon they had worked their way down the slope, leaving this reminder of their crossing.

August 1 the expedition reached the Coeur d'Alene mission and a junction with the earlier road. The northern route completed, the task became one of improving the existing road. Mullan was behind schedule and knew it. Hoping to provoke competition among his men, he divided them into six small contingents. One cut trees, another graded improvements, and four constructed bridges. Supply wagons followed them. The idea worked well. By September 15 all had crested the Bitterroot divide and started down the St. Regis de Borgia. Behind them lay twenty new bridges. The same competitive elements rendezvoused November 1 at the junction

of the St. Regis and the Bitterroot, after similar construction efforts along the eastern slope of the range.

Determined not to get caught in deep mountain snows, Mullan dispatched an advance party to the junction of the Hell Gate and Big Blackfoot rivers. There they constructed several log buildings to house workmen and supplies for the winter. Remaining workers reached the site November 22, making only minor improvements to the road along the Bitterroot. Mullan named the headquarters Cantonment Wright. Winter had still not arrived in the mountains, permitting Mullan to move his stock into the protection of the Bitterroot Valley and to spread his men out along the Hell Gate River between Cantonment Wright and Deer Lodge Valley. Beyond the cantonment, four other parties erected winter cabins and graded cuts as weather permitted. If all went well, Mullan hoped that spring would find road improvements nearly completed.

Despite good intentions, the expedition experienced severe hardships. A dry summer had withered much of the feed. Forty or fifty hungry cattle wandered off into the timber and were lost. Other animals died, unable to find forage. And winter, once it arrived in late November, "proved one of unusual and marked severity" in Mullan's own words. Snow continued to accumulate and did not melt until April. Indians could not remember a winter as cold, or recall trees "exploding." Frozen solid in the intense cold, trunks split with a loud report which echoed through the forest.

During January civilian employee Charles Schafft attempted to walk

Cantonment Wright; Mullan's winter quarters, 1861–62

from one of Mullan's forward camps to Deer Lodge Valley. As night closed in he realized the severity of the cold and stopped to build a fire. Attempting to remove his wet moccasins, he discovered them frozen to his feet. Alarmed, he retraced his route back to the construction camp, where his fellow workers placed both feet in a tub of cold water. As the feet thawed, flesh fell from the bones. On receiving word of the situation, Mullan dispatched soldiers from Cantonment Wright to bring Schafft in. Dr. George Hammond removed both legs above the knees, saving the patient's life. Co-workers took up a collection amounting to several hundred dollars, then transported the hapless victim to the Pend d'Oreille mission, where they left him in the care of the priests.

Despite hardships and tragedies,

Mullan's plan worked. By May 1862 five rock cuts involving over seven miles of excavation had been completed, eliminating ten crossings of the Hell Gate River. At the Big Blackfoot, the Cantonment Wright party completed a four-span, rock-pile bridge, 235 feet long, with whip-sawed planks three inches thick. Spring runoff prevented construction of an additional bridge across the Hell Gate near Deer Lodge Valley, so Mullan contracted the job to Samuel Hugo, a local resident.

Remaining work along the road to Fort Benton was minimal. On May 23 Mullan ordered Cantonment Wright abandoned. Dispatching two elements westward toward the Coeur d'Alene mission to check bridges and make small improvements en route, Mullan proceeded east to the Missouri River port. At Fort Benton,

Mullan had a mackinac boat constructed to transport discharged employees down the river to St. Louis. With sixteen remaining soldiers and six civilians, he departed Fort Benton in mid-June for his final traverse of the road. Several days out of Fort Benton he learned that four river-boats had arrived at the port with 364 emigrants bound for Idaho's new goldfields — not far from the place where Moise had promised to keep his secret three years before.

Mullan's leisurely trip back to Walla Walla revealed conditions which had plagued the entire effort. Spring runoff had damaged the Big Blackfoot bridge; six structures along the St. Regis and two along the Coeur d'Alene had been washed away entirely. Mullan now had neither the manpower nor the time to replace all of them. Again he contracted with Samuel Hugo to do the work under the supervision of Missoula County commissioners. West of the Bitterroot Range, Mullan reassembled his party and replaced missing bridges. Remembering the scant forage of 1861, he scattered grass seed on the open benches and valleys along the route. Future travellers enjoyed not only the ease of traveling a well-engineered road but also the convenience of feed for their stock.

In late August the remnant of Mullan's party reached Walla Walla. Here he received word of his promotion to captain, based on his road-building success. Mullan dismissed his men and sold all remaining equipment at public auction. "Thus ended my work in the field," he summarized in his notes. "Seven years of close and arduous attention, exploring and opening up a road of six hundred and twenty-four miles from the Columbia to the Missouri river at a cost of $230,000." Totaling the amount of construction, Mullan tabulated 120 miles of difficult timber: cutting 25 to 30 feet wide, and 30 measured miles of excavation 15 to 20 feet wide. In addition, more than 100 bridges and countless fords made travel easier.

Returning to Washington, D.C., by way of Fort Vancouver, Mullan set to work compiling the record of his work. In 1863 he published his *Report on the Construction of a Military Road from Fort Walla-Walla to Fort Benton,* filled with technical details of construction, particulars on requirements for railroad building, and glowing reports of the rich Pacific Northwest. Two years later the trickle of emigrants had turned into a flood, leading to the creation of three territories: Idaho, Montana, and Wyoming. To make his vast knowledge more available to the public and to further advertise his road, Mullan wrote a *Miners and Travelers Guide* in 1865. It contained all necessary details for travelers along the road and outright boosterism for the region with its "well-tilled fields, grand mountains and useful rivers, forests of orchards and oceans of grain, miles of sluice-boxes and tons of gold."

Capt. John Mullan became a victim of his own promotion. He resigned his commission shortly after turning in all his reports, returned to the Pacific Northwest, and married the daughter of a Washington farmer. Later he abandoned farming and the region to take up a law practice in San Francisco and finally in Washington, D.C.

In time the road which bore his name fell to disuse for lack of proper maintenance. But the route he pioneered remained viable.

In August 1883, the stocky, fifty-three-year-old lawyer boarded a westbound train. On September 7 he stood upon a crowded viewing stand erected at Gold Creek, Montana. He watched. A workman drove the last spike in the last rail of the Northern Pacific Railroad. A cheer went up from the crowd and the northern transcontinental railroad was complete. Its route? John Mullan smiled: Over the pass Gabriel had named in his honor nearly thirty years before; along rivers, through valleys of Montana, Idaho, and Washington where Mullan had pushed axmen, engineers, graders, and soldiers. He closed his eyes — the sound of the locomotive was no longer a dream.

THE SOUTH PLATTE RIVER TRAIL: THE INCREDIBLE HIGHWAY

By Nell Brown Propst

The South Platte Trail was only wagon ruts on the open prairie, and it ran alongside an unimpressive river which was described as "a mile wide and an inch deep." Yet the trail was part of the most heavily traveled road in the United States. Ninety percent of the Colorado gold seekers followed it, and from 1862 to 1865, when Indian attacks virtually closed down sections of the northern Overland Trail, most of that traffic was rerouted up the South Platte River.

It was a deceptive river. Its quicksand bed was known to swallow entire wagons while the helpless owners stood by and watched. On hot summer days only willow bushes graced its banks. In 1842 when John C. Fremont stopped to watch some Arapahos make a buffalo surround, his refuge from the 108-degree heat was

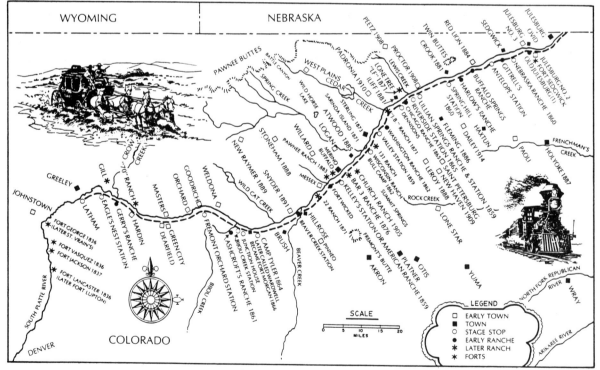

The South Platte River Trail

This map of the South Platte was researched by Nell Brown Propst and drawn by Gerald Jefferies.

under the overhanging banks of the stream.

One tree was so rare a landmark that it was listed in most of the itineraries published for gold seekers in 1858 and 1859. Reed's *Guide to the Kansas Gold Regions* described it:

> Near this spot upon an island stands a large and solitary cottonwood tree, upon the boughs of which, about 25 feet from the ground, reposes the body of an Indian chief, wrapped in a buffalo robe, thus far upon his road to spirit land.

The "highway" may have been a shock to some pilgrims, but its ruts were the recording of a mass migration of restless Americans searching for a new beginning. Places like Holon Godfrey's Fort Wicked bore testimony to the toughness and staying power of the frontiersmen. But numerous graves and burned out soddies became warning signals to the hopeful who thronged the trail from 1859 to 1869.

The river was a ribbon of life, as many discovered. In 1843 Fremont undertook a shorter route straight across the prairies from Missouri to the Rockies. Though he theoretically saved a couple of hundred miles, he actually spent twelve extra frustrating days searching for water and fighting the heat and dust. He learned, as did many who followed him, that the broad trail along the Platte was far superior to "shortcuts."

The millions of buffalo which grazed the Great Pasture between the Platte and Arkansas rivers made the first trail. In 1824 Col. William H. Ashley's men probably would

have perished in a blizzard if the buffalo, like so many snowplows, had not tramped out a path.

For several centuries a parade of people followed that path. In the 1500s the peaceable Jicarilla Apaches made summer trips from their home territory along the Arkansas to hunt in the South Platte area. In 1664 the Picuries, a Pueblo tribe, built a fort on the prairie (El Cuartelejo), and they, too, made hunting expeditions north to the South Platte.

But the Spanish and French were also claiming the land, and perhaps the Indians were not aware of the extent of their ambition. In fact, Indians acted as guides for Pedro de Villasur (probably the first white man to travel along the South Platte) when he was sent to investigate French intrusion into "Spanish" territory.

Villasur took with him on that semimilitary expedition many comforts of home: special foods, liquor, and brocade cloths on which he ceremoniously dined among the cacti and yucca. One mule was assigned to bear a complete silver service.

Finding that Pawnees and possibly French were camped where the Jesús María (the Spanish name for the South Platte) flowed into the San Lorenzo (the North Platte), he ignored the warnings of his Indian guides and camped in tall grass, with Pawnees clearly visible on an island. Just before dawn next morning, August 13, 1720, most of Villasur's forty-five white soldiers died with him. His guides, knowing only too well what was coming, managed to escape.

The French, who had been claiming the area as a part of Louisiana, swarmed over the prairie. Their diplomacy, so different from the arrogance of the Spaniards, won them friends among the red men. Many intermarried with Indians.

In 1739 the Mallet Brothers led a small French expedition into the Great Buffalo Pasture, following the South Platte at least as far as Lodgepole Creek near present-day Ovid, Colorado. They called the stream Padouca Fork, after the large tribe then moving into the area.

The Mallets translated the Indian name *Nithbaska,* which meant "river that spreads out in flatness," to Rivière Plat (shallow river), a name which stuck as the Platte. They thought the stream led to China and would open trade routes to Asia.

In 1763 the French, winding up their seven-year French and Indian War, transferred all of Louisiana west of the Mississippi back to the Spanish because they did not want England to gain control of the vast area. Napoleon repossessed it in 1800 but, realizing he could not defend it, soon sold the Louisiana Purchase to the United States. The land was a bargain, as Napoleon's minister, Talleyrand, declared — not quite three cents an acre.

The Indians were apparently unaware of those machinations or perhaps were unconcerned. The Kiowas and the Arapahos, the latter an Algonquin tribe, settled south of the Platte during the late 1700s.

Restless Americans began to roam over the new possession, but the first American military expedition did not travel up the South Platte until 1820, a century after Villasur's fateful

journey. Maj. Stephen Harriman Long's Topographical Engineers were members of one of the army's most exacting units, but they are best remembered for publicizing the vast plains as the Great American Desert. Today Long's name is immortalized by Long's Peak, the first landmark of the Rocky Mountains, which is visible far out on the South Platte. His French guide, Joseph Bijeau, received a lesser honor. His name, misspelled, was bestowed on a dry stream even less impressive than the South Platte: Bijou Creek, which joins the river near present-day Fort Morgan, Colorado.

About that time the Cheyenne Indians came south looking for the wild horses that roamed the Great Pasture. The Cheyennes were in the South Platte area for only fifty years, but during that Time of the Horse, they found a new life of following the buffalo and moving with the seasons. They became true prairie people. In 1863, when Territorial Governor John Evans tried to persuade the Indians to settle on farms, a Cheyenne named Bull Bear expressed the Indian contempt for a sedentary life when he told Elbridge Gerry, the governor's intermediary:

"Well, you can just go back to the governor and tell him we are not reduced quite that low yet."

Peaceable within their tribe, the Cheyennes became good warriors in order to survive the attacks of other Indians. The Kiowas and Apaches, on trips north, would travel in the mountains for fear of getting caught out on the plains by the prairie people.

The Cheyennes were governed by

a representative body, and several societies enforced rules and protected the tribe. In separation-of-powers tradition, a man could not be chief of a band and chief of one of the societies at the same time.

The system was said to have been established by Sweet Medicine (or Sweet Water), the messiah of the tribe, who was born of a virgin. Perhaps as a result of that belief, women held unusual positions of responsibility, and the Cheyennes placed great importance on their sanctity. A Cheyenne girl was much admired for her beauty and pride, but if a man took advantage of that beauty he could expect death. It was the one time that violence toward a tribe member was condoned.

The grassland along the South Platte was a heaven to the prairie people. The buffalo and antelope made it one of the finest hunting lands; snakes, birds, fish, and wild sand cherries varied the diet. As long as the Indians had buffalo hides for lodging and clothing, they could survive even when snow and sleet or rain and hail drove across the prairie. Their lives were built around the buffalo; it was their economy.

It was a good, free life, but the old men must have often thought of the final warning from Sweet Medicine: "Some day the Earth Men will come. Do not follow anything they do."

The earth men — the whites — were not long in coming. In late 1824 the first business venture came with Ashley's Rocky Mountain Fur Company. The guide was one of the most capable ever in the West, Thomas Fitzpatrick. A skilled trapper, he later headed the company. He became the

first Indian agent in what was to be Colorado and was trusted and respected by the red men.

In 1831 the Cheyennes took the first dangerous step of following the white men. Trapper John Gantt, dishonorably discharged from the army, was the first to introduce the Indians to liquor, mixing sugar with it to make them like it. The habit grew among the prairie people, and in five years' time they were making decisions and concessions simply because of whiskey. Rufus Sage, a trapper, wrote that the Cheyennes were never again as good a people. They had moved toward fulfilling Sweet Medicine's sad prophecy: "In the end your history will be forgotten."

Col. Henry Dodge led his First Dragoons up the river in 1835 with the aim of settling the Indians on the "worthless desert" between the Platte and the Arkansas. One of his officers, Lt. Lancaster Lupton, noted William Bent's prosperous trading center on the Arkansas and the next spring built Fort Lancaster, later called Fort Lupton, on the South Platte two miles below present-day Fort Lupton, Colorado. It thrived, and within a short time three other trading posts were located nearby: Fort Vasquez, built of cottonwood logs by Louis Vasquez in 1836 and later burned by Indians; St. Vrain's, another Bent enterprise, third in size to Bent's Fort and Fort Laramie and connected with Bent's by a once-a-week type of Pony Express; and the short-lived Fort Jackson.

Louis Vasquez got the idea of shipping down the South Platte and on April 26, 1840, launched a flat-bottomed boat, 36 by 8 feet, loaded with

700 buffalo robes and 400 dried buffalo tongues, which were often the only parts that the whites salvaged from the kill. E. Willard Smith described the journey:

> The water was very shallow and we proceeded with great difficulty, getting on sand bars every few minutes. We were obliged to wade and push the boat along most of the way.

Sometimes they had to unload all the robes and tongues in order to move the boat. Then within a few minutes the entire routine might have to be repeated. By the time the men reached St. Louis 69 days later, the 400 tongues had been eaten.

The boating idea died hard. Two years later Rufus Sage came upon a camp of Bent and St. Vrain trappers stuck five miles above Bijou Creek. The captain, Baptiste Charbonneau (who as a baby with his mother Sacajawea had gone on the Lewis and Clark Expedition), had been one of the seven on the original attempt to navigate the Platte. This time he had piled the furs on an island, where he hopefully awaited high water.

Fremont's expeditions were significant because he did the first extensive mapping. The later-well-known Colorado men in his group included Thomas Fitzpatrick and William Gilpin. The latter joined Fremont in 1843 at Elm Grove, Missouri. He was so enamored of the West that he had sold all his possessions — even his library — in order to outfit himself for crossing the plains. Indignant over the Great American Desert propaganda, he wrote several tracts, helping to change the name from desert to plains. He became so identified with the new country that years later President Lincoln appointed him the first territorial governor of Colorado.

The explorers had little trouble with Indians on the South Platte. On the 1843 expedition, a good-looking young Arapaho ran up to Tom Fitzpatrick with obvious joy and affection. Years before, the trapper had rescued three young children who had been lost on the prairie for a week and were starving. He took such a fancy to the oldest one, then about six, that he more or less adopted him and enrolled him in school in St. Louis. When the boy was about thirteen, on a trip west with Fitzpatrick, he entered an Arapaho village where his mother recognized him. He returned to the life of the Indians, but he never forgot Fitzpatrick, and he became a friend to the whites who later settled on the South Platte. Named Friday, for the day that Fitzpatrick found him, he was also known, according to Rufus Sage, as the "Arapaho American."

The dragoons came again in 1845, cutting down from Fort Laramie to the South Platte via Crow Creek. Designed to impress the Indians, the expedition was a beautiful sight. First, all by himself, a quarter mile ahead of the troops, rode Thomas Fitzpatrick — inevitably, it seems, the guide. After him came Col. Stephen W. Kearny, the commander, followed by his orderly and the bugler. Then the spectacular parade: a division on black horses marching by twos, followed by a division on grays, another on bays, one on sorrels, and a fifth on blacks again.

The Topographical Engineers sent

Lt. Francis T. Bryan in 1856. There had been war with Indians on the North Platte, but Bryan encountered no trouble on the South Platte.

The next year the story changed. Fearing that the Cheyennes would try to avenge their dead, Col. Edwin V. Sumner brought from Fort Leavenworth about four hundred cavalry and infantry soldiers. Part of the force, led by Maj. John Sedgwick, came up the Arkansas to the site which would soon be Denver, described by one of the soldiers as "literally a howling wilderness." He then proceeded down the South Platte to meet Sumner at his St. Vrain camp, named Buchanan in honor of the new president of the United States. Both forces had seen no Indians, and Sumner took part of his command south to the Smoky Hill River, where he engaged some Indians in battle.

Sedgwick became famous in the Civil War, but his men on the South Platte mission told of his loss of courage in danger, of turning his command over to others. Fort Sedgwick on the South Platte was later named for him.

Black Kettle, a principal chief of the Southern Cheyennes, was among the Indians in the battle. Perhaps more significant at the time was the presence of Fall Leaf, a Delaware Indian guide who would create a sensation by taking gold back to Kansas, helping to start the gold rush.

The expedition was noteworthy for a more ominous reason: Though the battle did not occur on the South Platte, it would have its effect on the people who would shortly be living there.

The next year, with the discovery of gold, the place called Denver was born. As many as two thousand men came out in the fall of 1858 and awaited spring, when they could begin to prospect. Some used the time to write guidebooks for future gold seekers. Most favored the old Overland Trail and a cutoff up the South Platte. If the Indians were stunned at the numbers in 1858, they must have been overwhelmed in 1859 when tens of thousands of people thronged across the prairies. Ninety percent of them followed the Platte.

John Jones and William Russell started the first stage line to Denver on the Smoky Hill but found the route dangerous and switched their Leavenworth and Pike's Peak Company to the Platte after only one month. *The Rocky Mountain News,* the paper in Denver, was complimentary of the new stage stations along the South Platte. Though crude, with earth floors, they had excellent wells and served good, hot food, the *News* declared.

By October the stage company was in financial trouble and was taken over by Russell, Majors, and Waddell, the freighters, who soon renamed it the Central Overland California and Pike's Peak Express. It, too, faced years of distress, and the employees joked that the initials, COC and PP, stood for Clean out of Cash and Poor Pay. But the COC and PP did quite well carrying private mail up the stretch of road to Denver, which was not yet included in the U.S. mail contract.

In early summer 1859 the trail was choked with "go-backs" who had found only disappointment in the goldfields. However, the major strike

Black Kettle, flying his American flag, arrived in Denver, September 28, 1864, to try to avert war.

of John H. Gregory at Central City set pulses racing once more. Over the next few years, hundreds of thousands came looking for life's big opportunity. Many of them found it — but not necessarily in the goldfields. Passage of the Homestead Act of 1862 insured that the migration would continue for decades. People told of wagons winding as far as the eye could see. Frank Root, messenger for the Overland Stage Line, was so impressed by the traffic that one day he counted the wagons. His total: 888.

It was said that the easiest way to get rich in a hurry was by freighting. The Russell, Majors, and Waddell line became the biggest in the world, with fifteen hundred employees and thousands of oxen and mules. Many a small operator got his start with only a wagon or two. Percival Lowe, who had been wagon master for Sumner, was one of the first. Bruce Fales Johnson, a civil engineer, came up the South Platte in search of gold but after a short time turned to freighting and ranching. Two of his best friends were also small operators: Jared ("Jud") Brush, who later owned a large ranch along the South Platte and became a lieutenant governor of Colorado; and Benjamin Eaton, who became a governor. The three made their pilgrimages across the plains together, two trips per year from 1862 to 1865, "walking every step of the way," Johnson said.

The Indians had suffered increasing anguish. The unintentional weapons of measles, whooping cough, and cholera were devastating to the red men, who had no defenses against the whites' diseases. Southern Cheyenne numbers, for instance, were reduced from five thousand in 1825 to half that number by 1845.

With the mass migration of the whites came another serious problem: The buffalo began to disappear. As the whites found prosperity, the Indians were starving. When William Bent, as Indian agent, came to the South Platte in July 1859 to make annuity payments, he found only forty-five lodges. Most of the men had gone south to try to find buffalo. The Great Buffalo Pasture was no more.

The red men, reduced to begging, began to camp near the whites in the winter. Bent, like Fitzpatrick, felt that agriculture was the only answer for them. Left Hand, one of the most capable Arapaho leaders, had taken his wife and five children on a wagon tour of Iowa and Nebraska farms in 1858. He agreed that Indian life would have to change but felt the cattle business would offer more of the traditional freedom which the red men had enjoyed.

Russell, Majors, and Waddell initiated the Pony Express in 1860. It was the imaginative Russell's next daring stunt after his expensive failures in the stage business, and it, too, was a glamorous success in every way except financially.

One of the riders was Jim Moore who, with his brother Charlie, established several stations and stores along the South Platte. His route ran between Julesburg and Mud Springs, thirty-two miles north of the Pole Creek Crossing. He attained fame one night when, ending his run to find no rider for the next relay, he swung into the saddle and took on another seventy-five miles.

The Pony Express did not bail the COC and PP out of trouble. Soon Ben Holladay, the entrepreneur admired by some and despised by others, was in control. He named the company the Overland Stage Line and built it into the largest in the United States. Later called the Holladay Overland Mail and Express, it had 2,670 route miles west of the Mississippi. The time came when Holladay's empire, too, collapsed, and Wells Fargo took over.

The men who ran the stage stations were destined to fight some lonely battles on the South Platte. One freighter told that only a dozen whites lived along the river in 1860. Even with an occasional "ranche" located on the trail, the proprietors were miles from neighbors.

The cutoff began at Julesburg, near the mouth of Lodgepole Creek. D. C. Oakes wrote in his guidebook:
Here you leave the old emigrant trail. Instead of crossing the river, keep up the south bank. The road follows the course of the river with but slight variations. A few scattering trees may be seen for the first fifty miles after which

there is no timber or wood of any kind. Plenty of buffalo chips for fuel, and excellent grass and water at almost any point.

Julesburg, at first the only store, was run by Jules Beni, a Frenchman suspected of fleecing the stage company. When Jack Slade, superintendent of the line between Julesburg and Latham, investigated, Beni shot him. Slade recovered and, his murderous instincts aroused, killed Beni after first cutting off his ears for mementos of the occasion. Slade was later assigned to the Virginia Dale Station (named for his wife) on the part of the trail which switched north along the front range to rejoin the old route.

Lillian Springs Ranche, which became a Western Company station, was thirty-four miles west of Julesburg. Henry Villard wrote in his guidebook that in 1859 it was an express station and that nothing could be bought there. He added, "Road very bad. Whole hills of sand." Lillian Springs was said to have been named for a young woman killed by Indians near the spot.

The American Ranche (or Kelley's) was sixty-five miles west of Julesburg, strategically located where the old Republican Fork Road joined the South Platte Trail. Kelley was a partner of the Moores, who also built Valley Station, fifteen miles downriver, and later Washington Ranche, three miles beyond. The American was also called Morrison's and Indian Ranche but not Morris, the name of the family who would suffer a tragic fate there.

A mile and a half above the Ameri-

can was Holon Godfrey's "ranche" where, for a modest price, he bought "footsores,": animals unable to travel further. Turned loose on the prairie, they recovered and were sold at the going rate. A ranche also had a blacksmith shop, bakery, eating house, and store, which stocked such varied items as food, liquor, playing cards, and goggles — the latter necessary because of heat, dust, and glare.

Thirty-five miles west of the American, near the mouth of Bijou Creek, Sam Ashcroft established a ranche. Upstream another thirty-two miles, Elbridge Gerry, probably the first permanent settler on the South Platte, operated his ranche and raised a large brood of children by a succession of Indian wives, sometimes two at a time.

Fort Latham, 135 miles west of Julesburg, was the last stage station before the road left the South Platte to rejoin the northern trail.

Other early establishments were Nebraska Ranche, a Western station operated by Ackley and Forbes five miles west of Julesburg; Twelve Mile Ranche (Simons and Hafford) fourteen miles further upriver; and Spring Hill, a COC and PP outfit five miles beyond. At the mouth of Beaver Creek was Beaver Creek Station, operated by Stevens and Moore. Scattered between there and Latham were three other stations: Bijou Creek; Fremont Orchard (so named because the gnarled cottonwoods there had looked like an orchard to Fremont); and Eagle's Nest.

The red men, seeing their Great Pasture threatened, watched the traffic in despair. The frontiersmen prospered and, according to the *News,* paid little attention when Indians killed two men in 1862. But it was soon evident that trouble was on the way.

It began in the spring of 1864. The Indians had spent a miserable winter of cold and hunger. Early in April there was a skirmish over some stock at the mouth of Crow Creek above Fremont's Orchard. White Antelope, a Cheyenne chief, later told Governor Evans that the unwarranted attack by the whites was the beginning of war on the plains of Colorado Territory.

Almost immediately came trouble at the ranches, the stealing of cattle, and the killing of two herders at Beaver Creek. Maj. Jacob A. Downing, fresh from Confederate battles in southern Colorado, led his men on a couple of futile trips downriver with guides Sam Ashcroft and Elbridge Gerry. He would no sooner return to Camp Sanford (near Gerry's Ranche) than the red men would strike again. Finally, Downing decided to use some of the Indians' own strategy: he would let them hunt for him. He mingled his horses with those at the American Ranche and hid his men behind the high corral. One man was on sentry duty at all times.

One day they captured an Indian, whom Sam Ashcroft recognized as Spotted Horse, a Cheyenne-Sioux who spoke English. Downing issued an ultimatum: either Spotted Horse would take him to the hiding place of the Indians, or he would burn him at the stake. Spotted Horse refused until the blaze began to lick at his shins.

He led the soldiers north of the river to a canyon on Cedar Creek. About ten miles from their destination the men openly camped and built bonfires. A little after midnight, they piled more wood on the fires, slipped into the ravine, and headed for battle. Spotted Horse, afraid the Cheyennes

Courtesy Ben Godfrey, great-grandson of the Godfreys
Holon and Matilda Godfrey's vigorous defense earned their trading post the name of FORT WICKED.

would kill him for his treachery, asked to be untied and given a gun. According to Downing, he fought against his own people.

Downing gave varied and probably exaggerated accounts of the battle. George Bent, half-breed son of William Bent, said hardly any Indians were present and few were killed. Downing came again a week later with reinforcements but found only empty lodges.

Sam Ashcroft gave a sad ending to the story: the homeless Spotted Horse, more and more despondent, tried to rejoin his band. They "had not forgotten and would not forgive," and they killed him.

In June the attacks began again. The worst tragedy was on Box Elder Creek, where Roman Nose, a Northern Cheyenne viewed as a renegade, killed the Hungate family, including two little girls. Simultaneous raids were made from Ashcroft's place to Washington Ranche, fifty miles down the trail. Cattle were shot, numerous horses driven away, and five emigrants killed.

On August 19, two Indians slipped into Elbridge Gerry's place to warn that a thousand Sioux, Cheyennes, and Arapahos, assembling up on Beaver Creek, would hit everything along the South Platte. The Indians gave Gerry a chance to escape, either because of friendship or his marriage to Indian women. Gerry, however, made a hasty ride up the river, warning everyone. Borrowing fresh horses three times, he reached the governor's home at midnight. Other riders and the telegraph spread the word. When the Indians appeared on the twenty-first they found the trail fortified.

Damage was minimal, but sixty horses and mules were taken from Gerry, a definite punishment for him. To the grateful frontiersmen, however, Gerry became "the Paul Revere of Colorado."

From August 11 to September 24 the trail was closed, and the whites took steps. Valley Station became a military outpost. Camp Rankin, later named Fort Sedgwick, was built opposite the mouth of Lodgepole Creek, one mile west of Julesburg. Camp Tyler, later called Wardwell and then Fort Morgan, was established near the mouth of Bijou Creek. It was named for Capt. C. M. Tyler, who organized Tyler's Rangers to patrol the South Platte until the War Department authorized Governor Evans to recruit a regiment of volunteers for one hundred days of service. Col. John M. Chivington, a 6-foot, 250-pound ex-Methodist minister, recruited and commanded the "Hundred Dayzers." The response was quick, because the trail was the lifeline of the territory. Most of what the people ate and wore had to come on freight wagons, which were stalled out on the river.

Black Kettle tried to make peace. On September 28 he initiated the Council on War and Peace in Denver. People snickered when he arrived, his American flag proudly flying on his wagon. That flag, which had been given him by an army officer, went with him everywhere.

He told the governor, "We must live near the buffalo or starve."

Despite the efforts of Black Kettle and other Indian leaders, incidents continued on the trail. The Hundred Dayzers were derisively called the

THE SOUTH PLATTE RIVER TRAIL: THE INCREDIBLE HIGHWAY   279

Bloodless Third because of their lack of action, but for some time the men had no horses and little equipment. When they finally headed down the South Platte, Chivington gave specific instructions to kill all Indians that they saw, including women and children. He was fond of saying, "Nits make lice."

Capt. David Nichols, later a lieutenant governor of Colorado, fought the first engagement, killing Big Wolf and his band of nine, which included four "nits."

As winter came on, the Indians gathered at Sand Creek near the Arkansas. The Hundred Dayzers were soon to be mustered out, and Chivington decided to strike while he still had forces. As the troops poured into the unsuspecting village, Black Kettle ran up his American flag and then a white flag of surrender. It was no use. Some of the most prominent Indians died on that cold morning: White Antelope, Left Hand, Little Wolf, One Eye, and Yellow Wolf. All had tried to establish friendly relations with the whites. Black Kettle survived, but his leadership was a victim of Sand Creek. Never again would he have the complete trust of his people.

Half naked and wounded, the surviving Indians dragged themselves out onto the prairie. The cold was paralyzing. George Bent said that Sand Creek was the worst disaster the Indians had ever endured. Those who survived would never forget, and the frontiersmen on the South Platte would feel their wrath.

The year-long attacks of 1864 were simply a prelude. The first month of 1865 was to be hell.

On the morning of January 7, Indians attacked the new fort at Julesburg, killing fifteen soldiers and three civilians. Upriver, they were enraged to find soldiers, discharged following Sand Creek, with the scalp of Little Wolf, easily recognizable by a shell that he always wore in his hair. They killed the men.

Valley Station wired Denver that a westbound coach was fired on, that a train in sight of the station was attacked, with two men killed. A large train camped five miles below was completely burned, and twelve teamsters and possibly some emigrants were killed. Valley Station was plundered and partially burned.

Proof of the security felt by the frontiersmen after Sand Creek may be found in the story of a wagonload of men surprised by fifty to seventy Indians near the American Ranche. They did not even have their guns loaded.

For a week the Indians moved great loads of goods south to their winter camp. When they returned they camped on White Butte Creek (Summit Springs) with Black Kettle who, not able to talk them out of the attacks, took his followers south to the Arkansas. On January 14 the warriors hit everything between Camp Wardwell and Valley Station.

Mark Coad had only one man to help him defend his Wisconsin Ranche, western headquarters for the Coad Brothers' freighting business. As the Indians set fire to building after building, the little group, including the employee's wife, three children, and an old man, retreated to their last stand in the storehouse. Mark shot 150 exhausting rounds from his muzzle-loading gun, and, when almost out of ammunition, stationed the other man with an ax while he made a daring run out the door to chase away three Indians about to set hay on fire against the building.

I took a Hawkins rifle, loaded and cocked, two pistols . . . jumped out the door, shot the first Indian with the rifle . . . jerked the pistols from my belt . . . shooting as fast as possible. We four were all mixed up together. I shot two down and wounded the other one. Then, squatting down close to the ground, jumped back into the store. As I went in the door, the fifteen Indians fired at me, but the shot passed over my head.

When the Indians retreated for the night, Coad slipped down the river to Valley Station. Soldiers from there rescued the others — none too soon, for the Indians burned the last building next morning.

Holon Godfrey led his three employees like a general, saving ammunition for sure shots and moving about to give the impression of many defenders. His teenage daughters helped by randomly poking up hats on brooms or shovel handles. When the Indians attempted to set fire, Holon, with a bucket in one hand and a rifle in the other, repeatedly sneaked out under cover of the smoke to wet the ground. When the Indians moved close and began firing lighted arrows at the roof, Holon's wife and children ran buckets of water to a ladder and passed them up to him. When ammunition got low, Matilda and the girls molded bullets.

Finally the Indians gave up. Godfrey's was one of only two places on the trail to survive undamaged. Thereafter, the red men called him Old Wicked. Proud of the name, he put a fourteen-foot board on which he painted FORT WICKED, and his

Photo by Robert McCaffree

The last battle on the Colorado plains was fought in the canyons of Summit Springs.

place was so known from that time on.

A mile and a half away, at the American Ranche, Gus Hall and another employee called simply Big Steve had just left for a wood-gathering trip up Cedar Canyon when one hundred Indians appeared. Eleven raced to the river, killing Steve and shooting Gus in the leg. The defenders of the American burst out of the flaming station into the corral, where the Indians quickly surrounded them. Gus watched them pull away and noted with despair a bright flash of color that had to be the dress of pretty Sarah Morris.

Gus knew that he was the only man left and that he would freeze there on the river. His only hope was Coad's, twelve miles away. For the next seventeen hours, he dragged his broken leg down the frozen South Platte. The sun was well up before he finally reached the freighting station. It was in ruins. Everyone was gone. Crawling inside a sod building, he found the walls still warm from the fire. The floor was littered with a foot of grain and flour, also warm. Gus burrowed into it and slept until finally he was rescued and taken to Omaha, where his leg was removed.

About January 27, the Indians moved from White Butte Creek to the north side of the river opposite Harlow's Ranche, which they attacked next morning, killing three men and capturing a woman. They burned Buffalo Springs Ranche and Antelope Station to the east and everything as far west as Washington Ranche, which was in for a three-day siege like Holon's. The store had the finest supply of canned goods on the

trail, and evidently the Indians wanted the food before burning the building. In desperation the Moores rigged up an old churn on a wagon to resemble a howitzer, and the trick helped.

However, on January 30 Jim Moore was badly wounded in the neck. A week or so later, a young woman on an armed train from Denver wrote of him as "the most terrible sight I have ever seen with his head swelled almost to the width of his shoulders."

George Bent told that never had the Indians eaten so well. At night they staged big celebrations. It was impossible for war parties to get lost. They could see the glow of campfires from miles away and could hear the drums beating out the scalp dances.

On February 2 the Indians moved camp to the mouth of Lodgepole Creek opposite Julesburg, where they systematically removed all usable goods and then burned each building. Finally they went on one last spree, with a party of Sioux mopping up downriver and Cheyennes and Arapahos destroying the telegraph line and burning wagons and buildings immediately west of Julesburg.

Next morning the people holed up in Fort Rankin ventured forth to find that the Indians had gone north. Bloody January was over. Almost everything on the trail would have to be rebuilt. Even sadder was the loss of life, particularly at the American Ranche. The wind blew the years away, the sod walls melted into the ground, and eventually all traces of the Morris family were gone. Like many who came to the West, they vanished with few to notice or mourn.

As traffic slowly resumed on the destroyed and bitterly cold trail, the Indians seemed to have vanished. The Galvanized Yankees (Southern prisoners of war sent west to regain their citizenship by protecting the trail) found little to do.

But it was Galvanized Yankees who rescued Sarah Morris, far to the north at Fort Rice in Dakota Territory. Her little adopted son had been taken from her. Her baby boy was killed. At times Sarah seemed normal, but again she would relive the terrible ordeal. Even when she returned to her home in Indiana, her suffering was not over. She would live with it for the rest of her life.

Nor were the Indian battles over. By the summer of 1865 the red men were again making hit-and-run attacks for a hundred miles each way from Julesburg. In February and March 1867 the trail was again closed. Perhaps it was a measure of the Indians' determination that one of the first places hit was Fort Wicked, which they usually avoided. Once again Holon survived.

Stages were the main victims because they lacked the protection that wagon trains enjoyed and because Wells Fargo did not pull them off the road as Ben Holladay had done. Five were in battles during the first few days of June, and several people were killed or wounded. One passenger aroused the indignation of the frontiersmen by expressing sympathy for the "abused" Indians when his stage stopped to watch a fight across the river with the "barbarous" whites. He was a son of Jefferson Davis, president of the Confederacy. Next day when his coach was attacked and Davis was wounded, he received little sympathy from people on the trail.

Two days later, Ed Kilburn, one of the most experienced stage drivers, pulled away from Fort Wicked, smiling when someone called, "Ed, look out for your scalp." Down the road, behind the ruins of the American, Indians were waiting. Ed's luck had run out.

Gus Hall, again on the river with a cork leg, was killed, ironically, as he cut wood in Cedar Canyon.

George Armstrong Custer had a disastrous experience on the trail. Anxious to return to his wife, Libby, he twisted orders to suit himself and led his men on a sixty-five-mile forced march to the South Platte. As the soldiers slept in exhaustion, Indians attacked Dennisons, only a mile away. Next morning Custer learned that a young lieutenant had left Fort Sedgwick to meet him on his supposed route. Realizing that the detail was in danger, he led another forced march. Too late, he found Lieutenant Kidder and his men, all dead. Many of Custer's troops deserted and headed for the goldfields. When horses collapsed, he shot them. He left injured men at ranches. Finally he raced alone on an unauthorized trip to Fort Riley to see Libby. For these exploits he was court-martialed.

Others who were to become famous traveled the South Platte during those years of sporadic warfare: young Henry Stanley, who rescued Dr. Livingstone in Africa; John Wesley Iliff, whose cattle herd and enormous range gave him the title of Cattle King; Buffalo Bill Cody, scout at the final battle of Summit Springs, who took credit for every aspect of the battle; and Brig. Gen. John Stephen Casement, who led the crew building the Union Pacific Railroad with as much authority as he had commanded his troops.

It was that railroad which ended the life of the trail. The golden spike driven in Utah on May 10, 1869, signified much more than the meeting of the Union Pacific and Central Pacific lines: It meant the end of stagecoaching and the end of the Overland Trail as the most heavily traveled road in the United States.

The Indian battles had little to do with it — not even Summit Springs on July 11, 1869. It was the last battle between the Plains Indians and the whites in Colorado. Tall Bull, chief of the Cheyenne Dog Soldiers, died, and his people were utterly defeated.

It was over. Never again would a Cheyenne maiden shyly lift her tent flap to admire the plaintive call of the flute. Not on the Great Buffalo Pasture. Not there the heady triumph of a buffalo surround — the gathering of all the bands for the big summer meeting — not there the cozy warmth of the lodge at night with the old storytellers passing on the heritage of the prairie people. Most of the old storytellers had died, perhaps with Sweet Medicine's warning still ringing in their ears: "Some day the Earth Men will come. Do not follow anything they do."

It was over for the whites as well. By early 1869 the frontiersmen had left. Along the quiet stretches of the South Platte Trail the occasional emigrant saw the ghostly remains of Fort Wicked and other places which had so recently catered to teeming traffic. Perhaps the most incredible aspect of the incredible highway was that it lasted for only ten years, but it changed the Great Pasture forever.

INDEX